William Robertson

The history of America

William Robertson

The history of America

ISBN/EAN: 9783744748995

Printed in Europe, USA, Canada, Australia, Japan

Cover: Foto ©ninafisch / pixelio.de

More available books at **www.hansebooks.com**

Harper's Stereotype Edition, with Engravings.

THE HISTORY

OF THE

DISCOVERY AND SETTLEMENT

OF

AMERICA

BY WILLIAM ROBERTSON, D.D.

PRINCIPAL OF THE UNIVERSITY AT EDINBURGH, ETC. ETC.

WITH AN ACCOUNT OF HIS LIFE AND WRITINGS.

TO WHICH ARE ADDED

QUESTIONS

FOR THE

EXAMINATION OF STUDENTS.

BY JOHN FROST, A.M.

COMPLETE IN ONE VOLUME.

NEW-YORK

PRINTED BY J. & J. HARPER, 82 CLIFF-STREET.

Sold by Collins & Hannay, Collins & Co., G. & C. & H. Carvill, White, Gallaher, & White, O. A. Roorbach, E. Bliss, and C. S Francis;—ALBANY, O. Steele, and Little & Cummings; —PHILADELPHIA, John Grigg, Towar & Hogan, E. L. Carey & A. Hart, T. Desilver, jr., and U. Hunt; — BOSTON, Richardson, Lord, & Holbrook, Carter, Hendee, & Babcock, and Hilliard, Gray, & Co.;—BALTIMORE, W. & J. Neal, J. Jewett, and Cushing & Sons.

1832.

THE
LIFE OF DR. WM. ROBERTSON.

WILLIAM ROBERTSON, the eldest son of the Reverend William Robertson, was born on the 8th of September, 1721, at Borthwick, in the shire of Mid Lothian, of which parish his father was the minister. By the paternal line he descended from a respectable family in the county of Fife, a branch of that which, for many generations, possessed the estate of Struan, in Perthshire. His mother was the daughter of David Pitcairn, esq. of Dreghorn. He had one brother and six sisters; all of whom were well settled in life, and most of whom lived to an advanced age.

It was at the parochial school of Borthwick that Robertson received the initiatory part of his education; but as soon as he was sufficiently forward to enter on the study of the learned languages, he was removed to the school of Dalkeith. The latter seminary was then under the superintendence of Mr. Leslie, whose eminence as a teacher was such as to attract pupils from all parts of Scotland; and the father of Robertson was consequently induced to send him to Dalkeith rather than to the Scottish metropolis.

When the future historian was twelve years old, his father was transferred from Borthwick to one of the churches of Edinburgh. In the autumn of 1733 he joined his parents; and, in October, he was admitted into the college and university of the northern capital.

Whatever were his first attempts at composition, and it is probable they were many, nothing has been preserved to show how early he began to exercise his talents, or with what degree of rapidity those talents were expanded. It is certain, however, that in the pursuit of knowledge he displayed that ardour and perseverance without which nothing great will ever be accomplished. A strong proof of this is afforded by some of his early commonplace books, which bear the dates of 1735, 1736, and 1737. The motto, *vita sine literis mors est*, which he prefixed to these books, sufficiently indicates by what an honourable ambition and love of literature he was inspired at a very tender and generally thoughtless age. The boy of fourteen, who can cherish the feeling which is implied by this motto, gives promise that his manhood will reflect lustre on himself and on the country of his birth.

Among the men of eminence, by whose instructions he profited at the university, were sir John Pringle, afterwards president of the Royal Society, but then professor of moral philosophy; Maclaurin, justly celebrated for the extent of his mathematical skill and the purity of his style and Dr. Stevenson, the learned and indefatigable professor of logic. To the masterly prelections of the latter, especially to his illustrations of the poetics of Aristotle, and of Longinus on the Sublime, Robertson often declared that he considered himself to be more deeply indebted than to any circumstance in the course of his academical career. It was indeed not towards the abstract sciences that the bent of his genius was directed. To mathematical and mechanical speculations he seems to have been at least cold, perhaps averse. Neither was he remarkable for metaphysical acuteness. His delight was to trace and elucidate moral and religious truths, to apply the process of reasoning to subjects more immediately connected with the every-day business of existence, to search into the causes and effects of historical events, to expatiate amidst the perennial beauties of classic lore, and, by meditating on the great models of oratorical art, to render himself master of all the powerful resources of a ready and persuasive eloquence.

With respect to eloquence, the possession of it was in fact indispensable to one who, as in all probability was the case with Robertson, had determined to assume a prominent station among the pastors and leaders of the Scottish church. The mere knowledge of rules, however, or even a thorough acquaintance with the rich stores of ancient and modern oratory, will not suffice to form an orator. It is by use alone that facility of speech and promptitude of reply can be acquired. It is the collision of minds which strikes out the "thoughts that breathe, and words that burn." During the last years, therefore, of his residing at college, he joined with some of his contemporaries in establishing a society, the avowed purpose of which, as we are told by Mr. Stewart, was " to cultivate the study of elocution, and to prepare themselves, by the habits of extemporary discussion and debate, for conducting the business of popular assemblies."

Of the colleagues of Robertson in this society many ultimately rose, like himself, to high reputation. Among them were Cleghorn, subsequently professor of moral philosophy at Edinburgh, Dr. John Blair, who became a member of the Royal Society, and a prebendary of Westminster, and who gave to the public "The Chronology and History of the World," Wilkie, the author of the Epigoniad, a faulty poem, but above contempt, Home, the author of Douglas, and Dr. Erskine, who, in after life, was at once the coadjutor, rival, opponent, and friend of Robertson.

This society continued in existence, and, no doubt, was beneficial to its members, till it was broken up by a quarrel, which had its rise from a religious source, and which, consequently, was of more than common bitterness. In 1741 that extraordinary man Whitefield, who was then in the zenith of his fame, paid a visit to Scotland, and his preaching excited in that country a feeling equally as strong as it had excited in England. On the subject of his merit violent parties immediately sprang up, especially among the clergy. By the one side he was considered as a clerical wonder, a kind of apostle, from whose evangelical labours the happiest result might be expected; by the other side he was calumniated as an impostor, and a worthless private character, while some, in the excess of their holy zeal, did not scruple to stigmatize him, even from the pulpit, as " an agent of the devil." It was natural that this question should be debated by Robertson and his associates; and it was, perhaps, not less natural that it should be argued with so much heat and asperity as not only to cause the dissolution of the society, but even, it is said, to interrupt, for some time, the intercourse of the members as private individuals. Of those who entertained doubts with regard to the personal conduct of Whitefield, and the utility of his efforts, Robertson was one. From his acknowledged moderation and evenness of temper we may, however, infer that his hostility to the preacher was carried on in a liberal spirit, and that he did not think it either necessary or decorous to brand him as an agent of the prince of darkness.

To excel in his written style as much as in his oral was one object of his ambition. The practice of clothing in an English dress the standard works of the ancients has been often recommended, as conducive to the improvement of style; and he seems to have believed it to be so, for it was adopted by him. He carried it so far as to entertain serious thoughts of preparing for the press a version of Marcus Antoninus. His scheme was, however, frustrated by the appearance of an anonymous translation at Glasgow. "In making choice of this author," says Mr. Stewart, "he was probably not a little influenced by that partiality with which (among the writers of heathen moralists) he always regarded the remains of the stoical philosophy."

Having completed his academic course, and richly stored his mind, he quitted the university, and, in 1741, before he had quite attained the age of twenty, a license to preach the gospel was given to him by the presbytery of Dalkeith. This kind of license, which does not authorize to administer the sacraments or to undertake the cure of souls, is granted to laymen; and the person who receives it may be considered as being placed by it in a state of probation.

After the lapse of two years, from the period of his leaving the university, when he was yet little more than twenty-two, he was, in 1743, presented, by the Earl of Hopetoun, to the living of Gladsmuir. Of this preferment the yearly value was not more than one hundred pounds. Scanty, however, as were its emoluments, it was most opportunely bestowed. He had not long resided at Gladsmuir when an unexpected and melancholy event occurred, which put to the trial at once his firmness and his benevolence. His father and mother expired within a few hours of each other, leaving behind them a family of six daughters and one son, without the means of providing for their education and maintenance. On this occasion Robertson acted in a manner which bore irrefragable testimony to the goodness of his heart, and which was also, as Mr. Stewart justly observes, "strongly marked with that manly decision in his plans, and that persevering steadiness in their execution, which were the characteristic features of his mind." Regardless of the privations to which he must necessarily submit, and the interruption which his literary and other projects must experience, he received his father's family into his house at Gladsmuir, educated his sisters under his own roof, and retained them there till opportunities arose of settling them respectably in the world. His merit is enhanced by the circumstance of his fraternal affection having imposed on him a sacrifice far more painful than that of riches or fame. He was tenderly attached to his cousin Miss Mary Nesbit, daughter of the Reverend Mr. Nesbit, one of the ministers of Edinburgh, and his attachment was returned; but it was not till 1751, when his family had ceased to stand in need of his protecting care, that he thought himself at liberty to complete a union which had, for several years, been the object of his ardent wishes. It is pleasant to know that the wife whom he so tardily obtained was every way worthy of such a husband, and that he suffered no interruption of his domestic happiness.

While he was laudably occupied in promoting the welfare of his orphan relatives, the rebellion broke out in Scotland. "It afforded him," says Mr. Stewart, "an opportunity of evincing the sincerity of that zeal for the civil and religious liberties of his country, which he had imbibed with the first principles of his education; and which afterwards, at the distance of more than forty years, when he was called on to employ his eloquence in the national commemoration of the revolution, seemed to rekindle the fires of his youth. His situation as a country clergyman confined indeed his patriotic exertions within a narrow sphere; but even here his conduct was guided by a mind superior to the scene in which he acted. On one occasion (when the capital was in danger of falling into the hands of the rebels) the present state of public affairs appeared so critical that he thought himself justified in laying aside for a time the pacific habits of his profession, and in quitting his parochial residence at Gladsmuir to join the volunteers of Edinburgh. And when, at last, it was determined that the city should be surrendered, he was one of the small band who repaired to Haddington, and offered their services to the commander of His Majesty's forces."

With the exception of this one troubled interval he continued, for many years, in the tranquil performance of his pastoral duties. The hours of his leisure were devoted to literary researches and to laying the solid fou dation of future eminence. It was his practice to rise early, and to read and write much before breakfast. The remainder of the day he devoted to the claims of his profession. As a minister of the gospel he was conscientious and active; not confining himself to the mere routine of his sacred office, but endeavouring by every means to extend the comforts and influence of religion. In the summer months it was customary for him, previous to the commencement of the church service, to assemble the youthful part of his flock for the purpose of explaining to them the doctrines of the catechism. By his zeal, his punctuality, and the suavity of his behaviour, he won the love of his parishioners; so that, in all their difficulties, it was to him that they resorted for consolation and for counsel. His pulpit eloquence was such as afforded delight to all classes of people; because, while it was adorned with those graces of style which are required to satisfy men of judgment and taste, it was rendered level to the comprehension of his humblest hearers, by the clearness of its argument and the perspicuity of its language.

The time at length arrived when the talents of Robertson were to be displayed on a more extensive and public scene of action, and he was to assume a leading share in the government of the Scottish church. He did not, however, come forward among his colleagues till he had attained the mature age of thirty, and had thoroughly prepared himself to sustain his new and important part with untiring vigour and a decisive effect. It was on the question of patronage that he first exerted his powers of eloquence in a deliberative assembly.

To enable the mere English reader to comprehend this subject, it may, perhaps, be proper to give some account of the constitution of the church of Scotland, and also of the right of patronage, out of which arose the contentions and heartburnings by which the church was disturbed for a considerable period.

The church of Scotland is ruled by a series of judicatories, rising by regular gradation from the kirk session, or parochial consistory, which is the lowest in order, to the general assembly, which is the highest. The kirk session is composed of the ministers and lay elders of parishes; a presbytery is formed of the ministers of contiguous parishes, with certain representatives from the kirk sessions; and a provincial synod is constituted by the union of a plurality of presbyteries. Crowning the whole is the general assembly. This body consists of three hundred and sixty-four members, of whom two hundred and two are ministers, and the remainder are laymen. Of this number two hundred and one ministers and eighty-nine lay elders are sent by the presbyteries; the royal boroughs elect sixty-seven laymen; the universities depute five persons, who may be either ecclesiastics or laymen; and the Scottish church of Campvere in Holland supplies two deputies, the one lay and the other clerical. The annual sittings of the assembly are limited to ten days; but whatever business it has left unsettled is transacted by a committee of the whole house (called the commission), which, in the course of the year, has four stated meetings. Among the lay members of the assembly are men of the highest consequence in the kingdom; lawyers, judges, and sometimes nobles.

Though all the ministers in Scotland are on a perfect equality with each other, yet each individual and each judicatory is bound to yield a prompt obedience to the superintending authority, and each court must punctually lay the record of its proceedings before the tribunal which is next in rank above it; but the general assembly has the power of deciding without appeal, of enforcing, uncontrolled, its decrees, and, with the concurrence of a majority of the presbyteries, of enacting laws for the government of the Scottish church.

The history of clerical patronage in Scotland since the overthrow of Catholicism, and of the struggles to which it has given rise, has been traced with so much clearness by Dr. Gleig that, though the passage is of some length, I shall give it in his own words. "The Reformation in Scotland," says he, "was irregular and tumultuous; and the great object of the powerful aristocracy of that kingdom seems to have been rather to get possession of the tithes, and the lands of the dignified clergy, than to purify the doctrine and reform the worship of the church. Of this Knox and the other reformed clergymen complained bitterly; and their complaints were extorted from them by their own sufferings. Never, I believe, were the established clergy of any Christian country reduced to such indigence as were those zealous and well meaning men, during the disastrous reign of queen Mary, and the minority of her son and successor; while the pittance that was promised to them, instead of being regularly paid, was often seized by the rapacity of the regents and the powerful barons who adhered to their cause, and the ministers left to depend for their subsistence on the generosity of the people.

"As nearly the whole of the ecclesiastical patronage of the kingdom had come into the possession of those barons, partly by inheritance from their ancestors, and partly with the church lands which, on the destruction of the monasteries, they had appropriated to themselves, it is not wonderful that, in an age when men were very apt to confound the illegal and mischievous conduct of him who exercised an undoubted right with the natural consequences of that right itself, strong prejudices were excited in the minds of the clergy and more serious part of the people against the law which vested in such sacrilegious robbers the right of presentation to parish churches. It is not indeed very accurately known by whom ministers were nominated to vacant churches for thirty years after the commencement of the Reformation, when there was hardly any settled government in the church or in the state. In some parishes they were probably called by the general voice of the people; in others, obtruded on them by the violence of the prevailing faction, to serve some political purpose of the day; and in others again appointed by the superintendent and his council: while in a few the legal patron may have exercised his right, without making any simoniacal contract with the presentee; which, however, there is reason to suspect was no uncommon practice.*

"Hitherto the government of the Protestant church of Scotland had fluctuated from one form to another, sometimes assuming the appearance of episcopacy under superintendents, and at other times being presbyterian in the strictest sense of the word. In the month of June, 1592, an act was passed, giving a legal sanction to the presbyterian form of government, and restoring the ancient law of patronage. By that act the patron of a vacant parish was authorized to present, to the presbytery comprehending that parish, a person properly qualified to be intrusted with the cure of souls; and the presbytery was enjoined, after subjecting the presentee to certain trials and examinations, of which its members were constituted the judges, 'to ordain and settle him as minister of the parish, provided no relevant objection should be stated to his life, doctrine, or qualifications.'

"Though we are assured by the highest authority† that this right of patronage, thus conferred by the fundamental charter of presbyterian government in Scotland, was early complained of as a grievance, it appears to have been regularly exercised until the era of the rebellion against Charles I. during the establishment as well of the presbyterian as of the episcopal church. It was indeed abolished by the usurping powers, which in 1649 established in its stead what was then called 'the gospel right of popular election;' but at the restoration it was re-established together with episcopacy, and was regularly exercised until the revolution, when epis-

---

* The reader will derive much valuable information on this subject from Dr. Cook's "History of the Reformation in Scotland." † Dr. Hill, Principal of St. Mary's College, in the University of St. Andrew's.

copacy was finally overthrown, and, by an act passed on the 26th of May, 'the presbyterian church, government, and discipline, by kirk sessions, presbyteries, provincial synods, and general assemblies,' established in its stead. The act of James VI. in 1592 was 'revived and confirmed in every head thereof, except in that part of it relating to patronages,' which were utterly abolished, though nothing was substituted in their stead until the 19th of July immediately succeeding.

"It was then statuted and declared, to use the language of the act, 'that, in the vacancy of any particular church, and for supplying the same with a minister, the protestant heritors and elders are to name and propose the person to the whole congregation, to be either approven or disapproven by them; and if they disapprove, they are to give in their reasons, to the effect the affairs may be cognosced by the presbytery of the bounds; at whose judgment, and by whose determination, the calling and entry of every particular minister is to be ordered and concluded. In recompense of which rights of presentation the heritors of every parish were to pay to the patron six hundred merks (£33 6s. 8d. sterling), against a certain time, and under certain proportions.

"Whether this sum, which at that period was very considerable, was actually paid to the patrons of the several parishes, I know not; but if it was, or indeed whether it was or not, had it been the intention of the legislature to produce dissension in the country, it could not have devised any thing better calculated to effect its purpose than this mode of appointing ministers to vacant churches. The heritors or landholders, if the price was paid, would naturally contend for the uncontrolled exercise of the right which they, and they only, had purchased; but it is not by any means probable that at such a period they could often agree in their choice of a minister for a vacant parish. The elders, who were men of inferior rank and inferior education, would, by the envy of the low, when comparing themselves with the high, be prompted to thwart the wishes of their landlords, which the act of parliament enabled them to do effectually; and the consequence must have been that two or three candidates for every vacant church were at once proposed to the people of the parish for their approbation or disapprobation. The people might either give the preference to one of the candidates proposed, or reject them all, for reasons of which the members of the presbytery were constituted the judges; and as it appears that the presbytery generally took part with the people, a source of everlasting contention was thus established between the country gentlemen and the parochial clergy; an evil than which a greater cannot easily be conceived. For these, and other reasons, this ill digested law was repealed in the tenth year of the reign of queen Anne, and the right of patronage restored as in all other established churches.

"By many of the clergy, however, patronage seems to have been considered as an appendage of prelacy; though it has obviously no greater connexion with that form of ecclesiastical polity than with any other that is capable of being allied with the state; and, till after the year 1730, ministers continued to be settled in vacant parishes in the manner prescribed by the act of king William and queen Mary. 'Even then,' says Dr. Hill, 'the church courts, although they could not entirely disregard the law, continued, in many instances, to render it ineffectual, and by their authority sanctioned the prevailing prejudices of the people against it. They admitted, as an incontrovertible principle in presbyterian church government, that a presentee, although perfectly well qualified, and unexceptionable in his life and doctrine, was nevertheless inadmissible to his clerical office, till the concurrence of the people who were to be under his ministry had been regularly ascertained.' The form of expressing this concurrence was by the subscription of a paper termed 'a call;' to which many of the old ministers paid greater respect than to the deed of presentation by the patron of the church.

"To render the call good, however, the unanimous consent of the landholders, elders, and people, was not considered as necessary, nor indeed ever looked for. Nay, it appears that even a majority was not in all cases deemed indispensable; for the presbytery often admitted to his charge, and proceeded to ordain the presentee whose call, by whatever number of parishioners, appeared to them to afford a reasonable prospect of his becoming, by prudent conduct, a useful parish minister. On the other hand, presbyteries sometimes set aside the presentation altogether, when they were not satisfied with the call; and when the patron insisted on his right, and the presbytery continued inflexible, the general assembly was, in such cases, under the necessity either of compelling the members of the presbytery, by ecclesiastical censures, to do their duty, or of appointing a committee of its own body to relieve them from that duty, by ordaining the presentee, and inducting him into the vacant church. To compulsion recourse had seldom been had; and the consequence was that individuals openly claimed a right to disobey the injunctions of the assembly, whenever they conceived their disobedience justified by a principle of conscience.

"Such was the state of ecclesiastical discipline in Scotland when Mr. Robertson first took an active part in the debates of the general assembly; and he very justly thought that its tendency was to overturn the presbyterian establishment, and introduce in its stead a number of independent congregational churches. He therefore supported the law of patronage, not merely because it was part of the law of the land, but because he thought it the most expedient method of filling the vacant churches. It did not appear to him that the people at large are competent judges of those qualities which a minister should possess in order to be a useful teacher of the truth as it is in Jesus, or of the precepts of a sound morality. He more than suspected that if the candidates for churches were taught to consider their success in obtaining a settlement as depending on a popular election, many of them would be tempted to adopt a manner of preaching calculated rather to please the people than to promote their edification. He thought that there is little danger to be apprehended from the abuse of the law of patronage; because the presentee must be chosen from among those whom the church had approved, and licensed as qualified for the office of a parish minister; because a presentee cannot be admitted to the benefice if any relevant objection to his life or doctrine be proved against him; and because, after ordination and admission, he is liable to be deposed for improper conduct, and the church declared vacant."

Whatever may be thought of the merits of the cause which Robertson espoused, it is impossible to doubt that he was a conscientious supporter of it. To undertake its defence some strength of nerve was, indeed, required. Success seemed, at the outset, to be scarcely within the verge of probability, and there was much danger of becoming unpopular. The result, nevertheless, gave ample proof of what may be accomplished by perseverance and talents. The first time that he came forward in the assembly was in May, 1751, when a debate arose on the conduct of a minister, who had disobeyed the sentence of a former assembly. Seizing this opportunity to enforce his principles of church discipline, Robertson, in a vigorous and eloquent speech, contended that if subordination were not rigidly maintained the presbyterian establishment would ultimately be overthrown, and, therefore, an exemplary punishment ought to be inflicted on the offending party. But, though he was heard with attention, his arguments produced so little present effect that, on the house being divided, he was left in a minority of no more than eleven against two hundred.

Though this decision was not calculated to encourage him, he determined to persist, and an occurrence very soon took place which enabled him to renew the contest. The presbytery of Dumferline having been guilty of disobedience, in refusing to admit a minister to the church of Inverkeithing, the commission of the assembly, which met in November, ordered them to cease from their opposition, and threatened, that, if they continued to be refractory, they should be subjected to a high censure Notwithstanding this, the presbytery again disobeyed the mandate of the superior court. Yet, instead of carrying its threat into effect, the commission came to a resolution that no censure should be inflicted.

Such a resolution as this, after the commission had gone so far as to resort to threats, was at least absurd. So fair an opening as this circumstance afforded was not neglected by Robertson. He accordingly drew up a protest, intituled, "Reasons of Dissent from the Judgment and Resolution of the Commission." This protest, which was signed by himself, Dr. Blair, Home, and a few other friends, is an able and closely reasoned production. It boldly declares the sentence of the commission to be inconsistent with the nature and first principles of society; charges the commission itself with having, by that sentence, gone beyond its powers, and betrayed the privileges and deserted the doctrines of the constitution; considers the impunity thus granted as encouraging and inviting contumacy; insists on the lawfulness and wisdom of ecclesiastical censures, and on the absolute necessity of preserving subordination and obedience in the church; and, finally, maintains that the exercise of no man's private judgment can justify him in disturbing all public order, that he who becomes a member of a church ought to conform to its decrees, or, "if he hath rashly joined himself, that he is bound, as an honest man and a good Christian, to withdraw, and to keep his conscience pure and undefiled."

When the assembly met, in 1752, the question was brought before it; and Robertson supported the principles of his protest with such cogency of argument, that he won over a majority to his side, and achieved a complete triumph. The judgment of the commission was reversed, Mr. Gillespie, one of the ministers of the presbytery of Dumferline, was deposed from his pastoral office, and ejected from his living, and three other individuals were suspended from their judicative capacity in the superior ecclesiastical courts. Gillespie, whose only crime was that of being absent on the day appointed for the induction of the presentee, was a pious and amiable man, and his deposition occasioned so much dissatisfaction, that it gave rise to a new sect of dissenters, afterwards known by the appellation of "the Presbytery of Relief;" a sect which still exists, and is of considerable magnitude.

From this time, though it was not till the year 1763 that he became its avowed leader, Robertson was, in fact, at the head of the assembly; which body, for the whole period of his ascendancy, he contrived to keep steady to his principles. In this task he was ably seconded by Dr. Drysdale, one of the ministers of Edinburgh. It was not, however, without many struggles that he retained his pre-eminence. Those which took place in 1765 and 1768 were peculiarly violent; motions having then been made, and vehemently contended for, to inquire into the causes of the rapid progress of secession from the established church; and, in order to counteract them, to introduce a more popular mode of inducting the parochial ministers. From what is mentioned by sir Henry Wellwood, in his "Memoirs of Dr. Erskine," it appears that the exertions of Robertson were kept continually on the stretch; and that for his victory he was partly indebted to cautious management, and to patience which nothing could tire. "During Dr. Robertson's time," says he, "the struggle with the people was perpetual; and the opposition to presentees so extremely pertinacious, as in a great measure to engross the business of the assemblies. The parties in the church were then more equally balanced than they have ever been since that period. The measures which were adopted, in the face of such perpetual opposition, it required no common talents to manage or defend; especially considering that the leaders in opposition were such men as Dr. Dick, Dr. Macqueen, Dr. Erskine, Mr. Stevenson of St. Madois, Mr. Freebairn of Dumbarton, Mr. Andrew Crosbie, &c. &c.; men of the first ability in the country, and some of them possessed of an eloquence for a popular assembly to which there was nothing superior in the church or in the state.

"Dr. Robertson's firmness was not easily shaken, but his caution and prudence never deserted him. He held it for a maxim, never wantonly to offend the prejudices of the people, and rather to endeavour to manage than directly to combat them. Some of the settlements in dispute were protracted for eight or ten years together; and though the general assemblies steadily pursued their system, and uniformly appointed the presentees to be inducted, their strongest sentences were not vindictive, and seldom went beyond the leading points to which they were directed."

In 1757 an event happened, which afforded to him an opportunity of manifesting the liberality of his spirit, and of exercising his influence over his colleagues, to moderate the vengeance which was threatened to be hurled on some of his brethren, for having been guilty of an act which was considered to be of the most profane nature. The chief offender was his friend Home, who was then minister of Athelstaneford. The crime consisted in Home having not only produced the tragedy of Douglas, but having also had the temerity to be present at the acting of it in the Edinburgh theatre. With him were involved several of his clerical intimates, who, as much from a desire to share with him any odium or peril which might be incurred, as from a natural curiosity, had been induced to accompany him to the theatre on the first night of the performance. The storm which this circumstance raised among the Scottish clergy can, in the present age, hardly be imagined. It seemed as if they had witnessed nothing less than the abomination of desolation standing in the holy place. The presbytery of Edinburgh hastened to summon before its tribunal such of its members as had committed this heinous offence, and it likewise despatched circulars to the presbyteries in the vicinity, recommending rigorous measures against all clergymen who had desecrated themselves by appearing in the polluted region of the theatre. The alarm thus sounded awakened all the bigotry of the circumjacent presbyteries. That of Haddington, to which Home belonged, cited him and his friend Carlyle, of Inveresk, to answer for their misconduct. That of Glasgow had no criminals to chastise, but it was resolved not to remain silent, and, therefore, with a zeal which assuredly was not according to knowledge, it fulminated forth a series of resolutions on this appalling subject. It lamented "the melancholy but notorious fact, that one, who is a minister of the church of Scotland, did himself write and compose a play entitled the Tragedy of Douglas, and got it to be acted in the theatre at Edinburgh; and that he, with several other ministers of the church, were present, and some of them oftener than once, at the acting of the said play before a numerous audience;" it affirmed, in direct hostility to historical evidence, that stage plays had "been looked upon by the Christian church, in all ages, and of all different communions, as extremely prejudicial to religion and morality; and, as a natural consequence from this, it called on the general assembly to reprobate publicly "a practice unbecoming the character of clergymen, and of such pernicious tendency to the great interests of religion, industry, and virtue." The cry of the church was echoed from the press, angry disputants were arrayed on both sides, and a multitude of ephemeral pamphlets and pasquinades was rapidly produced.

Throughout the whole of the ecclesiastical proceedings, which on this occasion were instituted in the presbyteries and in the general assembly,

Robertson exerted himself with more than common ardour and eloquence on behalf of his friends. Though, being restrained by a promise which he had given to his father, he had himself never been within the walls of a theatre, he did not hesitate to avow his belief that no culpability attached to the persons who were under prosecution. "The promise," said he, "which was exacted by the most indulgent of parents, I have hitherto religiously kept, and it is my intention to keep it till the day of my death. I am at the same time free to declare, that I perceive nothing sinful or inconsistent with the spirit of Christianity in writing a tragedy, which gives no encouragement to baseness or vice, and that I cannot concur in censuring my brethren for being present at the representation of such a tragedy, from which I was kept back by a promise, which, though sacred to me, is not obligatory on them."

Wholly to overcome the prevalent spirit of bigotry was more than Robertson could accomplish, but it is believed to have been at least greatly mitigated by his laudable efforts. To his persuasive eloquence is attributed, and no doubt justly, the comparative mildness of the sentence which was ultimately pronounced. A declaratory act was passed by the assembly, forbidding the clergy to visit the theatres, but not extending the prohibition to the writing of plays. The silence of the assembly on the latter head was at least one point gained in favour of liberal principles. As to the offending ministers, some of them were rebuked by the presbyteries to which they belonged, and one or two of them were suspended from their office for a few weeks. Home, however, being disgusted with the treatment which he had experienced, and having, perhaps, already been offered patronage in the British metropolis, resigned his living of Athelstaneford in June, 1757, and fixed his residence in London.

By the departure of Home, the Select Society, as it was called, lost one of its ablest members. This society was instituted at Edinburgh, in 1754, by Allan Ramsay, the painter, who was son to the poet of the same name. The object of it was philosophical and literary inquiry, and the improvement of the members in the art of speaking. It held its meetings in the Advocates' Library, and met regularly every Friday evening, during the sittings of the court of session. At the outset it consisted of only fifteen persons, of whom Robertson was one. It, however, soon acquired such high reputation, that its list of associates was swelled to more than a hundred and thirty names; among which were included those of the most eminent literary and political characters in the northern division of the kingdom. Of this number were Hume, Adam Smith, Wedderburn, afterwards Lord Chancellor, sir Gilbert Elliot, lord Elibank, lord Monboddo, lord Kames, lord Woodhouselee, Adam Ferguson, Wilkie, Dr. Cullen, and many others less gifted perhaps, but still rising far above mediocrity of talent. This society flourished in full vigour for some years; and is said by professor Stewart, to have produced such debates as have not often been heard in modern assemblies; debates, where the dignity of the speakers was not lowered by the intrigues of policy, or the intemperance of faction; and where the most splendid talents that have ever adorned this country were roused to their best exertions, by the liberal and ennobling discussions of literature and philosophy." That such an assemblage of learning and genius must have done much towards diffusing through Scotland a taste for letters, there cannot be the shadow of a doubt. Robertson took an active part, and was one of its presidents. As a speaker, it was remarked of him, that "whereas most of the others in their previous discourses exhausted the subject so much that there was no room for debate, he gave only such brief but artful sketches, as served to suggest ideas, without leading to a decision."

By a few members of the society, a Review was attempted in 1755, the principal contributors to which were Blair, Smith, and Robertson. This undertaking was designed to form a record of the progress of Scottish literature, and, occasionally, to criticise such English and foreign works as might appear to be worthy of notice. After having published two numbers, which appeared in July and December, the reviewers were under the necessity of relinquishing their plan. The failure is said to have arisen from their having lashed, with just but caustic severity, "some miserable effusions of fanaticism, which it was their wish to banish from the church." Their attack upon this mischievous trash excited such a vehement party outcry, that they thought it prudent to discontinue labours which, while they must fail of being useful, could not fail to expose them to vulgar odium, and involve them in endless disputes. Time, the great worker of changes, has since produced a marvellous alteration. At a period less than half a century later, the most prejudice-scorning and pungent of all Reviews was established in the Scottish capital, and was received with enthusiasm!

The first separate literary production of Robertson, or at least the first known production, was also laid before the public in 1755. It is a sermon which he preached in that year before the Scotch society for propagating Christian knowledge. He chose for his subject, "The situation of the world at the time of Christ's appearance, and its connexion with the success of his religion." Though this discourse never rises into a strain of glowing eloquence, it is a dignified and argumentative composition, in a chaste and animated style. If it does not flash and dazzle, it at least shines with a steady lustre. Its merit, indeed, affords us ample cause to regret that, before his removal from Gladsmuir, he lost a volume of sermons, on which much care is said to have been bestowed. The sole specimen which remains of his talents as a preacher has passed through five editions, and has been translated into the German language by Mr. Edeling.

The time now came when the high character for learning and talent, which Robertson had acquired among his friends, was to be ratified by the public voice. He had long been sedulously engaged on the History of Scotland, the plan of which he is said to have formed soon after his settling at Gladsmuir. By his letters to Lord Hailes we are, in some measure, enabled to trace his progress. It appears that as early as 1753 he had commenced his labours, and that by the summer of 1757 he had advanced as far as the narrative of Gowrie's conspiracy. In the spring of 1758 he visited London, to concert measures for publishing; and the History, in two volumes, quarto, was given to the world on the first of February, 1759, about three months subsequent to the completion of it. While the last sheets were in the press, the author received, by diploma, the degree of Doctor of Divinity from the University of Edinburgh.

At the period when Dr. Robertson commenced his career, this country could boast of few historians, possessed of philosophic views and an elegant style. Rapin, who, besides, wrote in his native language, Carte, and others, could not aspire to a loftier title than that of annalists; and the recent production from the pen of Smollet, though displaying talent, was by far too imperfect to give him a place among eminent historical writers. Hume alone had come near to the standard of excellence; and, after enduring a doubtful struggle, in the course of which his spirits were well nigh overpowered, had at length begun to enjoy the literary honours which he had so painfully acquired. For a considerable time past he had been occupied on the reigns of the Tudor race; and, as this subject is inseparably connected with Scottish history, Dr. Robertson was alarmed lest he himself should sustain injury from the volumes of his friend being published simultaneously with his own. The new candidate for fame endeavoured to induce Hume to proceed with some other portion of his narrative; and, having failed in this, he appears to have been desirous that he should at least be allowed to be the first to claim the notice of the public.

"I am (says Hume in a letter to him) nearly printed out, and shall be sure to send you a copy by the stage coach, or some other conveyance. I beg of you to make remarks as you go along. It would have been much better had we communicated before printing, which was always my desire, and was most suitable to the friendship which always did, and I hope always will subsist between us. I speak this chiefly on my own account. For though I had the perusal of your sheets before I printed, I was not able to derive sufficient benefits from them, or indeed to make any alteration by their assistance. There still remain, I fear, many errors, of which you could have convinced me if we had canvassed the matter in conversation. Perhaps I might also have been sometimes no less fortunate with you." He adds, "Millar was proposing to publish me about March; but I shall communicate to him your desire, even though I think it entirely groundless, as you will likewise think after you have read my volume. He has very needlessly delayed your publication till the first week of February, at the desire of the Edinburgh booksellers, who could no way be affected by a publication in London. I was exceedingly sorry not to be able to comply with your desire, when you expressed your wish that I should not write this period. I could not write downward. For when you find occasion, by new discoveries, to correct your opinion with regard to facts which passed in queen Elizabeth's days; who, that has not the best opportunities of informing himself, could venture to relate any recent transactions? I must therefore have abandoned altogether this scheme of the English History, in which I had proceeded so far, if I had not acted as I did. You will see what light and force this history of the Tudors bestows on that of the Stewarts. Had I been prudent I should have begun with it."

The alarm which Dr. Robertson conceived from the rivalship of his friend was, however, groundless. His success was not, like that of Hume, the slow growth of years. It was complete and immediate. So rapid was the sale of the book, that, before a month had elapsed, his publisher informed him that it was necessary to set about preparing for a second edition. It was read and admired by a part of the royal family; and plausive and grateful letters were showered on him from all quarters. Warburton, Horace Walpole, Lord Mansfield, Lord Lyttelton, Dr. Douglas, Hurd, and many other men of eminence, all concurred in swelling the chorus of praise. Among the foremost to blazon his merits was his amicable rival, Hume, whose letters bear repeated testimony to the warmth of his friendship, and his noble freedom from the base dominion of envy. "I am diverting myself," says he, "with the notion of how much you will profit by the applause of my enemies in Scotland. Had you and I been such fools as to have given way to jealousy, to have entertained animosity and malignity against each other, and to have rent all our acquaintance into parties, what a noble amusement we should have exhibited to the blockheads, which now they are likely to be disappointed of! All the people whose friendship or judgment either of us value are friends to both, and will be pleased with the success of both, as we will be with that of each other. I declare to you I have not of a long time had a more sensible pleasure than the good reception of your History has given me within this fortnight." In another place, with a sportiveness not unusual in his correspondence, he exclaims, "But though I have given this character of your work to Monsieur Helvetius, I warn you that this is the last time that, either to Frenchman or Englishman, I shall ever speak the least good of it. A plague take you! Here I sat near the historical summit of Parnassus, immediately under Dr. Smollet; and you have the impudence to squeeze yourself by me, and place yourself directly under his feet. Do you imagine that this can be agreeable to me! And must not I be guilty of great simplicity to contribute my endeavours to your thrusting me out of my place in Paris as well as at London? But I give you warning that you will find the matter somewhat difficult, at least in the former city. A friend of mine, who is there, writes home to his father the strangest accounts on that head; which my modesty will not permit me to repeat, but which it allowed me very deliciously to swallow."

The hold which the History of Scotland thus suddenly acquired on the public mind it yet retains. Fourteen editions were published during the life-time of the author, and the editions since his decease have been still more numerous. It has undoubtedly established itself as a classical English production. For a while, indeed, the voice of criticism was mute; and the historian had only to enjoy the luxury of his triumph. But, at length, some of his opinions, particularly his belief of the guilt of Mary, found opponents in the candid and well informed Tytler, the learned, acute, and eloquent Stuart, and the dogmatical Whitaker; the latter of whom, though master of talents, erudition, and forcible reasoning, almost rendered truth itself repulsive by the petulance and overbearingness of his manner, and the ruggedness of his style. Of his antagonists, however, the historian took not the slightest public notice, contenting himself with the silent correction of such passages in his work as his matured judgment had decided to be erroneous. In a letter to Gibbon he laconically notices Whitaker. "You will see," says he, "that I have got in Mr. Whitaker an adversary so bigoted and zealous, that though I have denied no article of faith, and am at least as orthodox as himself, yet he rails against me with all the asperity of theological hatred. I shall adhere to my fixed maxim of making no reply."

It was not merely a harvest of unproductive fame that was reaped by Dr. Robertson. He was no sooner known to the world than preferment was rapidly bestowed on him. In the autumn of 1758, while his work was in the hands of the printer, he was translated from Gladsmuir to one of the churches of the Scottish metropolis. I believe the church to which he was removed to have been that of the Old Gray Friars, in which, some years afterwards, his friend Dr. Erskine became his coadjutor. On the History issuing from the press, he was appointed chaplain of Stirling Castle, and, in 1761, one of his Majesty's chaplains in ordinary for Scotland. The dignity of Principal of the College of Edinburgh was conferred on him in 1762; and, two years subsequently to this, the office of Historiographer for Scotland, which, since the death of Crawfurd, in 1726, had been disused, was revived in his favour, with an annual stipend of two hundred pounds.

By the remuneration which he had received for his history, and the salaries which arose from his various appointments, Dr. Robertson was now in possession of an income far greater than had ever before been possessed by any Scotch presbyterian minister, and certainly not falling short of that which had been enjoyed by some bishops at the period when the church of Scotland was under episcopal government. A few of his indiscreet friends seem, however, to have thought that his talents were not adequately rewarded, and even that the clerical profession in the northern part of our island did not afford for them a sphere of action sufficiently extensive. The church of England held forth richer prospects to ambition and to mental endowments; and they were of opinion that, by transferring his services to that church, he might obtain a share in its highest dignities and emoluments. To this scheme allusions may be found in the letters which, about this time, were addressed to him by Dr. John Blair, Sir Gilbert Elliot, and Mr. Hume. But Dr. Robertson had a larger share of foresight and prudence than his advisers, and he rejected their dangerous though well intended counsel. It is, perhaps, more than doubtful whether, had it been executed, their plan would have produced the desired effect. This kind of transplanting has often been tried, but seldom, if ever, with any degree of success. The plant, vigorous on its native bed, languishes and is dwarfed on an alien soil. Dr. Robertson had now reached the mature age of forty-one; his opinions, his habits, his connexions, had all been formed with a reference to the circle in which he moved, and it was not probable that they could be suddenly bent with advantage in an opposite direction. In Scotland he had no competitors who could rise to a level with him; in England he would, perhaps, have had many; and he may be supposed to have thought with Cæsar, that it is better to be the first man in a village than the second at Rome. Nor was there any room in England for the exercise of that kind of eloquence in which he particularly excelled; the eloquence which is manifested in debate. By the force of his oratory he left far behind all his rivals and opponents, and wielded at will the general assembly of the Scottish church; but, since the convocation was shorn of its controversial and declamatory glories, since it was smitten with an incapacity of embarrassing the government, fostering theological rancour, and displaying the unseemly spectacle of Christian divines arrayed in worse than barbarian hostility to each other, there has not in this country existed any deliberative clerical body in which Dr. Robertson could have exerted those argumentative and rhetorical powers that, among his fellow ministers, obtained for him so entire an ascendancy. His preferment might also have stopped short of the point which his sanguine friends expected it to attain; and, whatever its degree, it would in all probability have been looked on with a jealous eye by many of his brethren on the south of the Tweed. There was, besides, another and still more powerful reason that must have influenced his decision. He had for nearly twenty years been a leading minister of the presbyterian establishment; and his now quitting it to enter into a prelatical church, which, as being deemed a scion from the hated stock of Rome, was still held in abomination by many of his countrymen, could scarcely have failed to be considered as an interested and base sacrifice of his principles and his character at the shrine of lucre and ambition. To be branded as a deserter by the zealots of the one institution, and by the envious of the other, was not a favourable auspice under which to commence his new career; and he therefore acted wisely, as well as honourably, in remaining a member of the Scottish church.

Having resolved to remain in Scotland, and to rely chiefly on his pen for the advancement of his fortune, Dr. Robertson had now to choose another theme on which his talents could be profitably employed. To the composition of history, in which he had met with such stimulating success, he wisely determined to adhere. It was, indeed, in that department that he was peculiarly qualified to excel, by his power of vivid description, and his happy delineation of character. His friends were consulted on this occasion; each had some favourite plan to suggest to him; and he seems to have been absolutely embarrassed by the affluence of subjects, many of which were worthy of his best exertions to illustrate and adorn them. If a ludicrous simile may be allowed, we may say that he found it no less difficult to fix his choice, than it was for Mr. Shandy to decide to what purpose he should apply the legacy which was left to him by his sister Dinah. Dr. John Blair strenuously recommended to him to write a complete History of England, and assured him that Lord Chesterfield had declared his readiness to move, in the house of peers, for public encouragement to him, in case of his undertaking a work which might with justice be considered as being a national one. But from adopting this project, though it was one which he had early cherished, Dr. Robertson was deterred by his honourable unwillingness to interfere with his friend Hume, who was now putting the finishing hand to his great labour. Hume himself advised him to undertake a series of modern lives, in the manner of Plutarch. "You see," said he, "that in Plutarch the life of Cæsar may be read in half an hour,

Were you to write the life of Henry the Fourth of France after that model, you might pillage all the pretty stories in Sully, and speak more of his mistresses than of his battles. In short, you might gather the flower of all modern history in this manner. The remarkable popes, the kings of Sweden, the great discoverers and conquerors of the New World, even the eminent men of letters might furnish you with matter, and the quick despatch of every different work would encourage you to begin a new one If one volume were successful, you might compose another at your leisure, and the field is inexhaustible. There are persons whom you might meet with in the corners of history, so to speak, who would be a subject of entertainment quite unexpected; and as long as you live, you might give and receive amusement by such a work." That so excellent an idea should not have been acted upon must be regretted by every one who is a lover of literature. By Horace Walpole two subjects, of no trivial interest, were pointed out. These were the History of Learning, and the History of the reigns of Nerva, Trajan, Adrian, and the two Antonines; the latter of which Walpole declared that he should be tempted to denominate the History of Humanity. Dr. Robertson himself seems, at one time, to have thought, though but transiently, of tracing the events which occurred in the age of Leo the Tenth. There is no reason to lament that he did not undertake this task, which was once meditated on by Warton, and has since been performed by a writer whom nature has largely gifted, and who possesses a profound knowledge of the records, arts, and language of Italy. But the two plans which had the ascendancy in his mind, and between which he long hesitated, were the History of Greece, and the History of Charles the Fifth. At length, notwithstanding the objections which were urged by Hume and Horace Walpole, he made choice of the reign of Charles as the subject of his second attempt.

When he had for about a year been engaged, partly in those preliminary researches which are necessary to give value to a work like that on which he was occupied, and partly in composition, his progress was suddenly suspended, by the intervention of a personage of such elevated rank as to render it almost impossible for him to decline a compliance with that which was required from him. It has been seen, that he was early desirous to be the historian of his native island, and that friendship alone prevented him from being so. He was now informed that the wishes of the British sovereign were in unison with his own. In the latter part of July, 1761, he was written to on this head by lord Cathcart. " Lord Bute told me the king's thoughts as well as his own," said lord Cathcart, " with respect to your History of Scotland, and a wish his majesty had expressed to see a History of England by your pen. His lordship assured me, every source of information which government can command would be open to you, and that great, laborious, and extensive as the work must be, he would take care your encouragement should be proportioned to it. He seemed to be aware of some objections you once had, founded on the apprehension of clashing or interfering with Mr. David Hume, who is your friend: but as your performance and his will be upon plans so different from each other, and as *his* will, in point of time, have so much the start of yours, these objections did not seem to him such as, upon reflection, were likely to continue to have much weight with you. I must add, that though I did not think it right to inquire into lord Bute's intentions before I knew a little of your mind, it appeared to me plain, that they were higher than any views which can open to you in Scotland, and which, I believe, he would think inconsistent with the attention the other subject would necessarily require."

A proposition thus powerfully enforced it would, under any circumstances, have been difficult for Dr. Robertson to reject. But, in fact, the reasons which formerly influenced his conduct had ceased to exist. Hume had now completed his history, it was before the public, and its fate must be irrevocably decided before a line of the rival narrative could be committed to paper. Dr. Robertson was convinced of this, and therefore he did not hesitate to embrace the opportunity which was offered to him. 'After the first publication of the History of Scotland, and the favourable reception it met with," said he in his answer to lord Cathcart, "I had both very tempting offers from booksellers, and very confident assurances of public encouragement, if I would undertake the History of England But as Mr. Hume, with whom, notwithstanding the contrariety of our sentiments both in religion and politics, I live in great friendship, was at that time in the middle of the subject, no consideration of interest or reputation would induce me to break in upon a field of which he had taken prior possession; and I determined that my interference with him should never be any obstruction to the sale or success of his work. Nor do I yet repent of my having resisted so many solicitations to alter this resolution. But the case I now think is entirely changed. His History will have been published several years before any work of mine on the same subject can appear; its first run will not be marred by any jostling with me, and it will have taken that station in the literary system which belongs to it. This objection, therefore, which I thought, and still think, so weighty at that time, makes no impression on me at present, and I can now justify my undertaking the English History, to myself, to the world, and to him. Besides, our manner of viewing the same subject is so different or peculiar, that (as was the case in our last books) both may maintain their own rank, have their own partisans, and possess their own merit, without hurting each other."

To enable him to accomplish so arduous a labour, he considered it necessary, not only that he should be established in such a manner as would divest him of all anxiety as to pecuniary concerns, but that he should likewise have the power of devoting to study a larger portion of his time than it was now possible for him to allot to that purpose. "Were I to carve out my own fortune," said he, "I should wish to continue one of his majesty's chaplains for Scotland, but to resign any charge as a minister of Edinburgh, which engrosses more of my time than one who is a stranger to the many minute duties of that office can well imagine. I would wish to apply my whole time to literary pursuits, which is at present parcelled out among innumerable occupations. In order to enable me to make this resignation some appointment must be assigned me for life. What that should be, it neither becomes me, nor do I pretend to say. One thing, however I wish with some earnestness, that the thing might be executed soon, both as it will give me great vigour in my studies to have my future fortune ascertained in so honourable a manner, and because, by allowing me to apply myself wholly to my present work, it will enable me to finish it in a less time, and to begin so much sooner to my new task." But though he was desirous to obtain some appointment, in order that he might not be "reduced entirely to the profession of an author," he at the same moment, with becoming spirit, declared that he did not wish to derive any emolument from it before he could commence the particular task for which the appointment was to be given. The proposal that he should remove to London, he was averse from complying with, though he did not put a direct negative on it; and he could not consent to begin the History of Britain till he had completed that of Charles the Fifth.

This scheme, which seems to have been almost brought to maturity, was, nevertheless, dropped; but for what reason is unknown. Mr. Stewart is disposed to believe that the failure of it may in part be attributed to the resignation of lord Bute. It was certainly so much a favourite with Dr. Robertson that he long cherished it, and abandoned it with reluctance We may, perhaps, be allowed to smile, or to wonder, that a sovereign should have selected a writer confessedly of Whig principles to compose a History of England, in opposition to one produced by a friend of arbitrary power; and we may also be allowed to doubt, whether, as far as regarded its sentiments, such a work, written by a Whig under the auspices of a court, would have proved quite satisfactory either to the monarch or to the people. There might, at least, have been some danger that it would have justified the sarcasm which was uttered by Horace Walpole, on another occasion "You must know, sir," said Dr. Robertson to nim, "that I look upon myself as a moderate Whig."—"Yes, doctor," replied Walpole, "I look on you as a *very* moderate Whig."

As soon as this negotiation was broken off, he bent all his exertions to the task which he had commenced. The public curiosity was highly excited, and it was long kept on the stretch before it was gratified. In the summer of 1761, he stated that one third of the work was finished, and that two years more would be required to bring the whole to perfection. But there never yet was an author who did not deceive himself, and consequently deceive others, as to the period at which his labour would be completed. The stupid, the thoughtless, and the malignant (and there are many persons, not literary, though connected with literature, who belong to these classes) consider as intended for the purpose of deception the erroneous estimate which authors are thus apt to form. They either cannot or will not be taught that, in spite of Dr. Johnson's bold assertion to the contrary, no man is at all hours capable of thinking deeply, or of clothing his thoughts in an attractive dress; that he who is dependent on his reputation for existence ought not to be compelled to hazard it by crude and slovenly efforts, the product of haste; that he who draws up a narrative from widely scattered, numerous, and conflicting documents must often, in painful research and in balancing evidence, spend more months than he had calculated on spending weeks; that the discovery of a single paper, the existence of which was previously unknown, may not only throw a new light upon a subject, but give to it an entirely new colour, and may compel a writer to modify, to arrange, and even to cancel, much that he had supposed to have received his last touches; and, therefore, that the delay which, as being a proof of literary indolence, is so frequently and so unfeelingly an object of censure, ought rather in many cases to be rewarded with praise, because it is a duty which an author conscientiously, and at his own cost, performs to society and to truth. Impediments of this kind no doubt retarded the progress of Dr. Robertson; to which must be added his multifarious avocations, as principal of the university, a minister of one of the churches of the Scottish metropolis, and an active member of the general assembly, in which body, as Mr. Stewart informs us, faction was running high at that epoch. The transactions relative to America he likewise found to be of too vast a magnitude, to allow of their being compressed into an episode. He was under the necessity of reserving them for a separate history; and this circumstance obliged him in some degree to make a change in his original plan. It is, therefore, not wonderful that the publication of his work was protracted six years beyond the time which he had himself assigned for it.

At length, early in 1769, appeared, in three volumes quarto, the History of Charles the Fifth. It had been perused, while in the press, by Hume, and probably by other friends, and had gained the warmest praise. "I got yesterday from Strahan," says Hume, in one of his letters, "about thirty sheets of your History, to be sent over to Suard, and last night and this morning have run them over with great avidity. I could not deny myself the satisfaction (which I hope also will not displease you) of expressing presently my extreme approbation of them. To say only they are very well written, is by far too faint an expression, and much inferior to the sentiments I feel: they are composed with nobleness, with dignity, with elegance, and with judgment, to which there are few equals. They even excel, and I think in a sensible degree, your History of Scotland. I propose to myself great pleasure in being the only man in England, during some months, who will be in the situation of doing you justice, after which you may certainly expect that my voice will be drowned in that of the public."

Hume's anticipation was prophetic. Soon after the work had come out, he wrote to his friend, in the following unequivocal terms. "The success has answered my expectations, and I, who converse with the great, the fair, and the learned, have scarcely heard an opposite voice, or even whisper, to the general sentiments. Only I have heard that the Sanhedrim at Mrs. Macaulay's condemns you as little less a friend to government and monarchy than myself." Horace Walpole was almost equally laudatory; lord Lyttelton testified his admiration; and, as Hume had long before done, recommended to the historian to write, in the manner of Plutarch, the lives of eminent persons. Voltaire, also, paid a flattering tribute. "It is to you and to Mr. Hume," said he, " that it belongs to write history You are eloquent, learned, and impartial. I unite with Europe in esteeming you." Nor was the fame of the author confined to his native island. Through the intervention of the baron D'Holbach, M. Suard was induced to translate the work into French, while it was being printed in England, and his masterly translation is said to have established his own literary character, and to have been the means of his obtaining a seat in the French academy. The remuneration which the author himself received was magnificent; especially in an age when it was not customary to give a large sum of money for the purchase of copyright. It is affirmed to have been no less than four thousand five hundred pounds.

It is not to be imagined, however, that the History of Charles the Fifth could entirely escape the severity of criticism, which appears to be the common lot of all literary productions. By the Abbé Mably it was attacked in rude and contemptuous language; which, without having the power to injure the work, was disgraceful to the person who descended to use it. Gilbert Stuart likewise assailed it; but with more skill than the French critic, and with a vigour which was animated by personal resentment. That his acuteness detected many inaccuracies, it would be absurd to dispute; but no one can doubt that he pushed his censure farther than was consonant with justice, when he characterized Dr. Robertson as an author " whose total abstinence from all ideas and inventions of his own permitted him to carry an undivided attention to other men's thoughts and speculations." Walpole, too, in later life, asserted that the reading of Dr. Robertson was not extensive, that the Introduction to the History of Charles abounds with gross errors, and that in many instances he has mistaken exceptions for rules. The work, however, still maintains its station; and, even admitting all that truth or ingenious prejudice can urge against it, who is there who will now have the boldness to deny that it forms a splendid addition to our historical treasures?

After having completed this arduous undertaking, Dr. Robertson allowed himself some respite from literary toil; a respite which, in fact, was necessary for the preservation of his health. His mind was, however, too active to remain long unoccupied, and he hastened to resume the pen. As a sequel to the history of Charles, he had promised to give to the public a narrative of the Spanish discoveries, conquests, and proceedings in America. This plan he soon resolved to enlarge, so as to include in it the transactions of all the European colonizers of the American continent. To the origin and progress of the British empire in that quarter, it was originally his intention to devote an entire volume. Than the History of the New World it was impossible for him to have chosen a subject more fertile, more attractive, or better calculated for the display of his peculiar talents

There was "ample room and verge enough" for eloquence to expatiate in. The rapidly succeeding events which he was to describe were scarcely less marvellous than those of an oriental fiction; one of his heroes, the dauntless explorer of unknown oceans, will always excite the wonder, admiration, and pity of mankind; others, though villains, were at least villains of no common powers; and the characters, the customs, the manners, the scenery, every thing in short that was connected with the work, possessed throughout the charm of novelty, and, in many instances, that of the most picturesque and forcible contrast.

To the first part of his subject, that which relates to the discovery of the New World, and the conquests and policy of the Spaniards, eight years of studious toil were devoted by Dr. Robertson. At length, in the spring of 1777, he put forth, in two quartos, the result of his labours. The public again received him with enthusiasm, and his literary friends again pressed forward to congratulate and to praise him. Hume was no longer in existence; but his place was supplied by Gibbon, who testified his entire approbation of the volumes even before he had wholly perused them. "I have seen enough," said he, " to convince me that the present publication will support, and, if possible, extend the fame of the author; that the materials are collected with care, and arranged with skill; that the progress of discovery is displayed with learning and perspicuity; that the dangers, the achievements, and the views of the Spanish adventurers, are related with a temperate spirit; and that the most original, perhaps the most curious portion of human manners, is at length rescued from the hands of sophists and declaimers."

But, perhaps, of all the applause which was bestowed on Dr. Robertson, none was more gratifying than that which was given by Burke; a man eminent at once as a writer, an orator, and a statesman. " I am perfectly sensible," says he, " of the very flattering distinction I have received in your thinking me worthy of so noble a present as that of your History of America. I have, however, suffered my gratitude to lie under some suspicion, by delaying my acknowledgment of so great a favour. But my delay was only to render my obligation to you more complete, and my thanks, if possible, more merited. The close of the session brought a great deal of very troublesome though not important business on me at once. I could not go through your work at one breath at that time, though I have done it since. I am now enabled to thank you, not only for the honour you have done me, but for the great satisfaction, and the infinite variety and compass of instruction, I have received from your incomparable work. Every thing has been done which was so naturally to be expected from the author of the History of Scotland, and of the Age of Charles the Fifth. I believe few books have done more than this, towards clearing up dark points, correcting errors, and removing prejudices. You have too he rare secret of rekindling an interest on subjects that had so often been treated, and in which every thing which could feed a vital flame appeared to have been consumed. I am sure I read many parts of your History with that fresh concern and anxiety which attend those who are not previously apprized of the event. You have, besides, thrown quite a new light on the present state of the Spanish provinces, and furnished both materials and hints for a rational theory of what may be expected from them in future

" The part which I read with the greatest pleasure is the discussion on the manners and character of the inhabitants of the New World. I have always thought with you, that we possess at this time very great advantages towards the knowledge of human nature. We need no longer go to history to trace it in all its ages and periods. History, from its comparative youth, is but a poor instructer. When the Egyptians called the Greeks children in antiquities, we may well call them children; and so we may call all those nations which were able to trace the progress of society only within their own limits. But now the great map of mankind is unrolled at once, and there is no state or gradation of barbarism, and no mode of refinement, which we have not at the same moment under our view; the very different civility of Europe and of China; the barbarism of Persia and of Abyssinia; the erratic manners of Tartary and of Arabia; the savage state of North America and New Zealand. Indeed you have made a noble use of the advantages you have had. You have employed philosophy to judge on manners, and from manners you have drawn new resources for philosophy. I only think that in one or two points you have hardly done justice to the savage character."

The honours which were paid to him by foreigners were equally gratifying. The Royal Academy of History at Madrid unanimously elected him a member on the eighth of August, in 1777, "in testimony of their approbation of the industry and care with which he had applied to the study of Spanish History, and as a recompense for his merit in having contributed so much to illustrate and spread the knowledge of it in foreign countries." It likewise appointed one of its members to translate the History of America into the Spanish language, and considerable progress is believed to have been made in the translation. But the latter measure excited alarm in an absurd and decrepit government, which sought for safety in concealment rather than in a bold and liberal policy, and, like the silly bird, imagined that by hiding its own head it could escape from the view of its pursuers. The translation was, therefore, officially ordered to be suppressed, with the vain hope of keeping the world still in the dark, with respect to the nature of the Spanish American commerce, and of the system of colonial administration.

It was not from Spain alone that he received testimonies of respect. In 1781, the Academy of Sciences at Padua elected him one of its foreign members; and, in 1783, the same compliment was paid to him by the Imperial Academy of Sciences at St. Petersburgh. The empress Catharine also, who, numerous as were her faults, was a woman of a strong and enlightened intellect, also conferred on him a flattering distinction. She ordered his friend, Dr. Rogerson, to transmit to him, as a mark of her esteem, a gold snuff box, richly set with diamonds; observing at the same time, that a person whose labours had afforded her so much satisfaction merited some attention from her. So much, indeed, was she delighted with the works of the Scottish author, that she did not hesitate to assign to him the place of first model in historical composition, to express much admiration of the sagacity and discernment which he displayed in painting the human mind and character, and to declare that the History of Charles the Fifth was the constant companion of her journeys, and that she was never tired of perusing it, particularly the introductory volume.

As soon as enthusiasm had subsided, criticism began its labours in search of defects. It was objected to the author, that he had shown a disposition to palliate or to veil the enormities of the Spaniards, in their American conquests, and that he had shed an illusive lustre round the daring and intelligent but sanguinary and unprincipled Cortes. Even Professor Stewart, notwithstanding his honourable affection for the memory of his friend, shrinks from vindicating him on this score, and contents himself with opposing to the charge "those warm and enlightened sentiments of humanity which in general animate his writings." Unwilling to censure severely, and unable to exculpate, Bryan Edwards suggests, as an apology for Dr. Robertson, that this is one of the cases in which the mind, shrinking from the contemplation of alleged horrors, wishes to resist conviction, and to relieve itself by incredulity. Dr. Gleig, however, the latest biographer of the historian, indignantly rejects this apology as absurd; and, more enterprising than his predecessors, partly labours to invalidate the accusation, by lessening the sum of Spanish cruelties, and partly to render it of no weight, by pleading that the writer probably considered the conquests of Mexico and Peru as means employed by Providence to accomplish the noblest and most beneficent purposes. That Dr. Robertson did really regard those conquests in such a light we may easily believe; since, in his sermon on the state of the world at the appearance of Christ, he manifests similar sentiments with respect to the measureless and unslumbering ambition of those universal robbers the Romans, whom he is pleased to style " the noblest people that ever entered on the stage of the world." But this defence is merely sophistical. Though we are not ignorant that a wise and benignant Providence educes good from evil, it is not the business of an historian to diminish the loathing which evil deeds ought to excite; nor does it appear that morality is likely to be much benefited, by teaching tyrants and murderers to imagine that, while they are giving the rein to their own furious and malignant passions, they are only performing their destined tasks as instruments of the Deity.

This was by no means all that was urged against the History of America. It is, in fact, not now attempted to be denied that, in many instances, Dr. Robertson was led astray by his partiality to the brilliant but fallacious theories of De Pauw and Buffon. Clavigero, in his History of Mexico, detected and somewhat harshly animadverted on several errors, a part of which were subsequently rectified. Bryan Edwards, too, pointed out some contradictions, and some erroneous statements. But the most severe censor is Mr. Southey, a man eminently well informed on ancient Spanish and American events. In his History of Brazil, after having described the mode of reckoning in use among the transatlantic tribes, he adds, " when Pauw reasoned upon the ignorance of the Americans in numbers, did he suppress this remarkable fact, or was he ignorant of it? The same question is applicable to Dr. Robertson, who, on this, and on many other subjects, in what he calls his History of America, is guilty of such omissions, and consequent misrepresentations, as to make it certain either that he had not read some of the most important documents to which he refers, or that he did not choose to notice the facts which he found there, because they were not in conformity to his own preconceived opinions. A remarkable example occurs respecting a circulating medium; when he mentions cocoa-nuts, which were used as money in Mexico, and says, ' this seems to be the utmost length which the Americans had advanced towards the discovery of any expedient for supplying the use of money.' Now, it is said by Cortes himself, that when he was about to make cannon, he had copper enough, but wanted tin; and having bought up all the plates and pots, which he could find among the soldiers, he began to inquire among the natives. He then found, that in the province of Tachco, little pieces of tin, like thin coin, were used for money, there and in other places. And this led him to a discovery of the mines from whence it was taken. The reputation of this author must rest upon his History of Scotland, if that can support it. His other works are grievously deficient."

Such are the defects which are attributed to Dr. Robertson's History On the other hand, it ought to be remembered, that many sources of knowledge, which were then hidden, have since become accessible, that no man is at all times exempted from the dominion of prejudice, that the most cautious vigilance may sink into a momentary slumber, and that to him who has achieved much, a tribute of gratitude is due, even though it may be discovered that he has left something undone. Were the History of the Spanish Conquests proved to be merely a fiction, it would nevertheless continue to be read, such attraction is there in the general elegance of the language, the skilful delineation of the characters, and the sustained interest and spirit of the narrative.

In the preface to this portion of his labours, he made known his intention to resume the subject at a future period; and he assigned the ferment which then agitated our North American colonies as a reason for suspending, at present, the execution of that part of his plan which related to British America. At the very beginning, in truth, of the contest with the colonies, he congratulated himself on his not having completed his narrative. "It is lucky," said he, in a letter to Mr. Strahan, "that my American History was not finished before this event. How many plausible theories that I should have been entitled to form, are contradicted by what has now happened." A fragment of this History, which, however, was carefully corrected by him, and which he preserved when he committed his manuscripts to the flames, was all that he subsequently wrote of the work; and this was published by his son to prevent it from falling into the hands of an editor who might make alterations and additions, and obtrude the whole on the public as the genuine composition of the author.

With respect to a separation between the mother country and the colonists, Dr. Robertson seems to have somewhat varied in his sentiments, and to have contemplated the probability of such an event with much more dislike in 1775 than he did in 1766. In the latter year, speaking of the repeal of the stamp act, he said, "I rejoice, from my love of the human species, that a million of men in America have some chance of running the same great career which other free people have held before them. I do not apprehend revolution or independence sooner than these must or should come. A very little skill and attention in the art of governing may preserve the supremacy of Britain as long as it ought to be preserved." But, in 1775, though he still acknowledged that the colonies must ultimately become independent, he was anxious that their liberation should be delayed till as distant a period as possible, and was clearly of opinion that they had as yet no right to throw off their allegiance. Nor was he sparing of his censure on the ministers for the want of policy and firmness, which he considered them to have displayed at the commencement of the quarrel. "I agree with you about the affairs of America," said he, in a letter, which was written in the autumn of 1775, "incapacity, or want of information, has led the people employed there to deceive the ministry. Trusting to them, they have been trifling for two years, when they should have been serious, until they have rendered a very simple piece of business extremely perplexed. They have permitted colonies, disjoined by nature and situation, to consolidate into a regular systematical confederacy; and when a few regiments stationed in each capital would have rendered it impossible for them to take arms, they have suffered them quietly to levy and train forces, as if they had not seen against whom they were prepared. But now we are fairly committed, and I do think it fortunate that the violence of the Americans has brought matters to a crisis too soon for themselves. From the beginning of the contest I have always asserted that independence was their object. The distinction between *taxation* and *regulation* is mere folly. There is not an argument against our right of taxation that does not conclude with tenfold force against our power of regulating their trade. They may profess or disclaim what they please, and hold the language that best suits their purpose; but, if they have any meaning, it must be that they should be free states, connected with us by blood, by habit, and by religion, but at liberty to buy and sell and trade where and with whom they please. This they will one day attain, but not just now, if there be any degree of political wisdom or vigour remaining. At the same time one cannot but regret that prosperous growing states should be checked in their career. As a lover of mankind, I bewail it; but as a subject of Great Britain, I must wish that their dependence on it should continue. If the wisdom of government can terminate the contest with honour instantly, that would be the most desirable issue. This, however, I take to be *now* impossible; and I will venture to foretell, that if our leaders do not at once exert the power of the British empire in its full force, the struggle will be long, dubious, and disgraceful We are past the hour of lenitives and half exertions. If the contest be protracted, the smallest interruption of the tranquillity that reigns in Europe, or even the appearance of it, may be fatal."

It must be owned, that language like this goes very far towards justifying the sarcasm of Horace Walpole, that the reverend historian was " a *very* moderate Whig." Perhaps, also, his belief that, at the outset, a few regiments in each capital would have sufficed to trample down the resistance of the Americans, may now appear difficult to be reconciled with a knowledge of military affairs, or of human nature. Yet we must, at the same time, remember that this erroneous idea was held by him in common with many other men of intellect, and that it was even brought forward in the British senate as an undeniable truth.

Though the American war precluded Dr. Robertson from bringing to a close his history of the British settlements, it is not easy to discover why he could not continue it to a certain point ; or why, at least, he could not proceed with that part of his narrative which related to the colonization of Brazil, and the violent struggles between the Dutch and the Portuguese in that country—an extensive subject, and worthy of his pen, as it would have afforded him abundant opportunities for the display of his delineative talents. Our curiosity on this head is not satisfied by the reason which, as we have recently seen, he himself gave, in his preface and in his letter to Mr. Strahan. That reason, however, he repeated in a correspondence with his friend Mr. Waddilove, and it is now in vain to seek for a better. It is certain that a wish to retire from literary toil was not his motive; for, at the same moment that he postponed his History of America, he declared that it was "neither his inclination nor his interest to remain altogether idle." As a proof of his sincerity, he projected a History of Great Britain, from the revolution to the accession of the House of Hanover, and even began to collect the necessary documents. Notwithstanding this seems to have been, for a while, a favourite scheme, it was speedily relinquished ; a circumstance which may justly be regretted. Hume then suggested the History of the Protestants in France. "The events," said he, " are important in themselves, and intimately connected with the great revolutions of Europe : some of the boldest or most amiable characters of modern times, the admiral Coligny, Henry IV., &c. would be your peculiar heroes ; the materials are copious, and authentic, and accessible ; and the objects appear to stand at that just distance which excites curiosity without inspiring passion."

The hint given by Hume was, however, not adopted. About the year 1779 or 1780, Dr. Robertson seems, indeed, to have seriously resolved to write no more for the public, but to pursue his studies at leisure, and for his own amusement. " His circumstances," says professor Stewart, " were independent: he was approaching to the age of sixty, with a constitution considerably impaired by a sedentary life; and a long application to the compositions he had prepared for the press had interfered with much of the gratification he might have enjoyed, if he had been at liberty to follow the impulse of his own taste and curiosity. Such a sacrifice must be more or less made by all who devote themselves to letters, whether with a view to emolument or to fame; nor would it perhaps be easy to make it, were it not for the prospect (seldom, alas! realized) of earning by their exertions, that learned and honourable leisure which he was so fortunate as to attain."

We must now contemplate Dr. Robertson in another point of view—that of his ecclesiastical and academical character ; in which, no less than in his literary capacity, he occupied a prominent station. The eminence, however, which he had not attained without difficulty, he did not hold entirely without danger. In one instance he was near falling a victim to his spirit of liberality. In 1778, the British legislature relieved the English Roman catholics from some of the severest of the barbarous penalties to which they had been subjected nearly a century before. Encouraged by this event, the Scottish catholics determined to petition parliament to extend the benefit to themselves. To this measure Dr. Robertson was friendly, and he successfully exerted his influence, and that of his partisans, to procure the rejection of a remonstrance against it, which was brought forward in the general assembly. But on this occasion, as, unhappily, on too many others, bigotry and ignorance triumphed over sound policy and Christian charity. The trumpet of fanaticism was immediately sounded, and men of the most opposite principles and interests hurried to obey the call. Presbyterians, seceders, and even episcopalians, the latter of whom were themselves under the lash of penal statutes, all combined in the crusade against papistry. Pamphlets and speeches were lavished, to prove that the constitution in church and state must inevitably perish, if an iota of relief were granted to the faithless members of an idolatrous and sanguinary church. The Roman catholics were so terrified at the fury that was thus aroused, that the principal gentlemen among them informed the ministry that they would desist from appealing to parliament; and they endeavoured to calm the popular tempest, by publishing in the daily papers an account of their proceedings. But the enlightened mob of Edinburgh had sagely resolved that the catholics should not even dare to wish for the slightest participation in the privileges of British subjects, without being punished for their temerity. Accordingly, on the 2d of February, 1779, multitudes of the lowest classes, headed by disguised leaders, assembled in the Scottish capital, burnt the house of the popish bishop and two chapels: and, in their even-handed justice, were on the point of committing to the flames an episcopal chapel, when they were propitiated, by being told that an episcopal clergyman was the author of one of the ablest tracts which had been published against popery. As, however, they could not consent to remit their vengeance, but only to change its object, they turned their wrath upon those who had expressed opinions favourable to the claims of the catholics. Dr. Robertson was marked out as one of the most guilty, and nothing less than the destruction of his property and life was considered as sufficient to atone for his crime. Fortunately his friends had provided for his safety, and, when the self-appointed champions of religion reached his house, it was found to be defended by a military force, which they had not enough of courage to look in the face. As they had come only to destroy and to murder, they, of course, retreated, when they discovered that, to accomplish their purpose, it would also be necessary to fight. Dr. Robertson is said to have manifested great firmness and tranquillity during this trying scene.

In selecting Dr. Robertson as the person most worthy of suffering by their summary process of punishment without trial, the mob of Edinburgh acted with a more than mobbish share of injustice. Though desirous that the catholics should be released from their thraldom, he was not disposed to put any thing to the hazard for the furtherance of that object, and had already withdrawn his patronage from such obnoxious clients. He was not one of those who, as Goldsmith says of Burke, are "too fond of the *right* to pursue the *expedient*." With him prudence was a governing principle. When, therefore, he saw that his countrymen were adverse to the measure, he advised the ministry to forbear from lending their countenance to it. In an eloquent speech, delivered in the general assembly, he afterwards explained and vindicated the view which he originally took of the subject, and the manner in which he finally acted. The perusal of that which he urged, on the latter point, will not merely show what were his motives in this instance, but also afford some insight into his general character. How far his system of policy is consonant with dignity or wisdom, which, indeed, are inseparable, I shall not stop to inquire. It might, perhaps, not improperly, be objected to him, that he mistakes the voice of a blind infuriated multitude for the voice of the people; though it is impossible for any two things to be more different in their nature. It might be asked, too, why the fanatical prejudices of a Scottish mob were to be treated with more respect than the complaints of the American colonists; why the one were to be indulged or complied with, while the other were to be silenced by "a few regiments stationed in each capital?" "As soon," says he, "as I perceived the extent and violence of the flame which the discussion of this subject had kindled in Scotland, my ideas concerning the expedience at this juncture of the measure in question, began to alter. For although I did think, and I do still believe, that if the protestants in this country had acquiesced in the repeal as quietly as our brethren in England and Ireland, a fatal blow would have been given to popery in the British dominions; I know, that in legislation, the sentiments and dispositions of the people, for whom laws are made, should be attended to with care. I remembered that one of the wisest men of antiquity declared, that he had framed for his fellow-citizens not the best laws, but the best laws which they could bear. I recollected with reverence, that the divine Legislator himself, accommodating his dispensations to the frailty of his subjects, had given the Israelites for a season *statutes which were not good*. Even the prejudices of the people are, in my opinion, respectable; and an indulgent legislator ought not unnecessarily to run counter to them. It appeared manifestly to be sound policy, in the present temper of the people, to sooth rather than to irritate them; and, however ill founded their apprehensions might be, some concession was now requisite in order to remove them."

This was, I believe, the last speech which he made in the General Assembly. While he was yet in the vigour of his faculties, and in the exercise of undiminished influence in that assembly, he came to a resolution to withdraw himself entirely from public business. It was in the year 1780, about the time when he ceased to be an historian, and when he was only fifty-nine, that he adopted this resolution. Several causes seem to have concurred in producing his retirement. It has been supposed by some, that he did not wish to remain on the scene till he was eclipsed by younger rivals; and it is known that he felt disgusted by the conduct of the violent men of his own party, who, though he had yielded many points to them against his better judgment, were nevertheless dissatisfied that he refused to resort to stronger measures than he deemed to be either right or prudent, and who, in consequence, tormented him with letters of remonstrance and reproach, which, as from their nature may easily be imagined, were written in a petulant and acrimonious style. In addition, there was one subject, which had long been a particular annoyance to him, and on which he had been more pertinaciously urged and fretted than on every other. This was a scheme for abolishing subscription to the Confession of Faith and Formula. Into this scheme, which he had avowed his determination to resist, whatever shape it might assume, many of his friends had zealously entered, and his patience was severely tried by their "beseeching or besieging" him with respect to so important an object. By his cautious and persuasive policy, he had for a considerable period prevented the controversy from being agitated in the assemblies; but he was of opinion that it would ultimately compel attention, and would give rise to vehement disputes; and it was this circumstance, as he himself confessed, that "at least confirmed his resolution to retire."

Having rendered triumphant a cause which, to say the least, had numerous enemies, it was hardly to be supposed that his character would not be aspersed by many of those who were mortified to witness his success.

Accordingly, the charge of having deserted the genuine principles of the Scottish church was often urged against him by some of his antagonists. Others, who had more of the zealot in their composition, did not stop here. These went so far as to accuse him of being indifferent to Christianity itself; and, in proof of this, they alleged his habits of intimacy with Hume, and his correspondence with Gibbon. It is difficult to say whether this stupid calumny ought to excite anger or contempt.

This, however, was the language of only malignant hearts, or little minds. By the great majority, even of those who were in opposition to him, full justice was done to his virtues, his talents, and the purity of his motives. Among those who, believing patronage to be a nuisance, were the most strenuous in contending with him, was Dr. Erskine, his college mate, and colleague in the ministry. That venerable and learned person always preserved for him a warm esteem, and, after the historian was no more, paid to his memory an animated and affectionate tribute from the pulpit. "His speeches in church courts," says Dr. Erskine, "were admired by those whom they did not convince, and acquired and preserved him an influence over a majority in them, which none before him enjoyed; though his measures were sometimes new, and warmly, and with great strength of argument, opposed, both from the press, and in the General Assembly. To this influence many causes contributed: his firm adherence to the principles of church policy, which he early adopted; his sagacity in forming plans; his steadiness in executing them; his quick discernment of whatever might hinder or promote his designs; his boldness in encountering difficulties; his presence of mind in improving every occasional advantage; the address with which, when he saw it necessary, he could make an honourable retreat; and his skill in stating a vote, and seizing the favourable moment for ending a debate and urging a decision. He guided and governed others, without seeming to assume any superiority over them; and fixed and strengthened his power, by often, in matters of form and expediency, preferring the opinions of those with whom he acted, to his own. In former times, hardly any rose up to speak in the General Assembly till called upon by the *Moderator*, unless men advanced in years, of high rank, or of established characters. His example and influence encouraged young men of abilities to take their share of public business; and thus deprived *Moderators* of an engine for preventing causes being fairly and impartially discussed. The power of others, who formerly had in some measure guided ecclesiastical affairs, was derived from ministers of state, and expired with their fall. He remained unhurt amidst frequent changes of administration. Great men in office were always ready to countenance him, to co-operate with him, and to avail themselves of his aid. But he judged for himself, and scorned to be their slave, or to submit to receive their instructions. Hence, his influence, not confined to men of mercenary views, extended to many of a free and independent spirit, who supported, because they approved, his measures; which others, from the same independent spirit, thought it their duty steadily to oppose.

"Deliberate in forming his judgment, but, when formed, not easily moved to renounce it, he sometimes viewed the altered plans of others with too suspicious an eye. Hence, there were able and worthy men, of whom he expressed himself less favourably, and whose later appearances in church judicatories he censured as inconsistent with principles they had formerly professed: while they maintained, that the system of managing church affairs was changed, not their opinions or conduct. Still, however, keen and determined opposition to his schemes of ecclesiastical policy neither extinguished his esteem nor forfeited his friendly offices, when he saw opposition carried on without rancour, and when he believed that it originated from conscience and principle, not from personal animosity, or envy, or ambition."

Of his private character, Dr. Erskine adds, that "he enjoyed the bounties of Providence, without running into riot; was temperate without austerity; condescending and affable without meanness; and in expense neither sordid nor prodigal. He could feel an injury, and yet bridle his passion; was grave, not sullen; steady, not obstinate; friendly, not officious; prudent and cautious, not timid."

Than the triumph which the principles of Dr. Robertson obtained in the General Assembly nothing could be more complete; and it was the more flattering, inasmuch as it was consummated after he had ceased to take a part in the debates. It had, from the year 1736, been the custom, annually, for the Assembly to instruct the Commission, "to make due application to the king and parliament for redress of the grievance of patronage, in case a favourable opportunity for doing so should occur." So cautious was the policy of Dr. Robertson, that, although he had entirely subverted the very groundwork on which this instruction was raised, he never chose to move that it should be expunged. He knew that it was popular with the great body of the people, and, therefore, he did not think it expedient to risk the chance of dissension in the Assembly, by an unnecessary and idle attack upon this shadow of a shade. In the year 1784, however, it was omitted, without any struggle being made in its favour, and it has never since been renewed.

Whether the system established by him has contributed to the harmony and welfare of the Scottish church is a question which yet remains undecided. It is urged, by the friends of the system, that it has given peace to the church; that the General Assembly is no longer occupied with angry appeals and tumultuous disputes; that instead of there being, as formerly, a necessity to call in a military force, to protect the presbytery in the act of induction, ministers are now peaceably settled; and that the worst that ever happens is the secession of the discontented part of the parishioners, and the consequent erection of a separate place of worship, which they frequent only till their zeal cools, and then desert to rejoin the kirk. But, on the other hand, it is contended, that the peace is rather in appearance than in reality; that, though the people have ceased to appeal to the Assembly, their silence arises from disgust and weariness, and not from satisfaction; that, grown too wise to enter into a protracted and fruitless contest, they immediately set themselves to rear a seceding meeting house, which often carries off a large proportion of the parishioners; and that, by this quiet but continual increase of seceding meetings, the influence of the established church has been gradually weakened and contracted, a spirit of disunion has been spread, and a heavy additional burden has been imposed on property of every kind.

But, whatever doubt may exist on this point, there seems to be none with respect to another. It is generally acknowledged that Dr. Robertson conduced greatly to give a more dignified character to the proceedings of the General Assembly, to introduce an impartial exercise of the judicial authority of the church, and to diffuse the principles of tolerance among men who had hitherto prided themselves on their utter contempt of them. In such respect are his decisions held, that they still form a sort of common law in the church; and the time which elapsed between his being chosen Principal of the University and his withdrawing from public life, is distinguished by the name of Dr. Robertson's administration

It is in his capacity of Principal that he is next to be considered. In this important office he displayed his wonted activity and talent. He began the performance of his duties, as his predecessors had done, by delivering annually a Latin discourse before the University. Of these orations, the first, the object of which was to recommend the study of classical learning, was delivered on the third of February, 1763. It is said, among numerous other splendid passages, to have contained a beautiful panegyric on the stoical philosophy. In the following year, his discourse "consisted chiefly of moral and literary observations, adapted to the particular circumstances of youth," and the style is affirmed to be "uncommonly elegant and impressive, and possessed of all the distinguishing characteristics of his English compositions." In 1765 and 1766, he chose for his theme the comparative advantages of public and private education; a subject which he treated in a masterly manner. After 1766 these annual lectures ceased his time being too fully occupied to allow of the continuance of them.

But, though his lectures were of necessity discontinued, he never remitted in his attention even to the minutest duties of his office. He appears, indeed, to have felt a filial anxiety to omit nothing which could assist in giving lustre to the University at which his own talents had been cultivated. With very slender funds, he made large additions to the public library; he planned or reformed most of the literary and medical societies, which have raised Edinburgh to such eminence as a seminary of learning, and a focus of literature; and he contrived to preserve an uninterrupted harmony among the numerous members of the body which he superintended. "The good sense, temper, and address," says professor Stewart, "with which he presided for thirty years at our university meetings, were attended with effects no less essential to our prosperity; and are attested by a fact which is perhaps without a parallel in the annals of any other literary community, that during the whole of that period there did not occur a single question which was not terminated by a unanimous decision."

To his exertions Scotland is also chiefly indebted for its Royal Society, which received its charter of incorporation in March, 1763. The basis of this establishment was the Philosophical Society, the founder of which was the celebrated Maclaurin. In his zeal to give all possible lustre to the new institution, by drawing together men of every species of merit, Dr. Robertson seems, for once, to have acted with less than his usual liberality. An antiquarian society, at the head of which was the earl of Buchan, had, two years before, been formed in the Scottish metropolis; and this body also was desirous to obtain the royal charter. The application which it made to the crown was, however, eagerly opposed, in a "Memorial from the principal and professors of the University of Edinburgh." This memorial is signed by Dr. Robertson; but it is so feeble in composition as well as in reasoning, that it is difficult to believe it to have flowed from his pen. The argument on which it wholly relies is, that "narrow countries" cannot supply materials for more than one society; that Scotland is such a country; and, therefore, that it "ought not to form its literary plans upon the model of the more extensive kingdoms in Europe, but in imitation of those which are more circumscribed." To this hostile proceeding the antiquaries responded, in a long memorial, which was penned with much acuteness, and was naturally expressive of some degree of resentment. They were successful in the contest, and their charter was granted.

The labours of Dr. Robertson, as a writer, were closed by a work which entered largely into antiquarian investigation, as connected with history In 1791 he published a quarto volume, containing his "Historical Disquisition concerning the Knowledge which the Ancients had of India; and the Progress of Trade with that Country prior to the Discovery of the Passage to it by the Cape of Good Hope." An Appendix was dedicated to observations on the civil policy, the laws and judicial proceedings, the arts, the sciences, and the religious institutions of the Indians. This subject, which occupied him twelve months, was suggested to him by the perusal of major Rennell's Memoirs for illustrating his History of Hindóstan, and was originally taken up with no other object than his own amusement and instruction. That it would become as popular as his other productions was, from its nature, not to be expected, but it obtained an honourable share of public approbation; and, though it has since been partly superseded by more elaborate inquiries, which, however, were grounded on more ample materials, it will always retain a certain degree of value, and will be considered as a proof of his industry, of his habits of research, and of the solidity of his judgment.

The latter years of Dr. Robertson's existence were passed in the well earned enjoyment of honourable leisure. But, though he ceased to write, he did not cease to be studious. Till the end of his life he is said to have risen early, and to have given up no part of his time to company before the hour of dinner. What he was in the moments of social ease has been so excellently described by professor Stewart, that his own words ought to be used. "A rich stock of miscellaneous information, acquired from books and from an extensive intercourse with the world, together with a perfect acquaintance at all times with the topics of the day, and the soundest sagacity and good sense applied to the occurrences of common life, rendered him the most instructive and agreeable of companions. He seldom aimed at art; but, with his intimate friends, he often indulged a sportive and fanciful species of humour. He delighted in good natured, characteristical anecdotes of his acquaintance, and added powerfully to their effect by his own enjoyment in relating them. He was, in a remarkable degree, susceptible of the ludicrous; but on no occasion did he forget the dignity of his character, or the decorum of his profession; nor did he ever lose sight of that classical taste which adorned his compositions. His turn of expression was correct and pure; sometimes, perhaps, inclining more than is expected, in the carelessness of a social hour, to formal and artificial periods; but it was stamped with his own manner no less than his premeditated style: it was always the language of a superior and a cultivated mind, and it embellished every subject on which he spoke. In the company of strangers, he increased his exertions to amuse and to inform; and the splendid variety of his conversation was commonly the chief circumstance on which they dwelt in enumerating his talents; and yet, I must acknowledge, for my own part, that much as I always admired his powers when they were thus called forth, I enjoyed his society less than when I saw him in the circle of his intimates, or in the bosom of his family."

It is not one of the least amiable features of his character, that, though he was not forward to volunteer his advice, yet, when he was consulted by his young acquaintance, as was very often the case, "he entered into their concerns with the most lively interest, and seemed to have a pleasure and a pride in imparting to them all the lights of his experience and wisdom."

It was about the end of the year 1791 that the health of Dr. Robertson began to manifest indications of decline. Strong symptoms of jaundice next appeared, his constitution was sapped, and a lingering and fatal illness ensued. His spirits, however, remained unbroken. Till within a few months of his death, he persisted in officiating as a minister. When his decaying strength no longer allowed him to perform his clerical duties, he retired to Grange House, in the neighbourhood of Edinburgh, that he might have the advantage of more quiet, a pure air, and the sight of those rural and picturesque objects in which he had ever delighted. "While he was able to walk abroad," says Mr. Stewart, "he commonly passed a part of the day in a small garden, enjoying the simple gratifications it afforded with all his wonted relish. Some who now hear me will long remember, among the trivial yet interesting incidents which marked these last weeks of his memorable life, his daily visits to the fruit trees (which were then in blossom), and the smile with which he, more than once, contrasted the interest he took in their progress, with the event which was to happen before their maturity." It was while he was thus lingering on the verge of the grave, that he was visited by two gentlemen from New-York, who were extremely anxious for an interview with him. He rallied all his powers to entertain his guests, and to inspire in their minds a feeling of kindness towards the parent land of the late colonists; and, on their rising to take leave, he said to them, in accents at once dignified and pathetic, "When you go home, tell your countrymen that you saw the wreck of Dr. Robertson." In less than two months that wreck disappeared in the ocean of eternity. He expired, with the fortitude which became him, on the 11th of July, 1793, in the seventy-first year of his age, and the fiftieth of his ministry.

So much has been written by others, respecting the literary merit of Dr. Robertson, that on this point it is unnecessary, even would my confined limits permit me, to enter into a lengthened discussion. His style has less of careless easy grace, but has more of equable dignity, than that of Hume; it does not display the masterly modulation, but it has none of the occasional obscurity and meretricious ornament, of that of Gibbon; it is well balanced, unstained by vulgarisms, more idiomatically English than might be expected from a native of Scotland, and is defective, perhaps, only in being too uniformly of an elevated tone. In arranging and linking together into one harmonious whole the scattered parts of his subject, he is eminently happy; and in delineating characters, manners, and scenery, in making vividly present to the mind that which he describes, he has few rivals, and no superiors. If all that has been urged against his works be admitted, and some of it cannot be denied, it may nevertheless safely be affirmed, that the balance heavily preponderates in his favour, and that he will always continue to rank in the first class of modern historians.

PREFACE.

In fulfilling the engagement which I had come under to the Public with respect to the History of America, it was my intention not to have published any part of the Work until the whole was completed. The present state of the British colonies has induced me to alter that resolution. While they are engaged in civil war with Great Britain, inquiries and speculations concerning their ancient forms of policy and laws, which exist no longer, cannot be interesting. The attention and expectation of mankind are now turned towards their future condition. In whatever manner this unhappy contest may terminate, a new order of things must arise in North America, and its affairs will assume another aspect. I wait with the solicitude of a good citizen, until the ferment subside, and regular government be re-established, and then I shall return to this part of my work, in which I had made some progress. That, together with the history of Portuguese America, and of the settlements made by the several nations of Europe in the West India Islands, will complete my plan.

The three volumes which I now publish contain an account of the discovery of the New World, and of the progress of the Spanish arms and colonies there. This is not only the most splendid portion of the American story, but so much detached, as by itself to form a perfect whole, remarkable for the unity of the subject. As the principles and maxims of the Spaniards in planting colonies, which have been adopted in some measure by every nation, are unfolded in this part of my work; it will serve as a proper introduction to the history of all the European establishments in America, and convey such information concerning this important article of policy, as may be deemed no less interesting than curious.

In describing the achievements and institutions of the Spaniards in the New World, I have departed in many instances, from the accounts of preceding historians, and have often related facts which seem to have been unknown to them. It is a duty I owe the Public to mention the sources from which I have derived such intelligence which justifies me either in placing transactions in a new light, or in forming any new opinion with respect to their causes and effects. This duty I perform with greater satisfaction, as it will afford an opportunity of expressing my gratitude to those benefactors who have honoured me with their countenance and aid in my researches.

As it was from Spain that I had to expect the most important information, with regard to this part of my work, I considered it as a very fortunate circumstance for me, when Lord Grantham, to whom I had the honour of being personally known, and with whose liberality of sentiment, and disposition to oblige, I was well acquainted, was appointed ambassador to the court of Madrid. Upon applying to him, I met with such a reception as satisfied me that his endeavours would be employed in the most proper manner, in order to obtain the gratification of my wishes; and I am perfectly sensible, that what progress I have made in my inquiries among the Spaniards, ought to be ascribed chiefly to their knowing how much his lordship interested himself in my success.

But did I owe nothing more to Lord Grantham than the advantages which I have derived from his attention in engaging Mr. Waddilove, the chaplain of his embassy, to take the conduct of my literary inquiries in Spain, the obligations I lie under to him would be very great. During five years that gentleman has carried on researches for my behoof, with such activity, perseverance, and knowledge of the subject, to which his attention was turned, as have filled me with no less astonishment than satisfaction. He procured for me the greater part of the Spanish books which I have consulted; and as many of them were printed early in the sixteenth century, and are become extremely rare, the collecting of these was such an occupation as alone required much time and assiduity. To his friendly attention I am indebted for copies of several valuable manuscripts, containing facts and details which I might have searched for in vain in works that have been made public. Encouraged by the inviting good will with which Mr. Waddilove conferred his favours, I transmitted to him a set of queries, with respect both to the customs and policy of the native Americans, and the nature of several institutions in the Spanish settlements, framed in such a manner that a Spaniard might answer them without disclosing any thing that was improper to be communicated to a foreigner. He translated these into Spanish, and obtained from various persons who had resided in most of the Spanish colonies, such replies as have afforded me much instruction.

Notwithstanding those peculiar advantages with which my inquiries were carried on in Spain, it is with regret I am obliged to add, that their success must be ascribed to the beneficence of individuals, not to any communication by public authority. By a singular arrangement of Philip II. the records of the Spanish monarchy are deposited in the *Archivo* of Simancas, near Valladolid, at the distance of a hundred and twenty miles from the seat of government and the supreme courts of justice. The papers relative to America, and chiefly to that early period of its history towards which my attention was directed, are so numerous, that they alone, according to one account, fill the largest apartment in the Archivo; and, according to another, they compose eight hundred and seventy-three large bundles. Conscious of possessing, in some degree, the industry which belongs to an historian, the prospect of such a treasure excited my most ardent curiosity. But the prospect of it is all that I have enjoyed. Spain, with an excess of caution, has uniformly thrown a veil over her transactions in America. From strangers they are concealed with peculiar solicitude. Even to her own subjects the Archivo of Simancas is not opened without a particular order from the crown; and, after obtaining that, papers cannot be copied without paying fees of office so exorbitant that the expense exceeds what it would be proper to bestow, when the gratification of literary curiosity is the only object. It is to be hoped, that the Spaniards will at last discover this system of concealment to be no less impolitic than illiberal. From what I have experienced in the course of my inquiries, I am satisfied, that upon a more minute scrutiny into their early operations in the New World, however reprehensible the actions of individuals may appear, the conduct of the nation will be placed in a more favourable light.

In other parts of Europe very different sentiments prevail. Having searched, without success, in Spain, for a letter of Cortes to Charles V., written soon after he landed in the Mexican Empire, which has not hitherto been published; it occurred to me, that as the Emperor was setting out for Germany at the time when the messengers from Cortes arrived in Europe, the letter with which they were intrusted might possibly be preserved in the Imperial library at Vienna. I communicated this idea to Sir Robert Murray Keith, with whom I have long had the honour to live in friendship, and I had soon the pleasure to learn, that upon his application her Imperial Majesty had been graciously pleased to issue an order, that not only a copy of that letter (if it were found), but of any other papers in the library which could throw light upon the History of America, should be transmitted to me. The letter from Cortes is not in the Imperial library; but an authentic copy, attested by a notary, of the letter written by the magistrates of the colony planted by him at Vera Cruz, which I have mentioned, p. 210, having been found, it was transcribed, and sent to me. As this letter is no less curious, and as little known as that which was the object of my inquiries, I have given some account, in its proper place, of what is most worthy of notice in it. Together with it, I received a copy of a letter from Cortes, containing a long account of his expedition to Honduras, with respect to which I did not think it necessary to enter into any particular detail; and likewise those curious Mexican paintings, which I have described, p. 321.

My inquiries at St. Petersburg were carried on with equal facility and success. In examining into the nearest communication between our continent and that of America, it became of consequence to obtain authentic information concerning the discoveries of the Russians in their navigation from Kamchatka towards the coast of America. Accurate relations of their first voyage, in 1741, have been published by Muller and Gmelin. Several foreign authors have entertained an opinion that the court of Russia studiously conceals the progress which has been made by more recent navigators, and suffers the Public to be amused with false accounts of their route. Such conduct appeared to me unsuitable to those liberal sentiments, and that patronage of science, for which the present sovereign of Russia is eminent; nor could I discern any political reason, that might render it improper to apply for information concerning the late attempts of the Russians to open a communication between Asia and America. My ingenious countryman, Dr. Rogerson, first physician to the Empress, presented my request to Her Imperial Majesty, who not only disclaimed any idea of concealment, but instantly ordered the journal of Captain Krenitzin, who conducted the only voyage of discovery made by public authority since the year 1741, to be translated, and his original chart to be copied for my use. By consulting them, I have been enabled to give a more accurate view of the progress and extent of the Russian discoveries than has hitherto been communicated to the Public.

From other quarters I have received information of great utility and importance. M. le Chevalier de Pinto, the minister from Portugal to the court of Great Britain, who commanded for several years at Matagrosso, a settlement of the Portuguese in the interior part of Brazil, where the Indians are numerous, and their original manners little altered by intercourse with Europeans, was pleased to send me very full answers to some queries concerning the character and institutions of the natives of America, which his polite reception of an application made to him in my name encouraged me to propose. These satisfied me, that he had contemplated with a discerning attention the curious objects which his situation presented to his view, and I have often followed him as one of my best instructed guides.

M. Suard, to whose elegant translation of the History of the Reign of Charles V., I owe the favourable reception of that work on the continent, procured me answers to the same queries from M. de Bougainville, who had opportunities of observing the Indians both of North and South America, and from M. Godin le Jeune, who resided fifteen years among Indians in Quito, and twenty years in Cayenne. The latter are more valuable from having been examined by M. de la Condamine, who, a few weeks before his death, made some short additions to them, which may be considered as the last effort of that attention to science which occupied a long life.

My inquiries were not confined to one region in America. Governor Hutchinson took the trouble of recommending the consideration of my queries to Mr. Hawley and Mr. Brainerd, two protestant missionaries employed among the Indians of the Five Nations, who favoured me with answers which discover a considerable knowledge of the people whose customs they describe. From William Smith, Esq. the ingenious historian of New York, I received some useful information. When I enter upon the History of our Colonies in North America, I shall have occasion to acknowledge how much I have been indebted to many other gentlemen of that country.

From the valuable Collection of Voyages made by Alexander Dalrymple, Esq., with whose attention to the History of Navigation and Discovery the Public is well acquainted, I have received some very rare books, particularly two large volumes of Memorials, partly manuscript and partly in print, which were presented to the court of Spain during the reigns of Philip III. and Philip IV. From these I have learned many curious particulars with respect to the interior state of the Spanish colonies, and the various schemes formed for their improvement. As this collection of Memorials formerly belonged to the Colbert Library, I have quoted them by that title.

All those books and manuscripts I have consulted with that attention which the respect due from an Author to the Public required; and by minute references to them, I have endeavoured to authenticate whatever I relate. The longer I reflect on the nature of historical composition, the more I am convinced that this scrupulous accuracy is necessary. The historian who records the events of his own time, is credited in proportion to the opinion which the Public entertains with respect to his means of information and his veracity. He who delineates the transactions of a remote period, has no title to claim assent, unless he produces evidence in proof of his assertions. Without this he may write an amusing tale, but cannot be said to have composed an authentic history. In those sentiments I have been confirmed by the opinion of an Author,* whom his industry, erudition, and discernment, have deservedly placed in a high rank among the most eminent historians of the age. Imboldened by a hint from him, I have published a catalogue of the Spanish books which I have consulted. This practice was frequent in the last century, and was considered as an evidence of laudable industry in an author; in the present, it may, perhaps, be deemed the effect of ostentation; but, as many of these books are unknown in Great Britain, I could not otherwise have referred to them as authorities, without encumbering the page with an insertion of their full titles. To any person who may choose to follow me in this path of inquiry, the catalogue must be very useful.

My readers will observe, that in mentioning sums of money, I have uniformly followed the Spanish method of computing by *pesos*. In America, the peso *fuerte*, or *duro*, is the only one known; and that is always meant when any sum imported from America is mentioned. The peso fuerte, as well as other coins, has varied in its numerary value; but I have been advised, without attending to such minute variations, to consider it as equal to four shillings and six-pence of our money. It is to be remembered, however, that, in the sixteenth century, the effective value of a peso, *i. e.* the quantity of labour which it represented, or of goods which it would purchase, was five or six times as much as at present.

N. B. Since this edition was put into the press, a History of Mexico, in two volumes in quarto, translated from the Italian of the Abbé D. Francesco Saverio Clavigero, has been published. From a person who is a native of New Spain, who has resided forty years in that country, and who is acquainted with the Mexican language, it was natural to expect much new information. Upon perusing his work, however, I find that it contains hardly any addition to the ancient History of the Mexican empire, as related by Acosta and Herrera, but what is derived from the improbable narratives and fanciful conjectures of Torquemada and Boturini. Having copied their splendid descriptions of the high state of civilization in the Mexican empire, M. Clavigero, in the abundance of his zeal for the honour of his native country, charges me with having mistaken some points, and with having misrepresented others, in the history of it. When an author is conscious of having exerted industry in research, and impartiality in decision, he may, without presumption, claim what praise is due to these qualities, and he cannot be insensible to any accusation that tends to weaken the force of his claim. A feeling of this kind has induced me to examine such strictures of M. Clavigero on my history of America as merited any attention, especially as these are made by one who seemed to possess the means of obtaining accurate information; and to show that the greater part of them is destitute of any just foundation. This I have done in notes upon the passages in my History which gave rise to his criticisms.

College of Edinburgh, *March* 1, 1788.

* Mr Gibbon

CONTENTS.

BOOK I.

PROGRESS of Navigation among the ancients—View of their discoveries as preparatory to those of the moderns—Imperfection of ancient navigation and geography—Doctrine of the zones—Further discoveries checked by the irruption of barbarous nations—Geographical knowledge still preserved in the East, and among the Arabians—Revival of commerce and navigation in Europe—favoured by the Croisades—extended by travellers into the East—promoted by the invention of the mariner's compass—First regular plan of discovery formed by Portugal—State of that kingdom-Schemes of Prince Henry-Early attempts feeble—Progress along the western coast of Africa—Hopes of discovering a new route to the East Indies—Attempts to accomplish this—prospects of success 17

BOOK II.

Birth and education of Columbus—acquires naval skill in the service of Portugal—conceives hopes of reaching the East Indies by holding a westerly course—his system founded on the ideas of the ancients, and knowledge of their navigation—and on the discoveries of the Portuguese—his negotiations with different courts—Obstacles which he had to surmount in Spain—Voyage of discovery—difficulties—success—return to Spain—Astonishment of mankind on this discovery of a new world—Papal grant of it—Second voyage—Colony settled—Further discoveries—War with the Indians—First tax imposed on them—Third voyage—He discovers the Continent—State of the Spanish colony—Errors in the first system of colonizing—Voyage of the Portuguese to the East Indies by the Cape of Good Hope—Effects of this—discoveries made by private adventurers in the New World—Name of America given to it—Machinations against Columbus—disgraced and sent in chains to Europe—Fourth voyage of Columbus—His discoveries—disasters—death 42

BOOK III.

State of the colony in Hispaniola—New war with the Indians—Cruelty of the Spaniards—Fatal regulations concerning the condition of the Indians—Diminution of that people—Discoveries and settlements—First colony planted on the Continent—Conquest of Cuba—Discovery of Florida—of the South Sea—Great expectations raised by this—Causes of disappointment with respect to these for some time—Controversy concerning the treatment of the Indians—Contrary decisions—Zeal of the ecclesiastics, particularly of Las Casas—Singular proceedings of Ximenes—Negroes imported into America—Las Casas' idea of a new colony—permitted to attempt it—unsuccessful—Discoveries towards the West—Yucatan—Campeachy-New Spain—preparations for invading it . 92

BOOK IV.

View of America when first discovered, and of the manners and policy of its most uncivilized inhabitants—Vast extent of America—grandeur of the objects it presents to view—its mountains—rivers—lakes—its form favourable to commerce—temperature—predominance of cold—causes of this—uncultivated—unwholesome—its animals—soil—Inquiry how America was peopled—various theories—what appears most probable—Condition and character of the Americans—All, the Mexicans and Peruvians excepted, in the state of savages—Inquiry confined to the uncivilized tribes—Difficulty of obtaining information—various causes of this—Method observed in the inquiry—I. The bodily constitution of the Americans considered—II. The qualities of their minds—III. Their domestic state—IV. Their political state and institutions—V. Their system of war and public security—VI. The arts with which they were acquainted—VII. Their religious ideas and institutions—VIII. Such singular and detached customs as are not reducible to any of the former heads—IX. General review and estimate of their virtues and defects 122

BOOK V.

History of the conquest of New Spain by Cortes 197

BOOK VI.

History of the conquest of Peru by Pizarro—and of the dissensions and civil wars of the Spaniards in that country—Origin, progress, and effects of these . 261

BOOK VII.

View of the institutions and manners of the Mexicans and Peruvians—Civilized states in comparison of other Americans—Recent origin of the Mexicans—Facts which prove their progress in civilization-View of their policy in its various branches—of their arts—Facts which indicate a small progress in civilization—What opinion should be formed on comparing these contradictory facts—Genius of their religion—Peruvian monarchy more ancient—its policy founded on religion—Singular effects of this—Peculiar state of property among the Peruvians—Their public works and arts—roads—bridges—buildings—Their un- warlike spirit—View of other dominions of Spain in America—Cinaloa and Sonora—California—Yucatan and Honduras—Chili—Tucuman—Kingdom of Tierra Firmé—New Kingdom of Granada 313

BOOK VIII.

View of the interior government, commerce, &c. of the Spanish colonies--Depopulation of America—first effects of their settlements—not the consequence of any system of policy—nor to be imputed to religion—Number of Indians still remaining—Fundamental maxims on which the Spanish system of colonization is founded—Condition of different orders of men in their colonies--Chapetones--Creoles—Negroes—Indians—Ecclesiastical state and policy—Character of secular and regular clergy—Small progress of Christianity among the natives—Mines, chief object of their attention—Mode of working these—their produce—Effects of encouraging this species of industry—Other commodities of Spanish America—First effects of this new commerce with America on Spain—Why the Spanish colonies have not been as beneficial to the parent state as those of other nations—Errors in the Spanish system of regulating this commerce—confined to one port—carried on by annual fleets—Contraband trade—Decline of Spain both in population and wealth—Remedies proposed—View of the wise regulations of the Bourbon princes—A new and more liberal system introduced—beneficial effects of this—probable consequences—Trade between New Spain and the Philippines--Revenue of Spain from America—whence it arises—to what it amounts 347

BOOK IX.

History of Virginia to the year 1688, 389

BOOK X.

History of New England to the year 1652 426

A CATALOGUE
OF
SPANISH BOOKS AND MANUSCRIPTS.

A CARETTE de Biscay, Relation des Voyages dans la Rivière de la Plata, et de là par Terre au Perou. Exst. Recueil de Thevenot. Part IV.
——— A Voyage up the River de la Plata, and thence by Land to Peru. 8vo. London, 1698.
Acosta (P. Jos. de) Historia Natural y Moral de las Indias. 4to. Madrid, 1590.
——— (Joseph de) Histoire Naturelle et Morale des Indes tant Orientales qu' Occidentales. 8vo. Paris, 1600.
———Novi Orbis Historia Naturalis et Moralis. Exst. in Collect. Theod. de Bry. Pars IX.
——— De Natura Novi Orbis, Libri duo, et de procuranda Indorum Salute, Libri sex. Salmant. 8vo. 1589.
——— (Christ.) Tratado de las Drogas y Medccinas, de las Indias Occidentales, con sus Plantas Dibuxadas al vivo. 4to. Burgos, 1578.
Acugna (P. Christoph.) Relation de la Revière des Amazones. 12mo. Tom. ii. Paris, 1682.
Acugna's Relation of the great River of the Amazons in South America. 8vo. London, 1698.
Alarchon (Fern.) Navigatione a Scoprere il Regno di sette Città. Ramusio iii. 363.
Albuquerque Coello (Duarté de) Memorial de Artes de la Guerra del Brasil. 4to. Mad. 1634.
Alcafarado (Franc.) An Historical Relation of the Discovery of the Isle of Madeira. 4to. Lond. 1675.
Alçedo y Herrera (D. Dionysio de) Aviso Historico-Politico-Geografico, con las Noticias mas particulares, del Peru, Tierra Firmé, Chili, y Nuevo Reyno de Granada. 4to. Mad. 1740.
Alçedo Compendi Historico de la Provincia y Puerto de Guayaquil. 4to. Mad. 1741.
——— Memorial sobre diferentes Puntos tocantes al estado de la real hazienda y del commercio, &c. en las Indias. fol.

Aldama y Guevara (D. Jos. Augustin de) Arde de la Lengua Mexicana. 12mo. Mexico, 1754.
Alvarado (Pedro de) Dos Relaciones a Hern. Cortes referiendole sus Expodiciones y Conquistas en varias Provincias de N. Espagna. Exst. Barcia Historiad. Primit. tom. i.
——— Lettere due, &c. Exst. Ramus. iii. 296.
Aparicio y Leon (D. Lorenzo de) Discurso Historico-Politico del Hospital San Lazaro de Lima. 8vo. Lim. 1761.
Aranzeles Reales de los Ministros de la Real Audiencia de N. Espagna. fol. Mex. 1727.
Argensola (Bartolome Leonardo de) Conquista de las Islas Malucas. fol. Mad. 1609.
——— Anales de Aragon. fol. Saragoça, 1630.
Arguello (Eman.) Sentum Confessionis. 12mo. Mex. 1703.
Arriago (P. Pablo Jos. de) Extirpacian de la Idolatria de Peru. 4to. Lima, 1621.
Avendagno (Didac.) Thesaurus Indicus, ceu Generalis Instructor pro Regimine Conscientiæ, in ijs quæ ad Indias spectant. fol. 2 vols. Antwerp, 1660.
Aznar (D. Bern. Fran.) Discurso tocante a la real hazienda y administracion de ella. 4to.

Bandini (Angelo Maria) Vita é Lettero di Armerigo Vespucci. 4to. Firenze. 1745.
Barcia (D. And. Gonzal.) Historiadores Primitivos de las Indias Occidontales, fol. 3 vols. Mad. 1749.
Barco-Continora (D. Martin de) Argentina y Conquista del Rio de la Plata: Poema. Exst. Barcia Historiad. Primit. iii.
Barros (Joao de) Decadas de Asia. fol. 4 vols. Lisboa, 1682.
Bellesteros (D. Thomas de) Ordenanzas del Peru. fol. 2 vols. Lima, 1685.
Beltran (P. F. Pedro) Arte de el Idioma Maya reducido a sucintas reglas, y Semilexicon. 4to. Mex. 1746.

Benzo (Hieron.) Novi Orbis Historiæ—De Bry America, Part IV, V, VI.

Betancurt y Figueroa (Don Luis) Derecho de las Inglesias Metropolitanas de las Indias. 4to. Mad. 1637.

Blanco (F. Matias Ruiz) Conversion de Piritu de Indios Cumanagotos y otros. 12mo. Mad. 1690.

Boturini Benaduci (Lorenzo) Idea de una nueva Historia general de la America Septentrional, fundada sobre material copiosa de Figuras, Symbolas, Caracteres, Cantares, y Manuscritos de Autores Indios. 4to. Mad. 1746.

Botello de Moraes y Vasconcellos (D. Francisco de) El Nuevo Mundo: Poema Heroyco. 4to. Barcelona, 1701.

Botero Benes (Juan) Description de Todas las Provincias, Reynos, y Ciudades del Mundo. 4to. Girona, 1748.

Brietius (Phil.) Paralela Geographiæ Voteris et Novæ. 4to. Paris, 1648.

Cabeza de Baca (Alvar. Nugnez) Relacion de los Naufragios. Exst. Barcia Hist. Prim. tom. i.

——— Examen Apologetico de la Historica Narration de los Naufragios. Exst. Barcia Hist. Prim. tom. i.

——— Commentarios de lo succedido duarante su gubierno del Rio de la Plata. Exst. ibid.

Cabo de Vacca, Relatione de. Exst. Ramus. iii. 310.

Cabota (Sebast.) Navigazione de. Exst. Ramus. ii. 211.

Cadamustus (Aloysius) Navigatio ad Terras incognitas. Exst. Nov. Orb. Grynæi, p. 1.

Calancha (F. Anton. de la) Cronica moralizada del Orden de San Augustin on el Peru. fol. Barcelona, 1638.

California—Diario Historico de los Viages de Mar y Tierra hechos en 1768, al Norte de California di orden del Marques de Croix Vi-rey de Nueva Espagna, &c. MS.

Calle (Juan Diaz de la) Memorial Informatorio de lo que a su Magestad Provien de la Nueva Espagna y Peru. 4to. 1645.

Campomanes (D. Pedro Rodrig.) Antiguedad Maritima de la Republica de Cartago, con en Periplo de su General Hannon traducido e illustrado. 4to. Mad. 1756.

——— Discurso sobre el fomento de la Industria popular. 8vo. Mad. 1774.

——— Discurso sobre la Educacion popular de los Artesanos. 8vo. 5 vol. Mad. 1775, &c.

Caracas—Real Cedula de Fundacion de la Real Compagnia Guipuscoana de Caracas. 12mo. Mad. 1765.

Caravantes (Fr. Lopez de) Relacion de las Provincias que tiene el Govierno del Peru, los Officios que en el se Provien, y la Hacienda que alli tiene su Magestad, lo que se Gasta de olla y le queda Libre, &c. &c. Dedicado al Marques de Santos Claros, Agno de 1611. MS.

Cardenas y Cano (Gabr.) Ensayo Chronologico para la Historia general de la Florida. fol. Mad. 1733.

Carranzana (D. Gonçalos) A Geographical Description of the Coasts, &c. of the Spanish West Indies. 8vo. Lond. 1740.

Casas (Bart. de las) Brevissima Relacion de la Destruycion de las Indias. 4to. 1552.

——— (Bart. de las) Narratio Iconibus illustrata per Theod. de Bry. 4to. Oppent. 1614.

——— (Bart. de las) An Account of the first Voyages and Discoveries of the Spaniards in America. 8vo. Lond. 1693.

Cassani (P. Joseph) Historia de la Provincia de Compagnia de Jesus en el Nuevo Reyno de Granada. fol. Mad. 1741.

Castanheda (Fern. Lop. de) Historia do Descobrimento e Conquista do India pelos Portugueses. fol. 2 vol. Lisb. 1552.

Castellanos (Juan de) Primera y Secunda de las Elegias de Varones Illustres de Indias. 4to. 2 vol. Mad. 1589.

Castillo (Bernal Dias del) Historia Verdadera de la Conquista de Nueva Espagna. fol. Mad. 1632.

Castro, Figueroa y Salazar (D. Pedro de) Relacion di su ancimiento y servicios. 12mo.

Cavallero (D. Jos. Garcia) Brieve Cotejo y Valance de las Pesas y Medidas di varias Naciones, reducidas a las que Corren en Castilla. 4to. Mad. 1731.

Cepeda (D. Fern.) Relacion Universal del Sitio en que esta fundada la Ciudad de Mexico. fol. 1637.

Cicça de Leon (Pedro de) Chronica del Peru. fol. Seville. 1533.

Cisneros (Diego) Sitio, Naturaleza, y Propriedades de la Ciudad de Mexico. 4to. Mexico. 1618.

Clemente (P. Claudio) Tablas Chronologicas, en que contienen los Sucesos Ecclesiasticos y Seculares de Indias. 4to. Val. 1689.

Cogullado (P. Fr. Diego Lopez) Historia de Yucatan. fol. Mad. 1688.

Colleçao dos Brives Pontificos e

Leyes Regias que Forao Expedidos y Publicadas desde o Anno 1741, sobre a la Liberdada das Pessoas bene e Commercio dos Indos de Bresil.

Colleccion General de la Providencias hasta aqui tomadas par el Gobierno sobre el Estragnimento, y Occupacion de Temporalidades de los Regulares de la Compagnia de Espagna, Indias, &c. Partes IV. 4to. Mad. 1767.

Colon (D. Fernando) La Historia del Almirante D. Christoval Colon. Exst. Barcia Hist. Prim. I. 1.

Columbus (Christ.) Navigatio qua multas Regiones hactenus incognitas invenit. Exst. Nov. Orb. Grynæi, p. 90.

———— (Ferd.) Life and Actions of his Father Admiral Christoph. Columbus. Exst. Churchill's Voyages, ii. 479.

Compagnia Real de Commercio para las Islas de Sto. Domingo Puerto-rico, y la Margarita. 12mo.

Compendio General de las Contribuciones y gattos que occasionan todos los effectos, frutos, caudales, &c. que trafican entre los reynos de Castilla y America. 4to.

Concilios Provinciales Primero y Segundo celebrados en la muy Noble y muy Leal Ciudad de Mexico en los Agnos de 1555 y 1565. fol. Mexico, 1769.

Concilium Mexicanum Provinciale tertium celebratum Mexici, anno 1585. fol. Mexici, 1770.

Continente Americano, Argonauta de las costas de Nueva Espagna y Tierra Firmé. 12mo.

Cordeyro (Antonio) Historia Insulana das Ilhas a Portugas sugeytas no Oceano Occidental. fol. Lisb. 1717.

Corita (Dr. Alonzo) Breve y sumaria Relacion de los Segnores, Manera, y Differencia de ellos, que havia en la Nueva Espagna, y otras Provincias sus Comarcanas, y de sus Leyes, Usos, y Costumbres, y de la Forma que tenian en Tributar sus Vasallos en Tiempo de su Gentilidad, &c. MS. 4to. pp. 307.

Coronada (Fr. Vasq. de) Sommario di due sue Lettere del Viaggio fatto del Fra. Marco da Nizza al sette Citta de Cevola. Exst. Ramusio iii. 354.

———— (Fr. Vasq. de) Relacion Viaggio alle sette Citta. Ramus. iii. 359.

Cortes (Hern.) Quattro Cartas dirigidas al Emperador Carlos V. en que ha Relacion de sus Conquistas en la Nueva Espagna. Exst. Barcia Hist. Prim. tom. i.

Cortessii (Ferd.) De Insulis nuper inventis Narrationes ad Car. V. fol. 1532.

Cortese (Fern.) Relacioni, &c. Exst. Ramusio ii. 225.

Cubero (D. Pedro) Peregrinacion del Mayor Parte del Mundo. Zaragosa. 4to. 1688.

Cumana, Govierno y Noticia de. fol. MS.

Davila Padilla (F. Aug.) Historia de la Fundacion y Discurso de Provincia de St. Jago de Mexico. fol. Bruss. 1625.

———— (Gil Gonzalez) Teatro Ecclesiastico de la Primitiva Iglesia de los Indias Occidentales. fol. 2 vols. 1649.

Documentos tocantes a la Persecucion, que los Regulares de la Compagnia suscitaron contra Don B. de Cardenas Obispo de Paraguay. 4to. Mad. 1768.

Echaveri (D. Bernardo Ibagnez de) El Reyno Jesuitico del Paraguay. Exst. tom. iv. Colleccion de Documentos. 4to. Mad. 1770.

Echave y Assu (D. Francisco de) La Estrella de Lima covertida en Sol sobre sur tres Coronas. fol. Amberes, 1688.

Eguiara El Egueren (D. J. Jos.) Bibliotheca Mexicana, sive Eruditorum Historia Virorum in America Boreali natorum, &c. tom. prim. fol. Mex. 1775. N. B. No more than one volume of this work has been published.

Ercilla y Zuniga (D. Alonzo de) La Araucana: Poema Eroico. fol. Mad. 1733.

———— 2 vols. 8vo. Mad. 1777.

Escalona (D. Gaspar de) Gazophylacium Regium Peruvicum. fol. Mad. 1775.

Faria y Sousa (Manuel de) Historia del Reyno de Portugal. fol. Amber. 1730.

Faria y Sousa, History of Portugal from the first Ages to the Revolution under John IV. 8vo. Lond. 1698.

Fernandez (Diego) Prima y secunda Parte de la Historia del Peru. fol. Sevill. 1571.

———— (P. Juan Patr.) Relacion Historial de las Missiones de los Indias que claman Chiquitos. 4to. Mad. 1726.

Feyjoo (Benit. Geron.) Espagnoles Americanos—Discurso VI. del. tom. iv. del Teatro Critico. Mad. 1769.

———— Solucion del gran Problema Historico sobre la Poblacion de la America—Discurso XV. del tom. v. de Teatro Critico.

———— (D. Miguel) Relacion Descriptiva de la Ciudad y Provincia Truxillo del Peru. fol. Mad. 1763.

Freyre (Ant.) Piratas de la America. 4to.

Frasso (D. Petro) De Regio Patronatu Indiarum. fol. 2 vols. Matriti, 1775.

Galvao (Antonio) Tratado dos Descobrimentos Antigos y Modernos. fol. Lisboa, 1731.

Galvano (Ant.) the Discoveries of the World from the first Original unto the Year 1555. Osborne's Collect. ii. 354.

Gamboa (D. Fran. Xavier de) Comentarios a los ordinanzas de Minas. fol. Mad. 1761.

Garcia (Gregorio) Historia Ecclesiastica y Seglar de la India Oriental y Occidental, y Predicacion de la Santa Evangelia en ella. 12mo. Baeca, 1626.

————— (Fr. Gregorio) Origen de los Indios del Nuevo Mundo. fol. Mad. 1729.

Gastelu (Ant. Velasquez) Arte de Lengua Mexicana. 4to. Puebla de los Angeles. 1716.

Gazeta de Mexico por los Annos 1728, 1729, 1730. 4to.

Girava (Hieronymo) Dos Libros de Cosmographia. Milan, 1556.

Godoy (Diego de) Relacion al H. Cortes, qua trata del Descubrimiento di diversas Ciudades, y Provincias, y Guerras que tuio con los Indios. Exst. Barcia. Hist. Prim. tom. i.

————— Lettera a Cortese, &c. Exst. Ramusio iii. 300.

Gomara (Fr. Lopez de) La Historia general de las Indias. 12mo. Anv.1554.

————— Historia general de las Indias. Exst. Barcia Hist. Prim. tom. ii.

————— (Fr. Lopez de) Chronica de la Nueva Espagna o Conquista de Mexico. Exst. Barcia Hist. Prim. tom. ii.

Guatemala—Razon puntual de los Successos mas memorabiles, y de los Estragos y dannos que ha padecido la Ciudad de Guatemala. fol. 1774.

Gumilla (P. Jos.) El Orinoco illustrado y defendido; Historia Natural, Civil, y Geographica de este Gran Rio, &c. 4to. 2 tom. Mad. 1745.

————— Histoire Naturelle, Civile, et Géographique de l'Orenoque. Traduite par M. Eidous. 12mo. tom. iii. Avig. 1758.

Gusman (Nugno de) Relacion scritta in Omitlan Provincia de Mechuacan della maggior Spagna nell 1530. Exst. Ramusio iii. 331.

Henis (P. Thadeus) Ephemerides Belli Guiaranici, ab Anno 1754. Exst.

Colleccion general de Docum, tom. iv.

Hernandes (Fran.) Plantarum Animalium, et Mineralium Mexicanorum Historia. fol. Rom. 1651.

Herrera (Anton. de) Historia general de los Hechos de los Castellanos en las Islas y Tierra Firma de Mar Oceano. fol. 4 vols. Mad. 1601.

————— Historia General, &c. 4 vols. Mad. 1730.

————— General History, &c. Translated by Stephens. 8vo. 6 vol. Lond. 1740.

————— Descriptio Indiæ Occidentalis. fol. Amst. 1622.

Huemez y Horcasitas (D. Juan Francisco de) Extracto de los Autos de Diligencias y reconocimientos de los rios, lagunas, vertientes, y desaguas de Mexico y su valle, &c. fol. Mex. 1748.

Jesuitas—Colleccion de las applicaciones que se van haciendo de los Cienes, Casas y Coligios que fueron de la Compagnia de Jesus, expatriados de estos Reales dominios. 4to. 2 vols. Lima, 1772 y 1773.

————— Colleccion General de Providencias hasta aqui tomadas por el Gobierno sobre el Estrannamiento y Occupacion de temporalidades, de los Regulares de la Compagnia de Espagna, Indias, e Islas Filipinas. 4to. Mad. 1767.

————— Retrato de los Jesuitas formado al natural. 4to. 2 vols. Mad. 1768.

————— Relacion Abbreviada da Republica que os Religiosos Jesuitas estabeleceraon. 12mo.

————— Idea del Origen, Gobierno, &c. de la Compagnia de Jesus. 8vo. Mad. 1768.

Lævinius (Apollonius) Libri V. de Peruviæ Invention. et rebus in eadem gestis. 12mo. Ant. 1567.

Leon (Fr. Ruiz de) Hernandia, Poema Heroyco de Conquista de Mexico. 4to. Mad. 1755.

————— (Ant. de) Epitome de la Bibliotheca Oriental y Occidental, Nautica y Geografica. fol. Mad. 1737.

Lima: A true Account of the Earthquake which happened there 28th of October, 1746. Translated from the Spanish. 8vo. London, 1748.

Lima Gozosa, Description de las festibas Demonstraciones, con que esta Ciudad celebrò la real Proclamacion de el Nombre Augusto del Catolico Monarcho D. Carlos III. Lim. 4to. 1760.

Llano Zapata (D. Jos. Euseb.) Preliminar al Tomo 1. de las Memorias Historico-Physicas, Critico-Apologeticas de la America Meridional. 8vo. Cadiz, 1759.

Lopez (D. Juan Luis) Discurso Historico Politico en defenso de la Jurisdicion Real. fol. 1685.

—— (Thom.) Atlas Geographico de la America Septentrional y Meridional. 12mo. Par. 1758.

Lorenzana (D. Fr. Ant.) Arzobispo de Mexico, ahora de Toledo, Historia do Nueva Espagna, escrita por su Esclarecido Conquistador Hernan. Cortes, Aumentada con otros Documentos y Notas. fol. Mex. 1770.

Lozano (P. Pedro) Description Chorographica, del Terretorios, Arboles, Animales del Gran Chaco, y de los Ritos y Costumbres de las innumerabiles Naciones que la habitan. 4to. Cordov. 1733.

—— Historia de la Compagnia de Jesus en la Provincia del Paraguay. fol. 2 vols. Mad. 1753.

Madriga (Pedro de) Description du Gouvernement du Pérou. Exst. Voyages qui ont servi à l'Etablissement de la Comp. des Indes, tom. ix. 105.

Mariana (P. Juan de) Discurso de los Enfermedades de la Compagnia de Jesus. 4to. Mad. 1658.

Martinez de la Puente (D. Jos.) Compendio de las Historias de los Descubrimientos, Conquistas, y Guerras de la India Oriental, y sus Islas, desde los Tiempos del Infante Don Enrique de Portugal su Inventor. 4to. Mad. 1681.

Martyr ab Angleria (Petr.) De Rebus Oceanicis et Novo Orbe Decades tres. 12mo. Colon. 1574.

—— De Insulis nuper inventis, et de Moribus Incolarum. Ibid. p. 329.

—— Opus Epistolarum. fol. Amst. 1670.

—— Il Sommario cavato della sua Historia del Nuevo Mundo. Ramusio iii. i.

Mata (D. Geron. Fern. de) Ideas politicas y morales. 12mo. Toledo, 1640.

Mechuacan—Relacion de las Ceremonias, Ritos, y Poblacion de los Indios de Mechuacan hecha al I. S. D. Ant. de Mendoza Vi-rey de Nueva Espagna. fol. MS.

Melendez (Fr. Juan) Tesoros Verdaderos de las Indias Historia de la Provincia de S. Juan Baptista del Peru, del Orden de Predicadores. fol. 3 vols. Rom. 1681.

Memorial Adjustado por D. A. Fern. de Heredia Gobernador de Nicaragua y Honduras. fol. 1753.

Memorial Adjustado contra los Officiales de Casa do Moneda a Mexico de el anno 1729. fol.

Mendoza (D. Ant. de) Lettera al Imperatore del Descoprimento della Terra Firma della N. Spagna verso Tramontano. Exst. Ramusio iii. 355.

—— (Juan Gonz. de) Historia del gran Reyno de China, con un Itinerario del Nuevo Mundo. 8vo. Rom. 1585.

Miguel (Vic. Jos.) Tablas de los Sucesos Ecclesiasticos en Africa, Indias Orientales y Occidentales. 4to. Val. 1689.

Miscellanea Economico-Politico, &c. fol. Pampl. 1749.

Molina (P. F. Anton.) Vocabulario Castellano y Mexicano. fol. 1571.

Monardes (El Dottor) Primera y Segunda y Tercera Parte de la Historia Medicinal, de las Cosas que se traen de nuestras Indias Occidentales, que sirven en Medicina. 4to. Sevilla, 1754.

Moncada (Sancho de) Restauracion Politica de Espagna, y de soos Publicos. 4to. Mad. 1746.

Morales (Ambrosio de) Coronica General de Espagna. fol. 4 vols. Alcala, 1574.

Moreno y Escandon (D. Fran. Ant.) Descripcion y Estado del Virreynato de Santa Fé, Nuevo Reyno de Granada, &c. fol. MS.

Munoz (D. Antonio) Discurso sobre Economia politica. 8vo. Mad. 1769.

Nizza (F. Marco) Rêlatione del Viaggio fatta per Terra al Cevole, Regno di cette Città. Exst. Ramus. iii. 356.

Nodal—Relacion del Viage que hicieron los Capitanes Barth. y Gonz. de Nodal al descubrimiento del Estrecho quo hoy es nombrado de Maire, y reconocimiento del de Magellanes. 4to. Mad.

Noticia Individual de los derechos segun lo reglado en ultimo proyecto de 1720. 4to. Barcelona, 1732.

Nueva Espagna—Historia de los Indios de Nueva Espagna dibidida en tres Partes. En la primera trata de los Ritos, Sacrificios y Idolatrias del Tiempo de su Gentilidad. En la segunda de su maravillosa Conversion a la Fé, y modo de celebrar las Fiestas de Neustra Santa Iglesia. En la tercera del Genio y Caracter de aquella Gente; y Figuras con que notaban sus Acontecimientos, con otras particularidades; y Noticias de las principales Ciudades an aquel Royno. Escrita en el Agno 1541 por uno de los doce Religiosos Franciscos que primero passaron a entender en su Conversion. MS. fol. pp. 618.

Ogna (Pedro de) Arauco Domado. Poëma. 12mo. Mad. 1605.

Ordenanzas del Consejo real de las Indias. fol. Mad. 1681.

Ortega (D. Casimiro de) Refumen Historico del primer Viago hecho al rededor del Mundo. 4to. Mad. 1769.

Ossorio (Jerome) History of the Portuguese during the Reign of Emmanuel. 8vo. 2 vols. Lond. 1752.

Ossorius (Hieron.) De Rebus Emanuelis Lusitaniæ Regis. 8vo. Col. Agr. 1752.

Ovalle (Alonso) Historica Relacion del Reyno de Chili. fol. Rom. 1646.

―――― An Historical Relation of the Kingdom of Chili. Exst. Churchill's Collect. iii. 1.

Oviedo y Bagnos (D. Jos.) Historia de la Conquista y Publicacion de Venezuela. fol. Mad. 1723.

―――― Sommaria, &c. Exst. Ramusio iii. 44.

―――― (Gonz. Fern. de) Relacion Sommaria de la Historia Natural de los Indias. Exst. Barcia Hist. Prim. tom. i.

―――― Historia Generale et Naturale dell Indie Occidentale. Exst. Ramusio iii. 74.

―――― Relatione della Navigatione per la grandissima Fiume Maragnon. Exst. Ramus. iii. 415.

Palacio (D. Raim. Mig.) Discurso Economico Politico. 4to. Mad. 1778.

Palafox y Mendoza (D. Juan) Virtudes del Indios, o Naturaliza y Costumbres de los Indios de N.Espagna. 4to.

―――― Vie de Venerable Dom. Jean Palafox Evêque de l'Angelopolis. 12mo. Cologne, 1772.

Pegna (Juan Nugnez de la) Conquista y Antiguedades de las Islas de Gran Canaria. 4to. Mad. 1676.

Pegna Montenegro (D. Alonso de la) Itinerario para Parochos de Indios, en que tratan les materias mas particulares, tocantes a ellos para se buen administracion. 4to. Amberes, 1754.

Penalosa y Mondragon (Fr. Benito de) Cinco Excellencias del Espagnol que des peublan a Espagna. 4to. Pampl. 1629

Peralta Barnuevo (D. Pedro de) Lima fundada, o Conquista del Peru, Poëma Eroyco. 4to. Lima, 1732.

―――― Calderon (D. Mathias de) El Apostol do las Indias y nuevos gentes San Francisco Xavier de la Compagnia de Jesus Epitome de sus Apostolicos Hechos. 4to. Pampl. 1665.

Pereira de Berrido (Bernard.) Annales Historicos do Estado do Maranchao. fol. Lisboa, 1749.

Peru ― Relatione d'un Capitano Spagnuolo del Descoprimento y Conquista del Peru. Exst. Ramus. iii. 371.

―――― Relatione d'un Secretario de Franc. Pizarro della Conquista del Peru. Exst. Ramusio iii. 371.

―――― Relacion del Peru. MS.

Pesquisa de los Oydores de Panama contra D. Jayme Mugnos, &c. por haverlos Commerciado illicitamente en tiempo do Guerra. fol. 1755.

Philipinas ― Carta que escribe un Religioso antiguo de Philipinas, a un Amigo suyo en Espagna, que le pregunta el Naturel y Genio de los Indios Naturales de estas Islas. MS. 4to.

Piedrahita (Luc. Fern.) Historia general de las Conquistas del Nuevo Reyno de Granada. fol. Ambres.

Pinelo (Ant. de Leon) Epitome de la Bibliotheca Oriental y Occidental en que se continen los Escritores de las Indias Orientales y Occidentales. fol. 2 vols. Mad. 1737.

Pinzonius socius Admirantis Columbi ― Navigatio et Res per eum repertæ. Exst. Nov. Orb. Grynæi, p. 119.

Pizarro y Orellana (D. Fern.) Varones illustres del N. Mundo. fol. Mad. 1639.

Planctus Judorum Christianorum in America Peruntina. 12mo.

Puente (D. Jos. Martinez de la) Compendio de las Historias de los Descubrimientos de la India Oriental y sus Islas. 4to. Mad. 1681.

Quir (Ferd de) Terra Australis incognita; or a new Southern Discovery, containing a fifth part of the World, lately found out. 4to. Lond. 1617.

Ramusio (Giov. Battista) Racolto delle Navigationi e Viaggi. fol. 3 vols. Venet. 1588.

Real Compagnia Guipuzcoana de Caracas, Noticias historiales Practicas, de los Sucesos y Adelantamientos de esta Compagnia desde su Fundacion en 1728 hasta 1764. 4to. 1765.

Recopilacion de Leyes de los Reynos de las Indias. fol. 4 vols. Mad. 1756.

Reglamento y Aranceles Reales para el Commercio de Espagna a Indias.

Relatione d'un Gentilhuomo del Sig. Fern. Cortese della gran Città Temistatan, Mexico, et della altre cose delle Nova Spagna. Exst. Ramus. iii. 304.

Remesal (Fr. Ant.) Historia general de las Indias Occidentales y particular de la Governacion de Chiapa a Guatimala.

Ribadeneyra (De Diego Portichuelo) de Relacion del Viage desde qui salio de Lima, hasta que llegò a Espagna.

Ribadeneyra y Barrientos (D. Ant. Joach.) Manuel Compendio de el Rogio Patronato Indiano. fol. Mad. 1755.

Ribas (Andr. Perez de) Historia de los Triumphos de Nuestra Sta Fe, entre Gentes la mas Barbaras, en las Missiones de Nueva Espagna. Mad. 1645.

Riol (D. Santiago) Representacion a Philipe V. sobre el Estado actual de los Papeles universales de la Monarchia. MS.

Ripia (Juan de la) Practica de la Administracion y Cobranza de las rentas reales. fol. Mad. 1768.

Rocha Pitta (Sebastiano de) Historia de America Portougueza desde o Anno de 1500 du su Descobrimento ate o de 1724. fol. Lisboa, 1730.

Rodriguez (Manuel) Explicacion de la Bulla de la Santa Cruzada. 1589.

——— (P. Man.) El Maragnon y Amozonas Historia de los Descubrimientos, Entradas y Reducion de Naciones.

Roman (Hieron.) Republicas del Mundo. fol. 3 vols. Mad. 1595.

Roma y Rosell (De Franc.) Las segnales de la felicidad de Espagna y medios de hacerlas efficaces. Mad. 1768.

Rosende (P. Ant. Gonz. de) Vida del Juan de Palafox Arzobispo de Mexico.

Rubaclava (Don Jos. Gutierrez de) Tratado Historico-Politico y Legal de el Commercio de las Indias Occidentales.

Ruiz (P. Ant.) Conquista Espiritual hecha por los Religiosos de la Compagnia de Jesus, en las Provincias de la Paraguay, Uraguay, Paraná y Tape.

Salazar de Mendoza (D. Pedro) Monarquia de Espagna, tom. i. ii. iii.

——— y Olarte (D. Ignacio) Historia de la Conquista de Mexico—Segunda parte. Cordov. 1743.

Salazar de Mendoza y Zevallos (D. Alonz. Ed. de) Constituciones y Ordenanzas antiguas Añadidas y Modernas de la Real Universidad y estudio general ste San Marcos de la Ciudad de los Reyes del Peru. fol. En la Ciudad de los Reyes, 1735.

Sanchez (Ant. Ribero) Dissertation sur l'Origine de la Maladie Venerienne, dans laquelle on prouve qu'elle n'a point été portée de l'Amerique. 1765.

Sarmiento de Gamboa (Pedro de) Viage el Estrecho de Magellanes. 1768.

Santa Cruz (El Marq.) Commercio Suelto y en Companias General. 1732.

Sta. Domingo, Puerto Rico, y Margarita, Real Compagnia de Commercio.

Schemidel (Hulderico) Historia y Discubrimiento del Rio de la Plata y Paraguay. Exst. Barcia Hist. Prim. tom. iii.

Sebara da Sylva (Jos. de) Recueil Chronologique et Analytique de tout ce qu'a fait en Portugal la Société dite de Jésus, depuis son Entrée dans ce Royaume en 1540 jusqu'à son Expulsion 1759. 12mo. 3 vols. Lisb. 1769.

Segni (D. Diego Raymundo) Antiquario Noticiosa General de Espagna y sus Indios. 12mo. 1769.

Sepulveda (Genesius) Dialogus de justis Belli Causis, præsertim in Indos Novi Orbis. MS.

——— (Jo. Genesius) Epist. Lib. VII.

Sepulveda de Regno, Libri III. 1570.

Seyxas y Lovero, (D. Fr.) Theatro Naval Hydrographico. 4to. 1648.

——— Descripcion Geographica y Derrotera de la Religion Austral Magellanica. 4to. Mad. 1690.

Simon (Pedro) Noticias Historiales de las Conquistas de Tierra Firmo en las Indias Occidentales. Cuença, 1627.

Solis (D. Ant. de) Historias de las Conquistas de Mexico. Mad. 1684.

——— History of the Conquest of Mexico.—Translated by Townshend. 1724

Solarzono y Pereyrra (Joan) Politica Indiana. fol. 2 vols. Mad. 1776.

——— De Indiarum Jure, sive de justa Indiarum Occidentalium Gubernatione.

——— Obras Varias posthumas. 1776.

Soto y Marne (P. Franc. de) Copia de la Relacion de Viage qui desde la Ciudad de Cadiz a la Cartagena de Indias hizo.

Spilbergen et Le Maire Speculum Orientalis Occidentalisque Navigationum.

Suarez de Figueroa (Chris.) Hechos de D. Garcia Hurtado de Mendoza.

Tanco (Luis Bezerra) Felicidad de Mexico en la admirable Aparicion de N. Signora de Guadalupe. Mad. 1745.

Tarragones (Hieron. Gir.) Dos Libros de Cosmographia. 4to. Milan, 1556.

Techo (F. Nichol. de), The History of the Provinces Paraguay, Tucuman, Rio de la Plata, &c. Exst. Churchill's Coll. vi. 3.

Torquemada (Juan de) Monarquia Indiana. fol. 3 vols. Mad. 1723.

Torres (Sim. Per. de) Viage del Mundo. Exst. Barcia Hist. Prim. iii.

——— (Franc. Caro de) Historia de las Ordenes Militares de Santiago, Calatrava y Alcantara, desde su Fundacion hasta el Rey D. Felipe II. Administrador perpetuo dellas. 1629.

Torribio (P. F. Jos.) Aparato para la Historia Natural Espagnala. fol. Mad. 1754.

——— Dissertacion Historico-Politica y en mucha parte Geographica de las Islas Philipinas. 12mo. Mad. 1753.

Totanes (F. Sebastian de) Manual Tagalog para auxilio de Provincia de las Philipinas. 4to. Samplai en las Philipinas. 1745.

Ulloa (D. Ant. de) Voyage Historique de l'Amerique Meridionale. 4to. 2 tom. Paris, 1752.

——— (D. Ant. de) Noticias Americanas, Entretenimientos Physicos-Historicos, sobre la America Meridional y la Septentrional Oriental. Mad. 1772.

——— (D. Bern. de) Restablecimiento de las Fabricas, Trafico, y Commercio maritimo de Espagna. Mad. 1740.

——— (Franc.) Navigatione per scoprire l'Isole delle Specierie fino all Mare detto Vermejo nel 1539. Exst. Ramus. iii. 339.

——— (D. Bernardo) Retablissement des Manufactures et du Commerce d'Espagne. 12mo. Amst. 1753.

Uztariz (D. Geron.) Theoria y Practica de Commercio y de Marina. fol. Mad. 1757.

——— The Theory and Practice of Commerce, and Maritime Affairs. 8vo. 2 vols. Lond. 1751.

Verages (D. Thom. Tamaio de) Restauracion de la Ciudad del Salvador y Baia de Todos Sanctos en la Provincia del Brasil. 4to. Mad. 1628.

Vargas Machuca (D. Bern. de) Milicia y Descripcion de las Indias. Mad. 1699.

Vega (Garcilasso de la) Histoire de la Conquête de la Floride. Traduite par Richelet. 12mo. 2 tom. Leyd. 1731.

——— Royal Commentaries of Peru, by Rycaut. fol. Lond. 1688.

Vega (L'Ynca Garcilasso de la) Histoires des Guerres Civiles des Espagnoles dans les Indes, par Baudoin. 1648.

Veitia Linage (Jos.) The Spanish Rule of Trade to the West Indies.

——— Declamacion Oratoria en Defensa de D. Jos. Fern. Veitia Linage.

Veitia Linage Norte de la Contratacion de las Indias Occidentales. fol. Sevill. 1672.

Venegas (Miguel), a Natural and Civil History of California. 8vo. 2 vols. Lond. 1759.

Verazzano (Giov.) Relatione delle Terra per lui scoperta nel 1524. Exst. Ramusio iii. p. 420.

Vesputius (Americus) Duæ Navigationes sub Auspiciis Ferdinandi, &c. Exst. de Bry America. Pars X.

——— Navigatio prima, secunda, tertia, quarta. Exst. Nov. Orb. Grynæi, p. 155.

Viage de Espagna. 12mo. 6 tom. Mad. 1776.

Victoria (Franc.) Relationes Theologicæ de Indis et de Jure Belli contra eos.

Viera y Clavijo (D. Jos.) Noticias de la Historia general de las Islas de Canaria.

Villalobos (D. Juan de) Manifesto sobre la introduccion de esclavos Negros en las Indias Occidentales. 4to. 1682.

Villagra (Gasp. de) Historia de Nueva Mexico, Poema. Alcala, 1610.

Villa Segnor y Sanchez (D. Jos. Ant.) Theatro Americano. Descripcion general de los Reynos y Provincias de la Nueva Espagna. 2 tom. Mex. 1746.

——— Ros puesta sobre el precio de Azogue. 4to.

Vocabulario Brasiliano y Portugues. 4to. MS.

Ward (D. Bernardo) Proyecto Economico sobre la poblacion de Espagna, la agricultura en todos sus ramos, y de mas establecimientos de industria, comercio con nuestra marina, arreglo de nuestra intereses en America, libertad del comercio en Indias, &c. MS.

Xeres (Franc. de) Verdadera Relacion de la Conquista del Peru y Provincia de Cuzco, Embiada al Emperador Carlos V. Exst. Barcia Hist. Prim. tom. iii.

——— Relatione, &c. &c. Exst. Ramusio iii. 372.

Zarate (Aug. de) Historia del Descubrimiento y Conquista de la Provincia del Peru. Exst. Barcia Hist. Prim. tom. iii.

——— Histoire de la Découverte et de la Conquête du Perou. Paris, 1742.

Zavala y Augnon (D. Miguel de) Representacion al Rey N. Segnor D. Philipe V. dirigida al mas seguro Aumento del Real Erario. 1732.

Zevallos (D. Pedro Ordognez de) Historia y Viago del Mundo. 1691.

THE HISTORY OF AMERICA.

BY WILLIAM ROBERTSON, D.D.
PRINCIPAL OF THE UNIVERSITY OF EDINBURGH, ETC. ETC.

THE
HISTORY OF AMERICA.

BOOK I.

The progress of men, in discovering and peopling the various parts of the earth, has been extremely slow. Several ages elapsed before they removed far from those mild and fertile regions in which they were originally placed by their Creator. The occasion of their first general dispersion is known; but we are unacquainted with the course of their migrations, or the time when they took possession of the different countries which they now inhabit. Neither history nor tradition furnishes such information concerning these remote events, as enables us to trace, with any certainty, the operations of the human race in the infancy of society.

We may conclude, however, that all the early migrations of mankind were made by land. The ocean which surrounds the habitable earth, as well as the various arms of the sea which separate one region from another, though destined to facilitate the communication between distant countries, seem, at first view, to be formed to check the progress of man, and to mark the bounds of that portion of the globe to which nature had confined him. It was long, we may believe, before men attempted to pass these formidable barriers, and became so skilful and adventurous as to commit themselves to the mercy of the winds and waves, or to quit their native shores in quest of remote and unknown regions.

Navigation and shipbuilding are arts so nice and complicated, that they require the ingenuity, as well as experience, of many successive ages to bring them to any degree of perfection. From the raft or canoe, which first served to carry a savage over the river that obstructed him in the chase, to the construction of a vessel capable of conveying a numerous crew with safety to a distant coast, the progress in improvement is immense. Many efforts would be made, many experiments would be tried, and much labour as well as invention would be employed, before men could accomplish this arduous and important undertaking. The rude and imperfect state in which navigation is still found among all nations which are not considerably civilized, corresponds with this account of its progress, and demonstrates that in early times the art was not so far improved as to enable men to undertake distant voyages, or to attempt remote discoveries.

As soon, however, as the art of navigation became known, a new species of correspondence among men took place. It is from this era that we must date the commencement of such an intercourse between nations as deserves the appellation of commerce. Men are, indeed, far advanced in improvement before commerce becomes an object of great importance to them. They must even have made some considerable progress towards civilization, before they acquire the idea of property, and ascertain it so perfectly as to be acquainted with the most simple of all contracts, that of exchanging by barter one rude commodity for another. But as soon as this important right is established, and every individual feels that he has an exclusive title to possess or to alienate whatever he has acquired by his own labour and dexterity, the wants and ingenuity of his nature suggest to him a new method of increasing his acquisitions and enjoyments, by disposing of what is superfluous in his own stores, in order to procure what is necessary or desirable in those of other men. Thus a commercial intercourse begins, and is carried on among the members of the same community. By degrees, they discover that neighbouring tribes possess what they themselves want, and enjoy comforts of which they wish to partake. In the same mode, and upon the same principles, that domestic traffic is carried on within the society, an external commerce is established with other tribes or nations. Their mutual interest and mutual wants render this intercourse desirable, and imperceptibly introduce the maxims and laws which facilitate its progress and render it secure. But no very extensive commerce can take place between contiguous provinces, whose soil and climate being nearly the same yield similar productions. Remote countries cannot convey their commodities, by land, to those places where on account of their rarity they are desired, and become valuable. It is to navigation that men are indebted for the power of transporting the superfluous stock of one part of the earth to supply the wants of another. The luxuries and blessings of a particular climate are no longer confined to itself alone, but the enjoyment of them is communicated to the most distant regions.

In proportion as the knowledge of the advantages derived from navigation and commerce continued to spread, the intercourse among nations extended. The ambition of conquest, or the necessity of procuring new settlements, were no longer the sole motives of visiting distant lands. The desire of gain became a new incentive to activity, roused adventurers, and sent them forth upon long voyages, in search of countries whose products or wants might increase that circulation which nourishes and gives vigour to commerce. Trade proved a great source of discovery: it opened unknown seas, it penetrated into new regions, and contributed more than any other cause to bring men acquainted with the situation, the nature, and commodities of the different parts of the globe. But even after a regular commerce was established in the world, after nations were considerably civilized, and the sciences and arts were cultivated with ardour and success, navigation continued to be so imperfect, that it can hardly be said to have advanced beyond the infancy of its improvement in the ancient world.

Among all the nations of antiquity, the structure of their vessels was extremely rude, and their method of working them very defective. They were unacquainted with several principles and operations in navigation, which are now considered as the first elements on which that science is founded. Though that property of the magnet by which it attracts iron was well known to the ancients, its more important and amazing virtue of pointing to the poles had entirely escaped their observation. Destitute of this faithful guide, which now conducts the pilot with so much certainty in the unbounded ocean, during the darkness of night, or when the heavens are covered with clouds, the ancients had no other method of regulating their course than by observing the sun and stars. Their navigation was of consequence uncertain and timid. They durst seldom quit sight of land, but crept along the coast, exposed to all the dangers, and retarded by all the obstructions, unavoidable in holding such an awkward course. An incredible length of time was requisite for performing voyages which are now finished in a short space. Even in the mildest climates, and in seas the least tempestuous, it was only during the summer months that the ancients ventured out of their harbours. The remainder of the year was lost in inactivity. It would have been deemed most inconsiderate rashness to have braved the fury of the winds and waves during winter.*

While both the science and practice of navigation continued to be so defective, it was an undertaking of no small difficulty and danger to visit any remote region of the earth. Under every disadvantage, however, the active spirit of commerce exerted itself. The Egyptians, soon after the establishment of their monarchy, are said to have opened a trade between the Arabian Gulf, or Red Sea, and the western coast of the great Indian continent. The commodities which they imported from the East, were carried by land from the Arabian Gulf to the banks of the Nile, and conveyed down that river to the Mediterranean. But if the Egyptians in early times applied themselves to commerce, their attention to it was of short duration. The fertile soil and mild climate of Egypt produced the necessaries and comforts of life with such profusion, as rendered its inhabitants so independent of other countries, that it became an established maxim among that people, whose ideas and institutions differed in almost every point from those of other nations, to renounce all intercourse with foreigners. In consequence of this, they never went out of their own country; they held all seafaring persons in detestation, as impious and profane; and fortifying their own harbours, they denied strangers admittance into them.† It was in the decline of their power, and when their veneration for ancient maxims had greatly abated, that they again opened their ports, and resumed any communication with foreigners.

The character and situation of the Phenicians were as favourable to the spirit of commerce and discovery as those of the Egyptians were adverse to it. They had no distinguishing peculiarity in their manners and institutions; they were not addicted to any singular and unsocial form of superstition; they could mingle with other nations without scruple or reluctance. The territory which they possessed was neither large nor fertile. Commerce was the only source from which they could derive opulence or power. Accordingly, the trade carried on by the Phenicians of Sidon and Tyre, was more extensive and enterprising than that of any state in the ancient world. The genius of the Phenicians, as well as the object of their policy and the spirit of their laws, were entirely commercial. They were a people of merchants, who aimed at the empire of the sea, and actually possessed it. Their ships not only frequented all the ports in the Mediterranean, but they were the first who ventured beyond the ancient boundaries of navigation, and, passing the Straits of Gades, visited the western coasts of Spain and Africa. In many of the places to which they resorted, they planted colonies, and communicated to the rude inhabitants some knowledge of their arts and improvements. While they extended their discoveries towards the north and the west, they did not neglect to penetrate into the more opulent and fertile regions of the south and east. Having rendered themselves masters of several commodious harbours towards the bottom of the Arabian Gulf, they, after the example of the Egyptians, established a regular intercourse with Arabia and the continent of India on the one hand, and with the eastern coast of Africa on the other. From these countries they imported many valuable commodities unknown to the rest of the world, and during a long period engrossed that lucrative branch of commerce without a rival. [1]

The vast wealth which the Phenicians acquired by monopolizing the trade carried on in the Red Sea, incited their neighbours the Jews, under the prosperous reigns of David and Solomon, to aim at being admitted to some share of it. This they obtained, partly by their conquest of Idumea, which stretches along the Red Sea, and partly by their alliance with Hi-

---

* Vegitius de Re milit. lib. iv.   † Diod. Sicul. lib. I. p. 78. ed. Wesselingii. Amst. 1756. Strabo, lib. xvii. p. 1142. ed. Amst. 1707.

ram, king of Tyre. Solomon fitted out fleets, which, under the direction of Phenician pilots, sailed from the Red Sea to Tarshish and Ophir. These, it is probable, were ports in India and Africa, which their conductors were accustomed to frequent, and from them the Jewish ships returned with such valuable cargoes as suddenly diffused wealth and splendour through the kingdom of Israel.* But the singular institutions of the Jews, the observance of which was enjoined by their divine Legislator, with an intention of preserving them a separate people, uninfected by idolatry, formed a national character, incapable of that open and liberal intercourse with strangers which commerce requires. Accordingly, this unsocial genius of the people, together with the disasters which befell the kingdom of Israel, prevented the commercial spirit which their monarchs laboured to introduce and to cherish, from spreading among them. The Jews cannot be numbered among the nations which contributed to improve navigation, or to extend discovery.

But though the instructions and example of the Phenicians were unable to mould the manners and temper of the Jews, in opposition to the tendency of their laws, they transmitted the commercial spirit with facility, and in full vigour, to their own descendants the Carthaginians. The commonwealth of Carthage applied to trade and naval affairs, with no less ardour, ingenuity, and success, than its parent state. Carthage early rivalled and soon surpassed Tyre in opulence and power, but seems not to have aimed at obtaining any share in the commerce with India. The Phenicians had engrossed this, and had such a command of the Red Sea as secured to them the exclusive possession of that lucrative branch of trade. The commercial activity of the Carthaginians was exerted in another direction. Without contending for the trade of the East with their mother country, they extended their navigation chiefly towards the west and north. Following the course which the Phenicians had opened, they passed the Straits of Gades, and pushing their discoveries far beyond those of the parent state, visited not only all the coasts of Spain, but those of Gaul, and penetrated at last into Britain. At the same time that they acquired knowledge of new countries in this part of the globe, they gradually carried their researches towards the south. They made considerable progress by land into the interior provinces of Africa, traded with some of them, and subjected others to their empire. They sailed along the western coast of that great continent almost to the tropic of Cancer, and planted several colonies, in order to civilize the natives and accustom them to commerce. They discovered the Fortunate Islands, now known by the name of the Canaries, the utmost boundary of ancient navigation in the western ocean.†

Nor was the progress of the Phenicians and Carthaginians in their knowledge of the globe, owing entirely to the desire of extending their trade from one country to another. Commerce was followed by its usual effects among both these people. It awakened curiosity, enlarged the ideas and desires of men, and incited them to bold enterprises. Voyages were undertaken, the sole object of which was to discover new countries, and to explore unknown seas. Such, during the prosperous age of the Carthaginian republic, were the famous navigations of Hanno and Himlico. Both their fleets were equipped by authority of the senate, and at public expense. Hanno was directed to steer towards the south, along the coast of Africa, and he seems to have advanced much nearer the equinoctial line than any former navigator.‡ Himlico had it in charge to proceed towards the north, and to examine the western coasts of the European continent.§ Of the same nature was the extraordinary navigation of the Phenicians

---

* Mémoire sur le Pays d'Ophir, par M. d'Anville, Mem. de l'Académ. des Inscript. &c. tom. xxx. 83. † Plinii Nat. Hist. lib. vi. c. 37. edit. in usum Delph. 4to. 1685. ‡ Plinii Nat. Hist. lib. v. c. 1. Hannonis Periplus ap. Geograph. minores, edit. Hudsoni, vol. I. p. 1. § Plinii Nat. Hist. lib. i. c. 67. Festus Avienus apud Bochart. Geogr. Sacer. lib. l. c. 60. p. 652. Oper. vol. III. L. Baj. 1707.

round Africa. A Phenician fleet, we are told, fitted out by Necho king of Egypt, took its departure about six hundred and four years before the Christian era, from a port in the Red Sea, doubled the southern promontory of Africa, and after a voyage of three years returned by the Straits of Gades to the mouth of the Nile.* Eudoxus of Cyzicus is said to have held the same course, and to have accomplished the same arduous undertaking.†

These voyages, if performed in the manner which I have related, may justly be reckoned the greatest effort of navigation in the ancient world; and if we attend to the imperfect state of the art at that time, it is difficult to determine whether we should most admire the courage and sagacity with which the design was formed, or the conduct and good fortune with which it was executed. But unfortunately all the original and authentic accounts of the Phenician and Carthaginian voyages, whether undertaken by public authority or in prosecution of their private trade, have perished. The information which we receive concerning them from the Greek and Roman authors is not only obscure and inaccurate, but if we except a short narrative of Hanno's expedition, is of suspicious authority.[2] Whatever acquaintance with the remote regions of the earth the Phenicians or Carthaginians may have acquired, was concealed from the rest of mankind with a mercantile jealousy. Every thing relative to the course of their navigation was not only a mystery of trade, but a secret of state. Extraordinary facts are related concerning their solicitude to prevent other nations from penetrating into what they wished should remain undivulged.‡ Many of their discoveries seem, accordingly, to have been scarcely known beyond the precincts of their own states. The navigation round Africa, in particular, is recorded by the Greek and Roman writers rather as a strange amusing tale, which they did not comprehend or did not believe, than as a real transaction which enlarged their knowledge and influenced their opinions.[3]. As neither the progress of the Phenician or Carthaginian discoveries, nor the extent of their navigation, were communicated to the rest of mankind, all memorials of their extraordinary skill in naval affairs seem, in a great measure, to have perished, when the maritime power of the former was annihilated by Alexander's conquest of Tyre, and the empire of the latter was overturned by the Roman arms.

Leaving, then, the obscure and pompous accounts of the Phenician and Carthaginian voyages to the curiosity and conjectures of antiquaries, history must rest satisfied with relating the progress of navigation and discovery among the Greeks and Romans, which, though less splendid, is better ascertained. It is evident that the Phenicians, who instructed the Greeks in many other useful sciences and arts, did not communicate to them that extensive knowledge of navigation which they themselves possessed; nor did the Romans imbibe that commercial spirit and ardour for discovery which distinguished their rivals the Carthaginians. Though Greece be almost encompassed by the sea, which formed many spacious bays and commodious harbours; though it be surrounded by a great number of fertile islands, yet, notwithstanding such a favourable situation, which seemed to invite that ingenious people to apply themselves to navigation, it was long before this art attained any degree of perfection among them. Their early voyages, the object of which was piracy rather than commerce, were so inconsiderable that the expedition of the Argonauts from the coast of Thessaly to the Euxine Sea, appeared such an amazing effort of skill and courage, as entitled the conductors of it to be ranked among the demigods, and exalted the vessel in which they sailed to a place among the heavenly constellations. Even at a later period, when the Greeks engaged in the famous enterprise against Troy, their knowledge in naval affairs seems not to have been much improved. According to the account of Homer, the only poet

* Herodot. lib. iv. c. 42. † Plinii Nat. Hist. lib. ii c. 67. ‡ Strab. Geogr. lib. iii. p. 265. lib. xviii. 1154.

to whom history ventures to appeal, and who, by his scrupulous accuracy in describing the manners and arts of early ages, merits this distinction, the science of navigation at that time had hardly advanced beyond its rudest state. The Greeks in the heroic age seem to have been unacquainted with the use of iron, the most serviceable of all the metals, without which no considerable progress was ever made in the mechanical arts. Their vessels were of inconsiderable burden, and mostly without decks. They had only one mast, which was erected or taken down at pleasure. They were strangers to the use of anchors. All their operations in sailing were clumsy and unskilful. They turned their observations towards stars, which were improper for regulating their course, and their mode of observing them was inaccurate and fallacious. When they had finished a voyage they drew their paltry barks ashore, as savages do their canoes, and these remained on dry land until the season of returning to sea approached. It is not then in the early heroic ages of Greece that we can expect to observe the science of navigation, and the spirit of discovery, making any considerable progress. During that period of disorder and ignorance, a thousand causes concurred in restraining curiosity and enterprise within very narrow bounds.

But the Greeks advanced with rapidity to a state of greater civilization and refinement. Government, in its most liberal and perfect form, began to be established in their different communities; equal laws and regular police were gradually introduced; the sciences and arts which are useful or ornamental in life were carried to a high pitch of improvement; and several of the Grecian commonwealths applied to commerce with such ardour and success, that they were considered, in the ancient world, as maritime powers of the first rank. Even then, however, the naval victories of the Greeks must be ascribed rather to the native spirit of the people, and to that courage which the enjoyment of liberty inspires, than to any extraordinary progress in the science of navigation. In the Persian war, those exploits, which the genius of the Greek historians has rendered so famous, were performed by fleets composed chiefly of small vessels without decks;* the crews of which rushed forward with impetuous valour, but little art, to board those of the enemy. In the war of Peloponnesus, their ships seem still to have been of inconsiderable burden and force. The extent of their trade, how highly soever it may have been estimated in ancient times, was in proportion to this low condition of their marine. The maritime states of Greece hardly carried on any commerce beyond the limits of the Mediterranean sea. Their chief intercourse was with the colonies of their countrymen planted in the Lesser Asia, in Italy, and Sicily. They sometimes visited the ports of Egypt, of the southern provinces of Gaul, and of Thrace; or, passing through the Hellespont, they traded with the countries situated around the Euxine sea. Amazing instances occur of their ignorance, even of those countries which lay within the narrow precincts to which their navigation was confined. When the Greeks had assembled their combined fleet against Xerxes at Egina, they thought it unadvisable to sail to Samos, because they believed the distance between that island and Egina to be as great as the distance between Egina and the Pillars of Hercules.† They were either utterly unacquainted with all the parts of the globe beyond the Mediterranean sea, or what knowledge they had of them was founded on conjecture, or derived from the information of a few persons whom curiosity and the love of science had prompted to travel by land into the Upper Asia, or by sea into Egypt, the ancient seats of wisdom and arts. After all that the Greeks learned from them, they appear to have been ignorant of the most important facts on which an accurate and scientific knowledge of the globe is founded.

The expedition of Alexander the Great into the East considerably en-

* Thucyd. lib. l. c. 14. † Herodot. lib. viii. c. 1.

larged the sphere of navigation and of geographical knowledge among the Greeks. That extraordinary man, notwithstanding the violent passions which incited him at some times to the wildest actions and the most extravagant enterprises, possessed talents which fitted him, not only to conquer, but to govern the world. He was capable of framing those bold and original schemes of policy, which gave a new form to human affairs. The revolution in commerce, brought about by the force of his genius, is hardly inferior to that revolution in empire occasioned by the success of his arms. It is probable that the opposition and efforts of the republic of Tyre, which checked him so long in the career of his victories, gave Alexander an opportunity of observing the vast resources of a maritime power, and conveyed to him some idea of the immense wealth which the Tyrians derived from their commerce, especially that with the East Indies. As soon as he had accomplished the destruction of Tyre, and reduced Egypt to subjection, he formed the plan of rendering the empire which he proposed to establish, the centre of commerce as well as the seat of dominion. With this view he founded a great city, which he honoured with his own name, near one of the mouths of the river Nile, that by the Mediterranean sea, and the neighbourhood of the Arabian Gulf, it might command the trade both of the East and West.* This situation was chosen with such discernment, that Alexandria soon became the chief commercial city in the world. Not only during the subsistence of the Grecian empire in Egypt and in the East, but amidst all the successive revolutions in those countries from the time of the Ptolemies to the discovery of the navigation by the Cape of Good Hope, commerce, particularly that of the East Indies, continued to flow in the channel which the sagacity and foresight of Alexander had marked out for it.

His ambition was not satisfied with having opened to the Greeks a communication with India by sea; he aspired to the sovereignty of those regions which furnished the rest of mankind with so many precious commodities, and conducted his army thither by land. Enterprising, however, as he was, he may be said rather to have viewed than to have conquered that country. He did not, in his progress towards the East, advance beyond the banks of the rivers that fall into the Indus, which is now the western boundary of the vast continent of India. Amidst the wild exploits which distinguish this part of his history, he pursued measures that mark the superiority of his genius as well as the extent of his views. He had penetrated as far into India as to confirm his opinion of its commercial importance, and to perceive that immense wealth might be derived from intercourse with a country where the arts of elegance, having been more early cultivated, were arrived at greater perfection than in any other part of the earth.† Full of this idea, he resolved to examine the course of navigation from the mouth of the Indus to the bottom of the Persian Gulf; and, if it should be found practicable, to establish a regular communication between them. In order to effect this, he proposed to remove the cataracts, with which the jealousy of the Persians, and their aversion to correspondence with foreigners, had obstructed the entrance into the Euphrates;‡ to carry the commodities of the East up that river, and the Tigris, which unites with it, into the interior parts of his Asiatic dominions; while, by the way of the Arabian Gulf and the river Nile, they might be conveyed to Alexandria, and distributed to the rest of the world. Nearchus, an officer of eminent abilities, was intrusted with the command of the fleet fitted out for this expedition. He performed this voyage, which was deemed an enterprise so arduous and important, that Alexander reckoned it one of the most extraordinary events which distinguished his reign. Inconsiderable as it may now appear, it was at that

---

* Strab. Geogr. lib. xvii. p 1143. 1149. † Strab. Geogr. lib. xv. p. 1036. Q. Curtius, lib. xviii. c. 9. ‡ Strab. Geogr. lib. xvi. p. 1075.

time an undertaking of no little merit and difficulty. In the prosecution of it, striking instances occur of the small progress which the Greeks had made in naval knowledge.[4] Having never sailed beyond the bounds of the Mediterranean, where the ebb and flow of the sea are hardly perceptible, when they first observed this phenomenon at the mouth of the Indus, it appeared to them a prodigy, by which the gods testified the displeasure of heaven against their enterprise.[5] During their whole course, they seem never to have lost sight of land, but followed the bearings of the coast so servilely, that they could not avail themselves of those periodical winds which facilitate navigation in the Indian ocean. Accordingly they spent no less than ten months in performing this voyage,* which, from the mouth of the Indus to that of the Persian Gulf, does not exceed twenty degrees. It is probable, that amidst the convulsions and frequent revolutions in the East, occasioned by the contests among the successors of Alexander, the navigation to India by the course which Nearchus had opened was discontinued. The Indian trade carried on at Alexandria, not only subsisted, but was so much extended, under the Grecian monarchs of Egypt, that it proved a great source of the wealth which distinguished their kingdom.

The progress which the Romans made in navigation and discovery, was still more inconsiderable than that of the Greeks. The genius of the Roman people, their military education, and the spirit of their laws, concurred in estranging them from commerce and naval affairs. It was the necessity of opposing a formidable rival, not the desire of extending trade, which first prompted them to aim at maritime power. Though they soon perceived, that in order to acquire the universal dominion after which they aspired, it was necessary to render themselves masters of the sea, they still considered the naval service as a subordinate station, and reserved for it such citizens as were not of a rank to be admitted into the legions.† In the history of the Roman republic, hardly one event occurs, that marks attention to navigation any further than it was instrumental towards conquest. When the Roman valour and discipline had subdued all the maritime states known in the ancient world; when Carthage, Greece, and Egypt had submitted to their power, the Romans did not imbibe the commercial spirit of the conquered nations. Among that people of soldiers, to have applied to trade would have been deemed a degradation to a Roman citizen. They abandoned the mechanical arts, commerce, and navigation, to slaves, to freedmen, to provincials, and to citizens of the lowest class. Even after the subversion of liberty, when the severity and haughtiness of ancient manners began to abate, commerce did not rise into high estimation among the Romans. The trade of Greece, Egypt, and the other conquered countries, continued to be carried on in its usual channels, after they were reduced into the form of Roman provinces. As Rome was the capital of the world, and the seat of government, all the wealth and valuable productions of the provinces flowed naturally thither. The Romans, satisfied with this, seem to have suffered commerce to remain almost entirely in the hands of the natives of the respective countries. The extent, however, of the Roman power, which reached over the greatest part of the known world, the vigilant inspection of the Roman magistrates, and the spirit of the Roman government, no less intelligent than active, gave such additional security to commerce as animated it with new vigour. The union among nations was never so entire, nor the intercourse so perfect, as within the bounds of this vast empire. Commerce, under the Roman dominion, was not obstructed by the jealousy of rival states, interrupted by frequent hostilities, or limited by partial restrictions. One superintending power moved and regulated the industry of mankind, and enjoyed the fruits of their joint efforts.

Navigation felt its influence, and improved under it. As soon as the

* Plin. Hist. Nat. lib. vi. c. 23.   † Polyb. lib. v.

Romans acquired a taste for the luxuries of the East, the trade with India through Egypt was pushed with new vigour, and carried on to greater extent. By frequenting the Indian continent, navigators became acquainted with the periodical course of the winds, which, in the ocean that separates Africa from India, blow with little variation during one half of the year from the east, and during the other half blow with equal steadiness from the west. Encouraged by observing this, the pilots who sailed from Egypt to India abandoned their ancient slow and dangerous course along the coast, and, as soon as the western monsoon set in, took their departure from Ocelis, at the mouth of the Arabian Gulf, and stretched boldly across the ocean.* The uniform direction of the wind, supplying the place of the compass, and rendering the guidance of the stars less necessary, conducted them to the port of Musiris, on the western shore of the Indian continent. There they took on board their cargo, and, returning with the eastern monsoon, finished their voyage to the Arabian Gulf within the year. This part of India, now known by the name of the Malabar coast, seems to have been the utmost limit of ancient navigation in that quarter of the globe. What imperfect knowledge the ancients had of the immense countries which stretch beyond this towards the East, they received from a few adventurers who had visited them by land. Such excursions were neither frequent nor extensive, and it is probable that, while the Roman intercourse with India subsisted, no traveller ever penetrated further than to the banks of the Ganges.†[6] The fleets from Egypt which traded at Musiris were loaded it is true, with the spices and other rich commodities of the continent and islands of the further India; but these were brought to that port, which became the staple of the commerce between the east and west, by the Indians themselves in canoes hollowed out of one tree.‡ The Egyptian and Roman merchants, satisfied with acquiring those commodities in this manner, did not think it necessary to explore unknown seas, and venture upon a dangerous navigation, in quest of the countries which produced them. But though the discoveries of the Romans in India were so limited, their commerce there was such as will appear considerable, even to the present age, in which the Indian trade has been extended far beyond the practice or conception of any preceding period. We are informed by one author of credit,§ that the commerce with India drained the Roman empire every year of more than four hundred thousand pounds; and by another, that one hundred and twenty ships sailed annually from the Arabian Gulf to that country.‖

The discovery of this new method of sailing to India, is the most considerable improvement in navigation made during the continuance of the Roman power. But in ancient times, the knowledge of remote countries was acquired more frequently by land than by sea;[7] and the Romans, from their peculiar disinclination to naval affairs, may be said to have neglected totally the latter, though a more easy and expeditious method of discovery. The progress, however, of their victorious armies through a considerable portion of Europe, Asia, and Africa, contributed greatly to extend discovery by land, and gradually opened the navigation of new and unknown seas. Previous to the Roman conquests, the civilized nations of antiquity had little communication with those countries in Europe which now form its most opulent and powerful kingdoms. The interior parts of Spain and Gaul were imperfectly known. Britain, separated from the rest of the world, had never been visited, except by its neighbours the Gauls, and by a few Carthaginian merchants. The name of Germany had scarcely been heard of. Into all these countries the arms of the Romans penetrated. They entirely subdued Spain and Gaul; they conquered the greatest and most fertile part of Britain; they advanced into Germany, as far as the

---

* Plin. Nat. Hist. lib. vi. c. 23.   † Strab. Geogr. lib. xv. p. 1006—1010.   ‡ Plin. Nat. Hist. lib. vi. c. 26.   § Ibid.   ‖ Strab. Geogr. lib. ii. p. 179.

banks of the river Elbe. In Africa, they acquired a considerable knowledge of the provinces, which stretched along the Mediterranean Sea, from Egypt westward to the Straits of Gades. In Asia, they not only subjected to their power most of the provinces which composed the Persian and the Macedonian empires, but after their victories over Mithridates and Tigranes, they seem to have made a more accurate survey of the countries contiguous to the Euxine and Caspian seas, and to have carried on a more extensive trade than that of the Greeks with the opulent and commercial nations then seated round the Euxine sea.

From this succinct survey of discovery and navigation, which I have traced from the earliest dawn of historical knowledge, to the full establishment of the Roman dominion, the progress of both appears to have been wonderfully slow. It seems neither adequate to what we might have expected from the activity and enterprise of the human mind, nor to what might have been performed by the power of the great empires which successively governed the world. If we reject accounts that are fabulous and obscure; if we adhere steadily to the light and information of authentic history, without substituting in its place the conjectures of fancy or the dreams of etymologists, we must conclude, that the knowledge which the ancients had acquired of the habitable globe was extremely confined. In Europe, the extensive provinces in the eastern part of Germany were little known to them. They were almost totally unacquainted with the vast countries which are now subject to the kings of Denmark, Sweden, Prussia, Poland, and the Russian empire. The more barren regions that stretch within the arctic circle, were quite unexplored. In Africa, their researches did not extend far beyond the provinces which border on the Mediterranean, and those situated on the western shore of the Arabian Gulf. In Asia, they were unacquainted, as I formerly observed, with all the fertile and opulent countries beyond the Ganges, which furnish the most valuable commodities that in modern times have been the great object of the European commerce with India; nor do they seem to have ever penetrated into those immense regions occupied by the wandering tribes, which they called by the general name of Sarmatians or Scythians, and which are now possessed by Tartars of various denominations, and by the Asiatic subjects of Russia.

But there is one opinion, that universally prevailed among the ancients, which conveys a more striking idea of the small progress they had made in the knowledge of the habitable globe than can be derived from any detail of their discoveries. They supposed the earth to be divided into five regions, which they distinguished by the name of Zones. Two of these, which were nearest the poles, they termed Frigid zones, and believed that the extreme cold which reigned perpetually there rendered them uninhabitable. Another, seated under the line, and extending on either side towards the tropics, they called the Torrid zone, and imagined it to be so burned up with unremitting heat, as to be equally destitute of inhabitants. On the two other zones, which occupied the remainder of the earth, they bestowed the appellation of Temperate, and taught that these, being the only regions in which life could subsist, were allotted to man for his habitation. This wild opinion was not a conceit of the uninformed vulgar, or a fanciful fiction of the poets, but a system adopted by the most enlightened philosophers, the most accurate historians and geographers in Greece and Rome. According to this theory, a vast portion of the habitable earth was pronounced to be unfit for sustaining the human species. Those fertile and populous regions within the torrid zone, which are now known not only to yield their own inhabitants the necessaries and comforts of life with most luxuriant profusion, but to communicate their superfluous stores to the rest of the world, were supposed to be the mansion of perpetual sterility and desolation. As all the parts of the globe with which the ancients were acquainted lay within the northern temperate zone, their opinion that the other temperate zone was filled with inhabitants, was founded on reasoning and conjecture, not on discovery. They even believed that, by the intolerable heat of the torrid zone such an insuperable barrier was placed between the two temperate regions of the earth as would prevent for ever any intercourse between their respective inhabitants. Thus, this extravagant theory not only proves that the ancients were unacquainted with the true state of the globe, but it tended to render their ignorance perpetual, by representing all attempts towards opening a communication with the remote regions of the earth, as utterly impracticable.[8]

But, however imperfect or inaccurate the geographical knowledge which the Greeks and Romans had acquired may appear, in respect of the present improved state of that science, their progress in discovery will seem considerable, and the extent to which they carried navigation and commerce must be reckoned great, when compared with the ignorance of early times. As long as the Roman Empire retained such vigour as to preserve its authority over the conquered nations, and to keep them united, it was an object of public policy, as well as of private curiosity, to examine and describe the countries which composed this great body. Even when the other sciences began to decline, geography, enriched with new observations, and receiving some accession from the experience of every age, and the reports of every traveller, continued to improve. It attained to the highest point of perfection and accuracy to which it ever arrived in the ancient world, by the industry and genius of Ptolemy the philosopher. He flourished in the second century of the Christian æra, and published a description of the terrestrial globe, more ample and exact than that of any of his predecessors.

But, soon after, violent convulsions began to shake the Roman state; the fatal ambition or caprice of Constantine, by changing the seat of government, divided and weakened its force; the barbarous nations, which Providence prepared as instruments to overturn the mighty fabric of the Roman power, began to assemble and to muster their armies on its frontier: the empire tottered to its fall. During this decline and old age of the Roman state, it was impossible that the sciences should go on improving. The efforts of genius were, at that period, as languid and feeble as those of government. From the time of Ptolemy, no considerable addition seems to have been made to geographical knowledge, nor did any important revolution happen in trade, excepting that Constantinople, by its advantageous situation, and the encouragement of the eastern emperors, became a commercial city of the first note.

At length, the clouds which had been so long gathering round the Roman empire burst into a storm. Barbarous nations rushed in from several quarters with irresistible impetuosity, and in the general wreck, occasioned by the inundation which overwhelmed Europe the arts, sciences, inventions, and discoveries of the Romans perished in a great measure, and disappeared.* All the various tribes which settled in the different provinces of the Roman empire were uncivilized, strangers to letters, destitute of arts, unacquainted with regular government, subordination, or laws. The manners and institutions of some of them were so rude as to be hardly compatible with a state of social union. Europe, when occupied by such inhabitants, may be said to have returned to a second infancy, and had to begin anew its career in improvement, science, and civility. The first effect of the settlement of those barbarous invaders was to dissolve the union by which the Roman power had cemented mankind together. They parcelled out Europe into many small and independent states, differing from each other in language and customs. No intercourse subsisted between the members of those divided and hostile communities. Accustomed to a simple mode

* Hist. of Charles V. vol. I.

of life, and averse to industry, they had few wants to supply, and few superfluities to dispose of. The names of *stranger* and *enemy* became once more words of the same import. Customs every where prevailed, and even laws were established, which rendered it disagreeable and dangerous to visit any foreign country.* Cities, in which alone an extensive commerce can be carried on, were few, inconsiderable, and destitute of those immunities which produce security or excite enterprise. The sciences, on which geography and navigation are founded, were little cultivated. The accounts of ancient improvements and discoveries, contained in the Greek and Roman authors, were neglected or misunderstood. The knowledge of remote regions was lost, their situation, their commodities, and almost their names, were unknown.

One circumstance prevented commercial intercourse with distant nations from ceasing altogether. Constantinople, though often threatened by the fierce invaders who spread desolation over the rest of Europe, was so fortunate as to escape their destructive rage. In that city the knowledge of ancient arts and discoveries was preserved; a taste for splendour and elegance subsisted; the productions and luxuries of foreign countries were in request; and commerce continued to flourish there when it was almost extinct in every other part of Europe. The citizens of Constantinople did not confine their trade to the islands of the Archipelago, or to the adjacent coasts of Asia; they took a wider range, and, following the course which the ancients had marked out, imported the commodities of the East Indies from Alexandria. When Egypt was torn from the Roman empire by the Arabians, the industry of the Greeks discovered a new channel by which the productions of India might be conveyed to Constantinople. They were carried up the Indus as far as that great river is navigable; thence they were transported by land to the banks of the river Oxus, and proceeded down its stream to the Caspian sea. There they entered the Volga, and, sailing up it, were carried by land to the Tanais, which conducted them into the Euxine sea, where vessels from Constantinople waited their arrival.† This extraordinary and tedious mode of conveyance merits attention, not only as a proof of the violent passion which the inhabitants of Constantinople had conceived for the luxuries of the East, and as a specimen of the ardour and ingenuity with which they carried on commerce; but because it demonstrates that, during the ignorance which reigned in the rest of Europe, an extensive knowledge of remote countries was still preserved in the capital of the Greek empire.

At the same time a gleam of light and knowledge broke in upon the East. The Arabians having contracted some relish for the sciences of the people whose empire they had contributed to overturn, translated the books of several of the Greek philosophers into their own language. One of the first was that valuable work of Ptolemy which I have already mentioned. The study of geography became, of consequence, an early object of attention to the Arabians. But that acute and ingenious people cultivated chiefly the speculative and scientific parts of geography. In order to ascertain the figure and dimensions of the terrestrial globe, they applied the principles of geometry, they had recourse to astronomical observations, they employed experiments and operations, which Europe in more enlightened times has been proud to adopt and to imitate. At that period, however, the fame of the improvements made by the Arabians did not reach Europe. The knowledge of their discoveries was reserved for ages capable of comprehending and of perfecting them.

By degrees the calamities and desolation brought upon the western provinces of the Roman empire by its barbarous conquerors were forgotten, and in some measure repaired. The rude tribes which settled there

* Hist. of Charles V. † Ramusio, vol. I. p. 372. F.

acquiring insensibly some idea of regular government, and some relish for the functions and comforts of civil life,-Europe began to awake from its torpid and inactive state. The first symptoms of revival were discerned in Italy. The northern tribes which took possession of this country, made progress in improvement with greater rapidity than the people settled in other parts of Europe. Various causes, which it is not the object of this work to enumerate or explain, concurred in restoring liberty and independence to the cities of Italy.* The acquisition of these roused industry, and gave motion and vigour to all the active powers of the human mind. Foreign commerce revived, navigation was attended to and improved. Constantinople became the chief mart to which the Italians resorted. There they not only met with a favourable reception, but obtained such mercantile privileges as enabled them to carry on trade with great advantage. They were supplied both with the precious commodities of the East, and with many curious manufactures, the product of ancient arts and ingenuity which still subsisted among the Greeks. As the labour and expense of conveying the productions of India to Constantinople by that long and indirect course which I have described, rendered them extremely rare, and of an exorbitant price, the industry of the Italians discovered other methods of procuring them in greater abundance and at an easier rate. They sometimes purchased them in Aleppo, Tripoli, and other ports on the coast of Syria, to which they were brought by a route not unknown to the ancients. They were conveyed from India by sea up the Persian Gulf, and, ascending the Euphrates and Tigris as far as Bagdat, were carried by land across the desert of Palmyra, and from thence to the towns on the Mediterranean. But, from the length of the journey, and the dangers to which the caravans were exposed, this proved always a tedious and often a precarious mode of conveyance. At length the Soldans of Egypt, having revived the commerce with India in its ancient channel, by the Arabian Gulf, the Italian merchants, notwithstanding the violent antipathy to each other with which Christians and the followers of Mahomet were then possessed, repaired to Alexandria, and enduring, from the love of gain, the insolence and exactions of the Mahometans, established a lucrative trade in that port. From that period the commercial spirit of Italy became active and enterprising. Venice, Genoa, Pisa, rose from inconsiderable towns to be populous and wealthy cities. Their naval power increased; their vessels frequented not only all the ports in the Mediterranean, but venturing sometimes beyond the Straits, visited the maritime towns of Spain, France, the Low Countries, and England; and, by distributing their commodities over Europe, began to communicate to its various nations some taste for the valuable productions of the East, as well as some ideas of manufactures and arts, which were then unknown beyond the precincts of Italy.

While the cities of Italy were thus advancing in their career of improvement, an event happened, the most extraordinary, perhaps, in the history of mankind, which, instead of retarding the commercial progress of the Italians, rendered it more rapid. The martial spirit of the Europeans, heightened and inflamed by religious zeal, prompted them to attempt the deliverance of the Holy Land from the dominion of Infidels. Vast armies, composed of all the nations in Europe, marched towards Asia upon this wild enterprise. The Genoese, the Pisans, and Venetians, furnished the transports which carried them thither. They supplied them with provisions and military stores. Besides the immense sums which they received on this account, they obtained commercial privileges and establishments of great consequence in the settlements which the Crusaders made in Palestine, and in other provinces of Asia. From those sources prodigious wealth flowed into the cities which I have mentioned. This was accompanied with a propor-

* Hist. of Charles V.

tional increase of power; and, by the end of the Holy War, Venice in particular became a great maritime state, possessing an extensive commerce and ample territories.* Italy was not the only country in which the Crusades contributed to revive and diffuse such a spirit as prepared Europe for future discoveries. By their expeditions into Asia, the other European nations became well acquainted with remote regions, which formerly they knew only by name, or by the reports of ignorant and credulous pilgrims. They had an opportunity of observing the manners, the arts, and the accommodations of people more polished than themselves. This intercourse between the East and West subsisted almost two centuries. The adventurers who returned from Asia communicated to their countrymen the ideas which they had acquired, and the habits of life they had contracted by visiting more refined nations. The Europeans began to be sensible of wants with which they were formerly unacquainted: new desires were excited; and such a taste for the commodities and arts of other countries gradually spread among them, that they not only encouraged the resort of foreigners to their harbours, but began to perceive the advantage and necessity of applying to commerce themselves.†

This communication, which was opened between Europe and the western provinces of Asia, encouraged several persons to advance far beyond the countries in which the Crusaders carried on their operations, and to travel by land into the more remote and opulent regions of the East. The wild fanaticism, which seems at that period to have mingled in all the schemes of individuals, no less than in all the counsels of nations, first incited men to enter upon those long and dangerous peregrinations. They were afterwards undertaken from prospects of commercial advantage, or from motives of mere curiosity. Benjamin, a Jew of Tudela, in the kingdom of Navarre, possessed with a superstitious veneration for the law of Moses, and solicitous to visit his countrymen in the East, whom he hoped to find in such a state of power and opulence as might redound to the honour of his sect, set out from Spain, in the year 1160, and, travelling by land to Constantinople, proceeded through the countries to the north of the Euxine and Caspian seas, as far as Chinese Tartary. From thence he took his route towards the south, and after traversing various provinces of the further India, he embarked on the Indian Ocean, visited several of its islands, and returned at the end of thirteen years, by the way of Egypt, to Europe, with much information concerning a large district of the globe altogether unknown at that time to the western world.‡ The zeal of the head of the Christian church co-operated with the superstition of Benjamin the Jew in discovering the interior and remote provinces of Asia. All Christendom having been alarmed with the accounts of the rapid progress of the Tartar arms under Zengis Khan [1246], Innocent IV., who entertained most exalted ideas concerning the plenitude of his own power, and the submission due to his injunctions, sent Father John de Plano Carpini, at the head of a mission of Franciscan monks, and Father Ascolino, at the head of another of Dominicans, to enjoin Kayuk Khan, the grandson of Zengis, who was then at the head of the Tartar empire, to embrace the Christian faith, and to desist from desolating the earth by his arms. The haughty descendant of the greatest conqueror Asia had ever beheld, astonished at this strange mandate from an Italian priest, whose name and jurisdiction were alike unknown to him, received it with the contempt which it merited, though he dismissed the mendicants who delivered it with impunity. But, as they had penetrated into the country by different routes, and followed for some time the Tartar camps, which were always in motion, they had opportunity of visiting a great part of Asia. Carpini, who proceeded by the way of Poland

---

* Essai de l'Histoire du Commerce de Venise, p. 52, &c.   † Hist. of Charles V.
‡ Bergeron, Recueil des Voyages, &c. tom I. p 1.

and Russia, travelled through its northern provinces as far as the extremities of Thibet. Ascolino, who seems to have landed somewhere in Syria, advanced through its southern provinces into the interior parts of Persia.*

Not long after [1253], St. Louis of France contributed further towards extending the knowledge which the Europeans had begun to acquire of those distant regions. Some designing impostor, who took advantage of the slender acquaintance of Christendom with the state and character of the Asiatic nations, having informed him that a powerful Khan of the Tartars had embraced the Christian faith, the monarch listened to the tale with pious credulity, and instantly resolved to send ambassadors to this illustrious convert, with a view of enticing him to attack their common enemy the Saracens in one quarter, while he fell upon them in another. As monks were the only persons in that age who possessed such a degree of knowledge as qualified them for a service of this kind, he employed in it Father Andrew, a Jacobine, who was followed by Father William de Rubruquis, a Franciscan. With respect to the progress of the former, there is no memorial extant. The journal of the latter has been published. He was admitted into the presence of Mangu, the third Khan in succession from Zengis, and made a circuit through the interior parts of Asia, more extensive than that of any European who had hitherto explored them.†

To those travellers whom religious zeal sent forth to visit Asia, succeeded others who ventured into remote countries from the prospect of commercial advantage, or from motives of mere curiosity. The first and most eminent of these was Marco Polo, a Venetian of a noble family. Having engaged early in trade [1265], according to the custom of his country, his aspiring mind wished for a sphere of activity more extensive than was afforded to it by the established traffic carried on in those ports of Europe and Asia which the Venetians frequented. This prompted him to travel into unknown countries, in expectation of opening a commercial intercourse with them more suited to the sanguine ideas and hopes of a young adventurer.

As his father had already carried some European commodities to the court of the great Khan of the Tartars, and had disposed of them to advantage, he resorted thither. Under the protection of Kublay Khan, the most powerful of all the successors of Zengis, he continued his mercantile peregrinations in Asia upwards of twenty-six years; and during that time advanced towards the east, far beyond the utmost boundaries to which any European traveller had ever proceeded. Instead of following the course of Carpini and Rubruquis, along the vast unpeopled plains of Tartary, he passed through the chief trading cities in the more cultivated parts of Asia, and penetrated to Cambalu, or Peking, the capital of the great kingdom of Cathay, or China, subject at that time to the successors of Zengis. He made more than one voyage on the Indian ocean; he traded in many of the islands from which Europe had long received spiceries and other commodities which it held in high estimation, though unacquainted with the particular countries to which it was indebted for those precious productions: and he obtained information concerning several countries which he did not visit in person, particularly the island Zipangri, probably the same now known by the name of Japan.‡ On his return, he astonished his contemporaries with his descriptions of vast regions whose names had never been heard of in Europe, and with such pompous accounts of their fertility, their populousness, their opulence, the variety of their manufactures, and the extent of their trade, as rose far above the conception of an uninformed age.

About half a century after Marco Polo [1322], Sir John Mandeville, an Englishman, encouraged by his example, visited most of the countries in the East which he had described, and, like him, published an account of

* Hakluyt, i. 71. Bergeron, tom. i. † Hakl. i. 71. Recueil des Voyages par Bergoron, tom. i.
‡ Viaggi di Marco Polo. Ramus. ii. 2. Bergeron. tom. ii.

them.* The narrations of those early travellers abound with many wild incoherent tales, concerning giants, enchanters, and monsters. But they were not from that circumstance less acceptable to an ignorant age, which delighted in what was marvellous. The wonders which they told, mostly on hearsay, filled the multitude with admiration. The facts which they related from their own observation attracted the attention of the more discerning. The former, which may be considered as the popular traditions and fables of the countries through which they had passed, were gradually disregarded as Europe advanced in knowledge. The latter, however incredible some of them may have appeared in their own time, have been confirmed by the observations of modern travellers. By means of both, however, the curiosity of mankind was excited with respect to the remote parts of the earth; their ideas were enlarged; and they were not only insensibly disposed to attempt new discoveries, but received such information as directed to that particular course in which these were afterwards carried on.

While this spirit was gradually forming in Europe, a fortunate discovery was made, which contributed more than all the efforts and ingenuity of preceding ages to improve and to extend navigation. That wonderful property of the magnet, by which it communicates such virtue to a needle or slender rod of iron as to point towards the poles of the earth, was observed. The use which might be made of this in directing navigation was immediately perceived. That valuable, but now familiar instrument, the *mariner's compass*, was constructed. When by means of it navigators found that, at all seasons and in every place, they could discover the north and south with so much ease and accuracy, it became no longer necessary to depend merely on the light of the stars and the observation of the seacoast. They gradually abandoned their ancient timid and lingering course along the shore, ventured boldly into the ocean, and, relying on this new guide, could steer in the darkest night, and under the most cloudy sky, with a security and precision hitherto unknown. The compass may be said to have opened to man the dominion of the sea, and to have put him in full possession of the earth by enabling him to visit every part of it. Flavio Gioia, a citizen of Amalfi, a town of considerable trade in the kingdom of Naples, was the author of this great discovery, about the year one thousand three hundred and two. It hath been often the fate of those illustrious benefactors of mankind who have enriched science and improved the arts by their inventions, to derive more reputation than benefit from the happy efforts of their genius. But the lot of Gioia has been still more cruel; through the inattention or ignorance of contemporary historians, he has been defrauded even of the fame to which he had such a just title. We receive from them no information with respect to his profession, his character, the precise time when he made this important discovery, or the accidents and inquiries which led to it. The knowledge of this event, though productive of greater effects than any recorded in the annals of the human race, is transmitted to us without any of those circumstances which can gratify the curiosity that it naturally awakens.† But though the use of the compass might enable the Italians to perform the short voyages to which they were accustomed with greater security and expedition, its influence was not so sudden or extensive as immediately to render navigation adventurous, and to excite a spirit of discovery. Many causes combined in preventing this beneficial invention from producing its full effect instantaneously. Men relinquish ancient habits slowly and with reluctance. They are averse to new experiments, and venture upon them with timidity. The commercial jealousy of the Italians, it is probable, laboured to conceal the

---

* Voyages and Travels, by Sir John Mandeville. † Collinas et Trombellus de Acus Nauticæ Inventore, Instit. Acad. Bonon. tom. ii. part iii. p. 372.

happy discovery of their countrymen from other nations. The art of steering by the compass with such skill and accuracy as to inspire a full confidence in its direction, was acquired gradually. Sailors unaccustomed to quit the sight of land, durst not launch out at once and commit themselves to unknown seas. Accordingly, near half a century elapsed from the time of Gioia's discovery, before navigators ventured into any seas which they had not been accustomed to frequent.

The first appearance of a bolder spirit may be dated from the voyages of the Spaniards to the Canary or Fortunate Islands. By what accident they were led to the discovery of those small isles, which lie near five hundred miles from the Spanish coast, and above a hundred and fifty miles from the coast of Africa, contemporary writers have not explained. But, about the middle of the fourteenth century, the people of all the different kingdoms into which Spain was then divided, were accustomed to make piratical excursions thither, in order to plunder the inhabitants, or to carry them off as slaves. Clement VI. in virtue of the right claimed by the Holy See to dispose of all countries possessed by infidels, erected those isles into a kingdom in the year one thousand three hundred and forty-four, and conferred it on Lewis de la Cerda descended from the royal family of Castile. But that unfortunate prince, destitute of power to assert his nominal title, having never visited the Canaries, John de Bethencourt, a Norman baron, obtained a grant of them from Henry III. of Castile.* Bethencourt, with the valour and good fortune which distinguished the adventurers of his country, attempted and effected the conquest; and the possession of the Canaries remained for some time in his family, as a fief held of the crown of Castile. Previous to this expedition of Bethencourt, his countrymen settled in Normandy are said to have visited the coast of Africa, and to have proceeded far to the south of the Canary Islands [1365]. But their voyages thither seem not to have been undertaken in consequence of any public or regular plan for extending navigation and attempting new discoveries. They were either excursions suggested by that roving piratical spirit which descended to the Normans from their ancestors, or the commercial enterprises of private merchants, which attracted so little notice that hardly any memorial of them is to be found in contemporary authors. In a general survey of the progress of discovery, it is sufficient to have mentioned this event; and leaving it among those of dubious existence, or of small importance, we may conclude, that though much additional information concerning the remote regions of the East had been received by travellers who visited them by land, navigation at the beginning of the fifteenth century had not advanced beyond the state to which it had attained before the downfal of the Roman empire.

At length the period arrived, when Providence decreed that men were to pass the limits within which they had been so long confined, and open to themselves a more ample field wherein to display their talents, their enterprise, and courage. The first considerable efforts towards this were not made by any of the more powerful states of Europe, or by those who had applied to navigation with the greatest assiduity and success. The glory of leading the way in this new career was reserved for Portugal, one of the smallest and least powerful of the European kingdoms. As the attempts of the Portuguese to acquire the knowledge of those parts of the globe with which mankind were then unacquainted, not only improved and extended the art of navigation, but roused such a spirit of curiosity and enterprise as led to the discovery of the New World, of which I propose to write the history, it is necessary to take a full view of the rise, the progress, and success of their various naval operations. It was in this school that the discoverer of America was trained; and unless we trace the steps by which

* Viera y Clavijo Notic. de la Histor. de Canaria, l. 268, &. Glas. Hist. c. 1.

Vol. I.—5

his instructors and guides advanced, it will be impossible to comprehend the circumstances which suggested the idea, or facilitated the execution, of his great design.

Various circumstances prompted the Portuguese to exert their activity in this new direction, and enabled them to accomplish undertakings apparently superior to the natural force of their monarchy. The kings of Portugal, having driven the Moors out of their dominions, had acquired power as well as glory, by the success of their arms against the infidels. By their victories over them, they had extended the royal authority beyond the narrow limits within which it was originally circumscribed in Portugal, as well as in other feudal kingdoms. They had the command of the national force, could rouse it to act with united vigour, and, after the expulsion of the Moors, could employ it without dread of interruption from any domestic enemy. By the perpetual hostilities carried on for several centuries against the Mahometans, the martial and adventurous spirit which distinguished all the European nations during the middle ages, was improved and heightened among the Portuguese. A fierce civil war towards the close of the fourteenth century, occasioned by a disputed succession, augmented the military ardour of the nation, and formed or called forth men of such active and daring genius as are fit for bold undertakings. The situation of the kingdom, bounded on every side by the dominions of a more powerful neighbour, did not afford free scope to the activity of the Portuguese by land, as the strength of their monarchy was no match for that of Castile. But Portugal was a maritime state, in which there were many commodious harbours; the people had begun to make some progress in the knowledge and practice of navigation, and the sea was open to them, presenting the only field of enterprise in which they could distinguish themselves.

Such was the state of Portugal, and such the disposition of the people, when John I. surnamed the Bastard, obtained secure possession of the crown by the peace concluded with Castile, in the year one thousand four hundred and eleven. He was a prince of great merit, who, by superior courage and abilities, had opened his way to a throne which of right did not belong to him. He instantly perceived that it would be impossible to preserve public order, or domestic tranquillity, without finding some employment for the restless spirit of his subjects. With this view he assembled a numerous fleet at Lisbon, composed of all the ships which he could fit out in his own kingdom, and of many hired from foreigners. This great armament was destined to attack the Moors settled on the coast of Barbary [1412.] While it was equipping, a few vessels were appointed to sail along the western shore of Africa bounded by the Atlantic ocean, and to discover the unknown countries situated there. From this inconsiderable attempt, we may date the commencement of that spirit of discovery which opened the barriers that had so long shut out mankind from the knowledge of one half of the terrestrial globe.

At the time when John sent forth these ships on this new voyage, the art of navigation was still very imperfect. Though Africa lay so near to Portugal, and the fertility of the countries already known on that continent invited men to explore it more fully, the Portuguese had never ventured to sail beyond Cape *Non.* That promontory, as its name imports, was hitherto considered as a boundary which could not be passed. But the nations of Europe had now acquired as much knowledge as emboldened them to disregard the prejudices and to correct the errors of their ancestors. The long reign of ignorance, the constant enemy of every curious inquiry and of every new undertaking, was approaching to its period. The light of science began to dawn. The works of the ancient Greeks and Romans began to be read with admiration and profit. The sciences cultivated by the Arabians were introduced into Europe by the Moors settled in Spain and Portugal, and by the Jews, who were very numerous in both these kingdoms. Geometry, astronomy, and geography, the sciences on which the art of navigation is founded, became objects of studious attention. The memory of the discoveries made by the ancients was revived, and the progress of their navigation and commerce began to be traced. Some of the causes which have obstructed the cultivation of science in Portugal, during this century and the last, did not exist, or did not operate in the same manner, in the fifteenth century; [9] and the Portuguese at that period seem to have kept pace with other nations on this side of the Alps in literary pursuits.

As the genius of the age favoured the execution of that new undertaking, to which the peculiar state of the country invited the Portuguese; it proved successful. The vessels sent on the discovery doubled that formidable Cape, which had terminated the progress of former navigators, and proceeded a hundred and sixty miles beyond it, to Cape Bojador. As its rocky cliffs, which stretched a considerable way into the Atlantic, appeared more dreadful than the promontory which they had passed, the Portuguese commanders durst not attempt to sail round it, but returned to Lisbon, more satisfied with having advanced so far, than ashamed of having ventured no further.

Inconsiderable as this voyage was, it increased the passion for discovery which began to arise in Portugal. The fortunate issue of the king's expedition against the Moors of Barbary added strength to that spirit in the nation, and pushed it on to new undertakings. In order to render these successful, it was necessary that they should be conducted by a person who possessed abilities capable of discerning what was attainable, who enjoyed leisure to form a regular system for prosecuting discovery, and who was animated with ardour that would persevere in spite of obstacles and repulses. Happily for Portugal, she found all those qualities in Henry Duke of Viseo, the fourth son of King John, by Philippa of Lancaster, sister of Henry IV. king of England. That prince, in his early youth, having accompanied his father in his expedition to Barbary, distinguished himself by many deeds of valour. To the martial spirit, which was the characteristic of every man of noble birth at that time, he added all the accomplishments of a more enlightened and polished age. He cultivated the arts and sciences, which were then unknown and despised by persons of his rank. He applied with peculiar fondness to the study of geography; and by the instruction of able masters, as well as by the accounts of travellers, he early acquired such knowledge of the habitable globe, as discovered the great probability of finding new and opulent countries, by sailing along the coast of Africa. Such an object was formed to awaken the enthusiasm and ardour of a youthful mind, and he espoused with the utmost zeal the patronage of a design which might prove as beneficial as it appeared to be splendid and honourable. In order that he might pursue this great scheme without interruption, he retired from court immediately after his return from Africa, and fixed his residence at Sagres, near Cape St. Vincent, where the prospect of the Atlantic ocean invited his thoughts continually towards his favourite project, and encouraged him to execute it. In this retreat he was attended by some of the most learned men in his country, who aided him in his researches. He applied for information to the Moors of Barbary, who were accustomed to travel by land into the interior provinces of Africa in quest of ivory, gold dust, and other rich commodities. He consulted the Jews settled in Portugal. By promises, rewards, and marks of respect, he allured into his service several persons, foreigners as well as Portuguese, who were eminent for their skill in navigation. In taking those preparatory steps, the great abilities of the prince were seconded by his private virtues. His integrity, his affability, his respect for religion, his zeal for the honour of his country, engaged persons of all ranks to applaud his design, and to favour the execution of it. His schemes were allowed, by the greater part of his countrymen, to proceed neither from ambition nor the desire of wealth, but to flow from the warm benevolence of a heart eager to promote the happiness of mankind, and which justly entitled him to assume a motto for his device, that described the quality by which he wished to be distinguished, *the talent of doing good.*

His first effort, as is usual at the commencement of any new undertaking, was extremely inconsiderable. He fitted out a single ship [1418], and giving the command of it to John Gonzales Zarco and Tristan Vaz, two gentlemen of his household, who voluntarily offered to conduct the enterprise, he instructed them to use their utmost efforts to double Cape Bojador, and thence to steer towards the south. They, according to the mode of navigation which still prevailed, held their course along the shore; and by following that direction, they must have encountered almost insuperable difficulties in attempting to pass Cape Bojador. But fortune came in aid, to their want of skill, and prevented the voyage from being altogether fruitless. A sudden squall of wind arose, drove them out to sea, and when they expected every moment to perish, landed them on an unknown island, which from their happy escape they named *Porto Santo.* In the infancy of navigation, the discovery of this small island appeared a matter of such moment, that they instantly returned to Portugal with the good tidings, and were received by Henry with the applause and honour due to fortunate adventurers. This faint dawn of success filled a mind ardent in the pursuit of a favourite object, with such sanguine hopes as were sufficient incitements to proceed. Next year [1419] Henry sent out three ships under the same commanders, to whom he joined Bartholomew Perestrellow, in order to take possession of the island which they had discovered. When they began to settle in Porto Santo, they observed towards the south a fixed spot in the horizon like a small black cloud. By degrees, they were led to conjecture that it might be land; and steering towards it, they arrived at a considerable island, uninhabited and covered with wood, which on that account they called *Madeira.** As it was Henry's chief object to render his discoveries useful to his country, he immediately equipped a fleet to carry a colony of Portuguese to these islands [1420]. By his provident care, they were furnished not only with the seeds, plants, and domestic animals common in Europe; but, as he foresaw that the warmth of the climate and fertility of the soil would prove favourable to the rearing of other productions, he procured slips of the vine from the island of Cyprus, the rich wines of which were then in great request, and plants of the sugar-cane from Sicily, into which it had been lately introduced. These throve so prosperously in this new country, that the benefit of cultivating them was immediately perceived, and the sugar and wine of Madeira quickly became articles of some consequence in the commerce of Portugal.†

As soon as the advantages derived from this first settlement to the west of the European continent began to be felt, the spirit of discovery appeared less chimerical, and became more adventurous. By their voyages to Madeira, the Portuguese were gradually accustomed to a bolder navigation, and, instead of creeping servilely along the coast, ventured into the open sea. In consequence of taking this course, Gilianez, who commanded one of prince Henry's ships, doubled Cape Bojador [1433], the boundary of the Portuguese navigation upwards of twenty years, and which had hitherto been deemed unpassable. This successful voyage, which the ignorance of the age placed on a level with the most famous exploits recorded in history, opened a new sphere to navigation, as it discovered the vast continent of Africa, still washed by the Atlantic ocean, and stretching towards the south. Part of this was soon explored; the Portuguese ad-

---

* Historical Relation of the first Discovery of Madeira, translated from the Portuguese of Fran. Alcaforano, p. 15, &c.   † Lud. Guicciardini Descritt. de Paesi Bassi, p. 180, 181.

vanced within the tropics, and in the space of a few years they discovered the river Senegal, and all the coast extending from Cape Blanco to Cape de Verd.

Hitherto the Portuguese had been guided in their discoveries, or encouraged to attempt them, by the light and information which they received from the works of the ancient mathematicians and geographers. But when they began to enter the torrid zone, the notion which prevailed among the ancients, that the heat which reigned perpetually there was so excessive as to render it uninhabitable, deterred them, for some time, from proceeding. Their own observations, when they first ventured into this unknown and formidable region, tended to confirm the opinion of antiquity concerning the violent operation of the direct rays of the sun. As far as the river Senegal, the Portuguese had found the coast of Africa inhabited by people nearly resembling the Moors of Barbary. When they advanced to the south of that river, the human form seemed to put on a new appearance. They beheld men with skins black as ebony, with short curled hair, flat noses, thick lips, and all the peculiar features which are now known to distinguish the race of negroes. This surprising alteration they naturally attributed to the influence of heat, and if they should advance nearer to the line, they began to dread that its effects would be still more violent. Those dangers were exaggerated; and many other objections against attempting further discoveries were proposed by some of the grandees, who, from ignorance, from envy, or from that cold timid prudence which rejects whatever has the air of novelty or enterprise, had hitherto condemned all prince Henry's schemes. They represented, that it was altogether chimerical to expect any advantage from countries situated in that region which the wisdom and experience of antiquity had pronounced to be unfit for the habitation of men; that their forefathers, satisfied with cultivating the territory which Providence had allotted them, did not waste the strength of the kingdom by fruitless projects in quest of new settlements; that Portugal was already exhausted by the expense of attempts to discover lands which either did not exist, or which nature destined to remain unknown; and was drained of men, who might have been employed in undertakings attended with more certain success, and productive of greater benefit. But neither their appeal to the authority of the ancients, nor their reasonings concerning the interests of Portugal, made any impression upon the determined philosophic mind of prince Henry. The discoveries which he had already made, convinced him that the ancients had little more than a conjectural knowledge of the torrid zone. He was no less satisfied that the political arguments of his opponents, with respect to the interest of Portugal, were malevolent and ill founded. In those sentiments he was strenuously supported by his brother Pedro, who governed the kingdom as guardian of their nephew Alphonso V. who had succeeded to the throne during his minority [1438]; and, instead of slackening his efforts, Henry continued to pursue his discoveries with fresh ardour.

But in order to silence all the murmurs of opposition, he endeavoured to obtain the sanction of the highest authority in favour of his operations. With this view he applied to the Pope, and represented, in pompous terms, the pious and unwearied zeal with which he had exerted himself during twenty years, in discovering unknown countries, the wretched inhabitants of which were utter strangers to true religion, wandering in heathen darkness, or led astray by the delusions of Mahomet. He besought the holy father, to whom, as the vicar of Christ, all the kingdoms of the earth were subject, to confer on the crown of Portugal a right to all the countries possessed by infidels, which should be discovered by the industry of its subjects, and subdued by the force of its arms. He entreated him to enjoin all Christian powers, under the highest penalties, not to molest Portugal while engaged in this laudable enterprise, and to prohibit them from settling in any of the countries which the Portuguese should discover. He promised that, in all their expeditions, it should be the chief object of his countrymen to spread the knowledge of the Christian religion, to establish the authority of the Holy See, and to increase the flock of the universal pastor. As it was by improving with dexterity every favourable conjuncture for acquiring new powers, that the court of Rome had gradually extended its usurpations, Eugene IV., the Pontiff to whom this application was made, eagerly seized the opportunity which now presented itself. He instantly perceived that, by complying with prince Henry's request, he might exercise a prerogative no less flattering in its own nature than likely to prove beneficial in its consequences. A bull was accordingly issued, in which, after applauding in the strongest terms the past efforts of the Portuguese, and exhorting them to proceed in that laudable career on which they had entered, he granted them an exclusive right to all the countries which they should discover, from Cape Non to the continent of India.

Extravagant as this donation, comprehending such a large portion of the habitable globe, would now appear, even in Catholic countries, no person in the fifteenth century doubted that the Pope in the plentitude of his apostolic power, had a right to confer it. Prince Henry was soon sensible of the advantages which he derived from this transaction. His schemes were authorized and sanctified by the bull approving of them. The spirit of discovery was connected with zeal for religion, which in that age was a principle of such activity and vigour as to influence the conduct of nations. All Christian princes were deterred from intruding into those countries which the Portuguese had discovered, or from interrupting the progress of their navigation and conquests.[10]

The fame of the Portuguese voyages soon spread over Europe. Men long accustomed to circumscribe the activity and knowledge of the human mind within the limits to which they had been hitherto confined, were astonished to behold the sphere of navigation so suddenly enlarged, and a prospect opened of visiting regions of the globe the existence of which was unknown in former times. The learned and speculative reasoned and formed theories concerning those unexpected discoveries. The vulgar inquired and wondered; while enterprising adventurers crowded from every part of Europe, soliciting prince Henry to employ them in this honourable service. Many Venetians and Genoese, in particular, who were at that time superior to all other nations in the science of naval affairs, entered aboard the Portuguese ships, and acquired a more perfect and extensive knowledge of their profession in that new school of navigation. In emulation of these foreigners, the Portuguese exerted their own talents. The nation seconded the designs of the prince. Private merchants formed companies [1446], with a view to search for unknown countries. The Cape de Verd Islands, which lie off the promontory of that name, were discovered [1449], and soon after the isles called Azores. As the former of these are above three hundred miles from the African coast, and the latter nine hundred miles from any continent, it is evident by their venturing so boldly into the open seas, that the Portuguese had by this time improved greatly in the art of navigation.

While the passion for engaging in new undertakings was thus warm and active, it received an unfortunate check by the death of prince Henry [1463], whose superior knowledge had hitherto directed all the operations of the discoverers, and whose patronage had encouraged and protected them. But notwithstanding all the advantages which they derived from these, the Portuguese during his life did not advance in their utmost progress towards the south, within five degrees of the equinoctial line; and after their continued exertions for half a century [from 1412 to 1463], hardly fifteen hundred miles of the coast of Africa were discovered. To an age acquainted with the efforts of navigation in its state of maturity and improvement, those essays of its early years must necessarily appear feeble and unskilful. But inconsiderable as they may be deemed, they were sufficient to turn the curiosity of the European nations into a new channel, to excite an enterprising spirit, and to point the way to future discoveries.

Alphonso, who possessed the throne of Portugal at the time of prince Henry's death, was so much engaged in supporting his own pretensions to the crown of Castile, or in carrying on his expeditions against the Moors in Barbary, that, the force of his kingdom being exerted in other operations, he could not prosecute the discoveries in Africa with ardour. He committed the conduct of them to Fernando Gomez, a merchant in Lisbon, to whom he granted an exclusive right of commerce with all the countries of which prince Henry had taken possession. Under the restraint and oppression of a monopoly, the spirit of discovery languished. It ceased to be a national object, and became the concern of a private man more attentive to his own gain than to the glory of his country. Some progress, however, was made. The Portuguese ventured at length [1471], to cross the line, and, to their astonishment, found that region of the torrid zone, which was supposed to be scorched with intolerable heat, to be not only habitable, but populous and fertile.

John II. who succeeded his father Alphonso [1481], possessed talents capable both of forming and executing great designs. As part of his revenues, while prince, had arisen from duties on the trade with the newly discovered countries, this naturally turned his attention towards them, and satisfied him with respect to their utility and importance. In proportion as his knowledge of these countries extended, the possession of them appeared to be of greater consequence. While the Portuguese proceeded along the coast of Africa, from Cape Non to the river of Senegal, they found all that extensive tract to be sandy, barren, and thinly inhabited by a wretched people professing the Mahometan religion, and subject to the vast empire of Morocco. But to the south of that river, the power and religion of the Mahometans were unknown. The country was divided into small independent principalities, the population was considerable, the soil fertile,* and the Portuguese soon discovered that it produced ivory, rich gums, gold, and other valuable commodities. By the acquisition of these, commerce was enlarged, and became more adventurous. Men, animated and rendered active by the certain prospect of gain, pursued discovery with greater eagerness than when they were excited only by curiosity and hope.

This spirit derived no small reinforcement of vigour from the countenance of such a monarch as John. Declaring himself the patron of every attempt towards discovery, he promoted it with all the ardour of his grand-uncle prince Henry, and with superior power. The effects of this were immediately felt. A powerful fleet was fitted out [1484], which after discovering the kingdoms of Benin and Congo, advanced above fifteen hundred miles beyond the line, and the Portuguese, for the first time, beheld a new heaven, and observed the stars of another hemisphere. John was not only solicitous to discover, but attentive to secure the possession of those countries. He built forts on the coast of Guinea; he sent out colonies to settle there; he established a commercial intercourse with the more powerful kingdoms; he endeavoured to render such as were feeble or divided tributary to the crown of Portugal. Some of the petty princes voluntarily acknowledged themselves his vassals. Others were compelled to do so by force of arms. A regular and well digested system was formed with respect to this new object of policy, and, by firmly adhering to it, the Portuguese power and commerce in Africa were established upon a solid foundation.

By their constant intercourse with the people of Africa, the Portuguese gradually acquired some knowledge of those parts of that country which

* Navigatio Aloysii Cadamusti apud Novum Orbem Grynæi, p. 2. 18. Navigat. all Isola di San Tome per un Pilotto Portug. Ramusio, i. 115

they had not visited. The information which they received from the natives, added to what they had observed in their own voyages, began to open prospects more extensive, and to suggest the idea of schemes more important than those which had hitherto allured and occupied them. They had detected the error of the ancients concerning the nature of the torrid zone. They found as they proceeded southwards, that the continent of Africa, instead of extending in breadth, according to the doctrine of Ptolemy,* at that time the oracle and guide of the learned in the science of geography, appeared sensibly to contract itself, and to bend towards the east. This induced them to give credit to the accounts of the ancient Phenician voyages round Africa, which had long been deemed fabulous, and led them to conceive hopes that, by following the same route, they might arrive at the East Indies, and engross that commerce which has been the source of wealth and power to every nation possessed of it. The comprehensive genius of prince Henry, as we may conjecture from the words of the Pope's bull, had early formed some idea of this navigation. But though his countrymen, at that period, were incapable of conceiving the extent of his views and schemes, all the Portuguese mathematicians and pilots now concurred in representing them as well founded and practicable. The king entered with warmth into their sentiments, and began to concert measures for this arduous and important voyage.

Before his preparations for this expedition were finished, accounts were transmitted from Africa, that various nations along the coast had mentioned a mighty kingdom situated on their continent, at a great distance towards the east, the king of which, according to their description, professed the Christian religion. The Portuguese monarch immediately concluded, that this must be the emperor of Abyssinia, to whom the Europeans, seduced by a mistake of Rubruquis, Marco Polo, and other travellers to the East, absurdly gave the name of Prester or Presbyter John; and, as he hoped to receive information and assistance from a Christian prince, in prosecuting a scheme that tended to propagate their common faith, he resolved to open, if possible, some intercourse with his court. With this view, he made choice of Pedro de Covillam and Alphonso de Payva, who were perfect masters of the Arabic language, and sent them into the East to search for the residence of this unknown potentate, and to make him proffers of friendship. They had in charge likewise to procure whatever intelligence the nations which they visited could supply, with respect to the trade of India, and the course of navigation to that continent.†

While John made this new attempt by land, to obtain some knowledge of the country which he wished so ardently to discover, he did not neglect the prosecution of this great design by sea. The conduct of a voyage for this purpose, the most arduous and important which the Portuguese had ever projected, was committed to Bartholomew Diaz [1486], an officer whose sagacity, experience, and fortitude rendered him equal to the undertaking. He stretched boldly towards the south, and proceeding beyond the utmost limits to which his countrymen had hitherto advanced, discovered near a thousand miles of new country. Neither the danger to which he was exposed, by a succession of violent tempests in unknown seas, and by the frequent mutinies of his crew, nor the calamities of famine which he suffered from losing his storeship, could deter him from prosecuting his enterprise. In recompense of his labours and perseverance, he at last descried that lofty promontory which bounds Africa to the south. But to descry it was all that he had in his power to accomplish. The violence of the winds, the shattered condition of his ships, and the turbulent spirit of the sailors, compelled him to return after a voyage of sixteen months, in which he discovered a far greater extent of country than any former navigator. Diaz had called the promontory which terminated his voyage *Cabo Tor-*

* Vide Nov. Orbis Tabul. Geograph. secund. Ptolem. Amst. 1730. † Faria y Sousa Port. Asia vol. i. p. 26. Lafitau Decouv. de Port. l. 46.

mentoso, or the Stormy Cape; but the king, his master, as he now entertained no doubt of having found the long-desired route to India, gave it a name more inviting, and of better omen, *The Cape of Good Hope*.*

Those sanguine expectations of success were confirmed by the intelligence which John received over land, in consequence of his embassy to Abyssinia. Covillam and Payva, in obedience to their master's instructions, had repaired to Grand Cairo. From that city they travelled along with a caravan of Egyptian merchants, and, embarking on the Red Sea, arrived at Aden, in Arabia. There they separated; Payva sailed directly towards Abyssinia; Covillam embarked for the East Indies, and, having visited Calecut, Goa, and other cities on the Malabar coast, returned to Sofala, on the east side of Africa, and thence to Grand Cairo, which Payva and he had fixed upon as their place of rendezvous. Unfortunately the former was cruelly murdered in Abyssinia; but Covillam found at Cairo two Portuguese Jews, whom John, whose provident sagacity attended to every circumstance that could facilitate the execution of his schemes, had despatched after them, in order to receive a detail of their proceedings, and to communicate to them new instructions. By one of these Jews, Covillam transmitted to Portugal a journal of his travels by sea and land, his remarks upon the trade of India, together with exact maps of the coasts on which he had touched; and from what he himself had observed, as well as from the information of skilful seamen in different countries, he concluded, that, by sailing round Africa, a passage might be found to the East Indies.†

The happy coincidence of Covillam's opinion and report with the discoveries which Diaz had lately made, left hardly any shadow of doubt with respect to the possibility of sailing from Europe to India. But the vast length of the voyage, and the furious storms which Diaz had encountered near the Cape of Good Hope, alarmed and intimidated the Portuguese to such a degree, although by long experience they were now become adventurous and skilful mariners, that some time was requisite to prepare their minds for this dangerous and extraordinary voyage. The courage, however, and authority of the monarch gradually dispelled the vain fears of his subjects, or made it necessary to conceal them. As John thought himself now upon the eve of accomplishing that great design which had been the principal object of his reign, his earnestness in prosecuting it became so vehement, that it occupied his thoughts by day, and bereaved him of sleep through the night. While he was taking every precaution that his wisdom and experience could suggest, in order to ensure the success of the expedition, which was to decide concerning the fate of his favourite project, the fame of the vast discoveries which the Portuguese had already made, the reports concerning the extraordinary intelligence which they had received from the East, and the prospect of the voyage which they now meditated, drew the attention of all the European nations, and held them in suspense and expectation. By some, the maritime skill and navigations of the Portuguese were compared with those of the Phenicians and Carthaginians, and exalted above them. Others formed conjectures concerning the revolutions which the success of the Portuguese schemes might occasion in the course of trade, and the political state of Europe. The Venetians began to be disquieted with the apprehension of losing their Indian commerce, the monopoly of which was the chief source of their power as well as opulence, and the Portuguese already enjoyed in fancy the wealth of the East. But during this interval, which gave such scope to the various workings of curiosity, of hope, and of fear, an account was brought to Europe of an event no less extraordinary than unexpected, the discovery of a New World situated on the West; and the eyes and admiration of mankind turned immediately towards that great object.

---

* Faria y Sousa Port. Asia vol. I. p. 26. † Ibid. p. 27. Lafitau Decouv. I. p. 48.

BOOK II.

AMONG the foreigners whom the fame of the discoveries made by the Portuguese had allured into their service, was Christopher Colon, or Columbus, a subject of the republic of Genoa. Neither the time nor place of his birth is known with certainty [11]; but he was descended of an honourable family, though reduced to indigence by various misfortunes. His ancestors having betaken themselves for subsistence to a seafaring life, Columbus discovered in his early youth the peculiar character and talents which mark out a man for that profession. His parents, instead of thwarting this original propensity of his mind, seem to have encouraged and confirmed it by the education which they gave him. After acquiring some knowledge of the Latin tongue, the only language in which science was taught at that time, he was instructed in geometry, cosmography, astronomy, and the art of drawing. To these he applied with such ardour and predilection, on account of their connexion with navigation, his favourite object, that he advanced with rapid proficiency in the study of them. Thus qualified, he went to sea at the age of fourteen [1461], and began his career on that element which conducted him to so much glory. His early voyages were to those ports in the Mediterranean which his countrymen the Genoese frequented. This being a sphere too narrow for his active mind, he made an excursion to the northern seas [1467], and visited the coast of Iceland, to which the English and other nations had begun to resort on account of its fishery. As navigation, in every direction, was now become enterprising, he proceeded beyond that island, the Thule of the ancients, and advanced several degrees within the polar circle. Having satisfied his curiosity, by a voyage which tended more to enlarge his knowledge of naval affairs than to improve his fortune, he entered into the service of a famous sea-captain of his own name and family. This man commanded a small squadron fitted out at his own expense, and by cruising sometimes against the Mahometans, sometimes against the Venetians, the rivals of his country in trade, had acquired both wealth and reputation. With him Columbus continued for several years, no less distinguished for his courage than for his experience as a sailor. At length, in an obstinate engagement off the coast of Portugal, with some Venetian caravals returning richly laden from the Low Countries, the vessel on board which he served took fire, together with one of the enemy's ships to which it was fast grappled. In this dreadful extremity his intrepidity and presence of mind did not forsake him. He threw himself into the sea, laid hold of a floating oar; and by the support of it, and his dexterity in swimming, he reached the shore, though above two leagues distant, and saved a life reserved for great undertakings.*

As soon as he recovered strength for the journey, he repaired to Lisbon, where many of his countrymen were settled. They soon conceived such a favourable opinion of his merit, as well as talents, that they warmly solicited him to remain in that kingdom, where his naval skill and experience could not fail of rendering him conspicuous. To every adventurer animated either with curiosity to visit new countries, or with ambition to distinguish himself, the Portuguese service was at that time extremely inviting. Columbus listened with a favourable ear to the advice of his friends, and, having gained the esteem of a Portuguese lady, whom he married, fixed his residence in Lisbon. This alliance, instead of detaching him from a seafaring life, contributed to enlarge the sphere of his naval knowledge, and to excite a

* Life of Columbus, c. v.

desire of extending it still further. His wife was a daughter of Bartholomew Perestrello, one of the captains employed by prince Henry in his early navigations, and who, under his protection, had discovered and planted the islands of Porto Santo and Madeira. Columbus got possession of the journals and charts of this experienced navigator; and from them he learned the course which the Portuguese had held in making their discoveries, as well as the various circumstances which guided or encouraged them in their attempts. The study of these soothed and inflamed his favourite passion; and while he contemplated the maps, and read the descriptions of the new countries which Perestrello had seen, his impatience to visit them became irresistible. In order to indulge it, he made a voyage to Madeira, and continued during several years to trade with that island, with the Canaries, the Azores, the settlements in Guinea, and all the other places which the Portuguese had discovered on the continent of Africa.*

By the experience which Columbus acquired, during such a variety of voyages to almost every part of the globe with which at that time any intercourse was carried on by sea, he was now become one of the most skilful navigators in Europe. But, not satisfied with that praise, his ambition aimed at something more. The successful progress of the Portuguese navigators had awakened a spirit of curiosity and emulation, which set every man of science upon examining all the circumstances that led to the discoveries which they had made, or that afforded a prospect of succeeding in any new and bolder undertaking. The mind of Columbus, naturally inquisitive, capable of deep reflection, and turned to speculations of this kind, was so often employed in revolving the principles upon which the Portuguese had founded their schemes of discovery, and the mode on which they had carried them on, that he gradually began to form an idea of improving upon their plan, and of accomplishing discoveries which hitherto they had attempted in vain.

To find out a passage by sea to the East Indies, was the important object in view at that period. From the time that the Portuguese doubled Cape de Verd, this was the point at which they aimed in all their navigations, and in comparison with it all their discoveries in Africa appeared inconsiderable. The fertility and riches of India had been known for many ages: its spices and other valuable commodities were in high request throughout Europe, and the vast wealth of the Venetians, arising from their having engrossed this trade, had raised the envy of all nations. But how intent soever the Portuguese were upon discovering a new route to those desirable regions, they searched for it only by steering towards the south, in hopes of arriving at India by turning to the east after they had sailed round the further extremity of Africa. This course was still unknown, and even if discovered, was of such immense length, that a voyage from Europe to India must have appeared at that period an undertaking extremely arduous, and of very uncertain issue. More than half a century had been employed in advancing from Cape Non to the equator; a much longer space of time might elapse before the more extensive navigation from that to India could be accomplished. These reflections upon the uncertainty, the danger, and tediousness of the course which the Portuguese were pursuing, naturally led Columbus to consider whether a shorter and more direct passage to the East Indies might not be found out. After revolving long and seriously every circumstance suggested by his superior knowledge in the theory as well as the practice of navigation; after comparing attentively the observations of modern pilots with the hints and conjectures of ancient authors, he at last concluded, that by sailing directly towards the west, across the Atlantic ocean, new countries, which probably formed a part of the great continent of India, must infallibly be discovered.

* Life of Columbus, c. iv. v.

Principles and arguments of various kinds, and derived from different sources, induced him to adopt this opinion, seemingly as chimerical as it was new and extraordinary. The spherical figure of the earth was known, and its magnitude ascertained with some degree of accuracy. From this it was evident, that the continents of Europe, Asia, and Africa, as far as they were known at that time, formed but a small portion of the terraqueous globe. It was suitable to our ideas concerning the wisdom and beneficence of the Author of Nature, to believe that the vast space still unexplored was not covered entirely by a waste unprofitable ocean, but occupied by countries fit for the habitation of man. It appeared likewise extremely probable that the continent on this side of the globe was balanced by a proportional quantity of land in the other hemisphere. These conclusions concerning the existence of another continent, drawn from the figure and structure of the globe, were confirmed by the observations and conjectures of modern navigators. A Portuguese pilot, having stretched further to the west than was usual at that time, took up a piece of timber artificially carved floating upon the sea; and as it was driven towards him by a westerly wind, he concluded that it came from some unknown land situated in that quarter. Columbus's brother-in-law had found to the west of the Madeira isles, a piece of timber fashioned in the same manner, and brought by the same wind; and had seen likewise canes of an enormous size floating upon the waves, which resembled those described by Ptolemy as productions peculiar to the East Indies.* After a course of westerly winds, trees torn up by the roots were often driven upon the coasts of the Azores; and at one time, the dead bodies of two men with singular features, resembling neither the inhabitants of Europe nor of Africa, were cast ashore there.

As the force of this united evidence, arising from theoretical principles and practical observations, led Columbus to expect the discovery of new countries in the western ocean, other reasons induced him to believe that these must be connected with the continent of India. Though the ancients had hardly ever penetrated into India further than the banks of the Ganges, yet some Greek authors had ventured to describe the provinces beyond that river. As men are prone, and at liberty, to magnify what is remote or unknown, they represented them as regions of an immense extent. Ctesias affirmed that India was as large as all the rest of Asia. Onesicritus, whom Pliny the naturalist follows,† contended that it was equal to a third part of the habitable earth. Nearchus asserted, that it would take four months to march in a straight line from one extremity of India to the other.‡ The journal of Marco Polo, who had proceeded towards the East far beyond the limits to which any European had ever advanced, seemed to confirm these exaggerated accounts of the ancients. By his magnificent descriptions of the kingdoms of *Cathay* and *Cipango*, and of many other countries the names of which were unknown in Europe, India appeared to be a region of vast extent. From these accounts, which, however defective, were the most accurate that the people of Europe had received at that period with respect to the remote parts of the East, Columbus drew a just conclusion. He contended that, in proportion as the continent of India stretched out towards the East, it must, in consequence of the spherical figure of the earth, approach near to the islands which had lately been discovered to the west of Africa; that the distance from the one to the other was probably not very considerable; and that the most direct as well as shortest course to the remote regions of the East was to be found by sailing due west. [12] This notion concerning the vicinity of India to the western parts of our continent, was countenanced by some eminent writers among the ancients, the sanction of whose authority was necessary, in that age, to procure a favourable reception to any tenet. Aristotle thought it probable that the Columns of

---

* Lib. i. c. 17.   † Nat. Hist. lib. vi. c. 17.   ‡ Strab. Geogr. lib. xv. p. 1011.

Hercules, or Straits of Gibraltar, were not far removed from the East Indies, and that there might be a communication by sea between them.* Seneca, in terms still more explicit, affirms, that with a fair wind one might sail from Spain to India in a few days.† The famous Atlantic island described by Plato, and supposed by many to be a real country, beyond which an unknown continent was situated, is represented by him as lying at no great distance from Spain. After weighing all these particulars, Columbus, in whose character the modesty and diffidence of true genius were united with the ardent enthusiasm of a projector, did not rest with such absolute assurance either upon his own arguments, or upon the authority of the ancients, as not to consult such of his contemporaries as were capable of comprehending the nature of the evidence which he produced in support of his opinion. As early as the year one thousand four hundred and seventy-four, he communicated his ideas concerning the probability of discovering new countries, by sailing westward, to Paul, a physician of Florence, eminent for his knowledge of cosmography, and who, from the learning as well as candour which he discovers in his reply, appears to have been well entitled to the confidence which Columbus placed in him. He warmly approved of the plan, suggested several facts in confirmation of it, and encouraged Columbus to persevere in an undertaking so laudable, and which must redound so much to the honour of his country and the benefit of Europe.‡

To a mind less capable of forming and of executing great designs than that of Columbus, all those reasonings and observations and authorities would have served only as the foundation of some plausible and fruitless theory, which might have furnished matter for ingenious discourse or fanciful conjecture. But with his sanguine and enterprising temper speculation led directly to action. Fully satisfied himself with respect to the truth of his system, he was impatient to bring it to the test of experiment, and to set out upon a voyage of discovery. The first step towards this was to secure the patronage of some of the considerable powers in Europe capable of undertaking such an enterprise. As long absence had not extinguished the affection which he bore to his native country, he wished that it should reap the fruits of his labours and invention. With this view, he laid his scheme before the senate of Genoa, and, making his country the first tender of his service, offered to sail under the banners of the republic in quest of the new regions which he expected to discover. But Columbus had resided for so many years in foreign parts, that his countrymen were unacquainted with his abilities and character; and, though a maritime people, were so little accustomed to distant voyages, that they could form no just idea of the principles on which he founded his hopes of success. They inconsiderately rejected his proposal, as the dream of a chimerical projector, and lost for ever the opportunity of restoring their commonwealth to its ancient splendour.§

Having performed what was due to his country, Columbus was so little discouraged by the repulse which he had received, that instead of relinquishing his undertaking he pursued it with fresh ardour. He made his next overture to John II. king of Portugal, in whose dominions he had been long established, and whom he considered on that account, as having the second claim to his service. Here every circumstance seemed to promise him a more favourable reception: he applied to a monarch of an enterprising genius, no incompetent judge in naval affairs, and proud of patronising every attempt to discover new countries. His subjects were the most experienced navigators in Europe, and the least apt to be intimidated either by the novelty or boldness of any maritime expedition. In Portugal, the professional skill of Columbus, as well as his personal good qualities, were thoroughly known: and as the former rendered it probable that his scheme was not

* Aristot. de Cœlo, lib. ii. c. 14. edit. Du Val. Par. 1629: vol. i. p. 472. † Senec. Quæst. Natur. lib. i. in proem. ‡ Life of Columbus. c. viii. § Herrera Hist. de las Indias Occid. dec. i. lib. i. c. vii.

altogether visionary, the latter exempted him from the suspicion of any sinister intention in proposing it. Accordingly, the king listened to him in the most gracious manner, and referred the consideration of his plan to Diego Ortiz, bishop of Ceuta, and two Jewish physicians, eminent cosmographers, whom he was accustomed to consult in matters of this kind. As in Genoa, ignorance had opposed and disappointed Columbus; in Lisbon, he had to combat with prejudice, an enemy no less formidable. The persons according to whose decision his scheme was to be adopted, or rejected, had been the chief directors of the Portuguese navigations, and had advised to search for a passage to India by steering a course directly opposite to that which Columbus recommended as shorter and more certain. They could not, therefore, approve of his proposal without submitting to the double mortification of condemning their own theory, and acknowledging his superior sagacity. After teasing him with captious questions, and starting innumerable objections, with a view of betraying him into such a particular explanation of his system as might draw from him a full discovery of its nature, they deferred passing a final judgment with respect to it. In the mean time they conspired to rob him of the honour and advantages which he expected from the success of his scheme, advising the king to despatch a vessel secretly, in order to attempt the proposed discovery by following exactly the course which Columbus seemed to point out. John, forgetting on this occasion the sentiments becoming a monarch, meanly adopted this perfidious counsel. But the pilot chosen to execute Columbus's plan had neither the genius nor the fortitude of its author. Contrary winds arose, no sight of approaching land appeared, his courage failed, and he returned to Lisbon, execrating the project as equally extravagant and dangerous.*

Upon discovering this dishonourable transaction, Columbus felt the indignation natural to an ingenuous mind, and in the warmth of his resentment determined to break off all intercourse with a nation capable of such flagrant treachery. He instantly quitted the kingdom, and landed in Spain towards the close of the year one thousand four hundred and eighty-four. As he was now at liberty to court the protection of any patron whom he could engage to approve of his plan, and to carry it into execution, he resolved to propose it in person to Ferdinand and Isabella, who at that time governed the united kingdoms of Castile and Aragon. But as he had already experienced the uncertain issue of application to kings and ministers, he took the precaution of sending into England his brother Bartholomew, to whom he had fully communicated his ideas, in order that he might negociate at the same time with Henry VII., who was reputed one of the most sagacious as well as opulent princes in Europe.

It was not without reason that Columbus entertained doubts and fears with respect to the reception of his proposals in the Spanish court. Spain was at that juncture engaged in a dangerous war with Granada, the last of the Moorish kingdoms in that country. The wary and suspicious temper of Ferdinand was not formed to relish bold or uncommon designs. Isabella, though more generous and enterprising, was under the influence of her husband in all her actions. The Spaniards had hitherto made no efforts to extend navigation beyond its ancient limits, and had beheld the amazing progress of discovery among their neighbours the Portuguese without one attempt to imitate or to rival them. The war with the Infidels afforded an ample field to the national activity and love of glory. Under circumstances so unfavourable, it was impossible for Columbus to make rapid progress with a nation naturally slow and dilatory in forming all its resolutions. His character, however, was admirably adapted to that of the people whose confidence and protection he solicited. He was grave, though courteous in his deportment; circumspect in his words and actions, irreproachable in his

* Life of Columbus, c. xi. Herrera, dec. i. lib. i. c. 7.

morals, and exemplary in his attention to all the duties and functions of religion. By qualities so respectable, he not only gained many private friends, but acquired such general esteem, that, notwithstanding the plainness of his appearance, suitable to the mediocrity of his fortune, he was not considered as a mere adventurer, to whom indigence had suggested a visionary project, but was received as a person to whose propositions serious attention was due.

Ferdinand and Isabella, though fully occupied by their operations against the Moors, paid so much regard to Columbus, as to remit the consideration of his plan to the queen's confessor, Ferdinand de Talavera. He consulted such of his countrymen as were supposed best qualified to decide with respect to a subject of this kind. But true science had hitherto made so little progress in Spain, that the pretended philosophers, selected to judge in a matter of such moment, did not comprehend the first principles upon which Columbus founded his conjectures and hopes. Some of them, from mistaken notions concerning the dimensions of the globe, contended that a voyage to those remote parts of the east which Columbus expected to discover, could not be performed in less than three years. Others concluded, that either he would find the ocean to be of infinite extent, according to the opinion of some ancient philosophers; or, if he should persist in steering towards the west beyond a certain point, that the convex figure of the globe would prevent his return, and that he must inevitably perish in the vain attempt to open a communication between the two opposite hemispheres which nature had for ever disjoined. Even without deigning to enter into any particular discussion, many rejected the scheme in general, upon the credit of a maxim, under which the ignorant and unenterprising shelter themselves in every age, "That it is presumptuous in any person, to suppose that he alone possesses knowledge superior to all the rest of mankind united." They maintained, that if there were really any such countries as Columbus pretended, they could not have remained so long concealed, nor would the wisdom and sagacity of former ages have left the glory of this invention to an obscure Genoese pilot.

It required all Columbus's patience and address to negotiate with men capable of advancing such strange propositions. He had to contend not only with the obstinacy of ignorance, but with what is still more intractable, the pride of false knowledge. After innumerable conferences, and wasting five years in fruitless endeavours to inform and to satisfy judges so little capable of deciding with propriety, Talavera at last made such an unfavourable report to Ferdinand and Isabella, as induced them to acquaint Columbus, that until the war with the Moors should be brought to a period it would be imprudent to engage in any new and extensive enterprise.

Whatever care was taken to soften the harshness of this declaration, Columbus considered it as a final rejection of his proposals. But, happily for mankind, that superiority of genius, which is capable of forming great and uncommon designs, is usually accompanied with an ardent enthusiasm, which can neither be cooled by delays nor damped by disappointment. Columbus was of this sanguine temper. Though he felt deeply the cruel blow given to his hopes, and retired immediately from a court where he had been amused so long with vain expectations, his confidence in the justness of his own system did not diminish, and his impatience to demonstrate the truth of it by an actual experiment became greater than ever. Having courted the protection of sovereign states without success, he applied next to persons of inferior rank, and addressed successively the Dukes of Medina Sidonia and Medina Celi, who, though subjects, were possessed of power and opulence more than equal to the enterprise which he projected. His negotiations with them proved as fruitless as those in which he had been hitherto engaged; for these noblemen were either as little convinced by Columbus's arguments as their superiors, or they were afraid of alarming the jealousy and offending the pride of Ferdinand, by countenancing a scheme which he had rejected.*

Amid the painful sensations occasioned by such a succession of disappointments, Columbus had to sustain the additional distress of having received no accounts of his brother whom he had sent to the court of England. In his voyage to that country, Bartholomew had been so unfortunate as to fall into the hands of pirates, who having stripped him of every thing detained him a prisoner for several years. At length he made his escape, and arrived in London, but in such extreme indigence, that he was obliged to employ himself, during a considerable time in drawing and selling maps, in order to pick up as much money as would purchase a decent dress in which he might venture to appear at court. He then laid before the king the proposals with which he had been intrusted by his brother; and notwithstanding Henry's excessive caution and parsimony, which rendered him averse to new or extensive undertakings, he received Columbus's overtures with more approbation than any monarch to whom they had hitherto been presented.

Meanwhile, Columbus being unacquainted with his brother's fate, and having now no prospect of encouragement in Spain, resolved to visit the court of England in person, in hopes of meeting with a more favourable reception there. He had already made preparations for this purpose, and taken measures for the disposal of his children during his absence, when Juan Perez, the guardian of the monastery of Rabida, near Palos, in which they had been educated, earnestly solicited him to defer his journey for a short time. Perez was a man of considerable learning, and of some credit with queen Isabella, to whom he was known personally. He was warmly attached to Columbus, with whose abilities as well as integrity he had many opportunities of being acquainted. Prompted by curiosity or by friendship, he entered upon an accurate examination of his system, in conjunction with a physician settled in the neighbourhood, who was a considerable proficient in mathematical knowledge. This investigation satisfied them so thoroughly, with respect to the solidity of the principles on which Columbus founded his opinion, and the probability of success in executing the plan which he proposed, that Perez, in order to prevent his country from being deprived of the glory and benefit which must accrue to the patrons of such a grand enterprise, ventured to write to Isabella, conjuring her to consider the matter anew with the attention which it merited.

Moved by the representations of a person whom she respected, Isabella desired Perez to repair immediately to the village of Santa Fe, in which, on account of the siege of Granada, the court resided at that time, that she might confer with him upon this important subject. The first effect of their interview was a gracious invitation of Columbus back to court, accompanied with the present of a small sum to equip him for the journey. As there was now a certain prospect that the war with the Moors would speedily be brought to a happy issue by the reduction of Granada, which would leave the nation at liberty to engage in new undertakings; this, as well as the mark of royal favour, with which Columbus had been lately honoured, encouraged his friends to appear with greater confidence than formerly in support of his scheme. The chief of these, Alonso de Quintanilla, comptroller of the finances in Castile, and Luis de Santangel, receiver of the ecclesiastical revenues in Aragon, whose meritorious zeal in promoting this great design entitles their names to an honourable place in history, introduced Columbus to many persons of high rank, and interested them warmly in his behalf.

But it was not an easy matter to inspire Ferdinand with favourable sentiments. He still regarded Columbus's project as extravagant and chime-

---

* Life of Columb. c. 13. Herrera, dec. 1. lib. 1, c. 7.

rical; and in order to render the efforts of his partisans ineffectual, he had the address to employ, in this new negotiation with him, some of the persons who had formerly pronounced his scheme to be impracticable. To their astonishment, Columbus appeared before them with the same confident hopes of success as formerly, and insisted upon the same high recompense. He proposed that a small fleet should be fitted out, under his command, to attempt the discovery, and demanded to be appointed hereditary admiral and viceroy of all the seas and lands which he should discover, and to have the tenths of the profits arising from them settled irrevocably upon himself and his descendants. At the same time, he offered to advance the eighth part of the sum necessary for accomplishing his design, on condition that he should be entitled to a proportional share of benefit from the adventure. If the enterprise should totally miscarry, he made no stipulation for any reward or emolument whatever. Instead of viewing this conduct as the clearest evidence of his full persuasion with respect to the truth of his own system, or being struck with that magnanimity which, after so many delays and repulses, would stoop to nothing inferior to its original claims, the persons with whom Columbus treated began meanly to calculate the expense of the expedition, and the value of the reward which he demanded. The expense, moderate as it was, they represented to be too great for Spain in the present exhausted state of its finances. They contended that the honours and emoluments claimed by Columbus were exorbitant, even if he should perform the utmost of what he had promised; and if all his sanguine hopes should prove illusive, such vast concessions to an adventurer would be deemed not only inconsiderate, but ridiculous. In this imposing garb of caution and prudence, their opinion appeared so plausible, and was so warmly supported by Ferdinand, that Isabella declined giving any countenance to Columbus, and abruptly broke off the negotiation with him which she had begun.

This was more mortifying to Columbus than all the disappointments which he had hitherto met with. The invitation to court from Isabella, like an unexpected ray of light, had opened such prospects of success as encouraged him to hope that his labours were at an end; but now darkness and uncertainty returned, and his mind, firm as it was, could hardly support the shock of such an unforeseen reverse. He withdrew in deep anguish from court, with an intention of prosecuting his voyage to England as his last resource.

About that time Granada surrendered, and Ferdinand and Isabella, in triumphal pomp, took possession of a city [Jan. 2, 1492], the reduction of which extirpated a foreign power from the heart of their dominions, and rendered them masters of all the provinces extending from the bottom of the Pyrenees to the frontiers of Portugal. As the flow of spirits which accompanies success elevates the mind, and renders it enterprising, Quintanilla and Santangel, the vigilant and discerning patrons of Columbus, took advantage of this favourable situation, in order to make one effort more in behalf of their friend. They addressed themselves to Isabella; and after expressing some surprise, that she, who had always been the munificent patroness of generous undertakings, should hesitate so long to countenance the most splendid scheme that had ever been proposed to any monarch; they represented to her, that Columbus was a man of a sound understanding and virtuous character, well qualified, by his experience in navigation, as well as his knowledge of geometry, to form just ideas with respect to the structure of the globe and the situation of its various regions; that, by offering to risk his own life and fortune in the execution of his scheme, he gave the most satisfying evidence both of his integrity and hope of success; that the sum requisite for equipping such an armament as he demanded was inconsiderable, and the advantages which might accrue from his undertaking were immense; that he demanded no recompense for his invention and labour, but what was to arise from the countries which he should discover; that, as it was worthy of her magnanimity to make this noble attempt to extend the sphere of human knowledge, and to open an intercourse with regions hitherto unknown, so it would afford the highest satisfaction to her piety and zeal, after re-establishing the Christian faith in those provinces of Spain from which it had been long banished, to discover a new world, to which she might communicate the light and blessings of divine truth; that if now she did not decide instantly, the opportunity would be irretrievably lost, that Columbus was on his way to foreign countries, where some prince, more fortunate or adventurous, would close with his proposals, and Spain would for ever bewail that fatal timidity which had excluded her from the glory and advantages that she had once in her power to have enjoyed.

These forcible arguments, urged by persons of such authority, and at a juncture so well chosen, produced the desired effect. They dispelled all Isabella's doubts and fears; she ordered Columbus to be instantly recalled, declared her resolution of employing him on his own terms, and, regretting the low estate of her finances, generously offered to pledge her own jewels in order to raise as much money as might be needed in making preparations for the voyage. Santangel, in a transport of gratitude, kissed the Queen's hand, and, in order to save her from having recourse to such a mortifying expedient for procuring money, engaged to advance immediately the sum that was requisite.*

Columbus had proceeded some leagues on his journey, when the messenger from Isabella overtook him. Upon receiving an account of the unexpected resolution in his favour, he returned directly to Santa Fe, though some remainder of diffidence still mingled itself with his joy. But the cordial reception which he met with from Isabella, together with the near prospect of setting out upon that voyage which had so long been the object of his thoughts and wishes, soon effaced the remembrance of all that he had suffered in Spain during eight tedious years of solicitation and suspense. The negotiation now went forward with facility and despatch, and a treaty or capitulation with Columbus was signed on the seventeenth of April, one thousand four hundred and ninety-two. The chief articles of it were:—
1. Ferdinand and Isabella, as sovereigns of the ocean, constituted Columbus their high admiral in all the seas, islands, and continents, which should be discovered by his industry; and stipulated that he and his heirs for ever should enjoy this office, with the same powers and prerogatives which belonged to the high admiral of Castile within the limits of his jurisdiction
2. They appointed Columbus their viceroy in all the islands and continents which he should discover; but if, for the better administration of affairs, it should hereafter be necessary to establish a separate governor in any of those countries, they authorized Columbus to name three persons of whom they would choose one for that office; and the dignity of viceroy, with all its immunities, was likewise to be hereditary in the family of Columbus. 3. They granted to Columbus and his heirs for ever, the tenth of the free profits accruing from the productions and commerce of the countries which he should discover. 4. They declared, that if any controversy or lawsuit shall arise with respect to any mercantile transaction in the countries which should be discovered, it should be determined by the sole authority of Columbus, or of judges to be appointed by him. 5. They permitted Columbus to advance one-eighth part of what should be expended in preparing for the expedition, and in carrying on commerce with the countries which he should discover, and entitled him, in return, to an eighth part of the profit.†

Though the name of Ferdinand appears conjoined with that of Isabella in this transaction, his distrust of Columbus was still so violent that he

---
* Herrera, doc. 1. lib. 1. c. 8. † Life of Columbus, c. 15. Herrera, dec. 1. lib. 1. c. 9.

refused to take any part in the enterprise as king of Aragon. As the whole expense of the expedition was to be defrayed by the crown of Castile, Isabella reserved for her subjects of that kingdom an exclusive right to all the benefits which might redound from its success.

As soon as the treaty was signed, Isabella, by her attention and activity in forwarding the preparations for the voyage, endeavoured to make some reparation to Columbus for the time which he had lost in fruitless solicitation. By the twelfth of May, all that depended upon her was adjusted; and Columbus waited on the king and queen in order to receive their final instructions. Every thing respecting the destination and conduct of the voyage they committed implicitly to the disposal of his prudence. But that they might avoid giving any just cause of offence to the king of Portugal, they strictly enjoined him not to approach near to the Portuguese settlements on the coast of Guinea, or in any of the other countries to which the Portuguese claimed right as discoverers. Isabella had ordered the ships of which Columbus was to take the command to be fitted out in the port of Palos, a small maritime town in the province of Andalusia. As the guardian Juan Perez, to whom Columbus had already been so much indebted, resided in the neighbourhood of this place, he, by the influence of that good ecclesiastic, as well as by his own connection with the inhabitants, not only raised among them what he wanted of the sum that he was bound by treaty to advance, but engaged several of them to accompany him in the voyage. The chief of these associates were three brothers of the name of Pinzon, of considerable wealth, and of great experience in naval affairs, who were willing to hazard their lives and fortunes in the expedition.

But after all the efforts of Isabella and Columbus, the armament was not suitable either to the dignity of the nation by which it was equipped, or to the importance of the service for which it was destined. It consisted of three vessels. The largest, a ship of no considerable burden, was commanded by Columbus, as admiral, who gave it the name of *Santa Maria,* out of respect for the Blessed Virgin, whom he honoured with singular devotion. Of the second, called the *Pinta,* Marton Pinzon was captain, and his brother Francis pilot. The third, named the *Nigna,* was under the command of Vincent Yanez Pinzon. These two were light vessels hardly superior in burden or force to large boats. The squadron, if it merits that name, was victualled for twelve months, and had on board ninety men, mostly sailors, together with a few adventurers who followed the fortune of Columbus, and some gentlemen of Isabella's court, whom she appointed to accompany him. Though the expense of the undertaking was one of the circumstances which chiefly alarmed the court of Spain, and retarded so long the negotiation with Columbus, the sum employed in fitting out this squadron did not exceed four thousand pounds.

As the art of ship-building in the fifteenth century was extremely rude, and the bulk of vessels was accommodated to the short and easy voyages along the coast which they were accustomed to perform, it is a proof of the courage, as well as enterprising genius of Columbus, that he ventured, with a fleet so unfit for a distant navigation, to explore unknown seas, where he had no chart to guide him, no knowledge of the tides and currents, and no experience of the dangers to which he might be exposed. His eagerness to accomplish the great design which had so long engrossed his thoughts, made him overlook or disregard every circumstance that would have intimidated a mind less adventurous. He pushed forward the preparations with such ardour, and was seconded so effectually by the persons to whom Isabella committed the superintendence of this business, that every thing was soon in readiness for the voyage. But as Columbus was deeply impressed with sentiments of religion, he would not set out upon an expedition so arduous, and of which one great object was to extend the knowledge of the Christian faith, without imploring publicly the guidance and protection of Heaven. With this view, he, together with all the persons under his command, marched in solemn procession to the monastery of Rabida. After confessing their sins, and obtaining absolution, they received the holy sacrament from the hands of the guardian, who joined his prayers to theirs for the success of an enterprise which he had so zealously patronized.

Next morning, being Friday the third day of August, in the year one thousand four hundred and ninety-two, Columbus set sail, a little before sunrise, in presence of a vast crowd of spectators, who sent up their supplications to Heaven for the prosperous issue of the voyage, which they wished rather than expected. Columbus steered directly for the Canary Islands, and arrived there [Aug. 13] without any occurrence that would have deserved notice on any other occasion. But, in a voyage of such expectation and importance, every circumstance was the object of attention. The rudder of the Pinta broke loose the day after she left the harbour; and that accident alarmed the crew, no less superstitious than unskilful, as a certain omen of the unfortunate destiny of the expedition. Even in the short run to the Canaries, the ships were found to be so crazy and ill appointed, as to be very improper for a navigation which was expected to be both long and dangerous. Columbus refitted them, however, to the best of his power; and having supplied himself with fresh provisions, he took his departure from Gomera, one of the most westerly of the Canary Islands, on the sixth day of September.

Here the voyage of discovery may properly be said to begin; for Columbus, holding his course due west, left immediately the usual track of navigation, and stretched into unfrequented and unknown seas. The first day, as it was very calm, he made but little way; but on the second he lost sight of the Canaries; and many of the sailors, dejected already, and dismayed, when they contemplated the boldness of the undertaking, began to beat their breasts, and to shed tears, as if they were never more to behold land. Columbus comforted them with assurances of success, and the prospect of vast wealth in those opulent regions whither he was conducting them. This early discovery of the spirit of his followers taught Columbus that he must prepare to struggle not only with the unavoidable difficulties which might be expected from the nature of his undertaking, but with such as were likely to arise from the ignorance and timidity of the people under his command; and he perceived that the art of governing the minds of men would be no less requisite for accomplishing the discoveries which he had in view, than naval skill and undaunted courage. Happily for himself, and for the country by which he was employed, he joined to the ardent temper and inventive genius of a projector, virtues of another species, which are rarely united with them. He possessed a thorough knowledge of mankind, an insinuating address, a patient perseverance in executing any plan, the perfect government of his own passions, and the talent of acquiring an ascendant over those of other men. All these qualities, which formed him for command, were accompanied with that superior knowledge of his profession, which begets confidence in times of difficulty and danger. To unskilful Spanish sailors, accustomed only to coasting voyages in the Mediterranean, the maritime science of Columbus, the fruit of thirty years' experience, improved by an acquaintance with all the inventions of the Portuguese, appeared immense. As soon as they put to sea, he regulated every thing by his sole authority; he superintended the execution of every order; and allowing himself only a few hours for sleep, he was at all other times upon deck. As his course lay through seas which had not formerly been visited, the sounding line, or instruments for observation, were continually in his hands. After the example of the Portuguese discoverers, he attended to the motion of tides and currents, watched the flight of birds, the appearance of fishes, of seaweeds, and of every thing that floated on the waves, and entered every occurrence, with a minute exactness, in the journal which he kept. As the length of the voyage could not fail of alarming sailors habituated only to short excursions, Columbus endeavoured to conceal from them the real progress which they made. With this view, though they run eighteen leagues on the second day after they left Gomera, he gave out that they had advanced only fifteen, and he uniformly employed the same artifice of reckoning short during the whole voyage. By the fourteenth of September the fleet was above two hundred leagues to the west of the Canary Isles, at a greater distance from land than any Spaniard had been before that time. There they were struck with an appearance no less astonishing than new. They observed that the magnetic needle, in their compasses, did not point exactly to the polar star, but varied towards the west; and as they proceeded, this variation increased. This appearance, which is now familiar, though it still remains one of the mysteries of nature, into the cause of which the sagacity of man hath not been able to penetrate, filled the companions of Columbus with terror. They were now in a boundless and unknown ocean, far from the usual course of navigation; nature itself seemed to be altered, and the only guide which they had left was about to fail them. Columbus, with no less quickness than ingenuity, invented a reason for this appearance, which, though it did not satisfy himself, seemed so plausible to them, that it dispelled their fears, or silenced their murmurs.

He still continued to steer due west, nearly in the same latitude with the Canary Islands. In this course he came within the sphere of the trade wind, which blows invariably from east to west, between the tropics and a few degrees beyond them. He advanced before this steady gale with such uniform rapidity that it was seldom necessary to shift a sail. When about four hundred leagues to the west of the Canaries, he found the sea so covered with weeds, that it resembled a meadow of vast extent, and in some places they were so thick as to retard the motion of the vessels. This strange appearance occasioned new alarm and disquiet. The sailors imagined that they were now arrived at the utmost boundary of the navigable ocean; that these floating weeds would obstruct their further progress, and concealed dangerous rocks, or some large track of land, which had sunk, they knew not how, in that place. Columbus endeavoured to persuade them, that what had alarmed ought rather to have encouraged them, and was to be considered as a sign of approaching land. At the same time, a brisk gale arose, and carried them forward. Several birds were seen hovering about the ship [13], and directing their flight towards the west. The desponding crew resumed some degree of spirit, and began to entertain fresh hopes.

Upon the first of October they were, according to the admiral's reckoning, seven hundred and seventy leagues to the west of the Canaries; but lest his men should be intimidated by the prodigious length of the navigation, he gave out that they had proceeded only five hundred and eighty-four leagues, and fortunately, for Columbus, neither his own pilot, nor those of the other ships, had skill sufficient to correct this error, and discover the deceit. They had now been above three weeks at sea; they had proceeded far beyond what former navigators had attempted or deemed possible; all their prognostics of discovery, drawn from the flight of birds and other circumstances, had proved fallacious; the appearances of land, with which their own credulity or the artifice of their commander had from time to time flattered and amused them, had been altogether illusive, and their prospect of success seemed now to be as distant as ever. These reflections occurred often to men who had no other object or occupation than to reason and discourse concerning the intention and circumstances of their expedition. They made impression at first upon the ignorant and timid, and, extending by degrees to such as were better informed or more resolute, the contagion spread at length from ship to ship. From secret whispers or murmurings, they proceeded to open cabals and public complaints. They taxed their sovereign with inconsiderate credulity, in paying such regard to the vain promises and rash conjectures of an indigent foreigner, as to hazard the lives of so many of her own subjects in prosecuting a chimerical scheme. They affirmed that they had fully performed their duty, by venturing so far in an unknown and hopeless course, and could incur no blame for refusing to follow any longer a desperate adventurer to certain destruction. They contended, that it was necessary to think of returning to Spain, while their crazy vessels were still in a condition to keep the sea, but expressed their fears that the attempt would prove vain, as the wind, which had hitherto been so favourable to their course, must render it impossible to sail in an opposite direction. All agreed that Columbus should be compelled by force to adopt a measure on which their common safety depended. Some of the more audacious proposed, as the most expeditious and certain method of getting rid at once of his remonstrances, to throw him into the sea, being persuaded that, upon their return to Spain, the death of an unsuccessful projector would excite little concern, and be inquired into with no curiosity.

Columbus was fully sensible of his perilous situation. He had observed, with great uneasiness, the fatal operation of ignorance and of fear in producing disaffection among his crew, and saw that it was now ready to burst out into open mutiny. He retained, however, perfect presence of mind. He affected to seem ignorant of their machinations. Notwithstanding the agitation and solicitude of his own mind, he appeared with a cheerful countenance, like a man satisfied with the progress he had made, and confident of success. Sometimes he employed all the arts of insinuation to soothe his men. Sometimes he endeavoured to work upon their ambition or avarice, by magnificent descriptions of the fame and wealth which they were about to acquire. On other occasions he assumed a tone of authority, and threatened them with vengeance from their sovereign, if, by their dastardly behaviour, they should defeat this noble effort to promote the glory of God, and to exalt the Spanish name above that of every other nation. Even with seditious sailors, the words of a man whom they had been accustomed to reverence, were weighty and persuasive, and not only restrained them from those violent excesses which they meditated, but prevailed with them to accompany their admiral for some time longer.

As they proceeded, the indications of approaching land seemed to be more certain, and excited hope in proportion. The birds began to appear in flocks, making towards the southwest. Columbus, in imitation of the Portuguese navigators, who had been guided, in several of their discoveries, by the motion of birds, altered his course from due west towards that quarter whither they pointed their flight. But, after holding on for several days in this new direction, without any better success than formerly, having seen no object, during thirty days, but the sea and the sky, the hopes of his companions subsided faster than they had risen; their fears revived with additional force; impatience, rage, and despair, appeared in every countenance. All sense of subordination was lost: the officers, who had hitherto concurred with Columbus in opinion, and supported his authority, now took part with the private men; they assembled tumultuously on the deck, expostulated with their commander, mingled threats with their expostulations, and required him instantly to tack about and to return to Europe. Columbus perceived that it would be of no avail to have recourse to any of his former arts, which, having been tried so often, had lost their effect; and that it was impossible to rekindle any zeal for the success of the expedition among men in whose breasts fear had extinguished every generous sentiment. He saw that it was no less vain to think of employing either gentle or severe measures to quell a mutiny so general and so violent. It was necessary, on all these accounts, to soothe passions which he could no longer command,

and to give way to a torrent too impetuous to be checked. He promised solemnly to his men that he would comply with their request, provided they would accompany him, and obey his command for three days longer, and if, during that time, land were not discovered, he would then abandon the enterprise, and direct his course towards Spain.*

Enraged as the sailors were, and impatient to turn their faces again towards their native country, this proposition did not appear to them unreasonable. Nor did Columbus hazard much in confining himself to a term so short. The presages of discovering land were now so numerous and promising, that he deemed them infallible. For some days the sounding line reached the bottom, and the soil which it brought up indicated land to be at no great distance. The flocks of birds increased, and were composed not only of seafowl, but of such land birds as could not be supposed to fly far from the shore. The crew of the Pinta observed a cane floating, which seemed to have been newly cut, and likewise a piece of timber artificially carved. The sailors aboard the Nigna took up the branch of a tree with red berries, perfectly fresh. The clouds around the setting sun assumed a new appearance; the air was more mild and warm, and during the night the wind became unequal and variable. From all these symptoms, Columbus was so confident of being near land, that on the evening of the eleventh of October, after public prayers for success, he ordered the sails to be furled, and the ships to lie to, keeping strict watch, lest they should be driven ashore in the night. During this interval of suspense and expectation, no man shut his eyes, all kept upon deck, gazing intently towards that quarter where they expected to discover the land, which had been so long the object of their wishes.

About two hours before midnight, Columbus, standing on the forecastle, observed a light at a distance, and privately pointed it out to Pedro Guttierez, a page of the Queen's wardrobe. Guttierez perceived it, and calling to Salcedo, comptroller of the fleet, all three saw it in motion, as if it were carried from place to place. A little after midnight the joyful sound of *land! land!* was heard from the Pinta, which kept always a head of the other ships. But, having been so often deceived by fallacious appearances, every man was now become slow of belief, and waited in all the anguish of uncertainty and impatience for the return of day. As soon as morning dawned [Oct. 12], all doubts and fears were dispelled. From every ship an island was seen about two leagues to the north, whose flat and verdant fields, well stored with wood, and watered with many rivulets, presented the aspect of a delightful country. The crew of the Pinta instantly began the *Te Deum*, as a hymn of thanksgiving to God, and were joined by those of the other ships, with tears of joy and transports of congratulation. This office of gratitude to Heaven was followed by an act of justice to their commander. They threw themselves at the feet of Columbus, with feelings of self-condemnation mingled with reverence. They implored him to pardon their ignorance, incredulity, and insolence, which had created him so much unnecessary disquiet, and had so often obstructed the prosecution of his well-concerted plan; and passing; in the warmth of their admiration, from one extreme to another, they now pronounced the man, whom they had so lately reviled and threatened, to be a person inspired by Heaven with sagacity and fortitude more than human, in order to accomplish a design so far beyond the ideas and conception of all former ages.

As soon as the sun arose, all their boats were manned and armed. They rowed towards the island with their colours displayed, with warlike music, and other martial pomp. As they approached the coast, they saw it covered with a multitude of people, whom the novelty of the spectacle had drawn together, whose attitudes and gestures expressed wonder and astonishment

* Oviedo, Hist. ap. Ramus, vol. iii. p. 81. E.

at the strange objects which presented themselves to their view. Columbus was the first European who set foot in the New World which he had discovered. He landed in a rich dress, and with a naked sword in his hand. His men followed, and kneeling down, they all kissed the ground which they had so long desired to see.. They next erected a crucifix, and prostrating themselves before it, returned thanks to God for conducting their voyage to such a happy issue. They then took solemn possession of the country, for the crown of Castile and Leon, with all the formalities which the Portuguese were accustomed to observe in acts of this kind, in their new discoveries.*

The Spaniards, while thus employed, were surrounded by many of the natives, who gazed in silent admiration upon actions which they could not comprehend, and of which they did not foresee the consequences. The dress of the Spaniards, the whiteness of their skins, their beards, their arms, appeared strange and surprising. The vast machines in which they had traversed the ocean, that seemed to move upon the waters with wings, and uttered a dreadful sound resembling thunder, accompanied with lightning and smoke, struck them with such terror, that they began to respect their new guests as a superior order of beings, and concluded that they were children of the Sun, who had descended to visit the earth.

The Europeans were hardly less amazed at the scene now before them. Every herb, and shrub, and tree, was different from those which flourished in Europe. The soil seemed to be rich, but bore few marks of cultivation. The climate, even to the Spaniards, felt warm, though extremely delightful. The inhabitants appeared in the simple innocence of nature, entirely naked. Their black hair, long and uncurled, floated upon their shoulders, or was bound in tresses around their heads. They had no beards, and every part of their bodies was perfectly smooth. Their complexion was of a dusky-copper colour, their features singular, rather than disagreeable, their aspect gentle and timid. Though not tall, they were well shaped and active. Their faces, and several parts of their body, were fantastically painted with glaring colours. They were shy at first through fear, but soon became familiar with the Spaniards, and with transports of joy received from them hawksbells, glass beads, or other baubles, in return for which they gave such provisions as they had, and some cotton yarn, the only commodity of value that they could produce. Towards evening, Columbus returned to his ship, accompanied by many of the islanders in their boats, which they called *canoes*, and though rudely formed out of the trunk of a single tree, they rowed them with surprising dexterity. Thus, in the first interview between the inhabitants of the old and new worlds, every thing was conducted amicably, and to their mutual satisfaction. The former, enlightened and ambitious, formed already vast ideas with respect to the advantages which they might derive from the regions that began to open to their view. The latter, simple and undiscerning, had no foresight of the calamities and desolation which were approaching their country.

Columbus, who now assumed the title and authority of admiral and viceroy, called the island which he had discovered *San Salvador*. It is better known by the name of *Guanahani*, which the natives gave to it, and is one of that large cluster of islands called the Lucaya or Bahama isles It is situated above three thousand miles to the west of Gomera; from which the squadron took its departure, and only four degrees to the south of it; so little had Columbus deviated from the westerly course, which he had chosen as the most proper.

Columbus employed the next day in visiting the coasts of the island; and from the universal poverty of the inhabitants, he perceived that this was not the rich country for which he sought. But, conformably to his theory

* Life of Columbus, c. 22, 23. Herrera, dec. 1. lib. 1. c. 22.

concerning the discovery of those regions of Asia which stretched towards the east, he concluded that San Salvador was one of the isles which geographers described as situated in the great ocean adjacent to India.* Having observed that most of the people whom he had seen wore small plates of gold, by way of ornament, in their nostrils, he eagerly inquired where they got that precious metal. They pointed towards the south, and made him comprehend by signs, that gold abounded in countries situated in that quarter. Thither he immediately determined to direct his course, in full confidence of finding there those opulent regions which had been the object of his voyage, and would be a recompense for all his toils and dangers. He took along with him seven of the natives of San Salvador, that, by acquiring the Spanish language, they might serve as guides and interpreters; and those innocent people considered it as a mark of distinction when they were selected to accompany him.

He saw several islands, and touched at three of the largest, on which he bestowed the names of St. Mary of the Conception, Fernandina, and Isabella. But, as their soil, productions, and inhabitants nearly resembled those of San Salvador, he made no stay in any of them. He inquired every where for gold, and the signs that were uniformly made by way of answer, confirmed him in the opinion that it was brought from the south. He followed that course, and soon discovered a country which appeared very extensive, not perfectly level, like those which he had already visited, but so diversified with rising grounds, hills, rivers, woods, and plains, that he was uncertain whether it might prove an island, or part of the continent. The natives of San Salvador, whom he had on board, called it *Cuba;* Columbus gave it the name of Juana. He entered the mouth of a large river with his squadron, and all the inhabitants fled to the mountains as he approached the shore. But as he resolved to careen the ships in that place, he sent some Spaniards, together with one of the people of San Salvador, to view the interior part of the country. They, having advanced above sixty miles from the shore, reported, upon their return, that the soil was richer and more cultivated than any they had hitherto discovered; that, besides many scattered cottages, they had found one village, containing above a thousand inhabitants; that the people, though naked, seemed to be more intelligent than those of San Salvador, but had treated them with the same respectful attention, kissing their feet, and honouring them as sacred beings allied to heaven; that they had given them to eat a certain root, the taste of which resembled roasted chestnuts, and likewise a singular species of corn called *maize,* which, either when roasted whole or ground into meal, was abundantly palatable; that there seemed to be no four-footed animals in the country, but a species of dogs, which could not bark, and a creature resembling a rabbit, but of a much smaller size; that they had observed some ornaments of gold among the people, but of no great value.†

These messengers had prevailed with some of the natives to accompany them, who informed Columbus, that the gold of which they made their ornaments was found in *Cubanacan.* By this word they meant the middle or inland part of Cuba; but Columbus, being ignorant of their language, as well as unaccustomed to their pronunciation, and his thoughts running continually upon his own theory concerning the discovery of the East Indies, he was led, by the resemblance of sound, to suppose that they spoke of the great Khan, and imagined that the opulent kingdom of *Cathay,* described by Marco Polo, was not very remote. This induced him to employ some time in viewing the country. He visited almost every harbour, from Porto del Principe, on the north coast of Cuba, to the eastern extremity of the island: but, though delighted with the beauty of the scenes which every where presented themselves, and amazed at the luxuriant fertility of the

* Pet. Mart. epist. 135.   † Life of Columbus, c. 24—28. Herrera, dec. 1. lib. l. c. 14.

soil, both which, from their novelty, made a more lively impression upon his imagination [14], he did not find gold in such quantity as was sufficient to satisfy either the avarice of his followers, or the expectations of the court to which he was to return. The people of the country, as much astonished at his eagerness in quest of gold as the Europeans were at their ignorance and simplicity, pointed towards the east, where an island which they called *Hayti* was situated, in which that metal was more abundant than among them. Columbus ordered his squadron to bend its course thither; but Marton Alonso Pinzon, impatient to be the first who should take possession of the treasures which this country was supposed to contain, quitted his companions, regardless of all the admiral's signals to slacken sail until they should come up with him.

Columbus, retarded by contrary winds, did not reach Hayti till the sixth of December. He called the port where he first touched St. Nicholas, and the island itself Espagnola, in honour of the kingdom by which he was employed; and it is the only country, of those he had yet discovered, which has retained the name that he gave it. As he could neither meet with the Pinta, nor have any intercourse with the inhabitants, who fled in great consternation towards the woods, he soon quitted St. Nicholas, and, sailing along the northern coast of the island, he entered another harbour, which he called Conception. Here he was more fortunate; his people overtook a woman who was flying from them, and after treating her with great gentleness, dismissed her with a present of such toys as they knew were most valued in those regions. The description which she gave to her countrymen of the humanity and wonderful qualities of the strangers; their admiration of the trinkets, which she showed with exultation; and their eagerness to participate of the same favours; removed all their fears, and induced many of them to repair to the harbour. The strange objects which they beheld, and the baubles which Columbus bestowed upon them, amply gratified their curiosity and their wishes. They nearly resembled the people of Guanabani and Cuba. They were naked like them, ignorant and simple; and seemed to be equally unacquainted with all the arts which appear most necessary in polished societies; but they were gentle, credulous, and timid, to a degree which rendered it easy to acquire the ascendant over them, especially as their excessive admiration led them into the same error with the people of the other islands, in believing the Spaniards to be more than mortals, and descended immediately from heaven. They possessed gold in greater abundance than their neighbours, which they readily exchanged for bells, beads, or pins; and in this unequal traffic both parties were highly pleased, each considering themselves as gainers by the transaction. Here Columbus was visited by a prince or *cazique* of the country. He appeared with all the pomp known among a simple people, being carried in a sort of palanquin upon the shoulders of four men, and attended by many of his subjects, who served him with great respect. His deportment was grave and stately, very reserved towards his own people, but with Columbus and the Spaniards extremely courteous. He gave the admiral some thin plates of gold, and a girdle of curious workmanship, receiving in return presents of small value, but highly acceptable to him.*

Columbus, still intent on discovering the mines which yielded gold, continued to interrogate all the natives with whom he had any intercourse, concerning their situation. They concurred in pointing out a mountainous country, which they called *Cibao*, at some distance from the sea, and further towards the east. Struck with this sound, which appeared to him the same with *Cipango*, the name by which Marco Polo, and other travellers to the east, distinguished the island of Japan, he no longer doubted with respect to the vicinity of the countries which he had discovered to the remote parts

* Life of Columbus, c. 32. Herrera, dec. 1. lib. 1. c. 15, &c.

of Asia; and, in full expectation of reaching soon those regions which had been the object of his voyage, he directed his course towards the east. He put into a commodious harbour, which he called St. Thomas, and found that district to be under the government of a powerful cazique, named *Guacanahari*, who, as he afterwards learned, was one of the five sovereigns among whom the whole island was divided. He immediately sent messengers to Columbus, who in his name delivered to him the present of a mask curiously fashioned with the ears, nose, and mouth of beaten gold, and invited him to the place of his residence, near the harbour now called Cape François, some leagues towards the east. Columbus despatched some of his officers to visit this prince, who, as he behaved himself with greater dignity, seemed to claim more attention. They returned with such favourable accounts both of the country and of the people, as made Columbus impatient for that interview with Guacanahari to which he had been invited.

He sailed for this purpose from St. Thomas, on the twenty-fourth of December, with a fair wind, and the sea perfectly calm; and as, amidst the multiplicity of his occupations, he had not shut his eyes for two days, he retired at midnight in order to take some repose, having committed the helm to the pilot, with strict injunctions not to quit it for a moment. The pilot, dreading no danger, carelessly left the helm to an unexperienced cabin boy, and the ship, carried away by a current, was dashed against a rock. The violence of the shock awakened Columbus. He ran up to the deck. There all was confusion and despair. He alone retained presence of mind. He ordered some of the sailors to take a boat, and carry out an anchor astern; but, instead of obeying, they made off towards the Nigna, which was about half a league distant. He then commanded the masts to be cut down, in order to lighten the ship; but all his endeavours were too late; the vessel opened near the keel, and filled so fast with water that its loss was inevitable. The smoothness of the sea, and the timely assistance of boats from the Nigna, enabled the crew to save their lives. As soon as the islanders heard of this disaster, they crowded to the shore, with their prince Guacanahari at their head. Instead of taking advantage of the distress in which they beheld the Spaniards, to attempt any thing to their detriment, they lamented their misfortune with tears of sincere condolence. Not satisfied with this unavailing expression of their sympathy, they put to sea a number of canoes, and, under the direction of the Spaniards, assisted in saving whatever could be got out of the wreck; and, by the united labour of so many hands, almost every thing of value was carried ashore. As fast as the goods were landed, Guacanahari in person took charge of them. By his orders they were all deposited in one place, and armed sentinels were posted, who kept the multitude at a distance, in order to prevent them not only from embezzling, but from inspecting too curiously what belonged to their guests. [15] Next morning this prince visited Columbus, who was now on board the Nigna, and endeavoured to console him for his loss, by offering all that he possessed to repair it.*

The condition of Columbus was such that he stood in need of consolation. He had hitherto procured no intelligence of the Pinta, and no longer doubted but that his treacherous associate had set sail for Europe, in order to have the merit of carrying the first tidings of the extraordinary discoveries which had been made, and to preoccupy so far the ear of their sovereign, as to rob him of the glory and reward to which he was justly entitled. There remained but one vessel, and that the smallest and most crazy of the squadron, to traverse such a vast ocean, and carry so many men back to Europe. Each of those circumstances was alarming, and filled the mind of Columbus with the utmost solicitude. The desire of overtaking Pinzon, and of effacing the unfavourable impressions which his misrepresentations might make in

* Herrera, dec. 1. lib. i. c. 18.

Spain, made it necessary to return thither without delay. The difficulty of taking such a number of persons on board the Nigna confirmed him in an opinion which the fertility of the country, and the gentle temper of the people, had already induced him to form. He resolved to leave a part of his crew in the island, that by residing there, they might learn the language of the natives, study their disposition, examine the nature of the country, search for mines, prepare for the commodious settlement of the colony with which he purposed to return, and thus secure and facilitate the acquisition of those advantages which he expected from his discoveries. When he mentioned this to his men, all approved of the design; and from impatience under the fatigue of a long voyage, from the levity natural to sailors, or from the hopes of amassing wealth in a country which afforded such promising specimens of its riches, many offered voluntarily to be among the number of those who should remain.

Nothing was now wanting towards the execution of this scheme, but to obtain the consent of Guacanahari; and his unsuspicious simplicity soon presented to the admiral a favourable opportunity of proposing it. Columbus having, in the best manner he could, by broken words and signs, expressed some curiosity to know the cause which had moved the islanders to fly with such precipitation upon the approach of his ships, the cazique informed him that the country was much infested by the incursions of certain people, whom he called *Carribeans*, who inhabited several islands to the south-east. These he described as a fierce and warlike race of men, who delighted in blood, and devoured the flesh of the prisoners who were so unhappy as to fall into their hands; and as the Spaniards at their first appearance were supposed to be Carribeans, whom the natives, however numerous, durst not face in battle, they had recourse to their usual method of securing their safety, by flying into the thickest and most impenetrable woods. Guacanahari, while speaking of those dreadful invaders, discovered such symptoms of terror, as well as such consciousness of the inability of his own people to resist them, as led Columbus to conclude that he would not be alarmed at the proposition of any scheme which afforded him the prospect of an additional security against their attacks. He instantly offered him the assistance of the Spaniards to repel his enemies: he engaged to take him and his people under the protection of the powerful monarch whom he served, and offered to leave in the island such a number of his men as should be sufficient, not only to defend the inhabitants from future incursions, but to avenge their past wrongs.

The credulous prince closed eagerly with the proposal, and thought himself already safe under the patronage of beings sprung from heaven, and superior in power to mortal men. The ground was marked out for a small fort, which Columbus called *Navidad*, because he had landed there on Christmas day. A deep ditch was drawn around it. The ramparts were fortified with pallisades, and the great guns, saved out of the admiral's ship, were planted upon them. In ten days the work was finished; that simple race of men labouring with inconsiderate assiduity in erecting this first monument of their own servitude. During this time, Columbus, by his caresses and liberality, laboured to increase the high opinion which the natives entertained of the Spaniards. But while he endeavoured to inspire them with confidence in their disposition to do good, he wished likewise to give them some striking idea of their power to punish and destroy such as were the objects of their indignation. With this view, in presence of a vast assembly, he drew up his men in order of battle, and made an ostentatious but innocent display of the sharpness of the Spanish swords, of the force of their spears, and the operation of their cross-bows. These rude people, strangers to the use of iron, and unacquainted with any hostile weapons but arrows of reed pointed with the bones of fishes, wooden swords, and javelins hardened in the fire, wondered and trembled. Before this surprise or fear had time to abate, he ordered the great guns to be fired. The sudden explosion struck them with such terror that they fell flat to the ground, covering their faces with their hands; and when they beheld the astonishing effect of the bullets among the trees, towards which the cannon had been pointed, they concluded that it was impossible to resist men, who had the command of such destructive instruments, and who came armed with thunder and lightning against their enemies.

After giving such impressions both of the beneficence and power of the Spaniards, as might have rendered it easy to preserve an ascendant over the minds of the natives, Columbus appointed thirty-eight of his people to remain in the island. He intrusted the command of these to Diego de Arado, a gentleman of Cordova, investing him with the same powers which he himself had received from Ferdinand and Isabella; and furnished him with every thing requisite for the subsistence or defence of this infant colony. He strictly enjoined them to maintain concord among themselves, to yield an unreserved obedience to their commander, to avoid giving offence to the natives by any violence or exaction, to cultivate the friendship of Guacanahari, but not to put themselves in his power by straggling in small parties, or marching too far from the fort. He promised to visit them soon with such a reinforcement of strength as might enable them to take full possession of the country, and to reap all the fruits of their discoveries. In the mean time he engaged to mention their names to the king and queen, and to place their merit and services in the most advantageous light.*

Having thus taken every precaution for the security of the colony, he left Navidad on the fourth of January, one thousand four hundred and ninety-three, and steering towards the east, discovered and gave names to most of the harbours on the northern coast of the island. On the sixth he descried the Pinta, and soon came up with her, after a separation of more than six weeks. Pinzon endeavoured to justify his conduct by pretending that he had been driven from his course by stress of weather, and prevented from returning by contrary winds. The admiral, though he still suspected his perfidious intentions, and knew well what he urged in his own defence to be frivolous as well as false, was so sensible that this was not a proper time for venturing upon any high strain of authority, and felt such satisfaction in this junction with his consort, which delivered him from many disquieting apprehensions, that, lame as Pinzon's apology was, he admitted of it without difficulty, and restored him to favour. During his absence from the admiral, Pinzon had visited several harbours in the island, had acquired some gold by trafficking with the natives, but had made no discovery of any importance.

From the condition of his ships, as well as the temper of his men, Columbus now found it necessary to hasten his return to Europe. The former having suffered much during a voyage of such an unusual length, were extremely leaky. The latter expressed the utmost impatience to revisit their native country, from which they had been so long absent, and where they had things so wonderful and unheard-of to relate. Accordingly, on the sixteenth of January, he directed his course towards the north-east, and soon lost sight of land. He had on board some of the natives, whom he had taken from the different islands which he discovered; and besides the gold, which was the chief object of research, he had collected specimens of all the productions which were likely to become subjects of commerce in the several countries, as well as many unknown birds, and other natural curiosities, which might attract the attention of the learned, or excite the wonder of the people. The voyage was prosperous to the fourteenth of February, and he had advanced near five hundred leagues across the Atlantic ocean, when the wind began to rise, and continued to blow with increasing

---

* Oviedo ap. Ramusio, iii. p. 82. P. Herrera, dec. l. lib. l. c. 20. Life of Columbus, c. 34.

rage, which terminated in a furious hurricane. Every thing that the naval skill and experience of Columbus could devise was employed in order to save the ships. But it was impossible to withstand the violence of the storm, and, as they were still far from any land, destruction seemed inevitable. The sailors had recourse to prayers to Almighty God, to the invocation of saints, to vows, and charms, to every thing that religion dictates, or superstition suggests to the affrighted mind of man. No prospect of deliverance appearing, they abandoned themselves to despair, and expected every moment to be swallowed up in the waves. Besides the passions which naturally agitate and alarm the human mind in such awful situations, when certain death, in one of his most terrible forms, is before it, Columbus had to endure feelings of distress peculiar to himself. He dreaded that all knowledge of the amazing discoveries which he had made was now to perish; mankind were to be deprived of every benefit that might have been derived from the happy success of his schemes, and his own name would descend to posterity as that of a rash deluded adventurer, instead of being transmitted with the honour due to the author and conductor of the most noble enterprise that had ever been undertaken. These reflections extinguished all sense of his own personal danger. Less affected with the loss of life than solicitous to preserve the memory of what he had attempted and achieved, he retired to his cabin and wrote upon a parchment a short account of the voyage which he had made, of the course which he had taken, of the situation and riches of the countries which he had discovered, and of the colony that he had left there. Having wrapped up this in an oiled cloth, which he enclosed in a cake of wax, he put it into a cask carefully stopped up, and threw it into the sea, in hopes that some fortunate accident might preserve a deposit of so much importance to the world.*[16]

At length Providence interposed to save a life reserved for other services. The wind abated, the sea became calm, and on the evening of the fifteenth, Columbus and his companions discovered land; and though uncertain what it was, they made towards it. They soon knew it to be St. Mary, one of the Azores or western isles, subject to the crown of Portugal. There, after a violent contest with the governor, in which Columbus displayed no less spirit than prudence, he obtained a supply of fresh provisions, and whatever else he needed. One circumstance, however, greatly disquieted him. The Pinta, of which he had lost sight on the first day of the hurricane, did not appear; he dreaded for some time that she had foundered at sea, and that all her crew had perished; afterwards, his former suspicions recurred, and he became apprehensive that Pinzon had borne away for Spain, that he might reach it before him, and by giving the first account of his discoveries, might obtain some share of his fame.

In order to prevent this, he left the Azores as soon as the weather would permit [Feb. 24]. At no great distance from the coast of Spain, when near the end of his voyage, and seemingly beyond the reach of any disaster, another storm arose, little inferior to the former in violence; and after driving before it during two days and two nights, he was forced to take shelter in the river Tagus [March 4]. Upon application to the King of Portugal, he was allowed to come up to Lisbon; and, notwithstanding the envy which it was natural for the Portuguese to feel, when they beheld another nation entering upon that province of discovery which they had hitherto deemed peculiarly their own, and in its first essay not only rivalling but eclipsing their fame, Columbus was received with all the marks of distinction due to a man who had performed things so extraordinary and unexpected. The King admitted him into his presence, treated him with the highest respect, and listened to the account which he gave of his voyage

* Life of Columbus, c. 37. Herrera, dec. 1. lib. ii. c. 1, 2.

with admiration mingled with regret. While Columbus, on his part, enjoyed the satisfaction of describing the importance of his discoveries, and of being now able to prove the solidity of his schemes to those very persons, who, with an ignorance disgraceful to themselves, and fatal to their country, had lately rejected them as the projects of a visionary or designing adventurer.*

Columbus was so impatient to return to Spain, that he remained only five days in Lisbon. On the fifteenth of March he arrived in the port of Palos, seven months and eleven days from the time when he set out thence upon his voyage. As soon as the ship was discovered approaching the port, all the inhabitants of Palos ran eagerly to the shore, in order to welcome their relations and fellow-citizens, and to hear tidings of their voyage. When the prosperous issue of it was known, when they beheld the strange people, the unknown animals, and singular productions, brought from the countries which had been discovered, the effusion of joy was general and unbounded. The bells were rung, the cannon fired; Columbus was received at landing with royal honours, and all the people in solemn procession, accompanied him and his crew to the church, where they returned thanks to Heaven, which had so wonderfully conducted and crowned with success a voyage of greater length and of more importance than had been attempted in any former age. On the evening of the same day, he had the satisfaction of seeing the Pinta, which the violence of the tempest had driven far to the north, enter the harbour.

The first care of Columbus was to inform the King and Queen, who were then at Barcelona, of his arrival and success. Ferdinand and Isabella, no less astonished than delighted with this unexpected event, desired Columbus, in terms the most respectful and flattering, to repair immediately to court, that from his own mouth they might receive a full detail of his extraordinary services and discoveries. During his journey to Barcelona, the people crowded from the adjacent country, following him every where with admiration and applause. His entrance into the city was conducted, by order of Ferdinand and Isabella, with pomp suitable to the great event, which added such distinguishing lustre to their reign. The people whom he brought along with him from the countries which he had discovered, marched first, and by their singular complexion, the wild peculiarity of their features, and uncouth finery, appeared like men of another species. Next to them were carried the ornaments of gold, fashioned by the rude art of the natives, the grains of gold found in the mountains, and dust of the same metal gathered in the rivers. After these appeared the various commodities of the new discovered countries, together with their curious productions. Columbus himself closed the procession, and attracted the eyes of all the spectators, who gazed with admiration on the extraordinary man, whose superior sagacity and fortitude had conducted their countrymen, by a route concealed from past ages, to the knowledge of a new world. Ferdinand and Isabella received him clad in their royal robes, and seated upon a throne, under a magnificent canopy. When he approached, they stood up, and raising him as he kneeled to kiss their hands, commanded him to take his seat upon a chair prepared for him, and to give a circumstantial account of his voyage. He delivered it with a gravity and composure no less suitable to the disposition of the Spanish nation than to the dignity of the audience in which he spoke, and with that modest simplicity which characterizes men of superior minds, who, satisfied with having performed great actions, court not vain applause by an ostentatious display of their exploits. When he had finished his narration, the king and queen, kneeling down, offered up solemn thanks to Almighty God for the discovery of those new regions, from which they expected so many advantages to flow in upon

* Life of Columbus, c. 40, 41. Herrera, dec. 1. lib. ii. c. 3

the kingdoms subject to their government. [17] Every mark of honour that gratitude or admiration could suggest was conferred upon Columbus. Letters patent were issued, confirming to him and to his heirs all the privileges contained in the capitulation concluded at Santa Fé; his family was ennobled; the king and queen, and after their example the courtiers, treated him on every occasion with all the ceremonious respect paid to persons of the highest rank. But what pleased him most, as it gratified his active mind, bent continually upon great objects, was an order to equip, without delay, an armament of such force as might enable him not only to take possession of the countries which he had already discovered, but to go in search of those more opulent regions which he still confidently expected to find.*

While preparations were making for this expedition, the fame of Columbus's successful voyage spread over Europe, and excited general attention. The multitude, struck with amazement when they heard that a new world had been found, could hardly believe an event so much above their conception. Men of science, capable of comprehending the nature, and of discerning the effects of this great discovery, received the account of it with admiration and joy. They spoke of his voyage with rapture, and congratulated one another upon their felicity in having lived in the period when, by this extraordinary event, the boundaries of human knowledge were so much extended, and such a new field of inquiry and observation opened, as would lead mankind to a perfect acquaintance with the structure and productions of the habitable globe.† [18] Various opinions and conjectures were formed concerning the new found countries, and what division of the earth they belonged to. Columbus adhered tenaciously to his original opinion, that they should be reckoned a part of those vast regions in Asia, comprehended under the general name of India. This sentiment was confirmed by the observations which he made concerning the productions of the countries he had discovered. Gold was known to abound in India, and he had met with such promising samples of it in the islands which he visited, as led him to believe that rich mines of it might be found. Cotton, another production of the East Indies, was common there. The pimento of the islands he imagined to be a species of the East Indian pepper. He mistook a root, somewhat resembling rhubarb, for that valuable drug, which was then supposed to be a plant peculiar to the East Indies.‡ The birds brought home by him were adorned with the same rich plumage which distinguishes those of India. The alligator of the one country appeared to be the same with the crocodile of the other. After weighing all these circumstances, not only the Spaniards, but the other nations of Europe, seem to have adopted the opinion of Columbus. The countries which he had discovered were considered as a part of India. In consequence of this notion, the name of Indies is given to them by Ferdinand and Isabella, in a ratification of their former agreement, which was granted to Columbus upon his return.§ Even after the error which gave rise to this opinion was detected, and the true position of the New World was ascertained, the name has remained, and the appellation of *West Indies* is given by all the people of Europe to the country, and that of *Indians* to its inhabitants.

The name by which Columbus distinguished the countries which he had discovered was so inviting, the specimens of their riches and fertility which he produced were so considerable, and the reports of his companions, delivered frequently with the exaggeration natural to travellers, so favourable, as to excite a wonderful spirit of enterprise among the Spaniards. Though little accustomed to naval expeditions, they were impatient to set out upon their voyage. Volunteers of every rank solicited to be employed. Allured by the inviting prospects which opened to their ambition and avarice,

---

* Life of Columbus, c. 42, 43. Herrera, dec. 1. lib. ii. c. 3. † 2 P. Mart. epist. 133, 134, 135. ‡ Herrera, dec. 1. lib. i. c. 20. Gomera Hist. c. 17. § Life of Columbus, c. 44.

neither the length nor danger of the navigation intimidated them. Cautious as Ferdinand was, and averse to every thing new or adventurous, he seems to have catched the same spirit with his subjects. Under its influence, preparations for a second expedition were carried on with rapidity unusual in Spain, and to an extent that would be deemed not inconsiderable in the present age. The fleet consisted of seventeen ships, some of which were of good burden. It had on board fifteen hundred persons, among whom were many of noble families, who had served in honourable stations. The greater part of these, being destined to remain in the country, were furnished with every thing requisite for conquest or settlement, with all kinds of European domestic animals, with such seeds and plants as were most likely to thrive in the climate of the West Indies, with utensils and instruments of every sort, and with such artificers as might be most useful in an infant colony.*

But, formidable and well provided as this fleet was, Ferdinand and Isabella did not rest their title to the possession of the newly discovered countries upon its operations alone. The example of the Portuguese, as well as the superstition of the age, made it necessary to obtain from the Roman pontiff a grant of those territories which they wished to occupy. The Pope, as the vicar and representative of Jesus Christ, was supposed to have a right of dominion over all the kingdoms of the earth. Alexander VI., a pontiff infamous for every crime which disgraces humanity, filled the Papal throne at that time. As he was born Ferdinand's subject, and very solicitous to secure the protection of Spain, in order to facilitate the execution of his ambitious schemes in favour of his own family, he was extremely willing to gratify the Spanish monarchs. By an act of liberality which cost him nothing, and that served to establish the jurisdiction and pretensions of the Papal See, he granted in full right to Ferdinand and Isabella all the countries inhabited by Infidels, which they had discovered, or should discover; and, in virtue of that power which he derived from Jesus Christ, he conferred on the crown of Castile vast regions, to the possession of which he himself was so far from having any title, that he was unacquainted with their situation, and ignorant even of their existence. As it was necessary to prevent this grant from interfering with that formerly made to the crown of Portugal, he appointed that a line, supposed to be drawn from pole to pole, a hundred leagues to the westward of the Azores, should serve as a limit between them; and, in the plenitude of his power, bestowed all to the east of this imaginary line upon the Portuguese, and all to the west of it upon the Spaniards.† Zeal for propagating the Christian faith was the consideration employed by Ferdinand in soliciting this bull, and is mentioned by Alexander as his chief motive for issuing it. In order to manifest some concern for this laudable object, several friars, under the direction of Father Boyl, a Catalonian monk of great reputation, as apostolical vicar, were appointed to accompany Columbus, and to devote themselves to the instruction of the natives. The Indians, whom Columbus had brought along with him, having received some tincture of Christian knowledge, were baptized with much solemnity, the king himself, the prince his son, and the chief persons of his court, standing as their godfathers. Those first fruits of the New World have not been followed by such an increase as pious men wished, and had reason to expect.

Ferdinand and Isabella having thus acquired a title, which was then deemed completely valid, to extend their discoveries and to establish their dominion over such a considerable portion of the globe, nothing now retarded the departure of the fleet. Columbus was extremely impatient to revisit the colony which he had left, and to pursue that career of glory upon which

---

* Herrera, dec. 1. lib. II. c. 5. Life of Columbus, c. 45. † Herrera, dec. 1. lib. II. c. 4.
Torquemada Mon. Ind. lib. xviii. c. 3.

he had entered. He set sail from the bay of Cadiz on the twenty-fifth of September, and touching again at the island of Gomera, he steered further towards the south than in his former voyage. By holding this course, he enjoyed more steadily the benefit of the regular winds, which reign within the tropics, and was carried towards a large cluster of islands, situated considerably to the east of those which he had already discovered. On the twenty-sixth day after his departure from Gomera [Nov. 2], he made land.[*] It was one of the Carribbee or Leeward Islands, to which he gave the name of Deseada, on account of the impatience of his crew to discover some part of the New World. After this he visited successively Dominica, Marigalante, Guadaloupe, Antigua, San Juan de Puerto Rico, and several other islands, scattered in his way as he advanced towards the north-west. All these he found to be inhabited by that fierce race of people whom Guacanahari had painted in such frightful colours. His descriptions appeared not to have been exaggerated. The Spaniards never attempted to land without meeting with such a reception as discovered the martial and daring spirit of the natives; and in their habitations were found relics of those horrid feasts which they had made upon the bodies of their enemies taken in war.

But as Columbus was eager to know the state of the colony which he had planted, and to supply it with the necessaries of which he supposed it to be in want, he made no stay in any of those islands, and proceeded directly to Hispaniola [Nov. 22].[†] When he arrived off Navidad, the station in which he had left the thirty-eight men under the command of Arada, he was astonished that none of them appeared, and expected every moment to see them running with transports of joy to welcome their countrymen. Full of solicitude about their safety, and foreboding in his mind what had befallen them, he rowed instantly to land. All the natives from whom he might have received information had fled. But the fort which he had built was entirely demolished, and the tattered garments, the broken arms and utensils scattered about it, left no room to doubt concerning the unhappy fate of the garrison.[‡] While the Spaniards were shedding tears over those sad memorials of their fellow-citizens, a brother of the cazique Guacanahari arrived. From him Columbus received a particular detail of what had happened after his departure from the island. The familiar intercourse of the Indians with the Spaniards tended gradually to diminish the superstitious veneration with which their first appearance had inspired that simple people. By their own indiscretion and ill conduct, the Spaniards speedily effaced those favourable impressions, and soon convinced the natives, that they had all the wants, and weaknesses, and passions of men. As soon as the powerful restraint which the presence and authority of Columbus imposed was withdrawn, the garrison threw off all regard for the officer whom he had invested with command. Regardless of the prudent instructions which he had given them, every man became independent, and gratified his desires without control. The gold, the women, the provisions of the natives, were all the prey of those licentious oppressors They roamed in small parties over the island, extending their rapacity and insolence to every corner of it. Gentle and timid as the people were, those unprovoked injuries at length exhausted their patience, and roused their courage. The cazique of Cibao, whose country the Spaniards chiefly infested on account of the gold which it contained, surprised and cut off several of them, while they straggled in as perfect security as if their conduct had been altogether inoffensive. He then assembled his subjects, and surrounding the fort, set it on fire. Some of the Spaniards were killed in defending it; the rest perished in attempting to make their escape by crossing an arm of the sea. Guacanahari, whom all their exactions had

---

[*] Oviedo ap. Ramus. ill. 85.   [†] P. Martyr, dec. p. 15. 18. Herrera, dec. 1. lib. ii. c. 7. Life of Columbus, c. 40. &c.   [‡] Hist. de Cura de los Palacios. MS.

not alienated from the Spaniards, took arms in their behalf, and, in endeavouring to protect them, had received a wound, by which he was still confined.*

Though this account was far from removing the suspicions which the Spaniards entertained with respect to the fidelity of Guacanahari, Columbus perceived so clearly that this was not a proper juncture for inquiring into his conduct with scrupulous accuracy, that he rejected the advice of several of his officers, who urged him to seize the person of that Prince, and to revenge the death of their countrymen by attacking his subjects. He represented to them the necessity of securing the friendship of some potentate of the country, in order to facilitate the settlement which they intended, and the danger of driving the natives to unite in some desperate attempt against them, by such an ill-timed and unavailing exercise of rigour. Instead of wasting his time in punishing past wrongs, he took precautions for preventing any future injury. With this view, he made choice of a situation more healthy and commodious than that of Navidad. He traced out the plan of a town in a large plain near a spacious bay, and obliging every person to put his hand to a work on which their common safety depended, the houses and ramparts were soon so far advanced, by their united labour, as to afford them shelter and security. This rising city, the first that the Europeans founded in the New World, he named Isabella, in honour of his patroness the Queen of Castile.†

In carrying on this necessary work, Columbus had not only to sustain all the hardships, and to encounter all the difficulties, to which infant colonies are exposed when they settle in an uncultivated country, but he had to contend with what was more insuperable, the laziness, the impatience, and mutinous disposition of his followers. By the enervating influence of a hot climate, the natural inactivity of the Spaniards seemed to increase. Many of them were gentlemen, unaccustomed to the fatigue of bodily labour, and all had engaged in the enterprise with the sanguine hopes excited by the splendid and exaggerated description of their countrymen who returned from the first voyage, or by the mistaken opinion of Columbus, that the country which he had discovered was either the Cipango of Marco Polo, or the Ophir,‡ from which Solomon imported those precious commodities which suddenly diffused such extraordinary riches through his kingdom. But when, instead of that golden harvest which they had expected to reap without toil or pains, the Spaniards saw that their prospect of wealth was remote as well as uncertain, and that it could not be attained but by the slow and persevering efforts of industry, the disappointment of those chimerical hopes occasioned such dejection of mind as bordered on despair, and led to general discontent. In vain did Columbus endeavour to revive their spirits by pointing out the fertility of the soil, and exhibiting the specimens of gold daily brought in from different parts of the island. They had not patience to wait for the gradual returns which the former might yield, and the latter they despised as scanty and inconsiderable. The spirit of disaffection spread, and a conspiracy was formed, which might have been fatal to Columbus and the colony. Happily he discovered it; and, seizing the ringleaders, punished some of them, sent others prisoners into Spain, whither he despatched twelve of the ships which had served as transports, with an earnest request for a reinforcement of men and a large supply of provisions.§

1494.] Meanwhile, in order to banish that idleness which, by allowing his people leisure to brood over their disappointment, nourished the spirit of discontent, Columbus planned several expeditions into the interior part of

---
* P. Martyr, dec. p. 22, &c.   Herrera, dec. 1. lib. II. c. 7. 9.   Life of Columbus, c. 49, 50.   † Life of Columbus, c. 51.   Herrera, dec. 1. lib. II. c. 10.   ‡ P. Martyr, dec. p. 29.   § Herrera, dec. 1. lib. II. c. 10, 11.

the country. He sent a detachment, under the command of Alonzo de Ojeda, a vigilant and enterprising officer, to visit the district of Çibao, which was said to yield the greatest quantity of gold, and followed him in person with the main body of his troops. In this expedition he displayed all the pomp of military magnificence that he could exhibit, in order to strike the imagination of the natives. He marched with colours flying, with martial music, and with a small body of cavalry that paraded sometimes in the front and sometimes in the rear. As those were the first horses which appeared in the New World, they were objects of terror no less than of admiration to the Indians, who, having no tame animals themselves, were unacquainted with that vast accession of power which man hath acquired by subjecting them to his dominion. They supposed them to be rational creatures. They imagined that the horse and the rider formed one animal, with whose speed they were astonished, and whose impetuosity and strength they considered as irresistible. But while Columbus endeavoured to inspire the natives with a dread of his power, he did not neglect the arts of gaining their love and confidence. He adhered scrupulously to the principles of integrity and justice in all his transactions with them, and treated them, on every occasion, not only with humanity, but with indulgence. The district of Cibao answered the description given of it by the natives. It was mountainous and uncultivated, but in every river and brook gold was gathered either in dust or in grains, some of which were of considerable size. The Indians had never opened any mines in search of gold. To penetrate into the bowels of the earth, and to refine the rude ore, were operations too complicated and laborious for their talents and industry, and they had no such high value for gold as to put their ingenuity and invention upon the stretch in order to obtain it.* The small quantity of that precious metal which they possessed, was either picked up in the beds of the rivers, or washed from the mountains by the heavy rains that fall within the tropics. But from those indications, the Spaniards could no longer doubt that the country contained rich treasures in its bowels, of which they hoped soon to be masters.† In order to secure the command of this valuable province, Columbus erected a small fort, to which he gave the name of St. Thomas, by way of ridicule upon some of his incredulous followers, who would not believe that the country produced gold, until they saw it with their own eyes, and touched it with their hands.‡

The account of those promising appearances of wealth in the country of Cibao came very seasonably to comfort the desponding colony, which was affected with distresses of various kinds. The stock of provisions which had been brought from Europe was mostly consumed; what remained was so much corrupted by the heat and moisture of the climate as to be almost unfit for use; the natives cultivated so small a portion of ground, and with so little skill, that it hardly yielded what was sufficient for their own subsistence; the Spaniards at Isabella had hitherto neither time nor leisure to clear the soil, so as to reap any considerable fruits of their own industry. On all these accounts, they became afraid of perishing with hunger, and were reduced already to a scanty allowance. At the same time, the diseases predominant in the torrid zone, and which rage chiefly in those uncultivated countries where the hand of industry has not opened the woods, drained the marshes, and confined the rivers within a certain channel, began to spread among them. Alarmed at the violence and unusual symptoms of those maladies, they exclaimed against Columbus and his companions in the former voyage, who, by their splendid but deceitful descriptions of Hispaniola, had allured them to quit Spain for a barbarous uncultivated land, where they must either be cut off by famine, or die of unknown distempers.

---

* Oviedo, lib. II. p. 90. A.   † P. Martyr, dec. p. 32.   ‡ Herrera, dec. l. lib. ii. c. 12. Life of Columbus, c. 53.

Several of the officers and persons of note, instead of checking, joined in those seditious complaints. Father Boyl, the apostolical vicar, was one of the most turbulent and outrageous. It required all the authority and address of Columbus to re-establish subordination and tranquillity in the colony. Threats and promises were alternately employed for this purpose; but nothing contributed more to soothe the malecontents than the prospect of finding, in the mines of Cibao, such a rich store of treasure as would be a recompense for all their sufferings, and efface the memory of former disappointments.

When, by his unwearied endeavours, concord and order were so far restored that he could venture to leave the island, Columbus resolved to pursue his discoveries, that he might be able to ascertain whether those new countries with which he had opened a communication were connected with any region of the earth already known, or whether they were to be considered as a separate portion of the globe hitherto unvisited. He appointed his brother Don Diego, with the assistance of a council of officers, to govern the island in his absence; and gave the command of a body of soldiers to Don Pedro Margarita, with which he was to visit the different parts of the island, and endeavour to establish the authority of the Spaniards among the inhabitants. . Having left them very particular instructions with respect to their conduct, he weighed anchor on the 24th of April, with one ship and two small barks under his command. During a tedious voyage of full five months, he had a trial of almost all the numerous hardships to which persons of his profession are exposed, without making any discovery of importance, except the island of Jamaica. As he ranged along the southern coast of Cuba [19], he was entangled in a labyrinth formed by an incredible number of small islands, to which he gave the name of the Queen's Garden. In this unknown course, among rocks and shelves, he was retarded by contrary winds, assaulted with furious storms, and alarmed with the terrible thunder and lightning which is often almost incessant between the tropics. At length his provisions fell short; his crew, exhausted with fatigue as well as hunger, murmured and threatened, and were ready to proceed to the most desperate extremities against him. Beset with danger in such various forms, he was obliged to keep continual watch, to observe every occurrence with his own eyes, to issue every order, and to superintend the execution of it. On no occasion was the extent of his skill and experience as a navigator so much tried. To these the squadron owed its safety. But this unremitted fatigue of body, and intense application of mind, overpowering his constitution, though naturally vigorous and robust, brought on a feverish disorder, which terminated in a lethargy, that deprived him of sense and memory, and had almost proved fatal to his life.*

But, on his return to Hispaniola [Sept. 27], the sudden emotion of joy which he felt upon meeting with his brother Bartholomew at Isabella, occasioned such a flow of spirits as contributed greatly to his recovery. It was now thirteen years since the two brothers, whom similarity of talents united in close friendship, had separated from each other, and during that long period there had been no intercourse between them. Bartholomew, after finishing his negotiation in the court of England, had set out for Spain by the way of France. At Paris he received an account of the extraordinary discoveries which his brother had made in his first voyage, and that he was then preparing to embark on a second expedition. Though this naturally induced him to pursue his journey with the utmost despatch, the admiral had sailed for Hispaniola before he reached Spain. Ferdinand and Isabella received him with the respect due to the nearest kinsman of a person whose merit and services rendered him so conspicuous; and as they knew what consolation his presence would afford to his brother, they persuaded him to

* Life of Columbus, c. 54, &c. Herrera, dec. 1. lib. ii. c. 13, 14 P. Martyr, dec. 1. p. 34, &c.

take the command of three ships, which they had appointed to carry provisions to the colony at Isabella.*

He could not have arrived at any juncture when Columbus stood more in need of a friend capable of assisting him with his counsels, or of dividing with him the cares and burdens of government. For although the provisions now brought from Europe afforded a temporary relief to the Spaniards from the calamities of famine, the supply was not in such quantity as to support them long, and the island did not hitherto yield what was sufficient for their sustenance. They were threatened with another danger, still more formidable than the return of scarcity, and which demanded more immediate attention. No sooner did Columbus leave the island on his voyage of discovery, than the soldiers under Margarita, as if they had been set free from discipline and subordination, scorned all restraint. Instead of conforming to the prudent instructions of Columbus, they dispersed in straggling parties over the island, lived at discretion upon the natives, wasted their provisions, seized their women, and treated that inoffensive race with all the insolence of military oppression.†

As long as the Indians had any prospect that their sufferings might come to a period by the voluntary departure of the invaders, they submitted in silence, and dissembled their sorrow; but they now perceived that the yoke would be as permanent as it was intolerable. The Spaniards had built a town, and surrounded it with ramparts. They had erected forts in different places. They had enclosed and sown several fields. It was apparent that they came not to visit the country, but to settle in it. Though the number of those strangers was inconsiderable, the state of cultivation among these rude people was so imperfect, and in such exact proportion to their own consumption, that it was with difficulty they could afford subsistence to their new guests. Their own mode of life was so indolent and inactive, the warmth of the climate so enervating, the constitution of their bodies naturally so feeble, and so unaccustomed to the laborious exertions of industry, that they were satisfied with a proportion of food amazingly small. A handful of maize, or a little of the insipid bread made of the cassada-root, was sufficient to support men whose strength and spirits were not exhausted by any vigorous efforts either of body or mind. The Spaniards, though the most abstemious of all the European nations, appeared to them excessively voracious. One Spaniard consumed as much as several Indians. This keenness of appetite surprised them so much, and seemed to be so insatiable, that they supposed the Spaniards had left their own country because it did not produce as much as was requisite to gratify their immoderate desire of food, and had come among them in quest of nourishment.‡ Self-preservation prompted them to wish for the departure of guests who wasted so fast their slender stock of provisions. The injuries which they suffered added to their impatience for this event. They had long expected that the Spaniards would retire of their own accord. They now perceived that, in order to avert the destruction with which they were threatened, either by the slow consumption of famine, or by the violence of their oppressors, it was necessary to assume courage, to attack those formidable invaders with united force, and drive them from the settlements of which they had violently taken possession.

Such were the sentiments which universally prevailed among the Indians, when Columbus returned to Isabella. Inflamed, by the unprovoked outrages of the Spaniards, with a degree of rage of which their gentle natures, formed to suffer and submit, seemed hardly susceptible, they waited only for a signal from their leaders to fall upon the colony. Some of the caziques had already surprised and cut off several stragglers. The dread of this impending danger united the Spaniards, and re-established the

* Herrera, dec. 1, lib. ii. c. 15. † P. Martyr, dec. p. 47. ‡ Herrera, dec. 1. lib. ii. c. 17.

authority of Columbus, as they saw no prospect of safety but in committing themselves to his prudent guidance. It was now necessary to have recourse to arms, the employing of which against the Indians Columbus had hitherto avoided with the greatest solicitude. Unequal as the conflict may seem, between the naked inhabitants of the New World armed with clubs, sticks hardened in the fire, wooden swords, and arrows pointed with bones or flints, and troops accustomed to the discipline, and provided with the instruments of destruction known in the European art of war, the situation of the Spaniards was far from being exempt from danger. The vast superiority of the natives in number compensated many defects. A handful of men was about to encounter a whole nation. One adverse event, or even any unforeseen delay in determining the fate of the war, might prove fatal to the Spaniards. Conscious that success depended on the vigour and rapidity of his operations, Columbus instantly assembled his forces. They were reduced to a very small number. Diseases, engendered by the warmth and humidity of the country, or occasioned by their own licentiousness, had raged among them with much violence; experience had not yet taught them the art either of curing these, or the precautions requisite for guarding against them; two-thirds of the original adventurers were dead, and many of those who survived were incapable of service.[*] The body which took the field [March 24, 1495] consisted only of two hundred foot, twenty horse, and twenty large dogs; and how strange soever it may seem to mention the last as composing part of a military force, they were not perhaps the least formidable and destructive of the whole, when employed against naked and timid Indians. All the caziques of the island, Guacanahari excepted, who retained an inviolable attachment to the Spaniards, were in arms to oppose Columbus, with forces amounting, if we may believe the Spanish historians, to a hundred thousand men. Instead of attempting to draw the Spaniards into the fastnesses of the woods and mountains, they were so imprudent as to take their station in the Vega Real, the most open plain in the country. Columbus did not allow them time to perceive their error, or to alter their position. He attacked them during the night, when undisciplined troops are least capable of acting with union and concert, and obtained an easy and bloodless victory. The consternation with which the Indians were filled by the noise and havoc made by the fire arms, by the impetuous force of the cavalry, and the fierce onset of the dogs was so great, that they threw down their weapons, and fled without attempting resistance. Many were slain; more were taken prisoners, and reduced to servitude [20]; and so thoroughly were the rest intimidated, that from that moment they abandoned themselves to despair, relinquishing all thoughts of contending with aggressors whom they deemed invincible.

Columbus employed several months in marching through the island, and in subjecting it to the Spanish government, without meeting with any opposition. He imposed a tribute upon all the inhabitants above the age of fourteen. Each person who lived in those districts where gold was found, was obliged to pay quarterly as much gold dust as filled a hawk's bell; from those in other parts of the country, twenty-five pounds of cotton were demanded. This was the first regular taxation of the Indians, and served as a precedent for exactions still more intolerable. Such an imposition was extremely contrary to those maxims which Columbus had hitherto inculcated with respect to the mode of treating them. But intrigues were carrying on in the court of Spain at this juncture, in order to undermine his power, and discredit his operations, which constrained him to depart from his own system of administration. Several unfavourable accounts of his conduct, as well as of the countries discovered by him, had been transmitted to Spain. Margarita and Father Boyl were now at court, and in order to justify their

[*] Life of Columbus, c. 61.

own conduct, or to gratify their resentment, watched with malevolent attention for every opportunity of spreading insinuations to his detriment. Many of the courtiers viewed his growing reputation and power with envious eyes. Fonseca, archdeacon of Seville, who was intrusted with the chief direction of Indian affairs, had conceived such an unfavourable opinion of Columbus, for some reason which the contemporary writers have not mentioned, that he listened with partiality to every invective against him. It was not easy for an unfriended stranger, unpractised in courtly arts, to counteract the machinations of so many enemies. Columbus saw that there was but one method of supporting his own credit, and of silencing all his adversaries. He must produce such a quantity of gold as would not only justify what he had reported with respect to the richness of the country, but encourage Ferdinand and Isabella to persevere in prosecuting his plans. The necessity of obtaining it forced him not only to impose this heavy tax upon the Indians, but to exact payment of it with extreme rigour; and may be pleaded in excuse for his deviating on this occasion from the mildness and humanity with which he uniformly treated that unhappy people.*

The labour, attention, and foresight which the Indians were obliged to employ in procuring the tribute demanded of them, appeared the most intolerable of all evils, to men accustomed to pass their days in a careless improvident indolence. They were incapable of such a regular and persevering exertion of industry, and felt it such a grievous restraint upon their liberty, that they had recourse to an expedient for obtaining deliverance from this yoke, which demonstrates the excess of their impatience and despair. They formed a scheme of starving those oppressors whom they durst not attempt to expel; and from the opinion which they entertained with respect to the voracious appetite of the Spaniards, they concluded the execution of it to be very practicable. With this view they suspended all the operations of agriculture; they sowed no maize, they pulled up the roots of the manioc or cassada which were planted, and, retiring to the most inaccessible parts of the mountains, left the uncultivated plains to their enemies. This desperate resolution produced in some degree the effects which they expected. The Spaniards were reduced to extreme want; but they received such seasonable supplies of provisions from Europe, and found so many resources in their own ingenuity and industry, that they suffered no great loss of men. The wretched Indians were the victims of their own ill-concerted policy. A great multitude of people, shut up in the mountainous or wooded part of the country, without any food but the spontaneous productions of the earth, soon felt the utmost distresses of famine. This brought on contagious diseases; and in the course of a few months more than a third part of the inhabitants of the island perished, after experiencing misery in all its various forms.†

But while Columbus was establishing the foundations of the Spanish grandeur in the New World, his enemies laboured with unwearied assiduity to deprive him of the glory and rewards which, by his services and sufferings, he was entitled to enjoy. The hardships unavoidable in a new settlement, the calamities occasioned by an unhealthy climate, the disasters attending a voyage in unknown seas, were all represented as the effects of his restless and inconsiderate ambition. His prudent attention to preserve discipline and subordination was denominated excess of rigour; the punishments which he inflicted upon the mutinous and disorderly were imputed to cruelty. These accusations gained such credit in a jealous court, that a commissioner was appointed to repair to Hispaniola, and to inspect into the conduct of Columbus. By the recommendation of his enemies, Aguado, a groom of the bedchamber, was the person to whom

---

* Herrera, dec. 1. lib. ii. c. 17.   † Herrera, dec. 1. lib. xi. c. 18.   Life of Columbus, c. 61. Oviedo, lib. iii. p. 93.   D. Benzon Hist. Novi Orbis, lib. i. c. 9.   P. Martyr, dec. p. 48.

this important trust was committed. But in this choice they seem to have been more influenced by the obsequious attachment of the man to their interest, than by his capacity for the station. Puffed up with such sudden elevation, Aguado displayed, in the exercise of this office, all the frivolous self-importance, and acted with all the disgusting insolence which are natural to little minds, when raised to unexpected dignity, or employed in functions to which they are not equal. By listening with eagerness to every accusation against Columbus, and encouraging not only the malecontent Spaniards, but even the Indians, to produce their grievances, real or imaginary, he fomented the spirit of dissension in the island, without establishing any regulations of public utility, or that tended to redress the many wrongs, with the odium of which he wished to load the admiral's administration. As Columbus felt sensibly how humiliating his situation must be, if he should remain in the country while such a partial inspector observed his motions and controlled his jurisdiction, he took the resolution of returning to Spain, in order to lay a full account of all his transactions, particularly with respect to the points in dispute between him and his adversaries, before Ferdinand and Isabella, from whose justice and discernment he expected an equal and a favourable decision [1496]. He committed the administration of affairs, during his absence, to Don Bartholomew, his brother, with the title of Adelantado, or Lieutenant-Governor. By a choice less fortunate, and which proved the source of many calamities to the colony, he appointed Francis Roldan chief justice, with very extensive powers.*

In returning to Europe, Columbus held a course different from that which he had taken in his former voyage. He steered almost due east from Hispaniola, in the parallel of twenty-two degrees of latitude; as experience had not yet discovered the more certain and expeditious method of stretching to the north, in order to fall in with the south-west winds. By this ill advised choice, which, in the infancy of navigation between the New and Old Worlds, can hardly be imputed to the admiral as a defect in naval skill, he was exposed to infinite fatigue and danger, in a perpetual struggle with the trade winds, which blow without variation from the east between the tropics. Notwithstanding the almost insuperable difficulties of such a navigation, he persisted in his course with his usual patience and firmness, but made so little way that he was three months without seeing land. At length his provisions began to fail, the crew was reduced to the scanty allowance of six ounces of bread a day for each person. The admiral fared no better than the meanest sailor. But, even in this extreme distress, he retained the humanity which distinguishes his character, and refused to comply with the earnest solicitations of his crew, some of whom proposed to feed upon the Indian prisoners whom they were carrying over, and others insisted to throw them overboard, in order to lessen the consumption of their small stock. He represented that they were human beings, reduced by a common calamity to the same condition with themselves, and entitled to share an equal fate. His authority and remonstrances dissipated those wild ideas suggested by despair. Nor had they time to recur; as he came soon within sight of the coast of Spain, when all their fears and sufferings ended.†

Columbus appeared at court with the modest but determined confidence of a man conscious not only of integrity, but of having performed great services. Ferdinand and Isabella, ashamed of their own facility in lending too favourable an ear to frivolous or unfounded accusations, received him with such distinguished marks of respect as covered his enemies with shame. Their censures and calumnies were no more heard of at that juncture. The gold, the pearls, the cotton, and other commodities of value

* Herrera, dec. 1. lib. II. c. 18. lib. III. c. 1.　　† Herrera, dec. 1. lib. III. c. 1. Life of Columbus, c. 64.

which Columbus produced, seemed fully to refute what the malecontents had propagated with respect to the poverty of the country. By reducing the Indians to obedience, and imposing a regular tax upon them, he had secured to Spain a large accession of new subjects, and the establishment of a revenue that promised to be considerable. By the mines which he had found out and examined, a source of wealth still more copious was opened. Great and unexpected as those advantages were, Columbus represented them only as preludes to future acquisitions, and as the earnest of more important discoveries, which he still meditated, and to which those he had already made would conduct him with ease and certainty.*

The attentive consideration of all these circumstances made such an impression, not only upon Isabella, who was flattered with the idea of being the patroness of all Columbus's enterprises, but even upon Ferdinand, who having originally expressed his disapprobation of his schemes, was still apt to doubt of their success, that they resolved to supply the colony of Hispaniola with every thing which could render it a permanent establishment, and to furnish Columbus with such a fleet, that he might proceed to search for those new countries of whose existence he seemed to be confident. The measures most proper for accomplishing both these designs were concerted with Columbus. Discovery had been the sole object of the first voyage to the New World; and though, in the second, settlement had been proposed, the precautions taken for that purpose had either been insufficient, or were rendered ineffectual by the mutinous spirit of the Spaniards, and the unforeseen calamities arising from various causes. Now a plan was to be formed of a regular colony, that might serve as a model in all future establishments. Every particular was considered with attention, and the whole arranged with a scrupulous accuracy. The precise number of adventurers who should be permitted to embark was fixed. They were to be of different ranks and professions, and the proportion of each was established according to their usefulness and the wants of the colony. A suitable number of women were to be chosen to accompany these new settlers. As it was the first object to raise provisions in a country where scarcity of food had been the occasion of so much distress, a considerable body of husbandmen was to be carried over. As the Spaniards had then no conception of deriving any benefit from those productions of the New World which have since yielded such large returns of wealth to Europe, but had formed magnificent ideas, and entertained sanguine hopes with respect to the riches contained in the mines which had been discovered, a band of workmen, skilled in the various arts employed in digging and refining the precious metals, was provided. All these emigrants were to receive pay and subsistence for some years, at the public expense.†

Thus far the regulations were prudent, and well adapted to the end in view. But as it was foreseen that few would engage voluntarily to settle in a country whose noxious climate had been fatal to so many of their countrymen, Columbus proposed to transport to Hispaniola such malefactors as had been convicted of crimes which, though capital, were of a less atrocious nature; and that for the future a certain proportion of the offenders usually sent to the galleys, should be condemned to labour in the mines which were to be opened. This advice, given without due reflection, was as inconsiderately adopted. The prisons of Spain were drained, in order to collect members for the intended colony; and the judges empowered to try criminals were instructed to recruit it by their future sentences. It was not, however, with such materials that the foundations of a society, destined to be permanent, should be laid. Industry, sobriety, patience, and mutual confidence, are indispensably requisite in an infant settlement, where purity of morals must contribute more towards establishing order than the operation

---

* Life of Columbus, c. 65. Herrera, dec. 1. lib. iii. c. 1.   † Herrera, dec. 1. lib. iii. c. 2.

or authority of laws. But when such a mixture of what is corrupt is admitted into the original constitution of the political body, the vices of those unsound and incurable members will probably infect the whole, and must certainly be productive of violent and unhappy effects. This the Spaniards fatally experienced; and the other European nations having successively imitated the practice of Spain in this particular, pernicious consequences have followed in their settlements, which can be imputed to no other cause.*

Though Columbus obtained, with great facility and despatch, the royal approbation of every measure and regulation that he proposed, his endeavours to carry them into execution were so long retarded, as must have tired out the patience of any man less accustomed to encounter and to surmount difficulties. Those delays were occasioned partly by that tedious formality and spirit of procrastination, with which the Spaniards conduct business, and partly by the exhausted state of the treasury, which was drained by the expense of celebrating the marriage of Ferdinand and Isabella's only son with Margaret of Austria, and that of Joanna, their second daughter, with Philip Archduke of Austria;† but must be chiefly imputed to the malicious arts of Columbus's enemies. Astonished at the reception which he met with upon his return, and overawed by his presence, they gave way, for some time, to a tide of favour too strong for them to oppose. Their enmity, however, was too inveterate to remain long inactive. They resumed their operations; and by the assistance of Fonseca, the minister for Indian affairs, who was now promoted to the bishopric of Badajos, they threw in so many obstacles to protract the preparations for Columbus's expedition, that a year elapsed‡ before he could procure two ships to carry over a part of the supplies destined for the colony, and almost two years were spent before the small squadron was equipped, of which he himself was to take the command.§

1498.] This squadron consisted of six ships only, of no great burden, and but indifferently provided for a long or dangerous navigation. The voyage which he now meditated was in a course different from any he had under taken. As he was fully persuaded that the fertile regions of India lay to the south-west of those countries which he had discovered, he proposed, as the most certain method of finding out these, to stand directly south from the Canary or Cape de Verd islands, until he came under the equinoctial line, and then to stretch to the west before the favourable wind for such a course, which blows invariably between the tropics. With this idea he set sail [May 30], and touched first at the Canary, and then at the Cape de Verd islands [July 4]. From the former he despatched three of his ships with a supply of provisions for the colony in Hispaniola; with the other three, he continued his voyage towards the south. No remarkable occurrence happened until they arrived within five degrees of the line [July 19]. There they were becalmed, and at the same time the heat became so excessive that many of their wine casks burst, the liquors in others soured, and their provisions corrupted.|| The Spaniards, who had never ventured so far to the south, were afraid that the ships would take fire, and began to apprehend the reality of what the ancients had taught concerning the destructive qualities of that torrid region of the globe. They were relieved, in some measure, from their fears by a seasonable fall of rain. This, however, though so heavy and unintermitting that the men could hardly keep the deck, did not greatly mitigate the intenseness of the heat. The admiral, who with his usual vigilance had in person directed every operation from the beginning of the voyage, was so much exhausted by

---

* Herrera, dec. 1. lib. III. c. 2. Touron Hist. Gener. de l'Amerique, t. p. 51.   † P. Martyr, epist. 168.   ‡ Life of Columbus, c. 65.   § Herrera, dec. 1. lib. iii. c. 9. || P. Martyr, dec. p. 70.

fatigue and want of sleep, that it brought on a violent fit of the gout, accompanied with a fever. All these circumstances constrained him to yield to the importunities of his crew, and to alter his course to the northwest, in order to reach some of the Caribbee islands, where he might refit, and be supplied with provisions.

On the first of August, the man stationed in the round top surprised them with the joyful cry of *Land!* They stood toward it, and discovered a considerable island, which the admiral called Trinidad, a name it still retains. It lies on the coast of Guiana, near the mouth of the Orinoco. This, though a river only of the third or fourth magnitude in the New World, far surpasses any of the streams in our hemisphere. It rolls towards the ocean such a vast body of water, and rushes into it with such impetuous force, that when it meets the tide, which on that coast rises to an uncommon height, their collision occasions a swell and agitation of the waves no less surprising than formidable. In this conflict, the irresistible torrent of the river so far prevails, that it freshens the ocean many leagues with its flood.* Columbus, before he could conceive the danger, was entangled among those adverse currents and tempestuous waves, and it was with the utmost difficulty that he escaped through a narrow strait, which appeared so tremendous that he called it La Boca del Drago. As soon as the consternation which this occasioned permitted him to reflect upon the nature of an appearance so extraordinary, he discerned in it a source of comfort and hope. He justly concluded that such a vast body of water as this river contained, could not be supplied by any island, but must flow through a country of immense extent, and of consequence that he was now arrived at that continent which it had long been the object of his wishes to discover. Full of this idea, he stood to the west along the coast of those provinces which are now known by the names of Paria and Cumana. He landed in several places, and had some intercourse with the people, who resembled those of Hispaniola in their appearance and manner of life. They wore, as ornaments, small plates of gold, and pearls of considerable value, which they willingly exchanged for European toys. They seemed to possess a better understanding and greater courage than the inhabitants of the islands. The country produced four-footed animals of several kinds, as well as a great variety of fowls and fruits.† The admiral was so much delighted with its beauty and fertility, that, with the warm enthusiasm of a discoverer, he imagined it to be the Paradise described in Scripture, which the Almighty chose for the residence of man while he retained innocence that rendered him worthy of such a habitation.‡ [21] Thus Columbus had the glory not only of discovering to mankind the existence of a new World, but made considerable progress towards a perfect knowledge of it; and was the first man who conducted the Spaniards to that vast continent which has been the chief seat of their empire, and the source of their treasures in this quarter of the globe. The shattered condition of his ships, scarcity of provisions, his own infirmities, together with the impatience of his crew, prevented him from pursuing his discoveries any further, and made it necessary to bear away for Hispaniola. In his way thither he discovered the islands of Cubagua and Margarita, which afterwards became remarkable for their pearl-fishery. When he arrived at Hispaniola [Aug. 30], he was wasted to an extreme degree, with fatigue and sickness; but found the affairs of the colony in such a situation as afforded him no prospect of enjoying that repose of which he stood so much in need.

Many revolutions had happened in that country during his absence. His brother, the adelantado, in consequence of an advice which the admiral gave before his departure, had removed the colony from Isabella to a more

---

* Gumilla Hist. de l'Orenoque, tom. I. p. 14. † Herrera, dec. 1. lib. III. c. 9—11. Life of Columbus, c. 66—73. ‡ Herrera, dec. 1. lib. III. c. 12. Gomara, c. 84.

commodious station, on the opposite side of the island, and laid the foundation of St. Domingo,* which was long the most considerable European town in the New World, and the seat of the supreme courts in the Spanish dominions there. As soon as the Spaniards were established in this new settlement, the adelantado, that they might neither languish in inactivity, nor have leisure to form new cabals, marched into those parts of the island which his brother had not yet visited or reduced to obedience. As the people were unable to resist, they submitted every where to the tribute which he imposed. But they soon found the burden to be so intolerable that, overawed as they were by the superior power of their oppressors, they took arms against them. Those insurrections, however, were not formidable. A conflict with timid and naked Indians was neither dangerous nor of doubtful issue.

But while the adelantado was employed against them in the field, a mutiny of an aspect far more alarming broke out among the Spaniards. The ringleader of it was Francis Roldan, whom Columbus had placed in a station which required him to be the guardian of order and tranquillity in the colony. A turbulent and inconsiderate ambition precipitated him into this desperate measure, so unbecoming his rank. The arguments which he employed to seduce his countrymen were frivolous and ill founded. He accused Columbus and his two brothers of arrogance and severity; he pretended that they aimed at establishing an independent dominion in the country; he taxed them with an intention of cutting off part of the Spaniards by hunger and fatigue, that they might more easily reduce the remainder to subjection; he represented it as unworthy of Castilians, to remain the tame and passive slaves of these Genoese adventurers. As men have always a propensity to impute the hardships of which they feel the pressure to the misconduct of their rulers; as every nation views with a jealous eye the power and exaltation of foreigners, Roldan's insinuations made a deep impression on his countrymen. His character and rank added weight to them. A considerable number of the Spaniards made choice of him as their leader; and, taking arms against the adelantado and his brother, seized the king's magazine of provisions, and endeavoured to surprise the fort at St. Domingo. This was preserved by the vigilance and courage of Don Diego Columbus. The mutineers were obliged to retire to the province of Xaragua, where they continued not only to disclaim the adelantado's authority themselves, but excited the Indians to throw off the yoke.†

Such was the distracted state of the colony when Columbus landed at St. Domingo. He was astonished to find that the three ships which he had despatched from the Canaries were not yet arrived. By the unskilfulness of the pilots, and the violence of currents, they had been carried a hundred and sixty miles to the west of St. Domingo, and forced to take shelter in a harbour of the province of Xaragua, where Roldan and his seditious followers were cantoned. Roldan carefully concealed from the commanders of the ships his insurrection against the adelantado, and, employing his utmost address to gain their confidence, persuaded them to set on shore a considerable part of the new settlers whom they brought over, that they might proceed by land to St. Domingo. It required but few arguments to prevail with those men to espouse his cause. They were the refuse of the jails of Spain, to whom idleness, licentiousness, and deeds of violence were familiar; and they returned eagerly to a course of life nearly resembling that to which they had been accustomed. The commanders of the ships perceiving, when it was too late, their imprudence in disembarking so many of their men, stood away for St. Domingo, and got safe into the port a few

---

* P. Martyr, dec. p. 56.   † Herrera, dec. 1. lib. iii. c. 5—8. Life of Columbus, c. 74—72. Gomara, c. 23. P. Martyr, p. 78.

days after the admiral; but their stock of provisions was so wasted during a voyage of such long continuance that they brought little relief to the colony.*

By this junction with a band of such bold and desperate associates, Roldan became extremely formidable, and no less extravagant in his demands. Columbus, though filled with resentment at his ingratitude, and highly exasperated by the insolence of his followers, made no haste to take the field. He trembled at the thoughts of kindling the flames of a civil war, in which, whatever party prevailed, the power and strength of both must be so much wasted as might encourage the common enemy to unite and complete their destruction. At the same time, he observed, that the prejudices and passions which incited the rebels to take arms, had so far infected those who still adhered to him, that many of them were adverse, and all cold to the service. From such sentiments, with respect to the public interest, as well as from this view of his own situation, he chose to negotiate rather than to fight. By a seasonable proclamation, offering free pardon to such as should merit it by returning to their duty, he made impression upon some of the malecontents. By engaging to grant such as should desire it the liberty of returning to Spain, he allured all those unfortunate adventurers, who, from sickness and disappointment, were disgusted with the country. By promising to re-establish Roldan in his former office, he soothed his pride; and, by complying with most of his demands in behalf of his followers, he satisfied their avarice. Thus, gradually and without bloodshed, but after many tedious negotiations, he dissolved this dangerous combination, which threatened the colony with ruin; and restored the appearance of order, regular government, and tranquillity.†

In consequence of this agreement with the mutineers, lands were allotted them in different parts of the island, and the Indians settled in each district were appointed to cultivate a certain portion of ground for the use of those new masters [1499]. The performance of this work was substituted in place of the tribute formerly imposed; and how necessary soever such a regulation might be in a sickly and feeble colony, it introduced among the Spaniards the *Repartimientos*, or distributions of Indians established by them in all their settlements, which brought numberless calamities upon that unhappy people, and subjected them to the most grievous oppression.‡ This was not the only bad effect of the insurrection in Hispaniola; it prevented Columbus from prosecuting his discoveries on the continent, as self-preservation obliged him to keep near his person his brother the adelantado, and the sailors whom he intended to have employed in that service. As soon as his affairs would permit, he sent some of his ships to Spain with a journal of the voyage which he had made, a description of the new countries which he had discovered, a chart of the coast along which he had sailed, and specimens of the gold, the pearls, and other curious or valuable productions which he had acquired by trafficking with the natives. At the same time he transmitted an account of the insurrection in Hispaniola; he accused the mutineers not only of having thrown the colony into such violent convulsions as threatened its dissolution, but of having obstructed every attempt towards discovery and improvement, by their unprovoked rebellion against their superiors, and proposed several regulations for the better government of the island, as well as the extinction of that mutinous spirit, which, though suppressed at present, might soon burst out with additional rage. Roldan and his associates did not neglect to convey to Spain, by the same ships, an apology for their own conduct, together with their recriminations upon the admiral and his brothers. Unfortunately for the honour of

---

* Herrera, dec. 1. lib. iii. c. 12. Life of Columbus, c. 78, 79.   † Herrera, dec. 1. lib. iii. c. 13, 14. Life of Columbus, c. 80. &c.   ‡ Herrera, dec. 1. lib. iii. c. 14, &c.

Spain and the happiness of Columbus, the latter gained most credit in the court of Ferdinand and Isabella, and produced unexpected effects.*

But, previous to the relating of these, it is proper to take a view of some events, which merit attention, both on account of their own importance, and their connection with the history of the New World. While Columbus was engaged in his successive voyages to the west, the spirit of discovery did not languish in Portugal, the kingdom where it first acquired vigour, and became enterprising. Self-condemnation and neglect were not the only sentiments to which the success of Columbus, and reflection upon their own imprudence in rejecting his proposals, gave rise among the Portuguese. They excited a general emulation to surpass his performances, and an ardent desire to make some reparation to their country for their own error. With this view, Emanuel, who inherited the enterprising genius of his predecessors, persisted in their grand scheme of opening a passage to the East Indies by the Cape of Good Hope, and soon after his accession to the throne equipped a squadron for that important voyage. He gave the command of it to Vasco de Gama, a man of noble birth, possessed of virtue, prudence, and courage, equal to the station. The squadron, like all those fitted out for discovery in the infancy of navigation, was extremely feeble, consisting only of three vessels, of neither burden nor force adequate to the service. As the Europeans were at that time little acquainted with the course of the trade-winds and periodical monsoons, which render navigation in the Atlantic ocean as well as in the sea that separates Africa from India, at some seasons easy, and at others not only dangerous but almost impracticable, the time chosen for Gama's departure was the most improper during the whole year. He set sail from Lisbon on the ninth of July, [1497], and, standing towards the south, had to struggle for four months with contrary winds before he could reach the Cape of Good Hope. Here their violence began to abate [Nov. 20]; and during an interval of calm weather, Gama doubled that formidable promontory, which had so long been the boundary of navigation, and directed his course towards the north-east, along the African coast. He touched at several ports; and after various adventures, which the Portuguese historians relate with high but just encomiums upon his conduct and intrepidity, he came to anchor before the city of Melinda. Throughout all the vast countries which extend along the coast of Africa, from the river Senegal to the confines of Zanguebar, the Portuguese had found a race of men rude and uncultivated, strangers to letters, to arts, and commerce, and differing from the inhabitants of Europe no less in their features and complexion than in their manners and institutions. As they advanced from this, they observed, to their inexpressible joy, that the human form gradually altered and improved; the Asiatic features began to predominate, marks of civilization appeared, letters were known, the Mahometan religion was established, and a commerce far from being inconsiderable was carried on. At that time several vessels from India were in the port of Melinda. Gama now pursued his voyage with almost absolute certainty of success, and, under the conduct of a Mahometan pilot, arrived at Calecut, upon the coast of Malabar, on the twenty-second of May, one thousand four hundred and ninety-eight. What he beheld of the wealth, the populousness, the cultivation, the industry, and arts of this highly civilized country, far surpassed any idea that he had formed, from the imperfect accounts which the Europeans had hitherto received of it. But as he possessed neither sufficient force to attempt a settlement, nor proper commodities with which he could carry on commerce of any consequence, he hastened back to Portugal, with an account of his success in performing a voyage, the longest, as well as most difficult, that had ever been made since the first invention of navigation. He landed at Lisbon on the four-

---

* Herrera, dec. 1. lib. iii. c. 14. Benzon. Hist. Nov. Orb. lib. i. c. 2.

teenth of September, one thousand four hundred and ninety-nine, two years two months and five days from the time he left that port.*

Thus, during the course of the fifteenth century, mankind made greater progress in exploring the state of the habitable globe, than in all the ages which had elapsed previous to that period. The spirit of discovery, feeble at first and cautious, moved within a very narrow sphere, and made its efforts with hesitation and timidity. Encouraged by success, it became adventurous, and boldly extended its operations. In the course of its progression, it continued to acquire vigour, and advanced at length with a rapidity and force which burst through all the limits within which ignorance and fear had hitherto circumscribed the activity of the human race. Almost fifty years were employed by the Portuguese in creeping along the coast of Africa from Cape Non to Cape de Verd, the latter of which lies only twelve degrees to the south of the former. In less than thirty years they ventured beyond the equinoctial line into another hemisphere, and penetrated to the southern extremity of Africa, at the distance of forty-nine degrees from Cape de Verd. During the last seven years of the century, a New World was discovered in the west, not inferior in extent to all the parts of the earth with which mankind were at that time acquainted. In the East, unknown seas and countries were found out, and a communication, long desired, but hitherto concealed, was opened between Europe and the opulent regions of India. In comparison with events so wonderful and unexpected, all that had hitherto been deemed great or splendid faded away and disappeared. Vast objects now presented themselves. The human mind, roused and interested by the prospect, engaged with ardour in pursuit of them, and exerted its active powers in a new direction.

This spirit of enterprise, though but newly awakened in Spain, began soon to operate extensively. All the attempts towards discovery made in that kingdom had hitherto been carried on by Columbus alone, and at the expense of the Sovereign. But now private adventurers, allured by the magnificent descriptions he gave of the regions which he had visited, as well as by the specimens of their wealth which he produced, offered to fit out squadrons at their own risk, and to go in quest of new countries. The Spanish court, whose scanty revenues were exhausted by the charge of its expeditions to the New World, which, though they opened alluring prospects of future benefit, yielded a very sparing return of present profit, was extremely willing to devolve the burden of discovery upon its subjects. It seized with joy an opportunity of rendering the avarice, the ingenuity, and efforts of projectors instrumental in promoting designs of certain advantage to the public, though of doubtful success with respect to themselves. One of the first propositions of this kind was made by Alonzo de Ojeda, a gallant and active officer, who had accompanied Columbus in his second voyage. His rank and character procured him such credit with the merchants of Seville, that they undertook to equip four ships, provided he could obtain the royal license, authorizing the voyage. The powerful patronage of the Bishop of Badajos easily secured success in a suit so agreeable to the court. Without consulting Columbus, or regarding the rights and jurisdiction which he had acquired by the capitulation in one thousand four hundred and ninety-two, Ojeda was permitted to set out for the New World. In order to direct his course, the bishop communicated to him the admiral's journal of his last voyage, and his charts of the countries which he had discovered. Ojeda struck out into no new path of navigation, but adhering servilely to the route which Columbus had taken, arrived on the coast of Paria [May]. He traded with the natives, and, standing to the west, proceeded as far as Cape de Vela, and ranged along a considerable extent of coast beyond that on which Columbus

* Ramusio, vol. 1. 113. D.

had touched. Having thus ascertained the opinion of Columbus, that this country was a part of the continent, Ojeda returned by way of Hispaniola to Spain [October], with some reputation as a discoverer, but with little benefit to those who had raised the funds for the expedition.*

Amerigo Vespucci, a Florentine gentleman, accompanied Ojeda in this voyage. In what station he served is uncertain; but as he was an experienced sailor, and eminently skilled in all the sciences subservient to navigation, he seems to have acquired such authority among his companions, that they willingly allowed him to have a chief share in directing their operations during the voyage. Soon after his return, he transmitted an account of his adventures and discoveries to one of his countrymen; and labouring with the vanity of a traveller to magnify his own exploits, he had the address and confidence to frame his narrative so as to make it appear that he had the glory of having first discovered the continent in the New World. Amerigo's account was drawn up not only with art, but with some elegance. It contained an amusing history of his voyage, and judicious observations upon the natural productions, the inhabitants, and the customs of the countries which he had visited. As it was the first description of any part of the New World that was published, a performance so well calculated to gratify the passion of mankind for what is new and marvellous, circulated rapidly, and was read with admiration. The country of which Amerigo was supposed to be the discoverer, came gradually to be called by his name. The caprice of mankind, often as unaccountable as unjust, has perpetuated this error. By the universal consent of nations, America is the name bestowed on this new quarter of the globe. The bold pretensions of a fortunate impostor, have robbed the discoverer of the New World of a distinction which belonged to him. The name of Amerigo has supplanted that of Columbus; and mankind may regret an act of injustice, which, having received the sanction of time, it is now too late to redress. [22]

During the same year, another voyage of discovery was undertaken. Columbus not only introduced the spirit of naval enterprise into Spain, but all the first adventurers who distinguished themselves in this new career were formed by his instructions, and acquired in his voyages the skill and information which qualified them to imitate his example. Alonso Nigno, who had served under the admiral in his last expedition, fitted out a single ship, in conjunction with Christopher Guerra, a merchant of Seville, and sailed to the coast of Paria. This voyage seems to have been conducted with greater attention to private emolument than to any general or national object. Nigno and Guerra made no discoveries of any importance; but they brought home such a return of gold and pearls as inflamed their countrymen with the desire of engaging in similar adventures.†

Soon after [Jan. 13, 1500], Vincent Yanez Pinzon, one of the admiral's companions in his first voyage, sailed from Palos with four ships. He stood boldly towards the south, and was the first Spaniard who ventured across the equinoctial line; but he seems to have landed on no part of the coast beyond the mouth of the Maragnon, or river of the Amazons. All these navigators adopted the erroneous theory of Columbus, and believed that the countries which they had discovered were part of the vast continent of India.‡

During the last year of the fifteenth century, that fertile district of America, on the confines of which Pinzon had stopped short, was more fully discovered. The successful voyage of Gama to the East Indies having encouraged the King of Portugal to fit out a fleet so powerful as not only to carry on trade but to attempt conquest, he gave the command of it to Pedro Alvarez Cabral. In order to avoid the coast of Africa, where he was

---
* Herrera, dec. 1. lib. iv. c. 1, 2, 3.   † P. Martyr, dec. p. 87. Herrera, dec. 1. lib. iv. c. 5
‡ Herrera, dec. 1. lib. iv. c. 6. P. Martyr, dec. p. 96.

certain of meeting with variable breezes or frequent calms, which might retard his voyage, Cabral stood out to sea, and kept so far to the west, that, to his surprise, he found himself upon the shore of an unknown country, in the tenth degree beyond the line. He imagined at first that it was some island in the Atlantic ocean, hitherto unobserved; but, proceeding along its coast for several days, he was led gradually to believe, that a country so extensive formed a part of some great continent. This latter opinion was well founded. The country with which he fell in belongs to that province in South America now known by the name of Brasil. He landed; and having formed a very high idea of the fertility of the soil, and agreeableness of the climate, he took possession of it for the crown of Portugal, and despatched a ship to Lisbon with an account of this event, which appeared to be no less important than it was unexpected.* Columbus's discovery of the New World was the effort of an active genius enlightened by science, guided by experience, and acting upon a regular plan executed with no less courage than perseverance. But from this adventure of the Portuguese, it appears that chance might have accomplished that great design which it is now the pride of human reason to have formed and perfected. If the sagacity of Columbus had not conducted mankind to America, Cabral, by a fortunate accident, might have led them, a few years later, to the knowledge of that extensive continent.†

While the Spaniards and Portuguese, by those successive voyages, were daily acquiring more enlarged ideas of the extent and opulence of that quarter of the globe which Columbus had made known to them, he himself, far from enjoying the tranquillity and honours with which his services should have been recompensed, was struggling with every distress in which the envy and malevolence of the people under his command, or the ingratitude of the court which he served, could involve him. Though the pacification with Roldan broke the union and weakened the force of the mutineers, it did not extirpate the seeds of discord out of the island. Several of the malecontents continued in arms, refusing to submit to the admiral. He and his brothers were obliged to take the field alternately, in order to check their incursions, or to punish their crimes. The perpetual occupation and disquiet which this created, prevented him from giving due attention to the dangerous machinations of his enemies in the court of Spain. A good number of such as were most dissatisfied with his administration had embraced the opportunity of returning to Europe with the ships which he despatched from St. Domingo. The final disappointment of all their hopes inflamed the rage of these unfortunate adventurers against Columbus to the utmost pitch. Their poverty and distress, by exciting compassion, rendered their accusations credible, and their complaints interesting. They teased Ferdinand and Isabella incessantly with memorials, containing the detail of their own grievances, and the articles of their charge against Columbus. Whenever either the king or queen appeared in public, they surrounded them in a tumultuary manner, insisting with importunate clamours for the payment of the arrears due to them, and demanding vengeance upon the author of their sufferings. They insulted the admiral's sons wherever they met them, reproaching them as the offspring of the projector, whose fatal curiosity had discovered those pernicious regions which drained Spain of its wealth, and would prove the grave of its people. These avowed endeavours of the malecontents from America to ruin Columbus, were seconded by the secret but more dangerous insinuations of that party among the courtiers, which had always thwarted his schemes, and envied his success and credit.‡

Ferdinand was disposed to listen, not only with a willing but with a partial ear, to these accusations. Notwithstanding the flattering accounts which

* Herrera, dec. 1. lib. iv. c. 7.   † Ibid. dec. 1. lib. vii. c. 5.   ‡ Life of Columbus, c. 85.

Columbus had given of the riches of America, the remittances from it had hitherto been so scanty that they fell far short of defraying the expense of the armaments fitted out. The glory of the discovery, together with the prospect of remote commercial advantages, was all that Spain had yet received in return for the efforts which she had made. But time had already diminished the first sensations of joy which the discovery of a New World occasioned, and fame alone was not an object to satisfy the cold interested mind of Ferdinand. The nature of commerce was then so little understood that, where immediate gain was not acquired, the hope of distant benefit, or of slow and moderate returns, was totally disregarded. Ferdinand considered Spain, on this account, as having lost by the enterprise of Columbus, and imputed it to his misconduct and incapacity for government, that a country abounding in gold had yielded nothing of value to its conquerors. Even Isabella, who from the favourable opinion which she entertained of Columbus had uniformly protected him, was shaken at length by the number and boldness of his accusers, and began to suspect that a disaffection so general must have been occasioned by real grievances which called for redress. The Bishop of Badajos, with his usual animosity against Columbus, encouraged these suspicions, and confirmed them.

As soon as the queen began to give way to the torrent of calumny, a resolution fatal to Columbus was taken. Francis de Bovadilla, a knight of Calatrava, was appointed to repair to Hispaniola, with full powers to inquire into the conduct of Columbus, and if he should find the charge of maladministration proved, to supersede him, and assume the government of the island. It was impossible to escape condemnation, when this preposterous commission made it the interest of the judge to pronounce the person whom he was sent to try, guilty. Though Columbus had now composed all the dissensions in the island; though he had brought both Spaniards and Indians to submit peaceably to his government; though he had made such effectual provision for working the mines, and cultivating the country, as would have secured a considerable revenue to the king, as well as large profits to individuals; Bovadilla, without deigning to attend to the nature or merit of those services, discovered from the moment that he landed in Hispaniola, a determined purpose of treating him as a criminal. He took possession of the admiral's house in St. Domingo, from which its master happened at that time to be absent, and seized his effects, as if his guilt had been already fully proved; he rendered himself master of the fort and of the King's stores by violence; he required all persons to acknowledge him as supreme governor; he set at liberty the prisoners confined by the admiral, and summoned him to appear before his tribunal, in order to answer for his conduct; transmitting to him, together with the summons, a copy of the royal mandate, by which Columbus was enjoined to yield implicit obedience to his commands.

Columbus, though deeply affected with the ingratitude and injustice of Ferdinand and Isabella, did not hesitate a moment about his own conduct. He submitted to the will of his sovereigns with a respectful silence, and repaired directly [October] to the court of that violent and partial judge whom they had authorized to try him. Bovadilla, without admitting him into his presence, ordered him instantly to be arrested, to be loaded with chains, and hurried on board a ship. Even under this humiliating reverse of fortune, the firmness of mind which distinguishes the character of Columbus did not forsake him. Conscious of his own integrity, and solacing himself with reflecting upon the great things which he had achieved, he endured this insult offered to his character, not only with composure but with dignity. Nor had he the consolation of sympathy to mitigate his sufferings. Bovadilla had already rendered himself so extremely popular, by granting various immunities to the colony, by liberal donations of Indians to all who applied for them, and by relaxing the reins of discipline and government, that the Spaniards, who were mostly adventurers, whom their indigence or crimes had compelled to abandon their native country, expressed the most indecent satisfaction with the disgrace and imprisonment of Columbus. They flattered themselves that now they should enjoy an uncontrolled liberty more suitable to their disposition and former habits of life. Among persons thus prepared to censure the proceedings, and to asperse the character of Columbus, Bovadilla collected materials for a charge against him. All accusations, the most improbable as well as inconsistent, were received. No informer, however infamous, was rejected. The result of this inquest, no less indecent than partial, he transmitted to Spain. At the same time he ordered Columbus, with his two brothers, to be carried thither in fetters; and, adding cruelty to insult, he confined them in different ships; and excluded them from the comfort of that friendly intercourse which might have soothed their common distress. But while the Spaniards in Hispaniola viewed the arbitrary and insolent proceedings of Bovadilla with a general approbation, which reflects dishonour upon their name and country, one man still retained a proper sense of the great actions which Columbus had performed, and was touched with the sentiments of veneration and pity due to his rank, his age, and his merit. Alonzo de Valejo, the captain of the vessel on board which the admiral was confined, as soon as he was clear of the island, approached his prisoner with great respect, and offered to release him from the fetters with which he was unjustly loaded. "No," replied Columbus with a generous indignation, "I wear these irons in consequence of an order from my sovereigns. They shall find me as obedient to this as to their other injunctions. By their command I have been confined, and their command alone shall set me at liberty."*

Nov. 23.] Fortunately, the voyage to Spain was extremely short. As soon as Ferdinand and Isabella were informed that Columbus was brought home a prisoner and in chains, they perceived at once what universal astonishment this event must occasion, and what an impression to their disadvantage it must make. All Europe, they foresaw, would be filled with indignation at this ungenerous requital of a man who had performed actions worthy of the highest recompense, and would exclaim against the injustice of the nation, to which he had been such an eminent benefactor, as well as against the ingratitude of the princes whose reign he had rendered illustrious. Ashamed of their own conduct, and eager not only to make some reparation for this injury, but to efface the stain which it might fix upon their character, they instantly issued orders to set Columbus at liberty [Dec. 17], invited him to court, and remitted money to enable him to appear there in a manner suitable to his rank. When he entered the royal presence, Columbus threw himself at the feet of his sovereigns. He remained for some time silent; the various passions which agitated his mind suppressing his power of utterance. At length he recovered himself, and vindicated his conduct in a long discourse, producing the most satisfying proofs of his own integrity as well as good intention, and evidence, no less clear, of the malevolence of his enemies, who, not satisfied with having ruined his fortune, laboured to deprive him of what alone was now left, his honour and his fame. Ferdinand received him with decent civility, and Isabella with tenderness and respect. They both expressed their sorrow for what had happened, disavowed their knowledge of it, and joined in promising him protection and future favour. But though they instantly degraded Bovadilla, in order to remove from themselves any suspicion of having authorized his violent proceedings, they did not restore to Columbus his jurisdiction and privileges as viceroy of those countries which he had discovered. Though willing to appear the avengers of Columbus's wrongs, that illiberal jealousy which

* Life of Columbus, c. 86. Herrera, dec. 1. lib. iv. c. 8—11. Gomara Hist. c. 23. Oviedo, lib. iii. c. 6.

prompted them to invest Bovadilla with such authority, as put it in his power to treat the admiral with indignity, still subsisted. They were afraid to trust a man to whom they had been so highly indebted; and retaining him at court under various pretexts, they appointed Nicholas de Ovando, a knight of the military order of Alcantara, governor of Hispaniola.*

Columbus was deeply affected with this new injury, which came from hands that seemed to be employed in making reparation for his past sufferings. The sensibility with which great minds feel every thing that implies any suspicion of their integrity, or that wears the aspect of an affront, is exquisite. Columbus had experienced both from the Spaniards, and their ungenerous conduct exasperated him to such a degree that he could no longer conceal the sentiments which it excited. Wherever he went he carried about with him, as a memorial of their ingratitude, those fetters with which he had been loaded. They were constantly hung up in his chamber, and he gave orders, that when he died they should be buried in his grave.†

1501.] Meanwhile the spirit of discovery, notwithstanding the severe check which it had received by the ungenerous treatment of the man who first excited it in Spain, continued active and vigorous. [January] Roderigo de Bastidas, a person of distinction, fitted out two ships in copartnery with John de la Cosa, who having served under the admiral in two of his voyages was deemed the most skilful pilot in Spain. They steered directly towards the continent, arrived on the coast of Paria, and, proceeding to the west, discovered all the coast of the province now known by the name of Tierra Firme, from Cape de Vela to the Gulf of Darien. Not long after Ojeda, with his former associate Amerigo Vespucci, set out upon a second voyage, and, being unacquainted with the destination of Bastidas, held the same course and touched at the same places. The voyage of Bastidas was prosperous and lucrative, that of Ojeda unfortunate. But both tended to increase the ardour of discovery; for in proportion as the Spaniards acquired a more extensive knowledge of the American continent, their idea of its opulence and fertility increased.‡

Before these adventurers returned from their voyages, a fleet was equipped, at the public expense, for carrying over Ovando, the new governor, to Hispaniola. His presence there was extremely requisite, in order to stop the inconsiderate career of Bovadilla, whose imprudent administration threatened the settlement with ruin. Conscious of the violence and iniquity of his proceedings against Columbus, he continued to make it his sole object to gain the favour and support of his countrymen, by accommodating himself to their passions and prejudices. With this view, he established regulations in every point the reverse of those which Columbus deemed essential to the prosperity of the colony. Instead of the severe discipline, necessary in order to habituate the dissolute and corrupted members of which the society was composed, to the restraints of law and subordination, he suffered them to enjoy such uncontrolled license as encouraged the wildest excesses. Instead of protecting the Indians, he gave a legal sanction to the oppression of that unhappy people. He took the exact number of such as survived their past calamities, divided them into distinct classes, distributed them in property among his adherents, and reduced all the people of the island to a state of complete servitude. As the avarice of the Spaniards was too rapacious and impatient to try any method of acquiring wealth but that of searching for gold, this servitude became as grievous as it was unjust. The Indians were driven in crowds to the mountains, and compelled to work in the mines, by masters who imposed their tasks without mercy or

* Herrera, dec. 1. lib. iv. c. 10—12. Life of Columbus, c. 87 † Life of Columbus, c. 86. p. 577. ‡ Herrera, dec. 1. lib. iv. c.

discretion. Labour so disproportioned to their strength and former habits of life, wasted that feeble race of men with such rapid consumption, as must have soon terminated in the utter extinction of the ancient inhabitants of the country.*

The necessity of applying a speedy remedy to those disorders hastened Ovando's departure. He had the command of the most respectable armament hitherto fitted out for the New World. It consisted of thirty-two ships, on board of which two thousand five hundred persons embarked with an intention of settling in the country. [1502.] Upon the arrival of the new governor with this powerful reinforcement to the colony, Bovadilla resigned his charge, and was commanded to return instantly to Spain, in order to answer for his conduct. Roldan and the other ringleaders of the mutineers, who had been most active in opposing Columbus, were required to leave the island at the same time. A proclamation was issued, declaring the natives to be free subjects of Spain, of whom no service was to be expected contrary to their own inclination, and without paying them an adequate price for their labour. With respect to the Spaniards themselves, various regulations were made, tending to suppress the licentious spirit which had been so fatal to the colony, and to establish that reverence for law and order on which society is founded, and to which it is indebted for its increase and stability. In order to limit the exorbitant gain which private persons were supposed to make by working the mines, an ordinance was published, directing all the gold to be brought to a public smelting-house, and declaring one half of it to be the property of the crown.†

While these steps were taking for securing the tranquillity and welfare of the colony which Columbus had planted, he himself was engaged in the unpleasant employment of soliciting the favour of an ungrateful court, and notwithstanding all his merit and services, he solicited in vain. He demanded, in terms of the original capitulation in one thousand four hundred and ninety-two, to be reinstated in his office of viceroy over the countries which he had discovered. By a strange fatality, the circumstance which he urged in support of his claim, determined a jealous monarch to reject it. The greatness of his discoveries, and the prospect of their increasing value, made Ferdinand consider the concessions in the capitulation as extravagant and impolitic. He was afraid of intrusting a subject with the exercise of a jurisdiction that now appeared to be so extremely extensive, and might grow to be no less formidable. He inspired Isabella with the same suspicions; and under various pretexts, equally frivolous and unjust, they eluded all Columbus's requisitions to perform that which a solemn compact bound them to accomplish. After attending the Court of Spain for near two years, as an humble suitor, he found it impossible to remove Ferdinand's prejudices and apprehensions; and perceived at length that he laboured in vain, when he urged a claim of justice or merit with an interested and unfeeling prince.

But even this ungenerous return did not discourage him from pursuing the great object which first called forth his inventive genius, and excited him to attempt discovery. To open a new passage to the East Indies was his original and favourite scheme. This still engrossed his thoughts; and either from his own observations in his voyage to Paria, or from some obscure hint of the natives, or from the accounts given by Bastidas and de la Cosa of their expedition, he conceived an opinion that beyond the continent of America there was a sea which extended to the East Indies, and hoped to find some strait or narrow neck of land, by which a communication might be opened with it and the part of the ocean already known. By a very fortunate conjecture, he supposed this strait or isthmus to be

* Herrera, dec. 1. lib. iv. c. 11, &c. Oviedo Hist. lib. iii. c. 6. p. 97. Benzon Hist. lib. l. c. 12. p. 51. † Solorzano Politica Indiana, lib. l. c. 12. Herrera, dec. 1. lib. iv. c. 12.

situated near the Gulf of Darien. Full of this idea, though he was now of an advanced age, worn out with fatigue, and broken with infirmities, he offered, with the alacrity of a youthful adventurer, to undertake a voyage which would ascertain this important point, and perfect the grand scheme which from the beginning he proposed to accomplish. Several circumstances concurred in disposing Ferdinand and Isabella to lend a favourable ear to this proposal. They were glad to have the pretext of any honourable employment for removing from court a man with whose demands they deemed it impolitic to comply, and whose services it was indecent to neglect. Though unwilling to reward Columbus, they were not insensible of his merit, and from their experience of his skill and conduct, had reason to give credit to his conjectures, and to confide in his success. To these considerations, a third must be added of still more powerful influence. About this time the Portuguese fleet, under Cabral, arrived from the Indies; and, by the richness of its cargo, gave the people of Europe a more perfect idea than they had hitherto been able to form, of the opulence and fertility of the East. The Portuguese had been more fortunate in their discoveries than the Spaniards. They had opened a communication with countries where industry, arts, and elegance flourished; and where commerce had been longer established, and carried to greater extent than in any region of the earth. Their first voyages thither yielded immediate as well as vast returns of profit, in commodities extremely precious and in great request. Lisbon became immediately the seat of commerce and wealth; while Spain had only the expectation of remote benefit, and of future gain, from the western world. Nothing, then, could be more acceptable to the Spaniards than Columbus's offer to conduct them to the East, by a route which he expected to be shorter, as well as less dangerous than that which the Portuguese had taken. Even Ferdinand was roused by such a prospect, and warmly approved of the undertaking.

But interesting as the object of this voyage was to the nation, Columbus could procure only four small barks, the largest of which did not exceed seventy tons in burden, for performing it. Accustomed to brave danger, and to engage in arduous undertakings with inadequate force, he did not hesitate to accept the command of this pitiful squadron. His brother Bartholomew, and his second son Ferdinand, the historian of his actions, accompanied him. He sailed from Cadiz on the ninth of May, and touched, as usual, at the Canary islands; from thence he proposed to have stood directly for the continent; but his largest vessel was so clumsy and unfit for service, as constrained him to bear away for Hispaniola, in hopes of exchanging her for some ship of the fleet that had carried out Ovando. When he arrived at St. Domingo [June 29], he found eighteen of these ships ready loaded, and on the point of departing for Spain. Columbus immediately acquainted the governor with the destination of his voyage, and the accident which had obliged him to alter his route. He requested permission to enter the harbour, not only that he might negotiate the exchange of his ship, but that he might take shelter during a violent hurricane, of which he discerned the approach from various prognostics which his experience and sagacity had taught him to observe. On that account, he advised him likewise to put off for some days the departure of tne fleet bound for Spain. But Ovando refused his request, and despised his counsel. Under circumstances in which humanity would have afforded refuge to a stranger, Columbus was denied admittance into a country of which he had discovered the existence and acquired the possession. His salutary warning, which merited the greatest attention, was regarded as the dream of a visionary prophet, who arrogantly pretended to predict an event beyond the reach of human foresight. The fleet set sail for Spain. Next night the hurricane came on, with dreadful impetuosity. Columbus, aware of the danger, took precautions against it, and saved his little squadron.

The fleet destined for Spain met with the fate which the rashness and obstinacy of its commanders deserved. Of eighteen ships two or three only escaped. In this general wreck perished Bovadilla, Roldan, and the greater part of those who had been the most active in persecuting Columbus, and oppressing the Indians. Together with themselves, all the wealth which they had acquired by their injustice and cruelty was swallowed up. It exceeded in value two hundred thousand *pesos;* an immense sum at that period, and sufficient not only to have screened them from any severe scrutiny into their conduct, but to have secured them a gracious reception in the Spanish court. Among the ships that escaped, one had on board all the effects of Columbus which had been recovered from the ruins of his fortune. Historians, struck with the exact discrimination of characters, as well as the just distribution of rewards and punishments, conspicuous in those events, universally attribute them to an immediate interposition of Divine Providence, in order to avenge the wrongs of an injured man, and to punish the oppressors of an innocent people. Upon the ignorant and superstitious race of men, who were witnesses of this occurrence, it made a different impression. From an opinion which vulgar admiration is apt to entertain with respect to persons who have distinguished themselves by their sagacity and inventions, they believed Columbus to be possessed of supernatural powers, and imagined that he had conjured up this dreadful storm by magical art and incantations in order to be avenged of his enemies.*

Columbus soon left Hispaniola [July 14], where he met with such an inhospitable reception, and stood towards the continent. After a tedious and dangerous voyage, he discovered Guanaia, an island not far distant from the coast of Honduras. There he had an interview with some inhabitants of the continent, who arrived in a large canoe. They appeared to be a people more civilized, and who had made greater progress in the knowledge of useful arts than any whom he had hitherto discovered. In return to the inquiries which the Spaniards made, with their usual eagerness, concerning the places where the Indians got the gold which they wore by way of ornament, they directed them to countries situated to the west, in which gold was found in such profusion that it was applied to the most common uses. Instead of steering in quest of a country so inviting, which would have conducted him along the coast of Yucatan to the rich Empire of Mexico, Columbus was so bent upon his favourite scheme of finding out the strait which he supposed to communicate with the Indian ocean, that he bore away to the east towards the gulf of Darien. In this navigation he discovered all the coast of the continent, from Cape Gracias a Dios to a harbour which, on account of its beauty and security, he called Porto Bello. He searched in vain for the imaginary strait, through which he expected to make his way into an unknown sea; and though he went on shore several times, and advanced into the country, he did not penetrate so far as to cross the narrow isthmus which separates the Gulf of Mexico from the great Southern ocean. He was so much delighted, however, with the fertility of the country, and conceived such an idea of its wealth from the specimens of gold produced by the natives, that he resolved to leave a small colony upon the river Belen, in the province of Veragua, under the command of his brother, and to return himself to Spain [1503], in order to procure what was requisite for rendering the establishment permanent. But the ungovernable spirit of the people under his command, deprived Columbus of the glory of planting the first colony on the continent of America. Their insolence and rapaciousness provoked the natives to take arms; and as these were a more hardy and warlike race of men than the inhabitants of the islands, they cut off part of the Spaniards, and obliged the rest to abandon a station which was found to be untenable.†

---

* Oviedo, lib. III. c. 7, 9. Herrera, dec. 1. lib. v. c. 1, 2. Life of Columbus, c. 88. † Herrera, dec. 1. lib. v. c. 5, &c. Life of Columbus, c. 89, &c. Oviedo, lib. III. c. 9.

This repulse, the first that the Spaniards met with from any of the American nations, was not the only misfortune that befell Columbus: it was followed by a succession of all the disasters to which navigation is exposed. Furious hurricanes, with violent storms of thunder and lightning, threatened his leaky vessels with destruction; while his discontented crew, exhausted with fatigue, and destitute of provisions, was unwilling or unable to execute his commands. One of his ships perished; he was obliged to abandon another, as unfit for service; and with the two which remained, he quitted that part of the continent, which, in his anguish, he named the Coast of Vexation,* and bore away for Hispaniola. New distresses awaited him in this voyage. He was driven back by a violent tempest from the coast of Cuba, his ships fell foul of one another, and were so much shattered by the shock that with the utmost difficulty they reached Jamaica [June 24], where he was obliged to run them aground, to prevent them from sinking. The measure of his calamities seemed now to be full. He was cast ashore upon an island at a considerable distance from the only settlement of the Spaniards in America. His ships were ruined beyond the possibility of being repaired. To convey an account of his situation to Hispaniola appeared impracticable; and without this it was in vain to expect relief. His genius, fertile in resources, and most vigorous in those perilous extremities when feeble minds abandon themselves to despair, discovered the only expedient which afforded any prospect of deliverance. He had recourse to the hospitable kindness of the natives, who, considering the Spaniards as beings of a superior nature, were eager, on every occasion, to minister to their wants. From them he obtained two of their canoes, each formed out of the trunk of a single tree hollowed with fire, and so misshapen and awkward as hardly to merit the name of boats. In these, which were fit only for creeping along the coast, or crossing from one side of a bay to another, Mendez, a Spaniard, and Fieschi, a Genoese, two gentlemen particularly attached to Columbus, gallantly offered to set out for Hispaniola, upon a voyage of above thirty leagues.† This they accomplished in ten days, after surmounting incredible dangers, and enduring such fatigues that several of the Indians who accompanied them sunk under it, and died. The attention paid to them by the governor of Hispaniola was neither such as their courage merited, nor the distress of the persons from whom they came required. Ovando, from a mean jealousy of Columbus, was afraid of allowing him to set foot in the island under his government. This ungenerous passion hardened his heart against every tender sentiment which reflection upon the services and misfortunes of that great man, or compassion for his own fellow-citizens, involved in the same calamities, must have excited. Mendez and Fieschi spent eight months in soliciting relief for their commander and associates, without any prospect of obtaining it.

During this period, various passions agitated the mind of Columbus and his companions in adversity. At first, the expectation of speedy deliverance, from the success of Mendez and Fieschi's voyage, cheered the spirits of the most desponding. After some time the most timorous began to suspect that they had miscarried in their daring attempt [1504]. At length, even the most sanguine concluded that they had perished. The ray of hope which had broke in upon them, made their condition appear now more dismal. Despair, heightened by disappointment, settled in every breast. Their last resource had failed, and nothing remained but the prospect of ending their miserable days among naked savages, far from their country and their friends. The seamen, in a transport of rage, rose in open mutiny, threatened the life of Columbus, whom they reproached as the author of all their calamities, seized ten canoes, which they had purchased from the Indians, and, despising his remonstrances and entreaties, made off with

---

* La Costa de los Contrastes.   † Oviedo, lib. III. c. 9.

them to a distant part of the island. At the same time the natives murmured at the long residence of the Spaniards in their country. As their industry was not greater than that of their neighbours in Hispaniola, like them they found the burden of supporting so many strangers to be altogether intolerable. They began to bring in provisions with reluctance, they furnished them with a sparing hand, and threatened to withdraw those supplies altogether. Such a resolution must have been quickly fatal to the Spaniards. Their safety depended upon the good will of the Indians; and unless they could revive the admiration and reverence with which that simple people had at first beheld them, destruction was unavoidable. Though the licentious proceedings of the mutineers had in a great measure effaced those impressions which had been so favourable to the Spaniards, the ingenuity of Columbus suggested a happy artifice, that not only restored but heightened the high opinion which the Indians had originally entertained of them. By his skill in astronomy, he knew that there was shortly to be a total eclipse of the moon. He assembled all the principal persons of the district around him on the day before it happened, and, after reproaching them for their fickleness in withdrawing their affection and assistance from men whom they had lately revered, he told them, that the Spaniards were servants of the Great Spirit who dwells in heaven, who made and governs the world; that he, offended at their refusing to support men who were the objects of his peculiar favour, was preparing to punish this crime with exemplary severity, and that very night the moon should withhold her light, and appear of a bloody hue, as a sign of the divine wrath and an emblem of the vengeance ready to fall upon them. To this marvellous prediction some of them listened with the careless indifference peculiar to the people of America; others, with the credulous astonishment natural to barbarians. But when the moon began gradually to be darkened, and at length appeared of a red colour, all were struck with terror. They ran with consternation to their houses, and returning instantly to Columbus loaded with provisions, threw them at his feet, conjuring him to intercede with the Great Spirit to avert the destruction with which they were threatened. Columbus, seeming to be moved by their entreaties, promised to comply with their desire. The eclipse went off, the moon recovered its splendour, and from that day the Spaniards were not only furnished profusely with provisions, but the natives, with superstitious attention, avoided every thing that could give them offence.*

During those transactions, the mutineers had made repeated attempts to pass over to Hispaniola in the canoes which they had seized. But, from their own misconduct or the violence of the winds and currents, their efforts were all unsuccessful. Enraged at this disappointment, they marched towards that part of the island where Columbus remained, threatening him with new insults and danger. While they were advancing, an event happened, more cruel and afflicting than any calamity which he dreaded from them. The governor of Hispaniola, whose mind was still filled with some dark suspicions of Columbus, sent a small bark to Jamaica, not to deliver his distressed countrymen, but to spy out their condition. Lest the sympathy of those whom he employed should afford them relief, contrary to his intention, he gave the command of this vessel to Escobar, an inveterate enemy of Columbus, who, adhering to his instructions with malignant accuracy, cast anchor at some distance from the island, approached the shore in a small boat, observed the wretched plight of the Spaniards, delivered a letter of empty compliments to the admiral, received his answer, and departed. When the Spaniards first descried the vessel standing towards the island, every heart exulted, as if the long expected hour of their deliverance had at length arrived; but when it disappeared so suddenly, they sunk into the

* Life of Columbus, c. 103.   Herrera, dec. 1. lib. vi. c. 5, 6.   Benzon, Hist. lib. i. c. 14.

deepest dejection, and all their hopes died away. Columbus alone, though he felt most sensibly this wanton insult which Ovando added to his past neglect, retained such composure of mind as to be able to cheer his followers. He assured them that Mendez and Fieschi had reached Hispaniola in safety; that they would speedily procure ships to carry them off; but, as Escobar's vessel could not take them all on board, that he had refused to go with her, because he was determined never to abandon the faithful companions of his distress. Soothed with the expectation of speedy deliverance, and delighted with his apparent generosity in attending more to their preservation than to his own safety, their spirits revived, and he regained their confidence.*

Without this confidence he could not have resisted the mutineers, who were now at hand. All his endeavours to reclaim those desperate men had no effect but to increase their frenzy. Their demands became every day more extravagant, and their intentions more violent and bloody. The common safety rendered it necessary to oppose them with open force. Columbus, who had been long afflicted with the gout, could not take the field. His brother, the adelantado, marched against them [May 20]. They quickly met. The mutineers rejected with scorn terms of accommodation, which were once more offered them, and rushed on boldly to the attack. They fell not upon an enemy unprepared to receive them. In the first shock, several of their most daring leaders were slain. The adelantado, whose strength was equal to his courage, closed with their captain, wounded, disarmed, and took him prisoner.† At sight of this, the rest fled with a dastardly fear suitable to their former insolence. Soon after, they submitted in a body to Columbus, and bound themselves by the most solemn oaths to obey all his commands. Hardly was tranquillity re-established when the ships appeared, whose arrival Columbus had promised with great address, though he could foresee it with little certainty. With transports of joy the Spaniards quitted an island in which the unfeeling jealousy of Ovando had suffered them to languish above a year, exposed to misery in all its various forms.

When they arrived at St. Domingo [Aug. 13], the governor, with the mean artifice of a vulgar mind, that labours to atone for insolence by servility, fawned on the man whom he envied, and had attempted to ruin. He received Columbus with the most studied respect, lodged him in his own house, and distinguished him with every mark of honour. But amidst those overacted demonstrations of regard, he could not conceal the hatred and malignity latent in his heart. He set at liberty the captain of the mutineers, whom Columbus had brought over in chains to be tried for his crimes; and threatened such as had adhered to the admiral with proceeding to a judicial inquiry into their conduct. Columbus submitted in silence to what he could not redress; but discovered an extreme impatience to quit a country which was under the jurisdiction of a man who had treated him, on every occasion, with inhumanity and injustice. His preparations were soon finished, and he set sail for Spain with two ships [Sept. 12]. Disasters similar to those which had accompanied him through life continued to pursue him to the end of his career. One of his vessels being disabled, was soon forced back to St. Domingo; the other, shattered by violent storms, sailed several hundred leagues with jury-masts, and reached with difficulty the port of St. Lucar [December].‡

There he received the account of an event the most fatal that could have befallen him, and which completed his misfortunes. This was the death of his patroness Queen Isabella [Nov. 9], in whose justice, humanity, and favour he confided as his last resource. None now remained to redress his wrongs, or to reward him for his services and sufferings, but Ferdinand, who

---

* Life of Columbus, c. 104. † Herrera, dec. 1. lib. vi. c. 17. ‡ Ibid. c. 107. Herrera, dec 1. lib. vi. c. 11. ‡ Ibid. c. 108. Herrera, dec. 1. lib. vi. c. 12.

had so long opposed and so often injured him. To solicit a prince thus prejudiced against him was an occupation no less irksome than hopeless. In this, however, was Columbus doomed to employ the close of his days. As soon as his health was in some degree re-established, he repaired to court; and though he was received there with civility barely decent, he plied Ferdinand with petition after petition, demanding the punishment of his oppressors, and the restitution of all the privileges bestowed upon him by the capitulation of one thousand four hundred and ninety-two. Ferdinand amused him with fair words and unmeaning promises. Instead of granting his claims, he proposed expedients in order to elude them, and spun out the affair with such apparent art, as plainly discovered his intention that it should never be terminated. The declining health of Columbus flattered Ferdinand with the hopes of being soon delivered from an importunate suitor, and encouraged him to persevere in this illiberal plan. Nor was he deceived in his expectations. Disgusted with the ingratitude of a monarch whom he had served with such fidelity and success, exhausted with the fatigues and hardships which* he had endured, and broken with the infirmities which these had brought upon him, Columbus ended his life at Valladolid on the twentieth of May, one thousand five hundred and six in the fifty-ninth year of his age. He died with a composure of mind suitable to the magnanimity which distinguished his character, and with sentiments of piety becoming that supreme respect for religion which he manifested in every occurrence of his life.*

BOOK III.

While Columbus was employed in his last voyage, several events worthy of notice happened in Hispaniola. The colony there, the parent and nurse of all the subsequent establishments of Spain in the New World, gradually acquired the form of a regular and prosperous society. The humane solicitude of Isabella to protect the Indians from oppression, and particularly the proclamation by which the Spaniards were prohibited to compel them to work, retarded, it is true, for some time the progress of improvement. The natives, who considered exemption from toil as extreme felicity, scorned every allurement and reward by which they were invited to labour. The Spaniards had not a sufficient number of hands either to work the mines or to cultivate the soil. Several of the first colonists who had been accustomed to the service of the Indians, quitted the island, when deprived of those instruments, without which they knew not how to carry on any operation. Many of the new settlers who came over with Ovando, were seized with the distempers peculiar to the climate, and in a short space above a thousand of them died. At the same time, the exacting one half of the product of the mines, as the royal share, was found to be a demand so exorbitant that no adventurers would engage to work them upon such terms. In order to save the colony from ruin, Ovando ventured to relax the rigour of the royal edicts [1505]. He made a new distribution of the Indians among the Spaniards, and compelled them to labour, for a stated time, in digging the mines, or in cultivating the ground; but in order to screen himself from the imputation of having subjected them again to servitude, he enjoined their masters to pay them a certain sum, as the price of their work. He

* Life of Columbus, c. 108. Herrera, dec. 1. lib. vi. c. 13, 14, 15.

reduced the royal share of the gold found in the mines from the half to the third part, and soon after lowered it to a fifth, at which it long remained. Notwithstanding Isabella's tender concern for the good treatment of the Indians, and Ferdinand's eagerness to improve the Royal revenue, Ovando persuaded the court to approve of both these regulations.*

But the Indians, after enjoying respite from oppression, though during a short interval, now felt the yoke of bondage to be so galling that they made several attempts to vindicate their own liberty. This the Spaniards considered as rebellion, and took arms in order to reduce them to subjection. When war is carried on between nations whose state of improvement is in any degree similar, the means of defence bear some proportion to those employed in the attack; and in this equal contest such efforts must be made, such talents are displayed, and such passions roused, as exhibit mankind to view in a situation no less striking than interesting. It is one of the noblest functions of history to observe and to delineate men at a juncture when their minds are most violently agitated, and all their powers and passions are called forth. Hence the operations of war, and the struggles between contending states, have been deemed by historians, ancient as well as modern, a capital and important article in the annals of human actions. But in a contest between naked savages, and one of the most warlike of the European nations, where science, courage, and discipline on one side, were opposed by ignorance, timidity, and disorder on the other, a particular detail of events would be as unpleasant as uninstructive. If the simplicity and innocence of the Indians had inspired the Spaniards with humanity, had softened the pride of superiority into compassion, and had induced them to improve the inhabitants of the New World. instead of oppressing them, some sudden acts of violence, like the too rigorous chastisements of impatient instructors, might have been related without horror. But, unfortunately, this consciousness of superiority operated in a different manner. The Spaniards were advanced so far beyond the natives of America in improvement of every kind, that they viewed them with contempt. They conceived the Americans to be animals of an inferior nature, who were not entitled to the rights and privileges of men. In peace they subjected them to servitude. In war they paid no regard to those laws which, by a tacit convention between contending nations, regulate hostility, and set some bounds to its rage. They considered them not as men fighting in defence of their liberty, but as slaves who had revolted against their masters. Their caziques, when taken, were condemned, like the leaders of banditti, to the most cruel and ignominious punishments; and all their subjects, without regarding the distinction of ranks established among them, were reduced to the same state of abject slavery. With such a spirit and sentiments were hostilities carried on against the cazique of Higuey, a province at the eastern extremity of the island. This war was occasioned by the perfidy of the Spaniards, in violating a treaty which they had made with the natives, and it was terminated by hanging up the cazique, who defended his people with bravery so far superior to that of his countrymen, as entitled him to a better fate.†

The conduct of Ovando, in another part of the island, was still more treacherous and cruel. The province anciently named Xaragua, which extends from the fertile plain where Leogane is now situated to the western extremity of the island, was subject to a female cazique, named Anacoana, highly respected by the natives. She, from that partial fondness with which the women of America were attached to the Europeans (the cause of which shall be afterwards explained), had always courted the friendship of the Spaniards, and loaded them with benefits. But some of the adherents of Roldan having settled in her country, were so much exasperated

* Herrera, dec. 1. lib. v. c. 3 † Ibid dec. 1. lib. vl. c. 9, 10.

at her endeavouring to restrain their excesses, that they accused her of having formed a plan to throw off the yoke, and to exterminate the Spaniards. Ovando, though he knew well what little credit was due to such profligate men, marched, without further inquiry, towards Xaragua, with three hundred foot and seventy horsemen. To prevent the Indians from taking alarm at this hostile appearance, he gave out that his sole intention was to visit Anacoana, to whom his countrymen had been so much indebted, in the most respectful manner, and to regulate with her the mode of levying the tribute payable to the king of Spain. Anacoana, in order to receive this illustrious guest with due honour, assembled the principal men in her dominions, to the number of three hundred; and advancing at the head of these, accompanied by a great crowd of persons of inferior rank, she welcomed Ovando with songs and dances, according to the mode of the country, and conducted him to the place of her residence. There he was feasted for some days, with all the kindness of simple hospitality, and amused with the games and spectacles usual among the Americans upon occasions of mirth and festivity. But amidst the security which this inspired, Ovando was meditating the destruction of his unsuspicious entertainer and her subjects; and the mean perfidy with which he executed this scheme, equalled his barbarity in forming it. Under colour of exhibiting to the Indians the parade of a European tournament, he advanced with his troops, in battle array, towards the house in which Anacoana and the chiefs who attended her were assembled. The infantry took possession of all the avenues which led to the village. The horsemen encompassed the house. These movements were the object of admiration, without any mixture of fear, until, upon a signal which had been concerted, the Spaniards suddenly drew their swords, and rushed upon the Indians, defenceless, and astonished at an act of treachery, which exceeded the conception of undesigning men. In a moment Anacoana was secured. All her attendants were seized and bound. Fire was set to the house; and without examination or conviction, all these unhappy persons, the most illustrious in their own country, were consumed in the flames. Anacoana was reserved for a more ignominious fate. She was carried in chains to St. Domingo, and, after the formality of a trial before Spanish judges, she was condemned, upon the evidence of those very men who had betrayed her, to be publicly hanged.*

Overawed and humbled by this atrocious treatment of their princes and nobles, who were objects of their highest reverence, the people in all the provinces of Hispaniola submitted, without further resistance, to the Spanish yoke. Upon the death of Isabella all the regulations tending to mitigate the rigour of their servitude were forgotten. The small gratuity paid to them as the price of their labour was withdrawn, and at the same time the tasks imposed upon them were increased [1506]. Ovando, without any restraint, distributed Indians among his friends in the island. Ferdinand, to whom the Queen had left by will one half of the revenue arising from the settlements in the New World, conferred grants of a similar nature upon his courtiers, as the least expensive mode of rewarding their services. They farmed out the Indians, of whom they were rendered proprietors, to their countrymen settled in Hispaniola; and that wretched people, being compelled to labour in order to satisfy the rapacity of both, the exactions of their oppressors no longer knew any bounds. But, barbarous as their policy was, and fatal to the inhabitants of Hispaniola, it produced, for some time, very considerable effects. By calling forth the force of a whole nation, and exerting itself in one direction, the working of the mines was carried on with amazing rapidity and success. During several years the gold brought into the royal smelting houses in Hispaniola amounted annually to four hundred

---

* Oviedo, lib. III. c. 12. Herrera, dec. 1. lib. vi. c. 4. Relacion de Destruyc. de las Indias por Bart. de las Casas, p. 8.

and sixty thousand pesos, above a hundred thousand pounds sterling; which, if we attend to the great change in the value of money since the beginning of the sixteenth century to the present times, must appear a considerable sum. Vast fortunes were created, of a sudden, by some. Others dissipated, in ostentatious profusion, what they acquired with facility. Dazzled by both, new adventurers crowded to America, with the most eager impatience, to share in those treasures which had enriched their countrymen; and, notwithstanding the mortality occasioned by the unhealthiness of the climate, the colony continued to increase.*

Ovando governed the Spaniards with wisdom and justice not inferior to the rigour with which he treated the Indians. He established equal laws; and, by executing them with impartiality, accustomed the people of the colony to reverence them. He founded several new towns in different parts of the island, and allured inhabitants to them by the concession of various immunities. He endeavoured to turn the attention of the Spaniards to some branch of industry more useful than that of searching for gold in the mines. Some slips of the sugarcane having been brought from the Canary islands by way of experiment, they were found to thrive with such increase in the rich soil and warm climate to which they were transplanted, that the cultivation of them soon became an object of commerce. Extensive plantations were begun; sugarworks, which the Spaniards called *ingenios*, from the various machinery employed in them, were erected, and in a few years the manufacture of this commodity was the great occupation of the inhabitants of Hispaniola, and the most considerable source of their wealth.†

The prudent endeavours of Ovando, to promote the welfare of the colony, were powerfully seconded by Ferdinand. The large remittances which he received from the New World opened his eyes, at length, with respect to the importance of those discoveries, which he had hitherto affected to undervalue. Fortune, and his own address, having now extricated him out of those difficulties in which he had been involved by the death of his Queen [1507], and by his disputes with his son-in-law about the government of her dominions,‡ he had full leisure to turn his attention to the affairs of America. To his provident sagacity Spain is indebted for many of those regulations which gradually formed that system of profound but jealous policy, by which she governs her dominions in the New World. He erected a court distinguished by the title of *Casa de Contratacion*, or Board of Trade, composed of persons eminent for rank and abilities, to whom he committed the administration of American affairs. This board assembled regularly in Seville, and was invested with a distinct and extensive jurisdiction. He gave a regular form to ecclesiastical government in America, by nominating archbishops, bishops, deans, together with clergymen of subordinate ranks, to take charge of the Spaniards established there, as well as of the natives who should embrace the Christian faith, but notwithstanding the obsequious devotion of the Spanish court to the papal see, such was Ferdinand's solicitude to prevent any foreign power from claiming jurisdiction, or acquiring influence, in his new dominions, that he reserved to the crown of Spain the sole right of patronage to the benefices in America, and stipulated that no papal bull or mandate should be promulgated there until it was previously examined and approved of by his council. With the same spirit of jealousy, he prohibited any goods to be exported to America, or any person to settle there without a special license from that council.§

But, notwithstanding this attention to the police and welfare of the colony, a calamity impended which threatened its dissolution. The original inha-

---

* Herrera, dec. 1. lib. vi. c. 18, &c.   † Oviedo, lib. iv. c. 8.   ‡ History of the Reign of Charles V. p. 6, &c.   § Herrera, dec. 1. lib. vi. c. 19, 20.

bitants, on whose labour the Spaniards in Hispaniola depended for their prosperity, and even their existence, wasted so fast that the extinction of the whole race, seemed to be inevitable. When Columbus discovered Hispaniola, the number of its inhabitants was computed to be at least a million.* They were now reduced to sixty thousand in the space of fifteen years. This consumption of the human species, no less amazing than rapid, was the effect of several concurring causes. The natives of the American islands were of a more feeble constitution than the inhabitants of the other hemisphere. They could neither perform the same work nor endure the same fatigue with men whose organs were of a more vigorous conformation. The listless indolence in which they delighted to pass their days, as it was the effect of their debility, contributed likewise to increase it, and rendered them from habit, as well as constitution, incapable of hard labour. The food on which they subsisted afforded little nourishment, and they were accustomed to take it in small quantities, not sufficient to invigorate a languid frame, and render it equal to the efforts of active industry. The Spaniards, without attending to those peculiarities in the constitution of the Americans, imposed tasks upon them which, though not greater than Europeans might have performed with ease, were so disproportioned to their strength, that many sunk under the fatigue, and ended their wretched days. Others, prompted by impatience and despair, cut short their own lives with a violent hand. Famine, brought on by compelling such numbers to abandon the culture of their lands, in order to labour in the mines, proved fatal to many. Diseases of various kinds, some occasioned by the hardships to which they were exposed, and others by their intercourse with the Europeans, who communicated to them some of their peculiar maladies, completed the desolation of the island. The Spaniards, being thus deprived of the instruments which they were accustomed to employ, found it impossible to extend their improvements, or even to carry on the works which they had already begun [1508]. In order to provide an immediate remedy for an evil so alarming, Ovando proposed to transport the inhabitants of the Lucayo islands to Hispaniola, under pretence that they might be civilized with more facility, and instructed to greater advantage in the Christian religion, if they were united to the Spanish colony, and placed under the immediate inspection of the missionaries settled there. Ferdinand, deceived by this artifice, or willing to connive at an act of violence which policy represented as necessary, gave his assent to the proposal. Several vessels were fitted out for the Lucayos, the commanders of which informed the natives, with whose language they were now well acquainted, that they came from a delicious country, in which the departed ancestors of the Indians resided, by whom they were sent to invite their descendants to resort thither, to partake of the bliss enjoyed there by happy spirits. That simple people listened with wonder and credulity; and, fond of visiting their relations and friends in that happy region, followed the Spaniards with eagerness. By this artifice above forty thousand were decoyed into Hispaniola, to share in the sufferings which were the lot of the inhabitants of that island, and to mingle their groans and tears with those of that wretched race of men.†

The Spaniards had, for some time, carried on their operations in the mines of Hispaniola with such ardour as well as success, that these seemed to have engrossed their whole attention. The spirit of discovery languished; and, since the last voyage of Columbus, no enterprise of any moment had been undertaken. But as the decrease of the Indians rendered it impossible to acquire wealth in that island with the same rapidity as formerly, this urged some of the more adventurous Spaniards to search for new countries, where their avarice might be gratified with more facility.

* Herrera, dec. 1. lib. x, c. 12.   † Ibid. lib. vii. c. 3.   Oviedo, lib. iii. c. 6.   Gomara Hist. c. 41.

Juan Ponce de Leon, who commanded under Ovando in the eastern district of Hispaniola, passed over to the island of St. Juan de Puerto Rico, which Columbus had discovered in his second voyage, and penetrated into the interior part of the country. As he found the soil to be fertile, and expected, from some symptoms, as well as from the information of the inhabitants, to discover mines of gold in the mountains, Ovando permitted him to attempt making a settlement in the island. This was easily effected by an officer eminent for conduct no less than for courage. In a few years Puerto Rico was subjected to the Spanish government, the natives were reduced to servitude; and being treated with the same inconsiderate rigour as their neighbours in Hispaniola, the race of original inhabitants, worn out with fatigue and sufferings, was soon exterminated.*

About the same time Juan Diaz de Solis, in conjunction with Vincent Yanez Pinzon, one of Columbus's original companions, made a voyage to the continent. They held the same course which Columbus had taken as far as the island of Guanaios; but, standing from thence to the west, they discovered a new and extensive province, afterwards known by the name of Yucatan, and proceeded a considerable way along the coast of that country.† Though nothing memorable occurred in this voyage, it deserves notice, because it led to discoveries of greater importance. For the same reason the voyage of Sebastian de Ocampo must be mentioned. By the command of Ovando he sailed round Cuba, and first discovered with certainty, that this country, which Columbus once supposed to be a part of the continent, was a large island.‡

This voyage round Cuba was one of the last occurrences under the administration of Ovando. Ever since the death of Columbus, his son, Don Diego, had been employed in soliciting Ferdinand to grant him the offices of viceroy and admiral in the New World, together with all the other immunities and profits which descended to him by inheritance, in consequence of the original capitulation with his father. But if these dignities and revenues appeared so considerable to Ferdinand, that, at the expense of being deemed unjust as well as ungrateful, he had wrested them from Columbus, it was not surprising that he should be unwilling to confer them on his son. Accordingly Don Diego wasted two years in incessant but fruitless importunity. Weary of this, he endeavoured at length to obtain by a legal sentence what he could not procure from the favour of an interested monarch. He commenced a suit against Ferdinand before the council which managed Indian affairs; and that court, with integrity which reflects honour upon its proceedings, decided against the king, and sustained Don Diego's claim of the viceroyalty, together with all the other privileges stipulated in the capitulation. Even after this decree Ferdinand's repugnance to put a subject in possession of such extensive rights might have thrown in new obstacles, if Don Diego had not taken a step which interested very powerful persons in the success of his claims. The sentence of the council of the Indies gave him a title to a rank so elevated, and a fortune so opulent, that he found no difficulty in concluding a marriage with Donna Maria, daughter of Don Ferdinand de Toledo, great commendator of Leon, and brother of the duke of Alva, a nobleman of the first rank, and nearly related to the king. The duke and his family espoused so warmly the cause of their new ally, that Ferdinand could not resist their solicitations [1509]. He recalled Ovando, and appointed Don Diego his successor, though even in conferring this favour he could not conceal his jealousy; for he allowed him to assume only the title of governor, not that of viceroy, which had been adjudged to belong to him.§

Don Diego quickly repaired to Hispaniola, attended by his brother, his uncles,

---

* Herrera, dec. 1. lib. vii. c. 1—4.   Gomara Hist. c. 44.   Relacion de B. de las Casas, p. 10.
† Ibid. dec. 1. lib. vi. c. 17.   ‡ Ibid. lib. vii. c. 1.   § Ibid. dec. 1. lib. vii. c. 4, &c.

his wife, whom the courtesy of the Spaniards honoured with the title of vice-queen, and a numerous retinue of persons of both sexes born of good families. He lived with a splendour and magnificence hitherto unknown in the New World; and the family of Columbus seemed now to enjoy the honours and rewards due to his inventive genius, of which he himself had been cruelly defrauded. The colony itself acquired new lustre by the accession of so many inhabitants, of a different rank and character from most of those who had hitherto migrated to America, and many of the most illustrious families in the Spanish settlements are descended from the persons who at that time accompanied Don Diego Columbus.*

No benefits accrued to the unhappy natives from this change of governors. Don Diego was not only authorized by a royal edict to continue the *repartimientos*, or distribution of Indians, but the particular number which he might grant to every person, according to his rank in the colony, was specified. He availed himself of that permission; and soon after he landed at St. Domingo, he divided such Indians as were still unappropriated, among his relations and attendants.†

The next care of the new governor was to comply with an instruction which he received from the king, about settling a colony in Cubagua, a small island which Columbus had discovered in his third voyage. Though this barren spot hardly yielded subsistence to its wretched inhabitants, such quantities of those oysters which produce pearls were found on its coast, that it did not long escape the inquisitive avarice of the Spaniards, and became a place of considerable resort. Large fortunes were acquired by the fishery of pearls, which was carried on with extraordinary ardour. The Indians, especially those from the Lucayo islands, were compelled to dive for them; and this dangerous and unhealthy employment was an additional calamity which contributed not a little to the extinction of that devoted race.‡

About this period, Juan Diaz de Solis and Pinzon set out, in conjunction, upon a second voyage. They stood directly south, towards the equinoctial line, which Pinzon had formerly crossed, and advanced as far as the fortieth degree of southern latitude. They were astonished to find that the continent of America stretched on their right hand through all this vast extent of ocean. They landed in different places, to take possession in name of their sovereign; but though the country appeared to be extremely fertile and inviting, their force was so small, having been fitted out rather for discovery than making settlements, that they left no colony behind them. Their voyage served, however, to give the Spaniards more exalted and adequate ideas with respect to the dimensions of this new quarter of the globe.§

Though it was about ten years since Columbus had discovered the main land of America, the Spaniards had hitherto made no settlement in any part of it. What had been so long neglected was now seriously attempted, and with considerable vigour; though the plan for this purpose was neither formed by the crown, nor executed at the expense of the nation, but carried on by the enterprising spirit of private adventurers. The scheme took its rise from Alonso de Ojeda, who had already made two voyages as a discoverer, by which he acquired considerable reputation, but no wealth. But his character for intrepidity and conduct easily procured him associates, who advanced the money requisite to defray the charges of the expedition. About the same time, Diego de Nicuessa, who had acquired a large fortune in Hispaniola, formed a similar design. Ferdinand encouraged both; and though he refused to advance the smallest sum, he was extremely liberal of titles and patents. He erected two governments on the continent, one extending from Cape de Vela to the Gulf of Darien, and the other from that to Cape Gracias a Dios. The former was given to Ojeda, the latter to Nicuessa.

* Oviedo, lib. iii. c. 1. † Recopilacion de Leyes, lib. vi. tit. 8. l. 1, 2. Herrera, dec. 1. lib. vii. c. 10. ‡ Herrera, dec. 1. lib. vii. c. 9. Gomara Hist. c. 78. § Ibid. dec. 1. lib. vii. c. 9.

Ojeda fitted out a ship and two brigantines, with three hundred men, Nicuessa, six vessels, with seven hundred and eighty men. They sailed about the same time from St. Domingo for their respective governments. In order to give their title to those countries some appearance of validity, several of the most eminent divines and lawyers in Spain were employed to prescribe the mode in which they should take possession of them.* There is not in the history of mankind any thing more singular or extravagant than the form which they devised for this purpose. They instructed those invaders, as soon as they landed on the continent, to declare to the natives the principal articles of the Christian faith; to acquaint them in particular, with the supreme jurisdiction of the Pope over all the kingdoms of the earth; to inform them of the grant which this holy pontiff had made of their country to the king of Spain; to require them to embrace the doctrines of that religion which the Spaniards made known to them; and to submit to the sovereign whose authority they proclaimed. If the natives refused to comply with this requisition, the terms of which must have been utterly incomprehensible to uninstructed Indians, then Ojeda and Nicuessa were authorized to attack them with fire and sword; to reduce them, their wives and children, to a state of servitude; and to compel them by force to recognise the jurisdiction of the church, and the authority of the monarch, to which they would not voluntarily subject themselves [23].

As the inhabitants of the continent could not at once yield assent to doctrines too refined for their uncultivated understandings, and explained to them by interpreters imperfectly acquainted with their language; as they did not conceive how a foreign priest, of whom they had never heard, could have any right to dispose of their country, or how an unknown prince should claim jurisdiction over them as his subjects; they fiercely opposed the new invaders of their territories. Ojeda and Nicuessa endeavoured to effect by force what they could not accomplish by persuasion. The contemporary writers enter into a very minute detail in relating their transactions; but as they made no discovery of importance, nor established any permanent settlement, their adventures are not entitled to any considerable place in the general history of a period where romantic valour, struggling with incredible hardships, distinguishes every effort of the Spanish arms. They found the natives in those countries of which they went to assume the government, to be of a character very different from that of their countrymen in the islands. They were free and warlike. Their arrows were dipped in a poison so noxious, that every wound was followed with certain death. In one encounter they slew above seventy of Ojeda's followers, and the Spaniards, for the first time, were taught to dread the inhabitants of the New World. Nicuessa was opposed by people equally resolute in defence of their possessions. Nothing could soften their ferocity. Though the Spaniards employed every art to soothe them, and to gain their confidence, they refused to hold any intercourse, or to exchange any friendly office, with men whose residence among them they considered as fatal to their liberty and independence [1510]. This implacable enmity of the natives, though it rendered an attempt to establish a settlement in their country extremely difficult as well as dangerous, might have been surmounted at length by the perseverance of the Spaniards, by the superiority of their arms, and their skill in the art of war. But every disaster which can be accumulated upon the unfortunate combined to complete their ruin. The loss of their ships by various accidents upon an unknown coast, the diseases peculiar to a climate the most noxious in all America, the want of provisions unavoidable in a country imperfectly cultivated, dissension among themselves, and the incessant hostilities of the natives, involved them in a succession of calamities, the bare recital of which strikes

* Herrera, dec. 1. lib. vii. c. 15.

one with horror. Though they received two considerable reinforcements from Hispaniola, the greater part of those who had engaged in this unhappy expedition perished, in less than a year, in the most extreme misery. A few who survived settled as a feeble colony at Santa Maria el Antigua, on the Gulf of Darien, under the command of Vasco Nugnez de Balboa, who, in the most desperate exigencies, displayed such courage and conduct as first gained the confidence of his countrymen, and marked him out as their leader in more splendid and successful undertakings. Nor was he the only adventurer in this expedition who will appear with lustre in more important scenes. Francisco Pizarro was one of Ojeda's companions, and in this school of adversity acquired or improved the talents which fitted him for the extraordinary actions which he afterwards performed. Hernan Cortes, whose name became still more famous, had likewise engaged early in this enterprise, which roused all the active youth of Hispaniola to arms; but the good fortune that accompanied him in his subsequent adventures interposed to save him from the disasters to which his companions were exposed. He was taken ill at St. Domingo before the departure of the fleet, and detained there by a tedious indisposition.*

Notwithstanding the unfortunate issue of this expedition, the Spaniards were not deterred from engaging in new schemes of a similar nature. When wealth is acquired gradually by the persevering hand of industry, or accumulated by the slow operations of regular commerce, the means employed are so proportioned to the end attained, that there is nothing to strike the imagination, and little to urge on the active powers of the mind to uncommon efforts. But when large fortunes were created almost instantaneously; when gold and pearls were procured in exchange for baubles; when the countries which produced these rich commodities, defended only by naked savages, might be seized by the first bold invader; objects so singular and alluring roused a wonderful spirit of enterprise among the Spaniards, who rushed with ardour into this new path that was opened to wealth and distinction. While this spirit continued warm and vigorous, every attempt either towards discovery or conquest was applauded, and adventurers engaged in it with emulation. The passion for new undertakings, which characterizes the age of discovery in the latter part of the fifteenth and beginning of the sixteenth century, would alone have been sufficient to prevent the Spaniards from stopping short in their career. But circumstances peculiar to Hispaniola, at this juncture, concurred with it in extending their navigation and conquests. The rigorous treatment of the inhabitants of that island having almost extirpated the race, many of the Spanish planters, as I have already observed, finding it impossible to carry on their works with the same vigour and profit, were obliged to look out for settlements in some country where people were not yet wasted by oppression. Others, with the inconsiderate levity natural to men upon whom wealth pours in with a sudden flow, had squandered in thoughtless prodigality what they acquired with ease, and were driven by necessity to embark in the most desperate schemes, in order to retrieve their affairs. From all these causes, when Don Diego Columbus proposed [1511] to conquer the island of Cuba, and to establish a colony there, many persons of chief distinction in Hispaniola engaged with alacrity in the measure. He gave the command of the troops destined for that service to Diego Velasquez, one of his father's companions in his second voyage, and who, having been long settled in Hispaniola, had acquired an ample fortune, with such reputation for probity and prudence, that he seemed to be well qualified for conducting an expedition of importance. Three hundred men were deemed sufficient for the conquest of an island of above seven hundred miles in

---

* Herrera, dec. 1. lib. vii. c. 11, &c. Gomara Hist. c. 57, 58, 59. Benzon. Hist. lib. i. c. 19—23. P. Martyr, decad. p. 122.

length, and filled with inhabitants. But they were of the same unwarlike character with the people of Hispaniola. They were not only intimidated by the appearance of their new enemies, but unprepared to resist them. For though, from the time that the Spaniards took possession of the adjacent island, there was reason to expect a descent on their territories, none of the small communities into which Cuba was divided, had either made any provision for its own defence, or had formed any concert for their common safety. The only obstruction the Spaniards met with was from Hatuey, a cazique, who had fled from Hispaniola, and had taken possession of the eastern extremity of Cuba. He stood upon the defensive at their first landing, and endeavoured to drive them back to their ships. His feeble troops, however, were soon broken and dispersed; and he himself being taken prisoner, Velasquez, according to the barbarous maxim of the Spaniards, considered him as a slave who had taken arms against his master, and condemned him to the flames. When Hatuey was fastened to the stake, a Franciscan friar, labouring to convert him, promised him immediate admittance into the joys of heaven, if he would embrace the Christian faith. "Are there any Spaniards," says he, after some pause, "in that region of bliss which you describe?"—"Yes," replied the monk, "but only such as are worthy and good."—"The best of them," returned the indignant cazique, "have neither worth nor goodness: I will not go to a place where I may meet with one of that accursed race."* This dreadful example of vengeance struck the people of Cuba with such terror that they scarcely gave any opposition to the progress of their invaders; and Velasquez, without the loss of a man, annexed this extensive and fertile island to the Spanish monarchy.†

The facility with which this important conquest was completed served as an incitement to other undertakings. Juan Ponce de Leon, having acquired both fame and wealth by the reduction of Puerto Rico, was impatient to engage in some new enterprise. He fitted out three ships at his own expense, for a voyage of discovery [1512], and his reputation soon drew together a respectable body of followers. He directed his course towards the Lucayo islands; and after touching at several of them, as well as of the Bahama isles, he stood to the south-west, and discovered a country hitherto unknown to the Spaniards, which he called Florida, either because he fell in with it on Palm Sunday, or on account of its gay and beautiful appearance. He attempted to land in different places, but met with such vigorous opposition from the natives, who were fierce and warlike, as convinced him that an increase of force was requisite to effect a settlement. Satisfied with having opened a communication with a new country, of whose value and importance he conceived very sanguine hopes, he returned to Puerto Rico through the channel now known by the name of the Gulf of Florida.

It was not merely the passion of searching for new countries that prompted Ponce de Leon to undertake this voyage; he was influenced by one of those visionary ideas, which at that time often mingled with the spirit of discovery, and rendered it more active. A tradition prevailed among the natives of Puerto Rico, that in the isle of Bimini, one of the Lucayos, there was a fountain of such wonderful virtue as to renew the youth and recall the vigour of every person who bathed in its salutary waters. In hopes of finding this grand restorative, Ponce de Leon and his followers ranged through the islands, searching with fruitless solicitude and labour for the fountain which was the chief object of their expedition. That a tale so fabulous should gain credit among simple and uninstructed Indians is not surprising. That it should make any impression upon an enlightened people appears in the present age altogether incredible. The fact, however, is

* B. de las Casas, p. 40. † Herrera, dec. 1. lib. ix. c. 2, 3, &c. Oviedo, lib. xvii. c. 3. p. 170.

certain; and the most authentic Spanish historians mention this extravagant sally of their credulous countrymen. The Spaniards at that period were engaged in a career of activity which gave a romantic turn to their imagination, and daily presented to them strange and marvellous objects. A New World was opened to their view. They visited islands and continents, of whose existence mankind in former ages had no conception. In those delightful countries nature seemed to assume another form: every tree and plant and animal was different from those of the ancient hemisphere. They seemed to be transported into enchanted ground; and after the wonders which they had seen, nothing, in the warmth and novelty of their admiration, appeared to them so extraordinary as to be beyond belief. If the rapid succession of new and striking scenes made such impression even upon the sound understanding of Columbus, that he boasted of having found the seat of Paradise, it will not appear strange that Ponce de Leon should dream of discovering the fountain of youth.*

Soon after the expedition to Florida, a discovery of much greater importance was made in another part of America. Balboa having been raised to the government of the small colony at Santa Maria in Darien, by the voluntary suffrage of his associates, was so extremely desirous to obtain from the crown a confirmation of their election, that he despatched one of his officers to Spain, in order to solicit a royal commission, which might invest him with a legal title to the supreme command. Conscious, however, that he could not expect success from the patronage of Ferdinand's ministers, with whom he was unconnected, or from negotiating in a court to the arts of which he was a stranger, he endeavoured to merit the dignity to which he aspired, and aimed at performing some signal service that would secure him the preference to every competitor. Full of this idea, he made frequent inroads into the adjacent country, subdued several of the caziques, and collected a considerable quantity of gold, which abounded more in that part of the continent than in the islands. In one of those excursions, the Spaniards contended with such eagerness about the division of some gold, that they were at the point of proceeding to acts of violence against one another. A young cazique who was present, astonished at the high value which they set upon a thing of which he did not discern the use, tumbled the gold out of the balance with indignation; and turning to the Spaniards, "Why do you quarrel (says he) about such a trifle? If you are so passionately fond of gold, as to abandon your own country, and to disturb the tranquillity of distant nations for its sake, I will conduct you to a region where the metal which seems to be the chief object of your admiration and desire is so common that the meanest utensils are formed of it." Transported with what they heard, Balboa and his companions inquired eagerly where this happy country lay, and how they might arrive at it. He informed them that at the distance of six suns, that is, of six days' journey, towards the south, they should discover another ocean, near to which this wealthy kingdom was situated; but if they intended to attack that powerful state, they must assemble forces far superior in number and strength to those with which they now appeared.†

This was the first information which the Spaniards received concerning the great southern ocean, or the opulent and extensive country known afterwards by the name of Peru. Balboa had now before him objects suited to his boundless ambition, and the enterprising ardour of his genius. He immediately concluded the ocean which the cazique mentioned, to be that for which Columbus had searched without success in this part of America, in hopes of opening a more direct communication with the East Indies; and he

---

* P. Martyr, decad. p. 202. Ensayo Chronol. para la Hist. de la Florida, par de Gab. Cardenas, p. 1. Oviedo, lib. xvi. c. 11. Herrera, dec. 1. lib. ix. c. 5. Hist. de la Conq. de la Florida, par Garc. de la Vega, lib. 1. c. 3. † Herrera, dec. 1. lib. ix. c. 2. Gomara, c. 60. P. Martyr, dec. p. 148.

jectured that the rich territory which had been described to him must be part of that vast and opulent region of the earth. Elated with the idea of performing what so great a man had attempted in vain, and eager to accomplish a discovery which he knew would be no less acceptable to the king than beneficial to his country, he was impatient until he could set out upon this enterprise, in comparison of which all his former exploits appeared inconsiderable. But previous arrangement and preparation were requisite to ensure success. He began with courting and securing the friendship of the neighbouring caziques. He sent some of his officers to Hispaniola with a large quantity of gold, as a proof of his past success, and an earnest of his future hopes. By a proper distribution of this, they secured the favour of the governor, and allured volunteers into the service. A considerable reinforcement from that island joined him, and he thought himself in a condition to attempt the discovery.

The isthmus of Darien is not above sixty miles in breadth; but this neck of land which binds together the continents of North and South America, is strengthened by a chain of lofty mountains stretching through its whole extent, which render it a barrier of solidity sufficient to resist the impulse of two opposite oceans. The mountains are covered with forests almost inaccessible. The valleys in that moist climate where it rains during two-thirds of the year, are marshy, and so frequently overflowed that the inhabitants find it necessary, in many places, to build their houses upon trees, in order to be elevated at some distance from the damp soil, and the odious reptiles engendered in the putrid waters.* Large rivers rush down with an impetuous current from the high grounds. In a region thinly inhabited by wandering savages, the hand of industry had done nothing to mitigate or correct those natural disadvantages. To march across this unexplored country with no other guides but Indians, whose fidelity could be little trusted, was, on all those accounts, the boldest enterprise on which the Spaniards had hitherto ventured in the New World. But the intrepidity of Balboa was such as distinguished him among his countrymen, at a period when every adventurer was conspicuous for daring courage [1513]. Nor was bravery his only merit; he was prudent in conduct, generous, affable, and possessed of those popular talents which, in the most desperate undertakings, inspire confidence and secure attachment. Even after the junction of the volunteers from Hispaniola, he was able to muster only a hundred and ninety men for his expedition. But they were hardy, veterans, inured to the climate of America, and ready to follow him through every danger. A thousand Indians attended them to carry their provisions; and, to complete their warlike array, they took with them several of those fierce dogs, which were no less formidable than destructive to their naked enemies.

Balboa set out upon this important expedition on the first of September, about the time that the periodical rains began to abate. He proceeded by sea, and without any difficulty, to the territories of a cazique whose friendship he had gained; but no sooner did he begin to advance into the interior part of the country, than he was retarded by every obstacle, which he had reason to apprehend, from the nature of the territory, or the disposition of its inhabitants. Some of the caziques, at his approach, fled to the mountains with all their people, and carried off or destroyed whatever could afford subsistence to his troops. Others collected their subjects, in order to oppose his progress; and he quickly perceived what an arduous undertaking it was to conduct such a body of men through hostile nations, across swamps, and rivers, and woods, which had never been passed but by straggling Indians. But by sharing in every hardship with the meanest soldier, by appearing the foremost to meet every danger, by promising confidently to his troops the enjoyment of honour and riches superior to

* P. Martyr, dec. p. 158.

what had been attained by the most successful of their countrymen, he inspired them with such enthusiastic resolution, that they followed him without murmuring. When they had penetrated a good way into the mountains, a powerful cazique appeared in a narrow pass, with a numerous body of his subjects, to obstruct their progress. But men who had surmounted so many obstacles, despised the opposition of such feeble enemies They attacked them with impetuosity, and, having dispersed them with much ease and great slaughter, continued their march. Though their guides had represented the breadth of the isthmus to be only a journey of six days, they had already spent twenty-five in forcing their way through the woods and mountains. Many of them were ready to sink under such uninterrupted fatigue in that sultry climate, several were taken ill of the dysentery and other diseases frequent in that country, and all became impatient to reach the period of their labours and sufferings. At length the Indians assured them, that from the top of the next mountain they should discover the ocean which was the object of their wishes. When, with infinite toil, they had climbed up the greater part of that steep ascent, Balboa commanded his men to halt, and advanced alone to the summit, that he might be the first who should enjoy a spectacle which he had so long desired. As soon as he beheld the South Sea stretching in endless prospect below him, he fell on his knees, and, lifting up his hands to heaven, returned thanks to God, who had conducted him to a discovery so beneficial to his country, and so honourable to himself. His followers, observing his transports of joy, rushed forward to join in his wonder, exultation, and gratitude. They held on their course to the shore with great alacrity, when Balboa, advancing up to the middle in the waves with his buckler and sword, took possession of that ocean in the name of the king his master, and vowed to defend it with these arms, against all his enemies.*

That part of the great Pacific or Southern Ocean which Balboa first discovered, still retains the name of the Gulf of St. Michael, which he gave to it, and is situated to the east of Panama. From several of the petty princes, who governed in the districts adjacent to that gulf, he extorted provisions and gold by force of arms. Others sent them to him voluntarily. To these acceptable presents, some of the caziques added a considerable quantity of pearls; and he learned from them, with much satisfaction, that pearl oysters abounded in the sea which he had newly discovered.

Together with the acquisition of this wealth, which served to soothe and encourage his followers, he received accounts which confirmed his sanguine hopes of future and more extensive benefits from the expedition. All the people on the coast of the South Sea concurred in informing him that there was a mighty and opulent kingdom situated at a considerable distance towards the south-east, the inhabitants of which had tame animals to carry their burdens. In order to give the Spaniards an idea of these, they drew upon the sand the figure of the llamas or sheep, afterwards found in Peru, which the Peruvians had taught to perform such services as they described. As the llama in its form nearly resembles a camel, a beast of burden deemed peculiar to Asia, this circumstance, in conjunction with the discovery of the pearls, another noted production of that country, tended to confirm the Spaniards in their mistaken theory with respect to the vicinity of the New World to the East Indies.†

But though the information which Balboa received from the people on the coast, as well as his own conjectures and hopes, rendered him extremely impatient to visit this unknown country, his prudence restrained him from

---

* Herrera, dec. 1. lib. x. c. 1, &c.　　Gomara, c. 62, &c.　P. Martyr, dec. p. 205, &c.　　† Ibid. dec. 1. lib. x. c. 2.

attempting to invade it with a handful of men exhausted by fatigue and weakened by diseases. [24] He determined to lead back his followers, at present, to their settlement of Santa Maria in Darien, and to return next season with a force more adequate to such an arduous enterprise. In order to acquire a more extensive knowledge of the isthmus, he marched back by a different route, which he found to be no less dangerous and difficult than that which he had formerly taken. But to men elated with success, and animated with hope, nothing is insurmountable. Balboa returned to Santa Maria [1514], from which he had been absent four months, with greater glory and more treasure than the Spaniards had acquired in any expedition in the New World. None of Balboa's officers distinguished themselves more in this service than Francisco Pizarro, or assisted with greater courage and ardour in opening a communication with those countries in which he was destined to act soon a more illustrious part.*

Balboa's first care was to send information to Spain of the important discovery which he had made: and to demand a reinforcement of a thousand men, in order to attempt the conquest of that opulent country concerning which he had received such inviting intelligence. The first account of the discovery of the New World hardly occasioned greater joy than the unexpected tidings that a passage was at last found to the great southern ocean. The communication with the East Indies, by a course to the westward of the line of demarcation drawn by the Pope, seemed now to be certain. The vast wealth which flowed into Portugal, from its settlements and conquests in that country, excited the envy and called forth the emulation of other states. Ferdinand hoped now to come in for a share in this lucrative commerce, and, in his eagerness to obtain it, was willing to make an effort beyond what Balboa required. But even in this exertion, his jealous policy, as well as the fatal antipathy of Fonseca, now Bishop of Burgos, to every man of merit who distinguished himself in the New World, was conspicuous. Notwithstanding Balboa's recent services, which marked him out as the most proper person to finish that great undertaking which he had begun, Ferdinand was so ungenerous as to overlook these, and to appoint Pedrarias Davila governor of Darien. He gave him the command of fifteen stout vessels and twelve hundred soldiers. These were fitted out at the public expense, with a liberality which Ferdinand had never displayed in any former armament destined for the New World; and such was the ardour of the Spanish gentlemen to follow a leader who was about to conduct them to a country where, as fame reported, they had only to throw their nets into the sea and draw out gold,† that fifteen hundred embarked on board the fleet, and, if they had not been restrained, a much greater number would have engaged in the service.‡

Pedrarias reached the Gulf of Darien without any remarkable accident, and immediately sent some of his principal officers ashore to inform Balboa of his arrival, with the king's commission to be governor of the colony.. To their astonishment, they found Balboa, of whose great exploits they had heard so much, and of whose opulence they had formed such high ideas, clad in a canvass jacket, and wearing coarse hempen sandals used only by the meanest peasants, employed, together with some Indians, in thatching his own hut with reeds. Even in this simple garb, which corresponded so ill with the expectations and wishes of his new guests, Balboa received them with dignity. The fame of his discoveries had drawn so many adventurers from the islands, that he could now muster four hundred and fifty men. At the head of those daring veterans, he was more than a match for the forces which Pedrarias brought with him. But, though his troops murmured loudly at the injustice of the king in superseding their commander,

---

* Herrera, dec. 1. lib. x. c. 3—6. Gomara, c. 64. P. Martyr, dec. p. 239, &c. † Ibid. c. 14.
‡ Ibid. c. 6, 7. P. Martyr, dec. p. 177. 296.

and complained that strangers would now reap the fruits of their toil and success, Balboa submitted with implicit obedience to the will of his sovereign, and received Pedrarias with all the deference due to his character.*
Notwithstanding this moderation, to which Pedrarias owed the peaceable possession of his government, he appointed a judicial inquiry to be made into Balboa's conduct, while under the command of Nicuessa, and imposed a considerable fine upon him, on account of the irregularities of which he had then been guilty. Balboa felt sensibly the mortification of being subjected to trial and to punishment in a place where he had so lately occupied the first station. Pedrarias could not conceal his jealousy of his superior merit ; so that the resentment of the one and the envy of the other gave rise to dissensions extremely detrimental to the colony. It was threatened with a calamity still more fatal. Pedrarias had landed in Darien at a most unlucky time of the year [July], about the middle of the rainy season, in that part of the torrid zone where the clouds pour down such torrents as are unknown in more temperate climates.† The village of Santa Maria was seated in a rich plain, environed with marshes and woods. The constitution of Europeans was unable to withstand the pestilential influence of such a situation, in a climate naturally so noxious, and at a season so peculiarly unhealthy. A violent and destructive malady carried off many of the soldiers who accompanied Pedrarias. An extreme scarcity of provision augmented this distress, as it rendered it impossible to find proper refreshment for the sick, or the necessary sustenance for the healthy.‡ In the space of a month, above six hundred persons perished in the utmost misery. Dejection and despair spread through the colony. Many principal persons solicited their dismission, and were glad to relinquish all their hopes of wealth, in order to escape from that pernicious region. Pedrarias endeavoured to divert those who remained from brooding over their misfortunes, by finding them employment. With this view, he sent several detachments into the interior parts of the country, to levy gold among the natives, and to search for the mines in which it was produced. Those rapacious adventurers, more attentive to present gain than to the means of facilitating their future progress, plundered without distinction wherever they marched. Regardless of the alliances which Balboa had made with several of the caziques, they stripped them of every thing valuable, and treated them, as well as their subjects, with the utmost insolence and cruelty. By their tyranny and exactions, which Pedrarias, either from want of authority or inclination, did not restrain, all the country from the Gulf of Darien to the lake of Nicaragua was desolated, and the Spaniards were inconsiderately deprived of the advantages which they might have derived from the friendship of the natives, in extending their conquests to the South Sea. Balboa, who saw with concern that such ill-judged proceedings retarded the execution of his favourite scheme, sent violent remonstrances to Spain against the imprudent government of Pedrarias, who had ruined a happy and flourishing colony. Pedrarias, on the other hand, accused him of having deceived the King, by magnifying his own exploits, as well as by a false representation of the opulence and value of the country.§
Ferdinand became sensible at length of his imprudence in superseding the most active and experienced officer he had in the New World, and, by way of compensation to Balboa, appointed him *Adelantado*, or Lieutenant-Governor of the countries upon the South Sea, with very extensive privileges and authority. At the same time he enjoined Pedrarias to support Balboa in all his operations, and to consult with him concerning every measure which he himself pursued. [1515] But to effect such a sudden

* Herrera, dec. 1. lib. x. c. 13, 14. † Richard, Hist. Naturelle de l'Air, tom. 1, p. 204.
‡ Herrera, dec. 1. lib. x. c. 14. P. Martyr, decad. p. 272. § Ibid. dec. 1. lib. x. c. 15. dec. 2. c. 1, &c. Gomara, c. 66. P. Martyr, dec. 3. c. 10. Relacion de B. de las Casas, p. 12.

transition from inveterate enmity to perfect confidence, exceeded Ferdinand's power. Pedrarias continued to treat his rival with neglect; and Balboa's fortune being exhausted by the payment of his fine, and other exactions of Pedrarias, he could not make suitable preparations for taking possession of his new government. At length, by the interposition and exhortations of the Bishop of Darien, they were brought to a reconciliation; and, in order to cement this union more firmly, Pedrarias agreed to give his daughter in marriage to Balboa. [1516.] The first effect of their concord was, that Balboa was permitted to make several small incursions into the country. These he conducted with such prudence, as added to the reputation which he had already acquired. Many adventurers resorted to him, and, with the countenance and aid of Pedrarias, he began to prepare for his expedition to the South Sea. In order to accomplish this, it was necessary to build vessels capable of conveying his troops to those provinces which he purposed to invade. [1517.] After surmounting many obstacles, and enduring a variety of those hardships which were the portion of the conquerors of America, he at length finished four small brigantines. In these, with three hundred chosen men, a force superior to that with which Pizarro afterwards undertook the same expedition, he was ready to sail towards Peru, when he received an unexpected message from Pedrarias.* As his reconciliation with Balboa had never been cordial, the progress which his son-in-law was making revived his ancient enmity, and added to its rancour. He dreaded the prosperity and elevation of a man whom he had injured so deeply. He suspected that success would encourage him to aim at independence upon his jurisdiction; and so violently did the passions of hatred, fear, and jealousy operate upon his mind, that, in order to gratify his vengeance, he scrupled not to defeat an enterprise of the greatest moment to his country. Under pretexts which were false, but plausible, he desired Balboa to postpone his voyage for a short time, and to repair to Acla, in order that he might have an interview with him. Balboa, with the unsuspicious confidence of a man conscious of no crime, instantly obeyed the summons; but as soon as he entered the place, he was arrested by order of Pedrarias, whose impatience to satiate his revenge did not suffer him to languish long in confinement. Judges were immediately appointed to proceed to his trial. An accusation of disloyalty to the king, and of an intention to revolt against the governor was preferred against him. Sentence of death was pronounced; and though the judges who passed it, seconded by the whole colony, interceded warmly for his pardon, Pedrarias continued inexorable; and the Spaniards beheld, with astonishment and sorrow, the public execution of a man whom they universally deemed more capable than any one who had borne command in America, of forming and accomplishing great designs.† Upon his death, the expedition which he had planned was relinquished. Pedrarias, notwithstanding the violence and injustice of his proceedings, was not only screened from punishment by the powerful patronage of the Bishop of Burgos and other courtiers, but continued in power. Soon after he obtained permission to remove the colony from its unwholesome station of Santa Maria to Panama, on the opposite side of the isthmus; and though it did not gain much in point of healthfulness by the change, the commodious situation of this new settlement contributed greatly to facilitate the subsequent conquests of the Spaniards in the extensive countries situated upon the Southern Ocean.‡

During these transactions in Darien [1515], the history of which it was proper to carry on in an uninterrupted tenour, several important events occurred with respect to the discovery, the conquest, and government of other provinces in the New World. Ferdinand was so intent upon opening

* Herrera, dec. 2. lib. 1. c. 3. lib. ii, c. 11. 12, 21.   † Ibid, dec. 2. lib. ii. c. 21, 22.   ‡ Ibid. lib. iv. c. 1.

a communication with the Molucca or Spice Islands by the west, that in the year one thousand five hundred and fifteen he fitted out two ships at his own expense, in order to attempt such a voyage, and gave the command of them to Juan Diaz de Solis, who was deemed one of the most skilful navigators in Spain. He stood along the coast of South America, and on the first of January, one thousand five hundred and sixteen, entered a river which he called Janeiro, where an extensive commerce is now carried on. From thence he proceeded to a spacious bay, which he supposed to be the entrance into a strait that communicated with the Indian Ocean; but, upon advancing further, he found it to be the mouth of Rio de Plata, one of the vast rivers by which the southern continent of America is watered. In endeavouring to make a descent in this country, De Solis and several of his crew were slain by the natives, who, in sight of the ships, cut their bodies in pieces, roasted and devoured them. Discouraged with the loss of their commander, and terrified at this shocking spectacle, the surviving Spaniards set sail for Europe, without aiming at any further discovery.* Though this attempt proved abortive, it was not without benefit. It turned the attention of ingenious men to this course of navigation, and prepared the way for a more fortunate voyage, by which, a few years posterior to this period, the great design that Ferdinand had in view was accomplished.

Though the Spaniards were thus actively employed in extending their discoveries and settlements in America, they still considered Hispaniola as their principal colony, and the seat of government. Don Diego Columbus wanted neither inclination nor abilities to have rendered the members of this colony, who were most immediately under his jurisdiction, prosperous and happy. But he was circumscribed in all his operations by the suspicious policy of Ferdinand, who on every occasion, and under pretexts the most frivolous, retrenched his privileges, and encouraged the treasurer, the judges, and other subordinate officers to counteract his measures, and to dispute his authority. The most valuable prerogative which the governor possessed was that of distributing Indians among the Spaniards settled in the island. The rigorous servitude of those unhappy men having been but little mitigated by all the regulations in their favour, the power of parcelling out such necessary instruments of labour at pleasure, secured to the governor great influence in the colony. In order to strip him of this, Ferdinand created a new office, with the power of distributing the Indians, and bestowed it upon Rodrigo Albuquerque, a relation of Zapata, his confidential minister. Mortified with the injustice as well as indignity of this invasion upon his rights, in a point so essential, Don Diego could no longer remain in a place where his power and consequence were almost annihilated. He repaired to Spain with the vain hopes of obtaining redress.† Albuquerque entered upon his office with all the rapacity of an indigent adventurer impatient to amass wealth. He began with taking the exact number of Indians in the island, and found that from sixty thousand, who in the year one thousand five hundred and eight survived after all their sufferings, they were now reduced to fourteen thousand. These he threw into separate divisions or lots, and bestowed them upon such as were willing to purchase them at the highest price. By this arbitrary distribution several of the natives were removed from their original habitations, many were taken from their ancient masters, and all of them subjected to heavier burdens, and to more intolerable labour, in order to reimburse their new proprietors.—Those additional calamities completed the misery, and hastened on the extinction of this wretched and innocent race of men.‡

The violence of these proceedings, together with the fatal consequences which attended them, not only excited complaints among such as thought

* Herrera, dec. 2. lib. i. c. 7.   P. Martyr, dec. p. 317.   † Ibid. dec. 1. lib. ix. c. 5. lib. x. c. 12.
‡ Ibid. dec. 1. lib. x. c. 12.

themselves aggrieved, but touched the hearts of all who retained any sentiments of humanity. From the time that ecclesiastics were sent as instructors into America, they perceived that the rigour with which their countrymen treated the natives, rendered their ministry altogether fruitless. The missionaries, in conformity to the mild spirit of that religion which they were employed to publish, early remonstrated against the maxims of the planters with respect to the Americans, and condemned the *repartimientos*, or *distributions*, by which they were given up as slaves to their conquerors, as no less contrary to natural justice and the precepts of Christianity than to sound policy. The Dominicans, to whom the instruction of the Americans was originally committed, were most vehement in testifying against the *repartimientos*. In the year one thousand five hundred and eleven, Montesino, one of their most eminent preachers, inveighed against this practice, in the great church of St. Domingo, with all the impetuosity of popular eloquence. Don Diego Columbus, the principal officers of the colony, and all the laymen who had been his hearers, complained of the monk to his superiors; but they, instead of condemning, applauded his doctrine as equally pious and seasonable. The Franciscans, influenced by the spirit of opposition and rivalship which subsists between the two orders, discovered some inclination to take part with the laity, and to espouse the defence of the *repartimientos*. But as they could not with decency give their avowed approbation to a system of oppression so repugnant to the spirit of religion, they endeavoured to palliate what they could not justify, and alleged, in excuse for the conduct of their countrymen, that it was impossible to carry on any improvement in the colony, unless the Spaniards possessed such dominion over the natives that they could compel them to labour.*

The Dominicans, regardless of such political and interested considerations, would not relax in any degree the rigour of their sentiments, and even refused to absolve, or admit to the sacrament, such of their countrymen as continued to hold the natives in servitude.† Both parties applied to the king for his decision in a matter of such importance. Ferdinand empowered a committee of his privy council, assisted by some of the most eminent civilians and divines in Spain, to hear the deputies sent from Hispaniola in support of their respective opinions. After a long discussion, the speculative point in controversy was determined in favour of the Dominicans, the Indians were declared to be a free people entitled to all the natural rights of men; but notwithstanding this decision, the *repartimientos* were continued upon their ancient footing.‡ As this determination admitted the principle upon which the Dominicans founded their opinion, they renewed their efforts to obtain relief for the Indians with additional boldness and zeal. At length, in order to quiet the colony, which was alarmed by their remonstrances and censures, Ferdinand issued a decree of his privy council [1513], declaring, that after mature consideration of the Apostolic Bull, and other titles by which the crown of Castile claimed a right to its possessions in the New World, the servitude of the Indians was warranted both by the laws of God and of man; that unless they were subjected to the dominion of the Spaniards, and compelled to reside under their inspection, it would be impossible to reclaim them from idolatry, or to instruct them in the principles of the Christian faith; that no further scruple ought to be entertained concerning the lawfulness of the *repartimientos*, as the king and council were willing to take the charge of that upon their own consciences; and that therefore the Dominicans and monks of other religious orders should abstain for the future from those invectives which, from an excess of charitable but ill-informed zeal, they had uttered against that practice.§

That his intention of adhering to this decree might be fully understood,

* Herrera, dec. 1. lib. viii. c. 11. Oviedo, lib. iii. c. 6. p. 97.   † Oviedo, lib. iii. c. 6. p. 97.
‡ Herrera, dec. 1. lib. viii. c. 12, lib. ix. c. 5.   § Ibid. dec. 1. lib. ix. c. 14.

Ferdinand conferred new grants of Indians upon several of his courtiers [25]. But, in order that he might not seem altogether inattentive to the rights of humanity, he published an edict, in which he endeavoured to provide for the mild treatment of the Indians under the yoke to which he subjected them; he regulated the nature of the work which they should be required to perform; he prescribed the mode in which they should be clothed and fed, and gave directions with respect to their instructions in the principles of Christianity.*

But the Dominicans, who from their experience of what was past judged concerning the future, soon perceived the inefficacy of those provisions, and foretold, that as long as it was the interest of individuals to treat the Indians with rigour, no public regulations could render their servitude mild or tolerable. They considered it as vain, to waste their own time and strength in attempting to communicate the sublime truths of religion to men whose spirits were broken and their faculties impaired by oppression. Some of them in despair, requested the permission of their superiors to remove to the continent, and to pursue the object of their mission among such of the natives as were not hitherto corrupted by the example of the Spaniards, or alienated by their cruelty from the Christian faith. Such as remained in Hispaniola continued to remonstrate, with decent firmness, against the servitude of the Indians.†

The violent operations of Albuquerque, the new distributor of Indians revived the zeal of the Dominicans against the *repartimientos*, and called forth an advocate for that oppressed people, who possessed all the courage the talents, and activity requisite in supporting such a desperate cause. This was Bartholomew de las Casas, a native of Seville, and one of the clergymen sent out with Columbus in his second voyage to Hispaniola, in order to settle in that island. He early adopted the opinion prevalent among ecclesiastics, with respect to the unlawfulness of reducing the natives to servitude; and that he might demonstrate the sincerity of his conviction, he relinquished all the Indians who had fallen to his own share in the division of the inhabitants among their conquerors, declaring that he should ever bewail his own misfortune and guilt, in having exercised for a moment this impious dominion over his fellow-creatures.‡ From that time he became the avowed patron of the Indians; and by his bold interpositions in their behalf, as well as by the respect due to his abilities and character he had often the merit of setting some bounds to the excesses of his countrymen. He did not fail to remonstrate warmly against the proceedings of Albuquerque; and though he soon found that attention to his own interest rendered this rapacious officer deaf to admonition, he did not abandon the wretched people whose cause he had espoused. He instantly set out for Spain, with the most sanguine hopes of opening the eyes and softening the heart of Ferdinand, by that striking picture of the oppression of his new subjects which he would exhibit to his view.§

He easily obtained admittance to the King, whom he found in a declining state of health. With much freedom, and no less eloquence, he represented to him all the fatal effects of the *repartimientos* in the New World, boldly charging him with the guilt of having authorized this impious measure, which had brought misery and destruction upon a numerous and innocent race of men, whom Providence had placed under his protection. Ferdinand, whose mind as well as body was much enfeebled by his distemper, was greatly alarmed at this charge of impiety, which at another juncture he would have despised. He listened with deep compunction to the discourse of Las Casas, and promised to take into serious consideration

---

* Herrera, dec. 1. lib. ix. c. 14.   † Id. ibid. Touron. Histoire Générale de l'Amérique, tom. 1 p. 252.   ‡ Fr. Aug. Davila Padilla Hist. de la Fundacion de la Provincia de St. Jago de Mexico, p. 303, 304. Herrera, dec. 1. lib. x. c. 12.   § Herrera, dec. 1. lib. x. c. 12. Dec. 2. lib. I. c. 11. Davila Padilla Hist. p. 304.

the means of redressing the evil of which he complained. But death prevented him from executing his resolution. Charles of Austria, to whom all his crowns devolved, resided at that time in his paternal dominions in the Low Countries. Las Casas, with his usual ardour, prepared immediately to set out for Flanders, in order to occupy the ear of the young monarch, when Cardinal Ximenes, who, as regent, assumed the reins of government in Castile, commanded him to desist from the journey, and engaged to hear his complaints in person.

He accordingly weighed the matter with attention equal to its importance; and as his impetuous mind delighted in schemes bold and uncommon, he soon fixed upon a plan which astonished the ministers trained up under the formal and cautious administration of Ferdinand. Without regarding either the rights of Don Diego Columbus, or the regulations established by the late King, he resolved to send three persons to America as superintendents of all the colonies there, with authority, after examining all circumstances on the spot, to decide finally with respect to the point in question. It was a matter of deliberation and delicacy to choose men qualified for such an important station. As all the laymen settled in America, or who had been consulted in the administration of that department, had given their opinion that the Spaniards could not keep possession of their new settlements, unless they were allowed to retain their dominion over the Indians, he saw that he could not rely on their impartiality, and determined to commit the trust to ecclesiastics. As the Dominicans and Franciscans had already espoused opposite sides in the controversy, he, from the same principle of impartiality, excluded both these fraternities from the commission. He confined his choice to the monks of St. Jerome, a small but respectable order in Spain. With the assistance of their general, and in concert with Las Casas, he soon pitched upon three persons whom he deemed equal to the charge. To them he joined Zuazo, a private lawyer of distinguished probity, with unbounded power to regulate all judicial proceedings in the colonies. Las Casas was appointed to accompany them, with the title of protector of the Indians.*

To vest such extraordinary powers, as might at once overturn the system of government established in the New World, in four persons, who, from their humble condition in life, were little entitled to possess this high authority, appeared to Zapata, and other ministers of the late king, a measure so wild and dangerous, that they refused to issue the despatches necessary for carrying it into execution. But Ximenes was not of a temper patiently to brook opposition to any of his schemes. He sent for the refractory ministers, and addressed him in such a tone that in the utmost consternation they obeyed his orders.† The superintendents, with their associate Zuazo and Las Casas, sailed for St. Domingo. Upon their arrival, the first act of their authority was to set at liberty all the Indians who had been granted to the Spanish courtiers, or to any person not residing in America. This, together with the information which had been received from Spain concerning the object of the commission, spread a general alarm. The colonists concluded that they were to be deprived at once of the hands with which they carried on their labour, and that, of consequence, ruin was unavoidable. But the fathers of St. Jerome proceeded with such caution and prudence as soon dissipated all their fears. They discovered, in every step of their conduct, a knowledge of the world, and of affairs, which is seldom acquired in a cloister; and displayed a moderation as well as gentleness still more rare among persons trained up in the solitude and austerity of a monastic life. Their ears were open to information from every quarter; they compared the different accounts which they received; and, after a mature consideration of the whole, they were fully satisfied that the state of the colony rendered it impossible to adopt the plan proposed by Las Casas,

* Herrera, dec. 2. lib. ii. c. 3.   † Ibid. dec. 2. lib. ii. c. 6.

and recommended by the Cardinal. They plainly perceived that the Spaniards settled in America were so few in number, that they could neither work the mines which had been opened, nor cultivate the country; that they depended for effecting both upon the labour of the natives, and, if deprived of it, they must instantly relinquish their conquests, or give up all the advantages which they derived from them; that no allurement was so powerful as to surmount the natural aversion of the Indians to any laborious effort, and that nothing but the authority of a master could compel them to work; and if they were not kept constantly under the eye and discipline of a superior, so great was their natural listlessness and indifference, that they would neither attend to religious instruction, nor observe those rites of Christianity which they had been already taught. Upon all those accounts, the superintendents found it necessary to tolerate the *repartimientos*, and to suffer the Indians to remain under subjection to their Spanish masters. They used their utmost endeavours, however, to prevent the fatal effects of this establishment, and to secure to the Indians the consolation of the best treatment compatible with a state of servitude. For this purpose, they revived former regulations, they prescribed new ones, they neglected no circumstance that tended to mitigate the rigour of the yoke; and by their authority, their example, and their exhortations, they laboured to inspire their countrymen with sentiments of equity and gentleness towards the unhappy people upon whose industry they depended. Zuazo, in his department, seconded the endeavours of the superintendents. He reformed the courts of justice in such a manner as to render their decisions equitable as well as expeditious, and introduced various regulations which greatly improved the interior policy of the colony. The satisfaction which his conduct and that of the superintendents gave was now universal among the Spaniards settled in the New World; and all admired the boldness of Ximenes in having departed from the ordinary path of business in forming his plan, as well as his sagacity in pitching upon persons whose wisdom, moderation, and disinterestedness rendered them worthy of this high trust.*

Las Casas alone was dissatisfied. The prudential consideration which influenced the superintendents made no impression upon him. He regarded their idea of accommodating their conduct to the state of the colony, as the maxim of an unhallowed timid policy, which tolerated what was unjust because it was beneficial. He contended that the Indians were by nature free, and, as their protector, he required the superintendents not to bereave them of the common privilege of humanity. They received his most virulent remonstrances without emotion, but adhered firmly to their own system. The Spanish planters did not bear with him so patiently, and were ready to tear him in pieces for insisting in a requisition so odious to them. Las Casas, in order to screen himself from their rage, found it necessary to take shelter in a convent; and perceiving that all his efforts in America were fruitless, he soon set out for Europe, with a fixed resolution not to abandon the protection of a people whom he deemed to be cruelly oppressed.†

Had Ximenes retained that vigour of mind with which he usually applied to business, Las Casas must have met with no very gracious reception upon his return to Spain. But he found the Cardinal languishing under a mortal distemper, and preparing to resign his authority to the young king, who was daily expected from the Low Countries. Charles arrived, took possession of the government, and, by the death of Ximenes, lost a minister whose abilities and integrity entitled him to direct his affairs. Many of the Flemish nobility had accompanied their sovereign to Spain. From that warm predilection to his countrymen, which was natural at his age, he consulted them with respect to all the transactions in his new kingdom; and they, with

---

* Herrera, dec. 2. lib. ii. c. 15. Remesal, Hist. Gener. lib. ii. c. 14, 15, 16. † Ibid. dec. 2. lib. ii. c. 16.

an indiscreet eagerness, intruded themselves into every business, and seized almost every department of administration.* The direction of American affairs was an object too alluring to escape their attention. Las Casas observed their growing influence; and though projectors are usually too sanguine to conduct their schemes with much dexterity, he possessed a bustling, indefatigable activity, which sometimes accomplishes its purposes with greater success than the most exquisite discernment and address. He courted the Flemish ministers with assiduity. He represented to them the absurdity of all the maxims hitherto adopted with respect to the government of America, particularly during the administration of Ferdinand, and pointed out the defects of those arrangements which Ximenes had introduced. The memory of Ferdinand was odious to the Flemings. The superior virtues and abilities of Ximenes had long been the object of their envy. They fondly wished to have a plausible pretext for condemning the measures both of the monarch and of the minister, and of reflecting some discredit on their political wisdom. The friends of Don Diego Columbus, as well as the Spanish courtiers who had been dissatisfied with the Cardinal's administration, joined Las Casas in censuring the scheme of sending superintendents to America. This union of so many interests and passions was irresistible; and in consequence of it the fathers of St. Jerome, together with their associate Zuazo, were recalled. Roderigo de Figueroa, a lawyer of some eminence, was appointed chief judge of the island, and received instructions, in compliance with the request of Las Casas, to examine once more, with the utmost attention, the point in controversy between him and the people of the colony, with respect to the treatment of the natives; and in the mean time to do every thing in his power to alleviate their sufferings, and prevent the extinction of the race.†

This was all that the zeal of Las Casas could procure at that juncture in favour of the Indians. The impossibility of carrying on any improvements in America, unless the Spanish planters could command the labour of the natives, was an insuperable objection to his plan of treating them as free subjects. In order to provide some remedy for this, without which he found it was in vain to mention his scheme, Las Casas proposed to purchase a sufficient number of negroes from the Portuguese settlements on the coast of Africa, and to transport them to America, in order that they might be employed as slaves in working the mines and cultivating the ground. One of the first advantages which the Portuguese had derived from their discoveries in Africa arose from the trade in slaves. Various circumstances concurred in reviving this odious commerce, which had been long abolished in Europe, and which is no less repugnant to the feelings of humanity than to the principles of religion. As early as the year one thousand five hundred and three, a few negro slaves had been sent into the New World.‡ In the year one thousand five hundred and eleven, Ferdinand permitted the importation of them in greater numbers.§ They were found to be a more robust and hardy race than the natives of America. They were more capable of enduring fatigue, more patient under servitude, and the labour of one negro was computed to be equal to that of four Indians.|| Cardinal Ximenes, however, when solicited to encourage this commerce, peremptorily rejected the proposition, because he perceived the iniquity of reducing one race of men to slavery, while he was consulting about the means of restoring liberty to another.¶ But Las Casas, from the inconsistency natural to men who hurry with headlong impetuosity towards a favourite point, was incapable of making this distinction. While he contended earnestly for the liberty of the people born in one quarter of the globe, he laboured to enslave the

---

* History of Charles V. † Herrera, dec. 2. lib. ii. c. 16. 19. 21. lib. iii. c. 7, 8.
‡ Ibid. dec. 1. lib. v. c. 12. § Ibid. lib. viii. c. 9. || Ibid. lib. ix. c. 5. ¶ Ibid. dec. 2. lib. ii c. 8.

inhabitants of another region; and in the warmth of his zeal to save the Americans from the yoke, pronounced it to be lawful and expedient to impose one still heavier upon the Africans. Unfortunately for the latter, Las Casas's plan was adopted. Charles granted a patent to one of his Flemish favourites, containing an exclusive right of importing four thousand negroes into America. The favourite sold his patent to some Genoese merchants for twenty-five thousand ducats, and they were the first who brought into a regular form that commerce for slaves between Africa and America, which has since been carried on to such an amazing extent.*

But the Genoese merchants [1518], conducting their operations, at first, with the rapacity of monopolists, demanded such a high price for negroes, that the number imported into Hispaniola made no great change upon the state of the colony. Las Casas, whose zeal was no less inventive than indefatigable, had recourse to another expedient for the relief of the Indians He observed, that most of the persons who had settled hitherto in America, were sailors and soldiers employed in the discovery or conquest of the country; the younger sons of noble families, allured by the prospect of acquiring sudden wealth; or desperate adventurers, whom their indigence or crimes forced to abandon their native land. Instead of such men, who were dissolute, rapacious, and incapable of that sober persevering industry which is requisite in forming new colonies, he proposed to supply the settlements in Hispaniola and other parts of the New World with a sufficient number of labourers and husbandmen, who should be allured by suitable premiums to remove thither. These, as they were accustomed to fatigue, would be able to perform the work to which the Indians, from the feebleness of their constitution, were unequal, and might soon become useful and opulent citizens. But though Hispaniola stood much in need of a recruit of inhabitants, having been visited at this time with the small-pox, which swept off almost all the natives who had survived their long continued oppression; and though Las Casas had the countenance of the Flemish ministers, this scheme was defeated by the bishop of Burgos, who thwarted all his projects.†

Las Casas now despaired of procuring any relief for the Indians in those places where the Spaniards were already settled. The evil was become so inveterate there as not to admit of a cure. But such discoveries were daily making in the continent as gave a high idea both of its extent and populousness. In all those vast regions there was but one feeble colony planted; and except a small spot on the isthmus of Darien, the natives still occupied the whole country. This opened a new and more ample field for the humanity and zeal of Las Casas, who flattered himself that he might prevent a pernicious system from being introduced there, though he had failed of success in his attempts to overturn it where it was already established. Full of this idea, he applied for a grant of the unoccupied country stretching along the seacoast from the Gulf of Paria to the western frontier of that province now known by the name of Santa Martha. He proposed to settle there with a colony composed of husbandmen, labourers, and ecclesiastics. He engaged in the space of two years to civilize ten thousand of the natives, and to instruct them so thoroughly in the arts of social life, that from the fruits of their industry an annual revenue of fifteen thousand ducats should arise to the king. In ten years he expected that his improvements would be so far advanced as to yield annually sixty thousand ducats. He stipulated, that no soldier or sailor should ever be permitted to settle in this district; and that no Spaniard whatever should enter it without his permission. He even projected to clothe the people whom he took along with him in some distinguishing garb, which did not resemble the Spanish dress, that they might appear to the natives to be a different race of men

* Herrera, dec. 1. lib. ii. c. 20. † Ibid. dec. 2. lib. ii. c. 21.

from those who had brought so many calamities upon their country.* From this scheme, of which I have traced only the great lines, it is manifest that Las Casas had formed ideas concerning the method of treating the Indians, similar to those by which the Jesuits afterwards carried on their great operations in another part of the same continent. He supposed that the Europeans, by availing themselves of that ascendant which they possessed in consequence of their superior progress in science and improvement, might gradually form the minds of the Americans to relish those comforts of which they were destitute, might train them to the arts of civil life, and render them capable of its functions.

But to the bishop of Burgos, and the council of the Indies, this project appeared not only chimerical, but dangerous in a high degree. They deemed the faculties of the Americans to be naturally so limited, and their indolence so excessive, that every attempt to instruct or to improve them would be fruitless. They contended, that it would be extremely imprudent to give the command of a country extending above a thousand miles along the coast to a fanciful presumptuous enthusiast, a stranger to the affairs of the world, and unacquainted with the arts of government. Las Casas, far from being discouraged with a repulse, which he had reason to expect, had recourse once more to the Flemish favourites, who zealously patronized his scheme merely because it had been rejected by the Spanish ministers. They prevailed with their master, who had lately been raised to the Imperial dignity, to refer the consideration of this measure to a select number of his privy counsellors; and Las Casas having excepted against the members of the council of the Indies, as partial and interested, they were all excluded. The decision of men chosen by recommendation of the Flemings was perfectly conformable to their sentiments. They warmly approved of Las Casas's plan, and gave orders for carrying it into execution, but restricted the territory allotted him to three hundred miles along the coast of Cumana; allowing him, however, to extend it as far as he pleased towards the interior part of the country.†

This determination did not pass uncensured. Almost every person who had been in the West Indies exclaimed against it, and supported their opinion so confidently, and with such plausible reasons, as made it advisable to pause and to review the subject more deliberately. Charles himself, though accustomed, at this early period of his life, to adopt the sentiments of his ministers with such submissive deference as did not promise that decisive vigour of mind which distinguished his riper years, could not help suspecting that the eagerness with which the Flemings took part in every affair relating to America flowed from some improper motive, and began to discover an inclination to examine in person into the state of the question concerning the character of the Americans, and the proper manner of treating them. An opportunity of making this inquiry with great advantage soon occurred [June 20]. Quevedo, the bishop of Darien, who had accompanied Pedrarias to the continent in the year one thousand five hundred and thirteen, happened to land at Barcelona, where the court then resided. It was quickly known that his sentiments concerning the talents and disposition of the Indians differed from those of Las Casas: and Charles naturally concluded that by confronting two respectable persons, who, during their residence in America, had full leisure to observe the manners of the people whom they pretended to describe, he might be able to discover which of them had formed his opinion with the greatest discernment and accuracy.

A day for this solemn audience was appointed. The emperor appeared with extraordinary pomp, and took his seat on a throne in the great hall of

---

* Herrera, dec. 2. lib. iv. c. 2.   † Gomara Hist. Gener. c. 77. Herrera, dec. 2. lib. iv c. 3. Oviedo, lib. xix. c. 5.

the palace. His principal courtiers attended. Don Diego Columbus, admiral of the Indies, was summoned to be present. The bishop of Darien was called upon first to deliver his opinion. He, in a short discourse, lamented the fatal desolation of America by the extinction of so many of its inhabitants; he acknowledged that this must be imputed, in some degree, to the extensive rigour and inconsiderate proceedings of the Spaniards; but declared that all the people of the New World whom he had seen, either in the continent or in the islands, appeared to him to be a race of men marked out, by the inferiority of their talents, for servitude, and whom it would be impossible to instruct or improve, unless they were kept under the continual inspection of a master. Las Casas, at greater length and with more fervour, defended his own system. He rejected with indignation the idea that any race of men was born to servitude as irreligious and inhuman. He asserted that the faculties of the Americans were not naturally despicable, but unimproved; that they were capable of receiving instruction in the principles of religion, as well as of acquiring the industry and arts which would qualify them for the various offices of social life; that the mildness and timidity of their nature rendered them so submissive and docile, that they might be led and formed with a gentle hand. He professed that his intentions in proposing the scheme now under consideration were pure and disinterested; and though from the accomplishment of his designs inestimable benefits would result to the crown of Castile, he never had claimed, nor ever would receive, any recompense on that account.

Charles, after hearing both, and consulting with his ministers, did not think himself sufficiently informed to establish any general arrangement with respect to the state of the Indians; but as he had perfect confidence in the integrity of Las Casas, and as even the bishop of Darien admitted his scheme to be of such importance that a trial should be made of its effects, he issued a patent [1522], granting him the district of Cumana formerly mentioned, with full power to establish a colony there according to his own plan.*

Las Casas pushed on the preparations for his voyage with his usual ardour. But, either from his own inexperience in the conduct of affairs, or from the secret opposition of the Spanish nobility, who universally dreaded the success of an institution that might rob them of the industrious and useful hands which cultivated their estates, his progress in engaging husbandmen and labourers was extremely slow, and he could not prevail on more than two hundred to accompany him to Cumana.

Nothing, however, could damp his zeal. With this slender train, hardly sufficient to take possession of such a large territory, and altogether unequal to any effectual attempt towards civilizing its inhabitants, he set sail. The first place at which he touched was the island of Puerto Rico. There he received an account of a new obstacle to the execution of his scheme, more insuperable than any he had hitherto encountered. When he left America, in the year one thousand five hundred and sixteen, the Spaniards had little intercourse with any part of the continent except the countries adjacent to the Gulf of Darien. But as every species of internal industry began to stagnate in Hispaniola, when, by the rapid decrease of the natives, the Spaniards were deprived of those hands with which they had hitherto carried on their operations, this prompted them to try various expedients for supplying that loss. Considerable numbers of negroes were imported; but, on account of their exorbitant price, many of the planters could not afford to purchase them. In order to procure slaves at an easier rate, some of the Spaniards in Hispaniola fitted out vessels to cruise along the coast

---

* Herrera, dec. 2. lib. iv. c. 3, 4, 5. Argensola Annales d'Aragon, 74. 97. Remisal Hist. Gener. lib. ii. c. 19, 20.

of the continent. In places where they found themselves inferior in strength, they traded with the natives, and gave European toys in exchange for the plates of gold worn by them as ornaments; but, wherever they could surprise or overpower the Indians, they carried them off by force, and sold them as slaves.* In those predatory excursions such atrocious acts of violence and cruelty had been committed, that the Spanish name was held in detestation all over the continent. Whenever any ships appeared, the inhabitants either fled to the woods, or rushed down to the shore in arms to repel those hated disturbers of their tranquillity. They forced some parties of the Spaniards to retreat with precipitation; they cut off others; and in the violence of their resentment against the whole nation, they murdered two Dominican missionaries, whose zeal had prompted them to settle in the province of Cumana.† This outrage against persons revered for their sanctity excited such indignation among the people of Hispaniola, who, notwithstanding all their licentious and cruel proceedings, were possessed with a wonderful zeal for religion, and a superstitious respect for its ministers, that they determined to inflict exemplary punishment, not only upon the perpetrators of that crime, but upon the whole race. With this view, they gave the command of five ships and three hundred men to Diego Ocampo, with orders to lay waste the country of Cumana with fire and sword, and to transport all the inhabitants as slaves to Hispaniola. This armament Las Casas found at Puerto Rico, in its way to the continent; and as Ocampo refused to defer his voyage, he immediately perceived that it would be impossible to attempt the execution of his pacific plan in a country destined to be the seat of war and desolation.‡

In order to provide against the effects of this unfortunate incident, he set sail directly for St. Domingo [April 12], leaving his followers cantoned out among the planters in Puerto Rico. From many concurring causes, the reception which Las Casas met with in Hispaniola was very unfavourable. In his negotiations for the relief of the Indians, he had censured the conduct of his countrymen settled there with such honest severity as rendered him universally odious to them. They considered their own ruin as the inevitable consequence of his success. They were now elated with hope of receiving a large recruit of slaves from Cumana, which must be relinquished if Las Casas were assisted in settling his projected colony there. Figueroa, in consequence of the instructions which he had received in Spain, had made an experiment concerning the capacity of the Indians, that was represented as decisive against the system of Las Casas. He collected in Hispaniola a good number of the natives, and settled them in two villages, leaving them at perfect liberty, and with the uncontrolled direction of their own actions. But that people, accustomed to a mode of life extremely different from that which takes place wherever civilization has made any considerable progress, were incapable of assuming new habits at once. Dejected with their own misfortunes as well as those of their country, they exerted so little industry in cultivating the ground, appeared so devoid of solicitude or foresight in providing for their own wants, and were such strangers to arrangement in conducting their affairs, that the Spaniards pronounced them incapable of being formed to live like men in social life, and considered them as children, who should be kept under the perpetual tutelage of persons superior to themselves in wisdom and sagacity.§

Notwithstanding all those circumstances, which alienated the persons in Hispaniola to whom Las Casas applied from himself and from his measures, he, by his activity and perseverance, by some concessions and many threats, obtained at length a small body of troops to protect him

* Herrera, dec. 3. lib. ii. c. 3. † Oviedo, Hist. lib. xix. p. 3 ‡ Herrera, dec. 2. lib. ix. c. 8, 9. § Ibid. dec. 2. lib. x c. 5.

and his colony at their first landing. But upon his return to Puerto Rico, he found that the diseases of the climate had been fatal to several of his people; and that others having got employment in that island, refused to follow him. With the handful that remained, he set sail and landed in Cumana. Ocampo had executed his commission in that province with such barbarous rage, having massacred many of the inhabitants, sent others in chains to Hispaniola, and forced the rest to fly for shelter to the woods, that the people of a small colony, which he had planted at a place which he named *Toledo*, were ready to perish for want in a desolated country. There, however, Las Casas was obliged to fix his residence, though deserted both by the troops appointed to protect him, and by those under the command of Ocampo, who foresaw and dreaded the calamities to which he must be exposed in that wretched station. He made the best provision in his power for the safety and subsistence of his followers, but as his utmost efforts availed little towards securing either the one or the other, he returned to Hispaniola, in order to solicit more effectual aid for the preservation of men who, from confidence in him, had ventured into a post of so much danger. Soon after his departure, the natives, having discovered the feeble and defenceless state of the Spaniards, assembled secretly, attacked them with the fury natural to men exasperated by many injuries, cut off a good number, and compelled the rest to fly in the utmost consternation to the island of Cubagua. The small colony settled there on account of the pearl fishery, catching the panic with which their countrymen had been seized, abandoned the island, and not a Spaniard remained in any part of the continent, or adjacent islands, from the Gulf of Paria to the borders of Darien. Astonished at such a succession of disasters, Las Casas was ashamed to show his face after this fatal termination of all his splendid schemes. He shut himself up in the convent of the Dominicans at St. Domingo, and soon after assumed the habit of that order.*

Though the expulsion of the colony from Cumana happened in the year one thousand five hundred and twenty-one, I have chosen to trace the progress of Las Casas's negotiations from their first rise to their final issue without interruption. His system was the object of long and attentive discussion; and though his efforts in behalf of the oppressed Americans, partly from his own rashness and imprudence, and partly from the malevolent opposition of his adversaries, were not attended with that success which he promised with too sanguine confidence, great praise is due to his humane activity, which gave rise to various regulations that were of some benefit to that unhappy people. I return now to the history of the Spanish discoveries as they occur in the order of time.†

Diego Velasquez, who conquered Cuba in the year one thousand five hundred and eleven, still retained the government of that island, as the deputy of Don Diego Columbus, though he seldom acknowledged his superior, and aimed at rendering his own authority altogether independent.‡ Under his prudent administration, Cuba became one of the most flourishing of the Spanish settlements. The fame of this allured thither many persons from the other colonies, in hopes of finding either some permanent establishment or some employment for their activity. As Cuba lay to the west of all the islands occupied by the Spaniards, and as the ocean which stretches beyond it towards that quarter had not hitherto been explored, these circumstances naturally invited the inhabitants to attempt new discoveries. An expedition for this purpose, in which activity and resolution might conduct to sudden wealth, was more suited to the genius of the age than the patient industry requisite in clearing ground and manufacturing sugar. Instigated

---

* Herrera, dec. 2. lib. x. c. 5. dec. 3. lib. ii. c. 3, 4, 5. Oviedo, Hist. lib. xix. c. 5. Gomara, c. 77. Davila Padilla, lib. i. c. 97. Remisal Hist. Gen. lib. xi. c. 22, 23. † Herrera, dec. 2. lib. x. c. 5. p. 329. ‡ Ibid, lib. ii. c. 19.

by this spirit, several officers, who had served under Pedrarias in Darien, entered into an association to undertake a voyage of discovery. They persuaded Franscisco Hernandez Cordova, an opulent planter in Cuba, and a man of distinguished courage, to join with them in the adventure, and chose him to be their commander. Velasquez not only approved of the design, but assisted in carrying it on. As the veterans from Darien were extremely indigent, he and Cordova advanced money for purchasing three small vessels, and furnished them with every thing requisite either for traffic or for war. A hundred and ten men embarked on board of them, and sailed from St. Jago de Cuba, on the eighth of February, one thousand five hundred and seventeen. By the advice of their chief pilot, Antonio Alaminos, who had served under the first admiral Columbus, they stood directly west, relying on the opinion of that great navigator, who uniformly maintained that a westerly course would lead to the most important discoveries.

On the twenty-first day after their departure from St. Jago, they saw land, which proved to be *Cape Catoche*, the eastern point of that large peninsula projecting from the continent of America, which still retains its original name of *Yucatan*. As they approached the shore, five canoes came off full of people decently clad in cotton garments; an astonishing spectacle to the Spaniards, who had found every other part of America possessed by naked savages. Cordova endeavoured by small presents to gain the good will of these people. They, though amazed at the strange objects now presented for the first time to their view, invited the Spaniards to visit their habitations, with an appearance of cordiality. They landed accordingly, and as they advanced into the country, they observed with new wonder some large houses built with stone. But they soon found that, if the people of Yucatan had made progress in improvement beyond their countrymen, they were likewise more artful and warlike. For though the cazique had received Cordova with many tokens of friendship, he had posted a considerable body of his subjects in ambush behind a thicket, who, upon a signal given by him, rushed out and attacked the Spaniards with great boldness, and some degree of martial order. At the first flight of their arrows, fifteen of the Spaniards were wounded; but the Indians were struck with such terror by the sudden explosion of the fire arms, and so surprised at the execution done by them, by the cross bows, and by the other weapons of their new enemies, that they fled precipitately. Cordova quitted a country where he had met with such a fierce reception, carrying off two prisoners, together with the ornaments of a small temple which he plundered in his retreat.

He continued his course towards the west, without losing sight of the coast, and on the sixteenth day arrived at Campeachy. There the natives received them more hospitably; but the Spaniards were much surprised, that on all the extensive coast along which they had sailed, and which they imagined to be a large island, they had not observed any river [26]. As their water had began to fail, they advanced, in hopes of finding a supply; and at length they discovered the mouth of a river at Potonchan, some leagues beyond Campeachy.

Cordova landed all his troops, in order to protect the sailors while employed in filling the casks; but notwithstanding this precaution, the natives rushed down upon them with such fury and in such numbers, that forty-seven of the Spaniards were killed upon the spot, and one man only of the whole body escaped unhurt. Their commander, though wounded in twelve different places, directed the retreat with presence of mind equal to the courage with which he had led them on in the engagement, and with much difficulty they regained their ships. After this fatal repulse, nothing remained but to hasten back to Cuba with their shattered forces. In their passage thither they suffered the most exquisite distress for want of water, that men, wounded and sickly, shut up in small vessels, and exposed to the heat of the torrid zone, can be supposed to endure. Some of them, sinking under these calamities, died by the way; Cordova, their commander, expired soon after they landed in Cuba.*

Notwithstanding the disastrous conclusion of this expedition, it contributed rather to animate than to damp a spirit of enterprise among the Spaniards. They had discovered an extensive country, situated at no great distance from Cuba, fertile in appearance, and possessed by a people far superior in improvement to any hitherto known in America. Though they had carried on little commercial intercourse with the natives, they had brought off some ornaments of gold, not considerable in value, but of singular fabric. These circumstances, related with the exaggeration natural to men desirous of heightening the merit of their own exploits, were more than sufficient to excite romantic hopes and expectations. Great numbers offered to engage in a new expedition. Velasquez, solicitous to distinguish himself by some service so meritorious as might entitle him to claim the government of Cuba independent of the admiral, not only encouraged their ardour, but at his own expense fitted out four ships for the voyage. Two hundred and forty volunteers, among whom were several persons of rank and fortune, embarked in this enterprise. The command of it was given to Juan de Grijalva, a young man of known merit and courage, with instructions to observe attentively the nature of the countries which he should discover, to barter for gold, and, if circumstances were inviting, to settle a colony in some proper station. He sailed from St. Jago de Cuba on the eighth of April, one thousand five hundred and eighteen. The pilot, Alaminos, held the same course as in the former voyage; but the violence of the currents carrying the ships to the south, the first land which they made was the island of *Cozumel*, to the east of Yucatan. As all the inhabitants fled to the woods and mountains at the approach of the Spaniards, they made no long stay there, and without any remarkable occurrence they reached Potonchan on the opposite side of the peninsula. The desire of avenging their countrymen, who had been slain there, concurred with their ideas of good policy, in prompting them to land, that they might chastise the Indians of that district with such exemplary rigour as would strike terror into all the people round them. But though they disembarked all their troops, and carried ashore some field pieces, the Indians fought with such courage, that the Spaniards gained the victory with difficulty, and were confirmed in their opinion that the inhabitants of this country would prove more formidable enemies than any they had met with in other parts of America. From Potonchan they continued their voyage towards the west, keeping as near as possible to the shore, and casting anchor every evening, from dread of the dangerous accidents to which they might be exposed in an unknown sea. During the day their eyes were turned continually towards land, with a mixture of surprise and wonder at the beauty of the country, as well as the novelty of the objects which they beheld. Many villages were scattered along the coast, in which they could distinguish houses of stone that appeared white and lofty at a distance. In the warmth of their admiration, they fancied these to be cities adorned with towers and pinnacles; and one of the soldiers happening to remark that this country resembled Spain in appearance, Grijalva, with universal applause, called it *New Spain*, the name which still distinguishes this extensive and opulent province of the Spanish empire in America [27]. They landed in a river which the natives called *Tabasco* [June 9]; and the fame of their

* Herrera, dec. 2. lib. ii. c. 17, 18. Hist. Verdadera de la Conquista de la Nueva Espana por Bernal Diaz del Costillo, cap. 1—7. Oviedo, lib. xvii, c. 3. Gomara, c. 52. P. Martyr de Insulis nuper inventis, p. 320.

victory at Potonchan having reached this place, the cazique not only received them amicably, but bestowed presents upon them of such value, as confirmed the high ideas which the Spaniards had formed with respect to the wealth and fertility of the country. These ideas were raised still higher by what occurred at the place where they next touched. This was considerably to the west of Tabasco, in the province since known by the name of Guaxaca. There they were received with the respect paid to superior beings. The people perfumed them, as they landed, with incense of gum copal, and presented to them as offerings the choicest delicacies of their country. They were extremely fond of trading with their new visitants, and in six days the Spaniards obtained ornaments of gold of curious workmanship, to the value of fifteen thousand pesos, in exchange for European toys of small price. The two prisoners whom Cordova had brought from Yucatan, had hitherto served as interpreters; but as they did not understand the language of this country, the Spaniards learned from the natives by signs, that they were subjects of a great monarch called Montezuma, whose dominions extended over that and many other provinces Leaving this place, with which he had so much reason to be pleased, Grijalva continued his course towards the west. He landed on a small island [June 19], which he named the Isle of Sacrifices, because there the Spaniards beheld, for the first time, the horrid spectacle of human victims, which the barbarous superstition of the natives offered to their gods. He touched at another small island, which he called St. Juan de Ulua. From this place he despatched Pedro de Alvarado, one of his officers, to Velasquez, with a full account of the important discoveries which he had made, and with all the treasure that he acquired by trafficking with the natives. After the departure of Alvarado, he himself, with the remaining vessels, proceeded along the coast as far as the river Panuco, the country still appearing to be well peopled, fertile, and opulent.

Several of Grijalva's officers contended that it was not enough to have discovered those delightful regions, or to have performed, at their different landing-places, the empty ceremony of taking possession of them for the crown of Castile, and that their glory was incomplete, unless they planted a colony in some proper station, which might not only secure the Spanish nation a footing in the country, but, with the reinforcements which they were certain of receiving, might gradually subject the whole to the dominion of their sovereign. But the squadron had now been above five months at sea; the greatest part of their provisions was exhausted, and what remained of their stores so much corrupted by the heat of the climate, as to be almost unfit for use; they had lost some men by death; others were sickly; the country was crowded with people who seemed to be intelligent as well as brave; and they were under the government of one powerful monarch, who could bring them to act against their invaders with united force. To plant a colony under so many circumstances of disadvantage, appeared a scheme too perilous to be attempted. Grijalva, though possessed both of ambition and courage, was destitute of the superior talents capable of forming or executing such a great plan. He judged it more prudent to return to Cuba, having fulfilled the purpose of his voyage, and accomplished all that the armament which he commanded enabled him to perform. He returned to St. Jago de Cuba, on the twenty-sixth of October, from which he had taken his departure about six months before.*

This was the longest as well as the most successful voyage which the Spaniards had hitherto made in the New World. They had discovered that Yucatan was not an island as they had supposed, but part of the great

---

* Herrera, dec. 11. lib. iii. c. 1, 2, 9, 10. Bernal Diaz, c. 8, 17. Oviedo Hist. lib. xvii. c. 9. 28 Gomara, c. 49

continent of America. From Potonchan they had pursued their course for many hundred miles along a coast formerly unexplored, stretching at first towards the west, and then turning to the north; all the country which they had discovered appeared to be no less valuable than extensive. As soon as Alvarado reached Cuba, Velasquez, transported with success so far beyond his most sanguine expectations, immediately despatched a person of confidence to carry this important intelligence to Spain, to exhibit the rich productions of the countries which had been discovered by his means, and to solicit such an increase of authority as might enable and encourage him to attempt the conquest of them. Without waiting for the return of his messenger, or for the arrival of Grijalva, of whom he was become so jealous or distrustful that he was resolved no longer to employ him, he began to prepare such a powerful armament as might prove equal to an enterprise of so much danger and importance.

But as the expedition upon which Velasquez was now intent terminated in conquests of greater moment than what the Spaniards had hitherto achieved, and led them to the knowledge of a people, who, if compared with those tribes of America with whom they were hitherto acquainted, may be considered as highly civilized; it is proper to pause before we proceed to the history of events extremely different from those which we have already related, in order to take a view of the state of the New World when first discovered, and to contemplate the policy and manners of the rude uncultivated tribes that occupied all the parts of it with which the Spaniards were at this time acquainted.

BOOK IV.

TWENTY-SIX years had elasped since Columbus had conducted the people of Europe to the New World. During that period the Spaniards had made great progress in exploring its various regions. They had visited all the islands scattered in different clusters through that part of the ocean which flows in between North and South America. They had sailed along the eastern coast of the continent from the river De la Plata to the bottom of the Mexican Gulf, and had found that it stretched without interruption through this vast portion of the globe. They had discovered the great Southern Ocean, which opened new prospects in that quarter. They had acquired some knowledge of the coast of Florida, which led them to observe the continent as it extended in an opposite direction; and though they pushed their discoveries no further towards the North, other nations had visited those parts which they neglected. The English, in a voyage the motives and success of which shall be related in another part of this History, had sailed along the coast of America from Labrador to the confines of Florida; and the Portuguese, in quest of a shorter passage to the East Indies, had ventured into the northern seas, and viewed the same regions.* Thus, at the period where I have chosen to take a view of the state of the New World, its extent was known almost from its northern extremity to thirty-five degrees south of the equator. The countries which stretch from thence to the southern boundary of America, the great empire of Peru, and the interior state of the extensive dominions subject to the sovereigns of Mexico, were still undiscovered.

* Herrera, doc. 1. lib. vi c. 16

AMERICA.

When we contemplate the New World, the first circumstance that strikes us is its immense extent. It was not a small portion of the earth, so inconsiderable that it might have escaped the observation or research of former ages, which Columbus discovered. He made known a new hemisphere, larger than either Europe, or Asia, or Africa, the three noted divisions of the ancient continent, and not much inferior in dimensions to a third part of the habitable globe.

America is remarkable, not only for its magnitude, but for its position. It stretches from the northern polar circle to a high southern latitude, above fifteen hundred miles beyond the furthest extremity of the old continent on that side of the line. A country of such extent passes through all the climates capable of becoming the habitation of man, and fit for yielding the various productions peculiar either to the temperate or to the torrid regions of the earth.

Next to the extent of the New World, the grandeur of the objects which it presents to view is most apt to strike the eye of an observer. Nature seems here to have carried on her operations upon a larger scale and with a bolder hand, and to have distinguished the features of this country by a peculiar magnificence. The mountains in America are much superior in height to those in the other divisions of the globe. Even the plain of Quito, which may be considered as the base of the Andes, is elevated further above the sea than the top of the Pyrenees. This stupendous ridge of the Andes, no less remarkable for extent than elevation, rises in different places more than one-third above the Peak of Teneriffe, the highest land in the ancient hemisphere. The Andes may literally be said to hide their heads in the clouds; the storms often roll, and the thunder bursts below their summits, which, though exposed to the rays of the sun in the centre of the torrid zone, are covered with everlasting snows [28].

From these lofty mountains descend rivers, proportionably large, with which the streams in the ancient continent are not to be compared, either for length of course, or the vast body of water which they roll towards the ocean. The Maragnon, the Orinoco, the Plata in South America, the Mississippi and St. Laurence in North America, flow in such spacious channels, that long before they feel the influence of the tide, they resemble arms of the sea rather than rivers of fresh water [29].

The lakes of the New World are no less conspicuous for grandeur than its mountains and rivers. There is nothing in other parts of the globe which resembles the prodigious chain of lakes in North America. They may properly be termed inland seas of fresh water; and even those of the second or third class in magnitude are of larger circuit (the Caspian Sea excepted) than the greatest lake of the ancient continent.

The New World is of a form extremely favourable to commercial intercourse. When a continent is formed, like Africa, of one vast solid mass, unbroken by arms of the sea penetrating into its interior parts, with few large rivers, and those at a considerable distance from each other, the greater part of it seems destined to remain for ever uncivilized, and to be debarred from any active or enlarged communication with the rest of mankind. When, like Europe, a continent is opened by inlets of the ocean of great extent, such as the Mediterranean and Baltic; or when, like Asia, its coasts is broken by deep bays advancing far into the country, such as the Black Sea, the Gulfs of Arabia, of Persia, of Bengal, of Siam, and of Leotang; when the surrounding seas are filled with large and fertile islands, and the continent itself watered with a variety of navigable rivers, those regions may be said to possess whatever can facilitate the progress of their inhabitants in commerce and improvement. In all these respects America may bear a comparison with the other quarters of the globe. The Gulf of Mexico, which flows in between North and South America, may be considered as a Mediterranean sea, which opens a maritime commerce with all the fertile countries by which it is encircled. The islands scattered in it are inferior only to those in the Indian Archipelago, in number, in magnitude, and in value. As we stretch along the northern division of the American hemisphere, the Bay of Chesapeak presents a spacious inlet, which conducts the navigator far into the interior parts of provinces no less fertile than extensive; and if ever the progress of culture and population shall mitigate the extreme rigour of the climate in the more northern districts of America, Hudson's Bay may become as subservient to commercial intercourse in that quarter of the globe, as the Baltic is in Europe. The other great portion of the New World is encompassed on every side by the sea, except one narrow neck which separates the Atlantic from the Pacific Ocean; and though it be not opened by spacious bays or arms of the sea, its interior parts are rendered accessible by a number of large rivers, fed by so many auxiliary streams, flowing in such various directions, that almost without any aid from the hand of industry and art, an inland navigation may be carried on through all the provinces from the river De la Plata to the Gulf of Paria. Nor is this bounty of nature confined to the southern division of America; its northern continent abounds no less in rivers which are navigable almost to their sources, and by its immense chain of lakes provision is made for an inland communication, more extensive and commodious than in any quarter of the globe. The countries stretching from the Gulf of Darien on one side, to that of California on the other, which form the chain that binds the two parts of the American continent together, are not destitute of peculiar advantages. Their coast on one side is washed by the Atlantic Ocean, on the other by the Pacific. Some of their rivers flow into the former, some into the latter, and secure to them all the commercial benefits that may result from a communication with both.

But what most distinguishes America from other parts of the earth is the peculiar temperature of its climate, and the different laws to which it is subject with respect to the distribution of heat and cold. We cannot determine with precision the portion of heat felt in any part of the globe, merely by measuring its distance from the equator. The climate of a country is affected, in some degree, by its elevation above the sea, by the extent of continent, by the nature of the soil, the height of adjacent mountains, and many other circumstances. The influence of these, however, is from various causes less considerable in the greater part of the ancient continent; and from knowing the position of any country there, we can pronounce with greater certainty what will be the warmth of its climate, and the nature of its productions.

The maxims which are founded upon observation of our hemisphere will not apply to the other. In the New World, cold predominates. The rigour of the frigid zone extends over half of those regions which should be temperate by their position. Countries where the grape and the fig should ripen, are buried under snow one half of the year; and lands situated in the same parallel with the most fertile and best cultivated provinces in Europe, are chilled with perpetual frosts, which almost destroy the power of vegetation [30]. As we advance to those parts of America which lie in the same parallel with provinces of Asia and Africa, blessed with a uniform enjoyment of such genial warmth as is most friendly to life and to vegetation, the dominion of cold continues to be felt, and winter reigns, though during a short period, with extreme severity. If we proceed along the American continent into the torrid zone, we shall find the cold prevalent in the New World extending itself also to this region of the globe, and mitigating the excess of its fervour. While the negro on the coast of Africa is scorched with unremitting heat, the inhabitant of Peru breathes an air equally mild and temperate, and is perpetually shaded under a canopy of gray clouds, which intercepts the fierce beams of the sun, without obstructing his friendly influence.* Along the eastern coast of America, the climate, though more similar to that of the torrid zone in other parts of the earth, is nevertheless considerably milder than in those countries of Asia and Africa which lie in the same latitude. If from the southern tropic we continue our progress to the extremity of the American continent, we meet with frozen seas, and countries horrid, barren, and scarcely habitable for cold, much sooner than in the north.†

Various causes combine in rendering the climate of America so extremely different from that of the ancient continent. Though the utmost extent of America towards the north be not yet discovered, we know that it advances much nearer to the pole than either Europe or Asia. Both these have large seas to the north, which are open during part of the year; and even when covered with ice, the wind that blows over them is less intensely cold than that which blows over land in the same high latitudes. But in America the land stretches from the river St. Laurence towards the pole, and spreads out immensely to the west. A chain of enormous mountains covered with snow and ice, runs through all this dreary region. The wind, in passing over such an extent of high and frozen land, becomes so impregnated with cold, that it acquires a piercing keenness, which it retains in its progress through warmer climates, and it is not entirely mitigated until it reach the Gulf of Mexico. Over all the continent of North America, a north-westerly wind and excessive cold are synonymous terms. Even in the most sultry weather, the moment that the wind veers to that quarter, its penetrating influence is felt in a transition from heat to cold no less violent than sudden. To this powerful cause we may ascribe the extraordinary dominion of cold, and its violent inroads into the southern provinces, in that part of the globe.‡

Other causes, no less remarkable, diminish the active power of heat in those parts of the American continent which lie between the tropics. In all that portion of the globe, the wind blows in an invariable direction from east to west. As this wind holds its course across the ancient continent, it arrives at the countries which stretch along the western shores of Africa, inflamed with all the fiery particles which it hath collected from the sultry plains of Asia, and the burning sands in the African deserts. The coast of Africa is, accordingly, the region of the earth which feels the most fervent heat, and is exposed to the unmitigated ardour of the torrid zone But this same wind, which brings such an accession of warmth to the countries lying between the river of Senegal and Cafraria, traverses the Atlantic Ocean before it reaches the American shore. It is cooled in its passage over this vast body of water, and is felt as a refreshing gale along the coast of Brazil [31], and Guiana, rendering these countries, though among the warmest in America, temperate, when compared with those which lie opposite to them in Africa [32]. As this wind advances in its course across America, it meets with immense plains covered with impenetrable forests, or occupied by large rivers, marshes, and stagnating waters, where it can recover no considerable degree of heat. At length it arrives at the Andes, which run from north to south through the whole continent. In passing over their elevated and frozen summits, it is so thoroughly cooled, that the greater part of the countries beyond them hardly feel the ardour to which they seem exposed by their situation.§ In the other provinces of America, from Tierra Ferme westward to the Mexican empire, the heat of the climate is tempered, in some places, by the elevation of the land above the sea, in others, by their extraordinary

---

* Voyage de Ulloa, tom. l. p. 453. Anson's Voyage, p. 184. † Anson's Voyage, p. 74; and Voyage de Quiros, chez. Hist. Gen. des Voyages, tom. xiv. p. 83. Richard Hist. Natur. de l'Air, ii. 305, &c. ‡ Charlevoix Hist. de Nouv. Fr. iii. 165. Hist. Généralé des Voyages, tom. xv 215, &c. § Acosta Hist. Novi Orbis, lib. ii. c. 11. Buffon Hist. Naturelle, &c. tom. ii. 512, &c. ix. 107, &c. Osborn's Collect. of Voyages, ii. p. 868.

humidity, and in all, by the enormous mountains scattered over this tract. The islands of America in the torrid zone are either small or mountainous, and are fanned alternately by refreshing sea and land breezes.

The causes of the extraordinary cold towards the southern limits of America, and in the seas beyond it, cannot be ascertained in a manner equally satisfying. It was long supposed that a vast continent, distinguished by the name of *Terra Australis Incognita*, lay between the southern extremity of America and the Antarctic pole. The same principles which account for the extraordinary degree of cold in the northern regions of America, were employed in order to explain that which is felt at Cape Horn and the adjacent countries. The immense extent of the southern continent, and the large rivers which it poured into the ocean, were mentioned and admitted by philosophers as causes sufficient to occasion the unusual sensation of cold, and the still more uncommon appearances of frozen seas in that region of the globe. But the imaginary continent to which such influence was ascribed, having been searched for in vain, and the space which it was supposed to occupy having been found to be an open sea, new conjectures must be formed with respect to the causes of a temperature of climate, so extremely different from that which we experience in countries removed at the same distance from the opposite pole [33].

After contemplating those permanent and characteristic qualities of the American continent, which arise from the peculiarity of its situation, and the disposition of its parts, the next object that merits attention is its condition when first discovered, as far as that depended upon the industry and operations of man. The effects of human ingenuity and labour are more extensive and considerable than even our own vanity is apt at first to imagine. When we survey the face of the habitable globe, no small part of that fertility and beauty which we ascribe to the hand of nature, is the work of man. His efforts, when continued through a succession of ages, change the appearance and improve the qualities of the earth. As a great part of the ancient continent has long been occupied by nations far advanced in arts and industry, our eye is accustomed to view the earth in that form which it assumes when rendered fit to be the residence of a numerous race of men, and to supply them with nourishment.

But in the New World, the state of mankind was ruder, and the aspect of nature extremely different. Throughout all its vast regions, there were only two monarchies remarkable for extent of territory, or distinguished by any progress in improvement. The rest of this continent was possessed by small independent tribes, destitute of arts and industry, and neither capable to correct the defects nor desirous to meliorate the condition of hat part of the earth allotted to them for their habitation. Countries occupied by such people were almost in the same state as if they had been without inhabitants. Immense forests covered a great part of the uncultivated earth; and as the hand of industry had not taught the rivers to run in a proper channel, or drained off the stagnating water, many of the most fertile plains were overflowed with inundations, or converted into marshes. In the southern provinces, where the warmth of the sun, the moisture of the climate, and the fertility of the soil, combine in calling forth the most vigorous powers of vegetation, the woods are so choked with its rank luxuriance as to be almost impervious, and the surface of the ground is hid from the eye under a thick covering of shrubs and herbs and weeds. In this state of wild unassisted nature, a great part of the large provinces in South America, which extend from the bottom of the Andes to the sea, still remain. The European colonies have cleared and cultivated a few spots along the coast; but the original race of inhabitants, as rude and indolent as ever, have done nothing to open or improve a country possessing almost every advantage of situation and climate. As we advance towards the northern provinces of America, nature continues to wear the same uncultivated aspect, and, in proportion as the rigour of the climate increases, appears more desolate and horrid. There the forests, though not encumbered with the same exuberance of vegetation, are of immense extent; prodigious marshes overspread the plains, and few marks appear of human activity in any attempt to cultivate or embellish the earth. No wonder that the colonies sent from Europe were astonished at their first entrance into the New World. It appeared to them waste, solitary, and uninviting. When the English began to settle in America, they termed the countries of which they took possession, *The Wilderness*. Nothing but their eager expectation of finding mines of gold could have induced the Spaniards to penetrate through the woods and marshes of America, where at every step they observed the extreme difference between the uncultivated face of nature, and that which it acquires under the forming hand of industry and art [34].

The labour and operations of man not only improve and embellish the earth, but render it more wholesome and friendly to life. When any region lies neglected and destitute of cultivation, the air stagnates in the woods; putrid exhalations arise from the waters; the surface of the earth, loaded with rank vegetation, feels not the purifying influence of the sun or of the wind; the malignity of the distempers natural to the climate increases, and new maladies no less noxious are engendered. Accordingly, all the provinces of America, when first discovered, were found to be remarkably unhealthy. This the Spaniards experienced in every expedition into the New World, whether destined for conquest or settlement. Though by the natural constitution of their bodies, their habitual temperance, and the persevering vigour of their minds, they were as much formed as any people in Europe for active service in a sultry climate, they felt severely the fatal and pernicious qualities of those uncultivated regions through which they marched, or where they endeavoured to plant colonies. Great numbers were cut off by the unknown and violent diseases with which they were infected. Such as survived the destructive rage of those maladies, were not exempted from the noxious influence of the climate. They returned to Europe, according to the description of the early Spanish historians, feeble, emaciated, with languid looks, and complexions of such a sickly yellow colour as indicated the unwholesome temperature of the countries where they had resided.*

The uncultivated state of the New World affected not only the temperature of the air, but the qualities of its productions. The principle of life seems to have been less active and vigorous there than in the ancient continent. Notwithstanding the vast extent of America, and the variety of its climates, the different species of animals peculiar to it are much fewer in proportion than those of the other hemisphere. In the islands there were only four kinds of quadrupeds known, the largest of which did not exceed the size of a rabbit. On the continent, the variety was greater; and though the individuals of each kind could not fail of multiplying exceedingly when almost unmolested by men, who were neither so numerous, nor so united in society, as to be formidable enemies to the animal creation, the number of distinct species must still be considered as extremely small. Of two hundred different kinds of animals spread over the face of the earth, only about one-third existed in America at the time of its discovery.† · Nature was not only less prolific in the New World, but she appears likewise to have been less vigorous in her productions. The animals originally belonging to this quarter of the globe appear to be of an inferior race, neither so robust nor so fierce as those of the other continent. America gives birth to no creature of such bulk as·

---

* Gomara Hist. c. 20. 22. Oviedo Hist. lib. ii. c. 13. lib. v. c. 10. P. Martyr, Epist. 545. Decad, p. 176. † Buffon Hist. Naturelle, tom. ix. p. 86.

to be compared with the elephant or rhinoceros, or that equals the lion
and tiger in strength and ferocity [35]. The *Tapyr* of Brazil, the largest
quadruped of the ravenous tribe in the New World, is not larger than a
calf of six months old. The *Puma* and *Jaguar*, its fiercest beasts of
prey, which Europeans have inaccurately denominated lions and tigers,
possess neither the undaunted courage of the former, nor the ravenous
cruelty of the latter.* They are inactive and timid, hardly formidable
to man, and often turn their backs upon the least appearance of resistance.†
The same qualities in the climate of America which stinted the growth,
and enfeebled the spirit, of its native animals, have proved pernicious to
such as have migrated into it voluntarily from the other continent, or have
been transported thither by the Europeans.‡ The bears, the wolves, the
deer of America, are not equal in size to those of the Old World.§ Most
of the domestic animals, with which the Europeans have stored the provinces wherein they settled, have degenerated with respect either to bulk
or quality, in a country whose temperature and soil seem to be less favourable to the strength and perfection of the animal creation [36].

The same causes which checked the growth and the vigour of the
more noble animals, were friendly to the propagation and increase of
reptiles and insects. Though this is not peculiar to the New World, and
those odious tribes, nourished by heat, moisture, and corruption, infest
every part of the torrid zone; they multiply faster, perhaps, in America,
and grow to a more monstrous bulk. As this country is on the whole less
cultivated and less peopled than the other quarters of the earth, the active
principle of life wastes its force in productions of this inferior form. The
air is often darkened with clouds of insects, and the ground covered with
shocking and noxious reptiles. The country around Porto Bello swarms
with toads in such multitudes as hide the surface of the earth. At Guayaquil, snakes and vipers are hardly less numerous. Carthagena is infested
with numerous flocks of bats, which annoy not only the cattle but the
inhabitants.‖ In the islands, legions of ants have at different times consumed every vegetable production [37], and left the earth entirely bare
as if it had been burned with fire. The damp forests and rank soil of
the countries on the banks of the Orinoco and Maragnon teem with
almost every offensive and poisonous creature which the power of a sultry
sun can quicken into life.¶

The birds of the New World are not distinguished by qualities so conspicuous and characteristical as those which we have observed in its quadrupeds. Birds are more independent of man, and less affected by the
changes which his industry and labour make upon the state of the earth.
They have a greater propensity to migrate from one country to another, and
can gratify this instinct of their nature without difficulty or danger. Hence
the number of birds common to both continents is much greater than that
of quadrupeds; and even such as are peculiar to America nearly resemble
those with which mankind were acquainted in similar regions of the ancient
hemisphere. The American birds of the torrid zone, like those of the
same climate in Asia and Africa, are decked in plumage which dazzles
the eye with the beauty of its colours; but nature, satisfied with clothing
them in this gay dress, has denied most of them that melody of sound and
variety of notes which catch and delight the ear. The birds of the temperate climates there, in the same manner as in our continent, are less

---

* Buffon Hist. Natur. tom. ix. p. 87.   Marcgravii Hist. Nat. Brazil, p. 229.   † Buffon Hist. Natur. ix. 13. 203.   Acosta Hist. lib. iv. c. 34.   Pisonis Hist. p. 6.   Herrera, dec. 4. lib. iv. c. 1. lib. x. c. 13.   ‡ Churchill, v. p. 691.   Ovalle Relat. of Chili, Church. iii. p. 10.   Somario de Oviedo, c. 14—22.   Voyage du Des Marchais, iii. 299.   § Buffon Hist. Natur. ix. 103.   Kalm's Travels i. 102.   Blet. voy. de France Equinox. p. 339.   ‖ Voyage de Ulloa, tom. i. p. 89.   Ib. p. 147. Herrera, dec. 11. lib. iii. c, 3, 19.   ¶ Voyage de Condamine, p. 167.   Gumilla, iii. 120, &c.   Hist. Gener. des Voyages, xiv. 317.   Dumont Mémoires sur la Louisiane, i. 109.   Somario de Oviedo, c. 52—62.

splendid in their appearance; but, in compensation for that defect, they have voices of greater compass, and more melodious. In some districts of America, the unwholesome temperature of the air seems to be unfavourable even to this part of the creation. The number of birds is less than in other countries, and the traveller is struck with the amazing solitude and silence of its forests.* It is remarkable, however, that America, where the quadrupeds are so dwarfish and dastardly, should produce the *Condor* which is entitled to pre-eminence over all the flying tribe, in bulk, in strength, and in courage.†

The soil in a continent so extensive as America must, of course, be extremely various. In each of its provinces we find some distinguishing peculiarities, the description of which belongs to those who write their particular history. In general we may observe, that the moisture and cold, which predominate so remarkably in all parts of America, must have great influence upon the nature of its soil; countries lying in the same parallel with those regions which never feel the extreme rigour of winter in the ancient continent, are frozen over in America during a great part of the year. Chilled by this intense cold, the ground never acquires warmth sufficient to ripen the fruits which are found in the corresponding parts of the other continent. If we wish to rear in America the productions which abound in any particular district of the ancient world, we must advance several degrees nearer to the line than in the other hemisphere, as it requires such an increase of heat to counterbalance the natural frigidity of the soil and climate [38]. At the Cape of Good Hope, several of the plants and fruits peculiar to the countries within the tropics are cultivated with success; whereas, at St. Augustine in Florida, and Charles Town in South Carolina, though considerably nearer the line, they cannot be brought to thrive with equal certainty [39]. But, if allowance be made for this diversity in the degree of heat, the soil of America is naturally as rich and fertile as in any part of the earth. As the country was thinly inhabited, and by a people of little industry, who had none of the domestic animals which civilized nations rear in such vast numbers, the earth was not exhausted by their consumption. The vegetable productions, to which the fertility of the soil gave birth, often remained untouched, and, being suffered to corrupt on its surface, returned with increase into its bosom.‡ As trees and plants derive a great part of their nourishment from air and water; if they were not destroyed by man and other animals, they would render to the earth more, perhaps, than they take from it, and feed rather than impoverish it. Thus the unoccupied soil of America may have gone on enriching for many ages. The vast number as well as enormous size of the trees in America, indicate the extraordinary vigour of the soil in its native state. When the Europeans first began to cultivate the New World, they were astonished at the luxuriant power of vegetation in its virgin mould; and in several places the ingenuity of the planter is still employed in diminishing and wasting its superfluous fertility, in order to bring it down to a state fit for profitable culture§ [40].

Having thus surveyed the state of the New World at the time of its discovery, and considered the peculiar features and qualities which distinguish and characterize it, the next inquiry that merits attention is, How was America peopled? By what course did mankind migrate from the one continent to the other? And in what quarter is it most probable that a communication was opened between them?

We know, with infallible certainty, that all the human race spring from

---

* Bouguer Voy. au Perou, 17. Chanvalon Voyage à la Martinique, p. 96. Warren's Descript. Surinam. Osborn's Collect. ii. 924. Lettres Edif. xxiv. p. 339. Charlev. Hist. de la Nouv. France, ii. 155. † Voyage de Ulloa, i. 363. Voyage de Condamine, 175. Buffon Hist. Nat. xvi. 184. Voyage du Des Marchais, iii. 390. ‡ Buffon, Hist. Natur. i. 242. Kalm, i. 151. § Charlevoix, Hist. de Nouv. Fran. iii. 405. Voyage du Des Marchais, iii. 229. Lery ap. de Bry. part iii. p. 174.

Vol. I.—17

the same source, and that the descendants of one man, under the protection, as well as in obedience to the command of Heaven, multiplied and replenished the earth. But neither the annals nor the traditions of nations reach back to those remote ages, in which they took possession of the different countries where they are now settled. We cannot trace the branches of this first family, or point out with certainty the time and manner in which they divided and spread over the face of the globe Even among the most enlightened people, the period of authentic history is extremely short; and every thing prior to that is fabulous or obscure. It is not surprising, then, that the unlettered inhabitants of America, who have no solicitude about futurity, and little curiosity concerning what is passed, should be altogether unacquainted with their own original. The people on the two opposite coasts of America, who occupy those countries in America which approach nearest to the ancient continent are so remarkably rude, that it is altogether vain to search among them for such information as might discover the place from whence they came, or the ancestors of whom they are descended.* Whatever light has been thrown on this subject is derived not from the natives of America, but from the inquisitive genius of their conquerors.

When the people of Europe unexpectedly discovered a New World, removed at a vast distance from every part of the ancient continent which was then known, and filled with inhabitants whose appearance and manners differed remarkably from the rest of the human species, the question concerning their original became naturally an object of curiosity and attention. The theories and speculations of ingenious men with respect to this subject, would fill many volumes; but are often so wild and chimerical, that I should offer an insult to the understanding of my readers, if I attempted either minutely to enumerate or to refute them. Some have presumptuously imagined, that the people of America were not the offspring of the same common parent with the rest of mankind, but that they formed a separate race of men, distinguishable by peculiar features in the constitution of their bodies, as well as in the characteristic qualities of their minds. Others contend, that they are descended from some remnant of the antediluvian inhabitants of the earth, who survived the deluge which swept away the greatest part of the human species in the days of Noah; and preposterously suppose rude, uncivilized tribes, scattered over an uncultivated continent, to be the most ancient race of people on the earth. There is hardly any nation from the north to the south pole, to which some antiquary, in the extravagance of conjecture, has not ascribed the honour of peopling America. The Jews, the Canaanites, the Phœnicians, the Carthaginians, the Greeks, the Scythians, in ancient times, are supposed to have settled in this western world. The Chinese, the Swedes, the Norwegians, the Welsh, the Spaniards, are said to have sent colonies thither in later ages, at different periods and on various occasions. Zealous advocates stand forth to support the respective claims of those people; and though they rest upon no better foundation than the casual resemblance of some customs, or the supposed affinity between a few words in their different languages, much erudition and more zeal have been employed, to little purpose, in defence of the opposite systems. Those regions of conjecture and controversy belong not to the historian. His is a more limited province, confined by what is established by certain or highly probable evidence. Beyond this I shall not venture, in offering a few observations which may contribute to throw some light upon this curious and much agitated question

1. There are authors who have endeavoured by mere conjecture to account for the peopling of America. Some have supposed that it was

---

* Vincgas's Hist. of California, i, 60.

originally united to the ancient continent, and disjoined from it by the shock of an earthquake, or the irruption of a deluge. Others have imagined, that some vessel being forced from its course by the violence of a westerly wind, might be driven by accident towards the American coast, and have given a beginning to population in that desolate continent.* But with respect to all those systems, it is in vain either to reason or inquire, because it is impossible to come to any decision. Such events as they suppose are barely possible, and may have happened. That they ever did happen, we have no evidence, either from the clear testimony of history, or from the obscure intimations of tradition.

2. Nothing can be more frivolous or uncertain than the attempts to discover the original of the Americans merely by tracing the resemblance between their manners and those of any particular people in the ancient continent. If we suppose two tribes, though placed in the most remote regions of the globe, to live in a climate nearly of the same temperature, to be in the same state of society, and to resemble each other in the degree of their improvement, they must feel the same wants, and exert the same endeavours to supply them. The same objects will allure, the same passions will animate them, and the same ideas and sentiments will arise in their minds. The character and occupations of the hunter in America must be little different from those of an Asiatic who depends for subsistence on the chase. A tribe of savages on the banks of the Danube must nearly resemble one upon the plains washed by the Mississippi. Instead then of presuming from this similarity, that there is any affinity between them, we should only conclude that the disposition and manners of men are formed by their situation, and arise from the state of society in which they live. The moment that begins to vary, the character of a people must change. In proportion as it advances in improvement, their manners refine, their powers and talents are called forth. In every part of the earth, the progress of man hath been nearly the same ; and we can trace him in his career from the rude simplicity of savage life, until he attains the industry, the arts, and the elegance of polished society. There is nothing wonderful, then, in the similitude between the Americans and the barbarous nations of our continent. Had Lafitau, Garcia, and many other authors attended to this, they would not have perplexed a subject, which they pretend to illustrate, by their fruitless endeavours to establish an affinity between various races of people, in the old and new continents, upon no other evidence than such a resemblance in their manners as necessarily arises from the similarity of their condition. There are, it is true, among every people, some customs which, as they do not flow from any natural want or desire peculiar to their situation, may be denominated usages of arbitrary institution. If between two nations settled in remote parts of the earth, a perfect agreement with respect to any of these should be discovered, one might be led to suspect that they were connected by some affinity. If, for example, a nation were found in America that consecrated the seventh day to religious worship and rest, we might justly suppose that it had derived its knowledge of this usage, which is of arbitrary institution, from the Jews. But, if it were discovered that another nation celebrated the first appearance of every new moon with extraordinary demonstrations of joy, we should not be entitled to conclude that the observation of this monthly festival was borrowed from the Jews, but ought to consider it merely as the expression of that joy which is natural to man on the return of the planet which guides and cheers him in the night. The instances of customs, merely arbitrary, common to the inhabitants of both hemispheres, are, indeed, so few and so equivocal, that no theory concerning the population of the New World ought to be founded upon them.

* Parson's Remains of Japhet, p. 240. Ancient Univers. Hist. vol. xx. p. 164; P. Feyjoo Teatro Critico, tom. v. p. 304, &c. Acosta Hist. Moral. Novi Orbis, lib. i. 16, c. 19.

3. The theories which have been formed with respect to the original of the Americans, from observation of their religious rites and practices, are no less fanciful and destitute of solid foundation. When the religious opinions of any people are neither the result of rational inquiry, nor derived from the instructions of revelation, they must needs be wild and extravagant. Barbarous nations are incapable of the former, and have not been blessed with the advantages arising from the latter. Still, however, the human mind, even where its operations appear most wild and capricious, holds a course so regular, that in every age and country the dominion of particular passions will be attended with similar effects. The savage of Europe or America, when filled with superstitious dread of invisible beings, or with inquisitive solicitude to penetrate into the events of futurity, trembles alike with fear, or glows with impatience. He has recourse to rites and practices of the same kind, in order to avert the vengeance which he supposes to be impending over him, or to divine the secret which is the object of his curiosity. Accordingly, the ritual of superstition in one continent seems, in many particulars, to be a transcript of that established in the other, and both authorize similar institutions, sometimes so frivolous as to excite pity, sometimes so bloody and barbarous as to create horror. But without supposing any consanguinity between such distant nations, or imagining that their religious ceremonies were conveyed by tradition from the one to the other, we may ascribe this uniformity, which in many instances seems very amazing, to the natural operation of superstition and enthusiasm upon the weakness of the human mind.

4. We may lay it down as a certain principle in this inquiry, that America was not peopled by any nation of the ancient continent which had made considerable progress in civilization. The inhabitants of the New World were in a state of society so extremely rude as to be unacquainted with those arts which are the first essays of human ingenuity in its advance towards improvement. Even the most cultivated nations of America were strangers to many of those simple inventions which were almost coeval with society in other parts of the world, and were known in the earliest periods of civil life with which we have any acquaintance. From this it is manifest, that the tribes which originally migrated to America, came off from nations which must have been no less barbarous than their posterity, at the time when they were first discovered by the Europeans. For, although the elegant or refined arts may decline or perish, amidst the violent shocks of those revolutions and disasters to which nations are exposed, the necessary arts of life, when once they have been introduced among any people, are never lost. None of the vicissitudes in human affairs affect these, and they continue to be practised as long as the race of men exists. If ever the use of iron had been known to the savages of America, or to their progenitors; if ever they had employed a plough, a loom, or a forge, the utility of those inventions would have preserved them, and it is impossible that they should have been abandoned or forgotten. We may conclude, then, that the Americans sprung from some people, who were themselves in such an early and unimproved state of society, as to be unacquainted with all those necessary arts, which continued to be unknown among their posterity when first visited by the Spaniards.

5. It appears no less evident that America was not peopled by any colony from the more southern nations of the ancient continent. None of the rude tribes settled in that part of our hemisphere can be supposed to have visited a country so remote. They possessed neither enterprise, nor ingenuity, nor power that could prompt them to undertake, or enable them to perform such a distant voyage. That the more civilized nations in Asia or Africa are not the progenitors of the Americans, is manifest not only from the observations which I have already made concerning their ignorance of the most simple and necessary arts, but from an additional circumstance,

Whenever any people have experienced the advantages which men enjoy by their dominion over the inferior animals, they can neither subsist without the nourishment which these afford, nor carry on any considerable operation independent of their ministry and labour. Accordingly, the first care of the Spaniards, when they settled in America, was to stock it with all the domestic animals of Europe; and if, prior to them, the Tyrians, the Carthaginians, the Chinese, or any other polished people, had taken possession of that continent, we should have found there the animals peculiar to those regions of the globe where they were originally seated. In all America, however, there is not one animal, tame or wild, which properly belongs to the warm or even the more temperate countries of the ancient continent. The camel, the dromedary, the horse, the cow, were as much unknown in America as the elephant or the lion. From which it is obvious, that the people who first settled in the western world did not issue from the countries where those animals abound, and where men, from having been long accustomed to their aid, would naturally consider it not only as beneficial, but as indispensably necessary to the improvement, and even the preservation of civil society.

6. From considering the animals with which America is stored, we may conclude that the nearest point of contact between the old and new continents is towards the northern extremity of both, and that there the communication was opened, and the intercourse carried on between them. All the extensive countries in America which lie within the tropics, or approach near to them, are filled with indigenous animals of various kinds, entirely different from those in the corresponding regions of the ancient continent. But the northern provinces of the New World abound with many of the wild animals which are common in such parts of our hemisphere, as lie in a similar situation. The bear, the wolf, the fox, the hare, the deer, the roebuck, the elk, and several other species, frequent the forests of North America, no less than those in the north of Europe and Asia.* It seems to be evident, then, that the two continents approach each other in this quarter, and are either united, or so nearly adjacent that these animals might pass from the one to the other.

7. The actual vicinity of the two continents is so clearly established by modern discoveries, that the chief difficulty with respect to the peopling of America is removed. While those immense regions which stretch eastward from the river Oby to the sea of Kamchatka were unknown or imperfectly explored, the north-east extremities of our hemisphere were supposed to be so far distant from any part of the New World, that it was not easy to conceive how any communication should have been carried on between them. But the Russians, having subjected the western part of Siberia to their empire, gradually extended their knowledge of that vast country, by advancing towards the east into unknown provinces. These were discovered by hunters in their excursions after game, or by soldiers employed in levying the taxes; and the court of Moscow estimated the importance of those countries, only by the small addition which they made to its revenue. At length Peter the Great ascended the Russian throne. His enlightened, comprehensive mind, intent upon every circumstance that could aggrandize his empire, or render his reign illustrious, discerned consequences of those discoveries which had escaped the observation of his ignorant predecessors. He perceived that in proportion as the regions of Asia extended towards the east, they must approach nearer to America; that the communication between the two continents, which had long been searched for in vain, would probably be found in this quarter; and that by opening it, some part of the wealth and commerce of the western world might be made to flow into his dominions by a new channel. Such an object suited

* Buffon, Hist. Nat. ix. p. 97, &c.

a genius that delighted in grand schemes. Peter drew up instructions with his own hand for prosecuting this design, and gave orders for carrying it into execution.*

His successors adopted his ideas and pursued his plan. The officers whom the Russian court employed in this service had to struggle with so many difficulties, that their progress was extremely slow. Encouraged by some faint traditions among the people of Siberia, concerning a successful voyage in the year one thousand six hundred and forty-eight, round the north-east promontory of Asia, they attempted to follow the same course. Vessels were fitted out, with this view, at different times, from the rivers Lena and Kolyma; but in a frozen ocean, which nature seems not to have destined for navigation, they were exposed to many disasters, without being able to accomplish their purpose. No vessel fitted out by the Russian court ever doubled this formidable Cape [41]; we are indebted for what is known of those extreme regions of Asia, to the discoveries made in excursions by land. In all those provinces an opinion prevails, that there are countries of great extent and fertility which lie at no considerable distance from their own coasts. These the Russians imagined to be part of America; and several circumstances concurred not only in confirming them in this belief, but in persuading them that some portion of that continent could not be very remote. Trees of various kinds unknown in those naked regions of Asia, are driven upon the coast by an easterly wind. By the same wind, floating ice is brought thither in a few days; flights of birds arrive annually from the same quarter; and a tradition obtains among the inhabitants, of an intercourse formerly carried on with some countries situated to the east.

After weighing all these particulars, and comparing the position of the countries in Asia which had been discovered, with such parts in the north-west of America as were already known, the Russian court formed a plan, which would have hardly occurred to a nation less accustomed to engage in arduous undertakings, and to contend with great difficulties. Orders were issued to build two vessels at the small village of Ochotz, situated on the sea of Kamchatka, to sail on a voyage of discovery. Though that dreary uncultivated region furnished nothing that could be of use in constructing them, but some larch trees: though not only the iron, the cordage, the sails, and all the numerous articles requisite for their equipment, but the provisions for victualling them were to be carried through the immense deserts of Siberia, down rivers of difficult navigation, and along roads almost impassable, the mandate of the sovereign, and the perseverance of the people, at last surmounted every obstacle. Two vessels were finished, and, under the command of the Captains Behring and Tschirikow, sailed from Kamchatka, in quest of the New World in a quarter where it had never been approached. They shaped their course towards the east; and though a storm soon separated the vessels, which never rejoined, and many disasters befell them, the expectations from the voyage were not altogether frustrated. Each of the commanders discovered land, which to them appeared to be part of the American continent; and, according to their observation, it seems to be situated within a few degrees of the north-west coast of California. Each set some of his people ashore: but in one place the inhabitants fled as the Russians approached; in another, they carried off those who landed, and destroyed their boats. The violence of the weather, and the distress of their crews, obliged both captains to quit this inhospitable coast. In their return they touched at several islands which stretch in a chain from east to west between the country which they had discovered and the coast of Asia. They had some intercourse with the natives, who seemed to them to resemble the North Americans. They

* Muller, Voyages et Découvertes par les Russes, tom. l. p. 4, 5. 141.

presented to the Russians the *calumet*, or pipe of peace, which is a symbol of friendship universal among the people of North America, and a usage of arbitrary institution peculiar to them.

Though the islands of this New Archipelago have been frequented since that time by the Russian hunters, the court of St. Petersburgh, during a period of more than forty years, seems to have relinquished every thought of prosecuting discoveries in that quarter. But in the year one thousand seven hundred and sixty-eight it was unexpectedly resumed. The sovereign who had been lately seated on the throne of Peter the Great, possessed the genius and talents of her illustrious predecessor. During the operations of the most arduous and extensive war in which the Russian empire was ever engaged, she formed schemes and executed undertakings, to which more limited abilities would have been incapable of attending but amidst the leisure of pacific times. A new voyage of discovery from the eastern extremity of Asia was planned, and Captain Krenitzin and Lieutenant Levasheff were appointed to command the two vessels fitted out for that purpose. In their voyage outward they held nearly the same course with the former navigators, they touched at the same islands, observed their situation and productions more carefully, and discovered several new islands with which Behring and Tschirikow had not fallen in. Though they did not proceed so far to the east as to revisit the country which Behring and Tschirikow supposed to be part of the American continent, yet, by returning in a course considerably to the north of theirs, they corrected some capital mistakes into which their predecessors had fallen, and have contributed to facilitate the progress of future navigators in those seas [42].

Thus the possibility of a communication between the continents in this quarter rests no longer upon mere conjecture, but is established by undoubted evidence.* Some tribe, or some families of wandering Tartars, from the restless spirit peculiar to their race, might migrate to the nearest islands, and, rude as their knowledge of navigation was, might, by passing from one to the other, reach at length the coast of America, and give a beginning to population in that continent. The distance between the Marian or Ladrone islands and the nearest land in Asia, is greater than that between the part of America which the Russians discovered, and the coast of Kamchatka; and yet the inhabitants of those islands are manifestly of Asiatic extract. If, notwithstanding their remote situation, we admit that the Marian islands were peopled from our continent, distance alone is no reason why we should hesitate about admitting that the Americans may derive their original from the same source. It is probable that future navigators in those seas, by steering further to the north, may find that the continent of America approaches still nearer to Asia. According to the information of the barbarous people who inhabit the country about the north-east promontory of Asia, there lies, off the coast, a small island, to which they sail in less than a day. From that they can descry a large continent which, according to their description, is covered with forests, and possessed by people whose language they do not understand.† By them they are supplied with the skins of martens, an animal unknown in the northern parts of Siberia, and which is never found but in countries abounding with trees. If we could rely on this account, we might conclude that the American continent is separated from ours only by a narrow strait, and all the difficulties with respect to the communication between them would vanish. What could be offered only as a conjecture, when this History was first published, is now known to be certain. The near approach of the two continents to each other has been discovered and traced in a voyage undertaken upon principles so pure and so liberal, and conducted with so much professional skill, as reflect lustre

---

* Muller's Voyages, tom. i. p. 248, &c. 267, 276.   † Ibid. tom. i. p. 166.

upon the reign of the sovereign by whom it was planned, and do honour to the officers intrusted with the execution of it [43].

It is likewise evident from recent discoveries, that an intercourse between our continent and America might be carried on with no less facility from the north-west extremities of Europe. As early as the ninth century [A. D. 830], the Norwegians discovered Greenland, and planted colonies there. The communication with that country, after a long interruption, was renewed in the last century. Some Lutheran and Moravian missionaries, prompted by zeal for propagating the Christian faith, have ventured to settle in this frozen and uncultivated region.* To them we are indebted for much curious information with respect to its nature and inhabitants. We learn that the north-west coast of Greenland is separated from America by a very narrow strait; that, at the bottom of the bay into which this strait conducts, it is highly probable that they are united;† that the inhabitants of the two countries have some intercourse with one another; that the Esquimaux of America perfectly resemble the Greenlanders in their aspect, dress, and mode of living; that some sailors who had acquired the knowledge of a few words in the Greenlandish language, reported that these were understood by the Esquimaux; that, at length [A. D. 1764], a Moravian missionary, well acquainted with the language of Greenland, having visited the country of the Esquimaux, found, to his astonishment, that they spoke the same language with the Greenlanders; that they were in every respect the same people, and he was accordingly received and entertained by them as a friend and a brother.‡

By these decisive facts, not only the consanguinity of the Esquimaux and Greenlanders is established, but the possibility of peopling America from the north of Europe is demonstrated. If the Norwegians, in a barbarous age, when science had not begun to dawn in the north of Europe, possessed such naval skill as to open a communication with Greenland, their ancestors, as much addicted to roving by sea, as the Tartars are to wandering by land, might, at some more remote period, accomplish the same voyage, and settle a colony there, whose descendants might, in progress of time, migrate into America. But if, instead of venturing to sail directly from their own coast to Greenland, we suppose that the Norwegians held a more cautious course, and advanced from Shetland to the Feroe islands, and from them to Iceland, in all which they had planted colonies; their progress may have been so gradual, that this navigation cannot be considered as either longer or more hazardous than those voyages which that hardy and enterprising race of men is known to have performed in every age.

8. Though it be possible that America may have received its first inhabitants from our continent, either by the north-west of Europe or the northeast of Asia, there seems to be good reason for supposing that the progenitors of all the American nations from Cape Horn to the southern confines of Labrador, migrated from the latter rather than the former. The Esquimaux are the only people in America, who in their aspect or character bear any resemblance to the northern Europeans. They are manifestly a race of men distinct from all the nations of the American continent, in language, in disposition, and in habits of life. Their original, then, may warrantably be traced up to that source which I have pointed out. But among all the other inhabitants of America, there is such a striking similitude in the form of their bodies and the qualities of their minds, that, notwithstanding the diversities occasioned by the influences of climate, or unequal progress in improvement, we must pronounce them to be descended from one source. There may be a variety in the shades, but we can every where trace the same original colour. Each tribe has something peculiar which distinguishes

* Crantz' Hist. of Greenl. i. 242. 244.   Prevot, Hist. Gén. des Voyages, tom. xv. 152, note (96).
† Eggede, p. 2, 3.   ‡ Crantz' Hist. of Greenl. p. 261, 262.

AMERICA.

it, but in all of them we discern certain features common to the whole race. It is remarkable, that in every peculiarity, whether in their persons or dispositions, which characterize the Americans, they have some resemblance to the rude tribes scattered over the north-east of Asia, but almost none to the nations settled in the northern extremities of Europe. We may, therefore, refer them to the former origin, and conclude that their Asiatic progenitors, having settled in those parts of America where the Russians have discovered the proximity of the two continents, spread gradually over its various regions. This account of the progress of population in America coincides with the traditions of the Mexicans concerning their own origin, which, imperfect as they are, were preserved with more accuracy, and merit greater credit, than those of any people in the New World. According to them, their ancestors came from a remote country situated to the north-west of Mexico. The Mexicans point out their various stations as they advanced from this into the interior provinces, and it is precisely the same route which they must have held if they had been emigrants from Asia. The Mexicans, in describing the appearance of their progenitors, their manners and habits of life at that period, exactly delineate those of the rude Tartars from whom I suppose them to have sprung.*

Thus have I finished a Disquisition which has been deemed of so much importance that it would have been improper to omit it in writing the history of America. I have ventured to inquire, but without presuming to decide. Satisfied with offering conjectures, I pretend not to establish any system. When an investigation is, from its nature, so intricate and obscure, that it is impossible to arrive at conclusions which are certain, there may be some merit in pointing out such as are probable.†

The condition and character of the American nations, at the time when they became known to the Europeans, deserve more attentive consideration than the inquiry concerning their original. The latter is merely an object of curiosity; the former is one of the most important as well as instructive researches which can occupy the philosopher or historian. In order to complete the history of the human mind, and attain to a perfect knowledge of its nature and operations, we must contemplate man in all those various situations wherein he has been placed. We must follow him in his progress through the different stages of society, as he gradually advances from the infant state of civil life towards its maturity and decline. We must observe, at each period, how the faculties of his understanding unfold; we must attend to the efforts of his active powers, watch the various movements of desire and affection, as they rise in his breast, and mark whither they tend, and with what ardour they are exerted. The philosophers and historians of ancient Greece and Rome, our guides in this as well as every other disquisition, had only a limited view of this subject, as they had hardly any opportunity of surveying man in his rudest and most early state. In all those regions of the earth with which they were well acquainted, civil society had made considerable advances, and nations had finished a good part of their career before they began to observe them. The Scythians and Germans, the rudest people of whom any ancient author has transmitted to us an authentic account, possessed flocks and herds, had acquired property of various kinds, and, when compared with mankind in their primitive state, may be reckoned to have attained to a great degree of civilization.

But the discovery of the New World enlarged the sphere of contemplation, and presented nations to our view, in stages of their progress, much less advanced than those wherein they have been observed in our continent. In America, man appears under the rudest form in which we

* Acosta, Hist. Nat. et Mor. lib. vii. c. 2, &c. Garcia, Origen de los Indios, lib. v. c. 3. Torquemada Monar Ind. lib. i. c. 2, &c. Boturini Benaduci Idea de una Hist. de la Amer. Septentr. sect. xvii. p. 127. † Mémoires sur la Louisiane, par Dumout, tom. 1. p. 112.

can conceive him to subsist. We behold communities just beginning to unite, and may examine the sentiments and actions of human beings in the infancy of social life, while they feel but imperfectly the force of its ties, and have scarcely relinquished their native liberty. That state of primeval simplicity, which was known in our continent only by the fanciful description of poets, really existed in the other. The greater part of its inhabitants were strangers to industry and labour, ignorant of arts, imperfectly acquainted with the nature of property, and enjoying almost without restriction or control the blessings which flowed spontaneously from the bounty of nature. There were only two nations in this vast continent which had emerged from this rude state, and had made any considerable progress in acquiring the ideas, and adopting the institutions, which belong to polished societies Their government and manners will fall naturally under our review in relating the discovery and conquest of the Mexican and Peruvian empires; and we shall have there an opportunity of contemplating the Americans in the state of highest improvement to which they ever attained.

At present, our attention and researches shall be turned to the small independent tribes which occupied every other part of America. Among these, though with some diversity in their character, their manners, and institutions, the state of society was nearly similar, and so extremely rude, that the denomination of *savage* may be applied to them all. In a general history of America, it would be highly improper to describe the condition of each petty community, or to investigate every minute circumstance which contributes to form the character of its members. Such an inquiry would lead to details of immeasurable and tiresome extent. The qualities belonging to the people of all the different tribes have such a near resemblance, that they may be painted with the same features. Where any circumstances seem to constitute a diversity in their character and manners worthy of attention, it will be sufficient to point these out as they occur, and to inquire into the cause of such peculiarities.

It is extremely difficult to procure satisfying and authentic information concerning nations while they remain uncivilized. To discover their true character under this rude form, and to select the features by which they are distinguished, requires an observer possessed of no less impartiality than discernment. For, in every stage of society, the faculties, the sentiments, and desires of men are so accommodated to their own state, that they become standards of excellence to themselves, they affix the idea of perfection and happiness to those attainments which resemble their own, and, wherever the objects and enjoyments to which they have been accustomed are wanting, confidently pronounce a people to be barbarous and miserable. Hence the mutual contempt with which the members of communities, unequal in their degrees of improvement, regard each other. Polished nations, conscious of the advantages which they derive from their knowledge and arts, are apt to view rude nations with peculiar scorn, and, in the pride of superiority, will hardly allow either their occupations, their feelings, or their pleasures, to be worthy of men. It has seldom been the lot of communities, in their early and unpolished state, to fall under the observation of persons endowed with force of mind superior to vulgar prejudices, and capable of contemplating man, under whatever aspect he appears, with a candid and discerning eye.

The Spaniards, who first visited America, and who had opportunity of beholding its various tribes while entire and unsubdued, and before any change had been made in their ideas or manners by intercourse with a race of men much advanced beyond them in improvement, were far from possessing the qualities requisite for observing the striking spectacle presented to their view. Neither the age in which they lived, nor the nation to which they belonged, had made such progress in true science, as inspires enlarged and liberal sentiments. The conquerors of the New World were mostly illiterate adventurers, destitute of all the ideas which should have directed them in contemplating objects so extremely different from those with which they were acquainted. Surrounded continually with danger or struggling with hardships, they had little leisure, and less capacity, for any speculative inquiry. Eager to take possession of a country of such extent and opulence, and happy in finding it occupied by inhabitants so incapable to defend it, they hastily pronounced them to be a wretched order of men, formed merely for servitude; and were more employed in computing the profits of their labour, than in inquiring into the operations of their minds, or the reasons of their customs and institutions. The persons who penetrated at subsequent periods into the interior provinces, to which the knowledge and devastations of the first conquerors did not reach, were generally of a similar character; brave and enterprising in a high degree, but so uninformed as to be little qualified either for observing or describing what they beheld.

Not only the incapacity but the prejudices of the Spaniards rendered their accounts of the people of America extremely defective. Soon after they planted colonies in their new conquests, a difference in opinion arose with respect to the treatment of the natives. One party, solicitous to render their servitude perpetual, represented them as a brutish, obstinate race, incapable either of acquiring religious knowledge, or of being trained to the functions of social life. The other, full of pious concern for their conversion, contended that, though rude and ignorant, they were gentle, affectionate, docile, and by proper instructions and regulations might be formed gradually into good Christians and useful citizens. This controversy, as I have already related, was carried on with all the warmth which is natural, when attention to interest on the one hand, and religious zeal on the other, animate the disputants. Most of the laity espoused the former opinion; all the ecclesiastics were advocates for the latter; and we shall uniformly find that, accordingly as an author belonged to either of these parties, he is apt to magnify the virtues or aggravate the defects of the Americans far beyond truth. Those repugnant accounts increase the difficulty of attaining a perfect knowledge of their character, and render it necessary to peruse all the descriptions of them by Spanish writers with distrust, and to receive their information with some grains of allowance.

Almost two centuries elapsed after the discovery of America, before the manners of its inhabitants attracted, in any considerable degree, the attention of philosophers. At length they discovered that the contemplation of the condition and character of the Americans, in their original state, tended to complete our knowledge of the human species; might enable us to fill up a considerable chasm in the history of its progress; and lead to speculations no less curious than important. They entered upon this new field of study with great ardour; but, instead of throwing light upon the subject, they have contributed in some degree to involve it in additional obscurity. Too impatient to inquire, they hastened to decide; and began to erect systems, when they should have been searching for facts on which to establish their foundations. Struck with the appearance of degeneracy in the human species throughout the New World, and astonished at beholding a vast continent occupied by a naked, feeble, and ignorant race of men, some authors, of great name, have maintained that this part of the globe had but lately emerged from the sea, and become fit for the residence of man; that every thing in it bore marks of a recent original; and that its inhabitants, lately called into existence, and still at the beginning of their career, were unworthy to be compared with the people of a more ancient and improved continent.* Others have imagined, that, under the influence of an unkindly climate, which checks and enervates

* M. de Buffon Hist. Nat. iii. 484, &c. ix. 103. 114.

the principle of life, man never attained in America the perfection which belongs to his nature, but remained an animal of an inferior order, defective in the vigour of his bodily frame, and destitute of sensibility, as well as of force, in the operations of his mind.* In opposition to both these, other philosophers have supposed that man arrives at his highest dignity and excellence long before he reaches a state of refinement; and, in the rude simplicity of savage life, displays an elevation of sentiment, an independence of mind, and a warmth of attachment, for which it is vain to search among the members of polished societies.† They seem to consider that as the most perfect state of man which is the least civilized. They describe the manners of the rude Americans with such rapture, as if they proposed them for models to the rest of the species. These contradictory theories have been proposed with equal confidence, and uncommon powers of genius and eloquence have been exerted, in order to clothe them with an appearance of truth.

As all those circumstances concur in rendering an inquiry into the state of the rude nations in America intricate and obscure, it is necessary to carry it on with caution. When guided in our researches by the intelligent observations of the few philosophers who have visited this part of the globe, we may venture to decide. When obliged to have recourse to the superficial remarks of vulgar travellers, of sailors, traders, buccaneers, and missionaries, we must often pause, and, comparing detached facts, endeavour to discover what they wanted sagacity to observe. Without indulging conjecture, or betraying a propensity to either system, we must study with equal care to avoid the extremes of extravagant admiration, or of supercilious contempt for those manners which we describe.

In order to conduct this inquiry with greater accuracy, it should be rendered as simple as possible. Man existed as an individual before he became the member of a community; and the qualities which belong to him under his former capacity should be known, before we proceed to examine those which arise from the latter relation. This is peculiarly necessary in investigating the manners of rude nations. Their political union is so incomplete, their civil institutions and regulations so few, so simple, and of such slender authority, that men in this state ought to be viewed rather as independent agents, than as members of a regular society. The character of a savage results almost entirely from his sentiments or feelings as an individual, and is but little influenced by his imperfect subjection to government and order. I shall conduct my researches concerning the manners of the Americans in this natural order, proceeding gradually from what is simple to what is more complicated.

I shall consider, I. The bodily constitution of the Americans in those regions now under review. II. The qualities of their minds. III. Their domestic state. IV. Their political state and institutions. V. Their system of war, and public security. VI. The arts with which they were acquainted. VII. Their religious ideas and institutions. VIII. Such singular detached customs as are not reducible to any of the former heads. IX. I shall conclude with a general review and estimate of their virtues and defects.

I. The bodily constitution of the Americans.—The human body is less affected by climate than that of any other animal. Some animals are confined to a particular region of the globe, and cannot exist beyond it; others, though they may be brought to bear the injuries of a climate foreign to them, cease to multiply when carried out of that district which nature destined to be their mansion. Even such as seem capable of being naturalized in various climates feel the effect of every remove from their proper station, and gradually dwindle and degenerate from the vigour and

---

* M. de P. Recherches Philos. sur les Améric. passim.   † M. Rousseau.

perfection peculiar to their species. Man is the only living creature whose frame is at once so hardy and so flexible, that he can spread over the whole earth, become the inhabitant of every region, and thrive and multiply under every climate. Subject, however, to the general law of Nature, the human body is not entirely exempt from the operation of climate; and when exposed to the extremes either of heat or cold, its size or vigour diminishes.

The first appearance of the inhabitants of the New World filled the discoverers with such astonishment that they were apt to imagine them a race of men different from those of the other hemisphere. Their complexion is of a reddish brown, nearly resembling the colour of copper.* The hair of their heads is always black, long, coarse, and uncurled. They have no beard, and every part of their body is perfectly smooth. Their persons are of a full size, extremely straight, and well proportioned [44]. Their features are regular, though often distorted by absurd endeavours to improve the beauty of their natural form, or to render their aspect more dreadful to their enemies. In the islands, where four-footed animals were both few and small, and the earth yielded her productions almost spontaneously, the constitution of the natives, neither braced by the active exercises of the chase, nor invigorated by the labour of cultivation, was extremely feeble and languid. On the continent, where the forests abound with game of various kinds, and the chief occupation of many tribes was to pursue it, the human frame acquired greater firmness. Still, however, the Americans were more remarkable for agility than strength. They resembled beasts of prey, rather than animals formed for labour [45]. They were not only averse to toil, but incapable of it; and when roused by force from their native indolence, and compelled to work, they sunk under tasks which the people of the other continent would have performed with ease.† This feebleness of constitution was universal among the inhabitants of those regions in America which we are surveying, and may be considered as characteristic of the species there.‡

The beardless countenance and smooth skin of the American seems to indicate a defect of vigour, occasioned by some vice in his frame. He is destitute of one sign of manhood and of strength. This peculiarity, by which the inhabitants of the New World are distinguished from the people of all other nations, cannot be attributed, as some travellers have supposed, to their mode of subsistence.§ For though the food of many Americans be extremely insipid, as they are altogether unacquainted with the use of salt, rude tribes in other parts of the earth have subsisted on aliments equally simple, without this mark of degradation, or any apparent symptom of a diminution in their vigour.

As the external form of the Americans leads us to suspect that there is some natural debility in their frame, the smallness of their appetite for food has been mentioned by many authors as a confirmation of this suspicion. The quantity of food which men consume varies according to the temperature of the climate in which they live, the degree of activity which they exert, and the natural vigour of their constitutions. Under the enervating heat of the torrid zone, and when men pass their days in indolence and ease, they require less nourishment than the active inhabitants of temperate or cold countries. But neither the warmth of their climate, nor their extreme laziness, will account for the uncommon defect of appetite among the Americans. The Spaniards were astonished with observing this, not only in the islands, but in several parts of the continent. The constitutional temperance of the natives far exceeded, in their opinion,

---

* Oviedo Somario p. 46. D. Life of Columbus, c. 24. † Oviedo Som. p. 51. C; Voy. de Correal, ii. 138. Wafer's Description, p. 131. ‡ B. Las Casas Brev. Relac. p. 4. Torquem. Monar. L 580. Oviedo Somario, p. 41. Histor. lib. lii. c. 6. Herrera, dec. 1. lib. xl. c. 5. Simon. p. 41. § Charlev. Hist. de Nouv. Fr. lii. 310.

the abstinence of the most mortified hermits :* while, on the other hand, the appetite of the Spaniards appeared to the Americans insatiably voracious; and they affirmed, that one Spaniard devoured more food in a day than was sufficient for ten Americans.†

A proof of some feebleness in their frame, still more striking, is the insensibility of the Americans to the charms of beauty, and the power of love. That passion which was destined to perpetuate life, to be the bond of social union, and the source of tenderness and joy, is the most ardent in the human breast. Though the perils and hardships of the savage state, though excessive fatigue on some occasions, and the difficulty at all times of procuring subsistence, may seem to be adverse to this passion, and to have a tendency to abate its vigour, yet the rudest nations in every other part of the globe seem to feel its influence more powerfully than the inhabitants of the New World. The negro glows with all the warmth of desire natural to his climate; and the most uncultivated Asiatics discover that sensibility, which, from their situation on the globe, we should expect them to have felt. But the Americans are, in an amazing degree, strangers to the force of this first instinct of nature. In every part of the New World the natives treat their women with coldness and indifference. They are neither the objects of that tender attachment which takes place in civilized society, nor of that ardent desire conspicuous among rude nations. Even in climates where this passion usually acquires its greatest vigour, the savage of America views his female with disdain, as an animal of a less noble species. He is at no pains to win her favour by the assiduity of courtship, and still less solicitous to preserve it by indulgence and gentleness.‡ Missionaries themselves, notwithstanding the austerity of monastic ideas, cannot refrain from expressing their astonishment at the dispassionate coldness of the American young men in their intercourse with the other sex.§ Nor is this reserve to be ascribed to any opinion which they entertain with respect to the merit of female chastity. That is an idea too refined for a savage, and suggested by a delicacy of sentiment and affection to which he is a stranger.

But in inquiries concerning either the bodily or mental qualities of particular races of men, there is not a more common or more seducing error, than that of ascribing to a single cause, those characteristic peculiarities which are the effect of the combined operation of many causes. The climate and soil of America differ in so many respects from those of the other hemisphere, and this difference is so obvious and striking, that philosophers of great eminence have laid hold on this as sufficient to account for what is peculiar in the constitution of its inhabitants. They rest on physical causes alone, and consider the feeble frame and languid desire of the Americans, as consequences of the temperament of that portion of the globe which they occupy. But the influences of political and moral causes ought not to have been overlooked. These operate with no less effect than that on which many philosophers rest as a full explanation of the singular appearances which have been mentioned. Wherever the state of society is such as to create many wants and desires, which cannot be satisfied without regular exertions of industry, the body accustomed to labour becomes robust and patient of fatigue. In a more simple state, where the demands of men are so few and so moderate that they may be gratified, almost without any effort, by the spontaneous productions of nature, the powers of the body are not called forth, nor can they attain their proper strength. The natives of Chili and of North America, the two

* Ramusio, lii. 304. F. 306. A. Simon Conquista, &c. p. 39. Hakluyt, iii. 468. 508. † Herrera, dec. 1. lib. ii. c. 16. ‡ Hennepin Mœurs des Sauvages, 32, &c. Rochefort Hist. des Isles Antilles, p. 461. Voyage de Correal, ii. 141. Ramusio, iii. 309. F. Lozano Descr. del Gran Chaco, 71. Falkner's Descr. of Patagon, p. 125. Lettere di P. Cataneo ap. Muratori Il Christian. Felice, i. 305. § Chanvalon, p. 51. Lettr. Edif. tom. xxiv. 318. Tertre, ii. 377. Venegas, i. 81. Ribas Hist. de los Triumf. p. 11.

temperate regions in the New World, who live by hunting, may be deemed an active and vigorous race, when compared with the inhabitants of the isles, or of those parts of the continent where hardly any labour is requisite to procure subsistence. The exertions of a hunter are not, however, so regular, or so continued, as those of persons employed in the culture of the earth, or in the various arts of civilized life; and though his agility may be greater than theirs, his strength is on the whole inferior. If another direction were given to the active powers of man in the New World, and his force augmented by exercise, he might acquire a degree of vigour which he does not in his present state possess. The truth of this is confirmed by experience. Wherever the Americans have been gradually accustomed to hard labour, their constitutions become robust, and they have been found capable of performing such tasks, as seemed not only to exceed the powers of such a feeble frame as has been deemed peculiar to their country, but to equal any effort of the natives either of Africa or of Europe [46].

The same reasoning will apply to what has been observed concerning their slender demand for food. As a proof that this should be ascribed as much to their extreme indolence, and often total want of occupation, as to any thing peculiar in the physical structure of their bodies, it has been observed, that in those districts where the people of America are obliged to exert any unusual effort of activity, in order to procure subsistence, or wherever they are employed in severe labour, their appetite is not inferior to that of other men, and in some places, it has struck observers as remarkably voracious.*

The operation of political and moral causes is still more conspicuous in modifying the degree of attachment between the sexes. In a state of high civilization, this passion, inflamed by restraint, refined by delicacy, and cherished by fashion, occupies and engrosses the heart. It is no longer a simple instinct of nature; sentiment heightens the ardour of desire, and the most tender emotions of which our frame is susceptible soothe and agitate the soul. This description, however, applies only to those, who, by their situation, are exempted from the cares and labours of life. Among persons of inferior order, who are doomed by their condition to incessant toil, the dominion of this passion is less violent; their solicitude to procure subsistence, and to provide for the first demand of nature, leaves little leisure for attending to its second call. But if the nature of the intercourse between the sexes varies so much in persons of different rank in polished societies, the condition of man while he remains uncivilized must occasion a variation still more apparent. We may well suppose, that amidst the hardships, the dangers, and the simplicity of domestic life, where subsistence is always precarious and often scanty, where men are almost continually engaged in the pursuit of their enemies, or in guarding against their attacks, and where neither dress nor reserve are employed as arts of female allurement, that the attention of the Americans to their women would be extremely feeble, without imputing this solely to any physical defect or degradation in their frame.

It is accordingly observed, that in those countries of America where, from the fertility of the soil, the mildness of the climate, or some further advances which the natives have made in improvement, the means of subsistence are more abundant, and the hardships of savage life are less severely felt, the animal passion of the sexes becomes more ardent. Striking examples of this occur among some tribes seated on the banks of great rivers well stored with food, among others who are masters of hunting grounds abounding so much with game, that they have a regular and plentiful supply of nourishment with little labour. The superior degree

* Gumilla, ii. 12. 70. 247. Lafitau, i. 515. Ovalle Church. ii. 81. Muratori, i. 995.

of security and affluence which those tribes enjoy is followed by their natural effects. The passions implanted in the human frame by the hand of nature acquire additional force; new tastes and desires are formed; the women, as they are more valued and admired, become more attentive to dress and ornament; the men beginning to feel how much of their own happiness depends upon them, no longer disdain the arts of winning their favour and affection. The intercourse of the sexes becomes very different from that which takes place among their ruder countrymen; and as hardly any restraint is imposed on the gratification of desire, either by religion or laws or decency, the dissolution of their manners is excessive.*

Notwithstanding the feeble make of the Americans, hardly any of them are deformed, or mutilated, or defective in any of their senses. All travellers have been struck with this circumstance, and have celebrated the uniform symmetry and perfection of their external figure. Some authors search for the cause of this appearance in their physical condition. As the parents are not exhausted or over fatigued with hard labour, they suppose that their children are born vigorous and sound. They imagine that, in the liberty of savage life, the human body, naked and unconfined from its earliest age, preserves its natural form; and that all its limbs and members acquire a juster proportion than when fettered with artificial restraints, which stint its growth and distort its shape.† Something, without doubt, may be ascribed to the operation of these causes; but the true reasons of this apparent advantage, which is common to all savage nations, lie deeper, and are closely interwoven with the nature and genius of that state. The infancy of man is so long and so helpless, that it is extremely difficult to rear children among rude nations. Their means of subsistence are not only scanty, but precarious. Such as live by hunting must range over extensive countries, and shift often from place to place. The care of children, as well as every other laborious task, is devolved upon the women. The distresses and hardships of the savage life, which are often such as can hardly be supported by persons in full vigour, must be fatal to those of more tender age. Afraid of undertaking a task so laborious, and of such long duration, as that of rearing their offspring, the women, in some parts of America, procure frequent abortions by the use of certain herbs, and extinguish the first sparks of that life which they are unable to cherish.‡ Sensible that only stout and well formed children have force of constitution to struggle through such a hard infancy, other nations abandon and destroy such of their progeny as appear feeble or defective, as unworthy of attention.§ Even when they endeavour to rear all their children without distinction, so great a proportion of the whole number perishes under the rigorous treatment which must be their lot in the savage state, that few of those who laboured under any original frailty attain the age of manhood.|| Thus, in polished societies, where the means of subsistence are secured with certainty, and acquired with ease; where the talents of the mind are often of more importance than the powers of the body; children are preserved notwithstanding their defects or deformity, and grow up to be useful citizens. In rude nations, such persons are either cut off as soon, as they are born, or, becoming a burden to themselves and to the community, cannot long protract their lives. But in those provinces of the New World, where, by the establishment of the Europeans, more regular provision has been made for the subsistence of its inhabitants, and they are restrained from laying violent hands on their children, the Americans are so far from being eminent for any superior perfection in their form, that one should rather suspect some peculiar imbecility in the race, from the

---

* Biet. 389. Charlev. iii. 423. Dumont. Mém. sur Louisiane, i. 155. † Piso, p. 6.
‡ Ellis's Voyage to Hudson's Bay, 198. Herrera, dec. 7. lib. ix. c. 4. § Gumilla Hist. ii. 234.
Techo's Hist. of Paraguay, &c. Churchill's Collect. vi. 108. || Creuxii. Hist. Canad. p. 57.

extraordinary number of individuals who are deformed, dwarfish, mutilated, blind, or deaf.*

How feeble soever the constitution of the Americans may be, it is remarkable that there is less variety in the human form throughout the New World than in the ancient continent. When Columbus and the other discoverers first visited the different countries of America which lie within the torrid zone, they naturally expected to find people of the same complexion with those in the corresponding regions of the other hemisphere. To their amazement, however, they discovered that America contained no negroes;† and the cause of this singular appearance became as much the object of curiosity as the fact itself was of wonder. In what part or membrane of the body that humour resides which tinges the complexion of the negro with a deep black, it is the business of anatomists to inquire and describe. The powerful operation of heat appears manifestly to be the cause which produces this striking variety in the human species. All Europe, a great part of Asia, and the temperate countries of Africa, are inhabited by men of a white complexion. All the torrid zone in Africa, some of the warmer regions adjacent to it, and several countries in Asia, are filled with people of a deep black colour. If we survey the nations of our continent, making our progress from cold and temperate countries towards those parts which are exposed to the influence of vehement and unremitting heat, we shall find that the extreme whiteness of their skin soon begins to diminish; that its colour deepens gradually as we advance; and, after passing through all the successive gradations of shade, terminates in a uniform unvarying black. But in America, where the agency of heat is checked and abated by various causes, which I have already explained, the climate seems to be destitute of that force which produces such wonderful effects on the human frame. The colour of the natives of the torrid zone in America is hardly of a deeper hue than that of the people in the more temperate parts of their continent. Accurate observers, who had an opportunity of viewing the Americans in very different climates, and in provinces far removed from each other, have been struck with the amazing similarity of their figure and aspect [47].

But though the hand of nature has deviated so little from one standard in fashioning the human form in America, the creation of fancy hath been various and extravagant. The same fables that were current in the ancient continent, have been revived with respect to the New World, and America too has been peopled with human beings of monstrous and fantastic appearance. The inhabitants of certain provinces were described to be pigmies of three feet high; those of others to be giants of an enormous size. Some travellers published accounts of people with only one eye; others pretended to have discovered men without heads, whose eyes and mouths were planted in their breasts. The variety of Nature in her productions is indeed so great, that it is presumptuous to set bounds to her fertility, and to reject indiscriminately every relation that does not perfectly accord with our own limited observation and experience. But the other extreme, of yielding a hasty assent on the slighest evidence to whatever has the appearance of being strange and marvellous, is still more unbecoming a philosophical inquirer; as, in every period, men are more apt to be betrayed into error by their weakness in believing too much, than by their arrogance in believing too little. In proportion as science extends, and nature is examined with a discerning eye, the wonders which amused ages of ignorance disappear. The tales of credulous travellers concerning America are forgotten; the monsters which they describe have been searched for in vain; and those provinces where they pretend to have

* Voy. de Ulloa, i, 232.   † P. Martyr, dec. p. 71.

found inhabitants of singular forms, are now known to be possessed by a people nowise different from the other Americans.

Though those relations may, without discussion, be rejected as fabulous, there are other accounts of varieties in the human species in some parts of the New World, which rest upon better evidence, and merit more attentive examination. This variety has been particularly observed in three different districts. The first of these is situated in the isthmus of Darien, near the centre of America. Lionel Wafer, a traveller possessed of more curiosity and intelligence than we should have expected to find in an associate of Buccaneers, discovered there a race of men few in number, but of a singular make. They are of low stature, according to his description, of a feeble frame, incapable of enduring fatigue. Their colour is a dead milk white; not resembling that of fair people among the Europeans, but without any tincture of a blush or sanguine complexion. Their skin is covered with a fine hairy down of a chalky white; the hair of their heads, their eyebrows, and eye-lashes, are of the same hue. Their eyes are of a singular form, and so weak that they can hardly bear the light of the sun; but they see clearly by moonlight, and are most active and gay in the night.* No race similar to this has been discovered in any other part of America. Cortes, indeed, found some persons exactly resembling the white people of Darien among the rare and monstrous animals which Montezuma had collected.† But as the power of the Mexican empire extended to the provinces bordering on the isthmus of Darien, they were probably brought thence. Singular as the appearance of those people may be, they cannot be considered as constituting a distinct species. Among the negroes of Africa, as well as the natives of the Indian islands, nature sometimes produces a small number of individuals, with all the characteristic features and qualities of the white people of Darien. The former are called *Albinos* by the Portuguese, the latter *Kackerlakes* by the Dutch. In Darien the parents of those *Whites* are of the same colour with the other natives of the country; and this observation applies equally to the anomalous progeny of the Negroes and Indians. The same mother who produces some children of a colour that does not belong to the race, brings forth the rest with a complexion peculiar to her country.‡ One conclusion may then be formed with respect to the people described by Wafer, the *Albinos* and the *Kackerlakes;* they are a degenerated breed, not a separate class of men; and from some disease or defect of their parents, the peculiar colour and debility which mark their degradation are transmitted to them. As a decisive proof of this, it has been observed, that neither the white people of Darien, nor the Albinos of Africa, propagate their race: their children are of the colour and temperament peculiar to the natives of their respective countries§ [48].

The second district that is occupied by inhabitants differing in appearance from the other people of America, is situated in a high northern latitude, extending from the coast of Labrador towards the pole, as far as the country is habitable. The people scattered over those dreary regions are known to the Europeans by the name of *Esquimaux*. They themselves, with that idea of their own superiority, which consoles the rudest and most wretched nations, assume the name of *Keralit* or *Men*. They are of a middle size, and robust, with heads of a disproportioned bulk, and feet as remarkably small. Their complexion though swarthy, by being continually exposed to the rigour of a cold climate, inclines to the European white rather than to the copper colour of America, and the men have beards which are sometimes bushy and long.‖ From these marks of

---
* Wafer's Descript. of Isth. ap. Dampier, iii. p. 346. † Cortes ap. Ramus. iii. p. 241. E.
‡ Margrav. Hist. Rer. Nat. Bras. lib. viii. c. 4. • § Wafer, p. 348. Demanet Hist. de l'Afrique, ii. 234. Recherch. Philos. sur les Amer. ii. 1, &c. ‖ Ellis Voy. to Huds. Bay, p. 131. 139. De la Potherie, tom. 1. p. 79. Wales Journ. of a Voy. to Churchill River, Phil. Trans. vol lx. 100.

distinction, as well as from one still less equivocal, the affinity of their language to that of the Greenlanders, which I have already mentioned, we may conclude, with some degree of confidence, that the Esquimaux are a race different from the rest of the Americans.

We cannot decide with equal certainty concerning the inhabitants of the third district, situated at the southern extremity of America. These are the famous *Patagonians*, who, during two centuries and a half, have afforded a subject of controversy to the learned, and an object of wonder to the vulgar. They are supposed to be one of the wandering tribes which occupy the vast but least known region of America, which extends from the river de la Plata to the Straits of Magellan. Their proper station is in that part of the interior country which lies on the banks of the river Negro; but, in the hunting season, they often roam as far as the straits which separate Tierra del Fuego from the main land. The first accounts of this people were brought to Europe by the companions of Magellan,* who described them as a gigantic race, above eight feet high, and of strength in proportion to their enormous size. Among several tribes of animals, a disparity in bulk as considerable may be observed. Some large breeds of horses and dogs exceed the more diminutive races in stature and strength, as far as the Patagonian is supposed to rise above the usual standard of the human body. But animals attain the highest perfection of their species only in mild climates, or where they find the most nutritive food in greatest abundance. It is not then in the uncultivated waste of the Magellanic regions, and among a tribe of improvident savages, that we should expect to find man possessing the highest honours of his race, and distinguished by a superiority of size and vigour, far beyond what he has reached in any other part of the earth. The most explicit and unexceptionable evidence is requisite, in order to establish a fact repugnant to those general principles and laws, which seem to affect the human frame in every other instance, and to decide with respect to its nature and qualities. Such evidence has not hitherto been produced. Though several persons, to whose testimony great respect is due, have visited this part of America since the time of Magellan, and have had interviews with the natives; though some have affirmed, that such as they saw were of gigantic stature, and others have formed the same conclusion from measuring their footsteps, or from viewing the skeletons of their dead; yet their accounts vary from each other in so many essential points, and are mingled with so many circumstances manifestly false or fabulous, as detract much from their credit. On the other hand, some navigators, and those among the most eminent of their order for discernment and accuracy, have asserted that the natives of Patagonia, with whom they had intercourse, though stout and well made, are not of such extraordinary size as to be distinguished from the rest of the human species [49]. The existence of this gigantic race of men seems, then, to be one of those points in natural history, with respect to which a cautious inquirer will hesitate, and will choose to suspend his assent until more complete evidence shall decide whether he ought to admit a fact, seemingly inconsistent with what reason and experience have discovered concerning the structure and condition of man, in all the various situations in which he has been observed.

In order to form a complete idea with respect to the constitution of the inhabitants of this and the other hemisphere, we should attend not only to the make and vigour of their bodies, but consider what degree of health they enjoy, and to what period of longevity they usually arrive. In the simplicity of the savage state, when man is not oppressed with labour, or enervated by luxury, or disquieted with care, we are apt to imagine that this life will flow on almost untroubled by disease or suffering, until his

* Falkner's Description of Patagonia, p. 102.

days be terminated in extreme old age by the gradual decays of nature. We find, accordingly, among the Americans, as well as among other rude people, persons whose decrepit and shrivelled form seems to indicate an extraordinary length of life. But as most of them are unacquainted with the art of numbering, and all of them as forgetful of what is past, as they are improvident of what is to come, it is impossible to ascertain their age with any degree of precision.* It is evident that the period of their longevity must vary considerably, according to the diversity of climates, and their different modes of subsistence. They seem, however, to be every where exempt from many of the distempers which afflict polished nations. None of the maladies, which are the immediate offspring of luxury, ever visited them; and they have no names in their languages by which to distinguish this numerous train of adventitious evils.

But whatever be the situation in which man is placed, he is born to suffer; and his diseases in the savage state, though fewer in number, are, like those of the animals whom he nearly resembles in his mode of life, more violent and more fatal. If luxury engenders and nourishes distempers of one species, the rigour and distresses of savage life bring on those of another. As men in this state are wonderfully improvident, and their means of subsistence precarious, they often pass from extreme want to exuberant plenty, according to the vicissitudes of fortune in the chase, or in consequence of the various degrees of abundance with which the earth affords to them its productions in different seasons. Their inconsiderate gluttony in the one situation, and their severe abstinence in the other, are equally pernicious. For though the human constitution may be accustomed by habit, like that of animals of prey, to tolerate long famine, and then to gorge voraciously, it is not a little affected by such sudden and violent transitions. The strength and vigour of savages are at some seasons impaired by what they suffer from a scarcity of food; at others they are afflicted with disorders arising from indigestion and a superfluity of gross aliment. These are so common, that they may be considered as the unavoidable consequence of their mode of subsisting, and cut off considerable numbers in the prime of life. They are likewise extremely subject to consumptions, to pleuritic, asthmatic, and paralytic disorders,† brought on by the immoderate hardships and fatigue which they endure in hunting and in war; or owing to the inclemency of the seasons to which they are continually exposed. In the savage state, hardships and fatigue violently assault the constitution. In polished societies, intemperance undermines it. It is not easy to determine which of them operates with most fatal effect, or tends most to abridge human life. The influence of the former is certainly most extensive. The pernicious consequences of luxury reach only a few members in any community; the distresses of savage life are felt by all. As far as I can judge, after very minute inquiry, the general period of human life is shorter among savages than in well regulated and industrious societies.

One dreadful malady, the severest scourge with which, in this life, offended Heaven chastens the indulgence of criminal desire, seems to have been peculiar to the Americans. By communicating it to their conquerors, they have not only amply avenged their own wrongs, but, by adding this calamity to those which formerly imbittered human life, they have, perhaps, more than counterbalanced all the benefits which Europe has derived from the discovery of the New World. This distemper, from the country in which it first raged, or from the people by whom it was supposed to have been spread over Europe, has been sometimes called the Neapolitan, and sometimes the French disease. At its first appearance, the infection was

---

* Ulloa Notic. Americ. 323. Bancroft Nat. Hist. of Guiana, 334. † Charlev. N. Fr. iii. 364.
Lafitau, ii. 360. De la Potherie, ii. 37.

so malignant, its symptoms so violent, its operation so rapid and fatal, as to baffle all the efforts of medical skill. Astonishment and terror accompanied this unknown affliction in its progress, and men began to dread the extinction of the human race by such a cruel visitation. Experience, and the ingenuity of physicians, gradually discovered remedies of such virtue as to cure or to mitigate the evil. During the course of two centuries and a half, its virulence seems to have abated considerably. At length, in the same manner with the leprosy, which raged in Europe for some centuries, it may waste its force and disappear; and in some happier age, this western infection, like that from the east, may be known only by description [50].

II. After considering what appears to be peculiar in the bodily constitution of the Americans, our attention is naturally turned towards the powers and qualities of their minds. As the individual advances from the ignorance and imbecility of the infant state to vigour and maturity of understanding, something similar to this may be observed in the progress of the species. With respect to it, too, there is a period of infancy, during which several powers of the mind are not unfolded, and all are feeble and defective in their operation. In the early ages of society, while the condition of man is simple and rude, this reason is but little exercised, and his desires move within a very narrow sphere. Hence arise two remarkable characteristics of the human mind in this state. Its intellectual powers are extremely limited; its emotions and efforts are few and languid. Both these distinctions are conspicuous among the rudest and most unimproved of the American tribes, and constitute a striking part of their description.

What, among polished nations, is called speculative reasoning or research, is altogether unknown in the rude state of society, and never becomes the occupation or amusement of the human faculties, until man be so far improved as to have secured, with certainty, the means of subsistence, as well as the possession of leisure and tranquillity. The thoughts and attention of a savage are confined within the small circle of objects immediately conducive to his preservation or enjoyment. Every thing beyond that escapes his observation, or is perfectly indifferent to him. Like a mere animal, what is before his eyes interests and affects him; what is out of sight, or at a distance, makes little impression.* There are several people in America whose limited understandings seem not to be capable of forming an arrangement for futurity; neither their solicitude nor their foresight extends so far. They follow blindly the impulse of the appetite which they feel, but are entirely regardless of distant consequences, and even of those removed in the least degree from immediate apprehension. While they highly prize such things as serve for present use, or minister to present enjoyment, they set no value upon those which are not the object of some immediate want.† When, on the approach of the evening, a Caribbee feels himself disposed to go to rest, no consideration will tempt him to sell his hammock. But, in the morning, when he is sallying out to the business or pastime of the day, he will part with it for the slightest toy that catches his fancy.‡ At the close of winter, while the impression of what he has suffered from the rigour of the climate is fresh in the mind of the North American, he sets himself with vigour to prepare materials for erecting a comfortable hut to protect him against the inclemency of the succeeding season; but, as soon as the weather becomes mild, he forgets what is past, abandons his work, and never thinks of it more until the return of cold compels him, when too late, to resume it.§

If in concerns the most interesting, and seemingly the most simple, the

---

* Ullo Noticias Americ. 222. † Venegas Hist. of Calif. I. 66. Supp. Church. Coll. v. 693. Borde Descr. des Caraibes, p. 16. Ellis Voy. 194, ‡ Labat Voyages, II. 114, 115. Tertre, ii. 385. § Adair's Hist. of Amer. Indians, 417

reason of man, while rude and destitute of culture, differs so little from the thoughtless levity of children, or the improvident instinct of animals, its exertions in other directions cannot be very considerable. The objects towards which reason turns, and the disquisitions in which it engages, must depend upon the state in which man is placed, and are suggested by his necessities and desires. Disquisitions, which appear the most necessary and important to men in one state of society, never occur to those in another. Among civilized nations, arithmetic, or the art of numbering, is deemed an essential and elementary science: and in our continent, the invention and use of it reaches back to a period so remote as is beyond the knowledge of history. But among savages, who have no property to estimate, no hoarded treasures to count, no variety of objects or multiplicity of ideas to enumerate, arithmetic is a superfluous and useless art. Accordingly, among some tribes in America it seems to be quite unknown. There are many who cannot reckon further than three; and have no denomination to distinguish any number above it.*' Several can proceed as far as ten, others to twenty. When they would convey an idea of any number beyond these, they point to the hair of their head, intimating that it is equal to them, or with wonder declare it to be so great that it cannot be reckoned.† Not only the Americans, but all nations while extremely rude, seem to be unacquainted with the art of computation.‡ As soon, however, as they acquire such acquaintance or connexion with a variety of objects, that there is frequent occasion to combine or divide them, their knowledge of numbers increases, so that the state of this art among any people may be considered as one standard by which to estimate the degree of their improvement. The Iroquoise, in North America, as they are much more civilized than the rude inhabitants of Brazil, Paraguay, or Guiana, have likewise made greater advances in this respect; though even their arithmetic does not extend beyond a thousand, as in their petty transactions they have no occasion for any higher number.§ The Cherokee, a less considerable nation on the same continent, can reckon only as far as a hundred, and to that extent have names for the several numbers; the smaller tribes in their neighbourhood can rise no higher than ten‖ [51].

In other respects, the exercise of the understanding among rude nations is still more limited. The first ideas of every human being must be such as he receives by the senses. But in the mind of man, while in the savage state, there seem to be hardly any ideas but what enter by this avenue. The objects around him are presented to his eye. Such as may be subservient to his use, or can gratify any of his appetites, attract his notice; he views the rest without curiosity or attention. Satisfied with considering them under that simple mode in which they appear to him, as separate and detached, he neither combines them so as to form general classes, nor contemplates their qualities apart from the subject in which they inhere, nor bestows a thought upon the operations of his own mind concerning them. Thus he is unacquainted with all the ideas which have been denominated *universal*, or *abstract*, or *of reflection*. The range of his understanding must, of course, be very confined, and his reasoning powers be employed merely on what is sensible. This is so remarkably the case with the ruder nations of America, that their languages (as we shall afterwards find) have not a word to express any thing but what is material or corporeal. *Time, space, substance,* and a thousand terms, which represent abstract and universal ideas, are altogether unknown to them.¶ A naked savage, cowering over the fire in his miserable cabin, or stretched under a few

---

* Condam. p. 67.   Stadius ap. de Bry, ix. 128.   Lery, ibid. 251.   Biet. 362.   Lettr. Edif. 23. 314.   † Dumont Louis. l. 187.   Herrera, dec. 1. lib. iii. c. 3.   Biet. 396.   Borde, 6.   ‡ This is the case with the Greenlanders, Crantz, l. 225, and with Kamchatkadales, M. l'Abbé Chappé, iii. 17.   § Charley. Nouv. Franc. iii. 402.   ‖ Adair's Hist. of Amer. Indians, 77.   ¶ Condam. p. 54.

branches which afford him a temporary shelter, has as little inclination as capacity for useless speculation. His thoughts extend not beyond what relates to animal life; and when they are not directed towards some of its concerns, his mind is totally inactive. In situations where no extraordinary effort either of ingenuity or labour is requisite, in order to satisfy the simple demands of nature, the powers of the mind are so seldom roused to any exertion, that the rational faculties continue almost dormant and unexercised. The numerous tribes scattered over the rich plains of South America, the inhabitants of some of the islands, and of several fertile regions on the continent, come under this description. Their vacant countenance, their staring unexpressive eye, their listless inattention, and total ignorance of subjects which seemed to be the first which should occupy the thoughts of rational beings, made such impression upon the Spaniards, when they first beheld those rude people, that they considered them as animals of an inferior order, and could not believe that they belonged to the human species.* It required the authority of a papal bull to counteract this opinion, and to convince them that the Americans were capable of the functions and entitled to the privileges of humanity.† Since that time, persons more enlightened and impartial than the discoverers or conquerors of America, have had an opportunity of contemplating the most savage of its inhabitants, and they have been astonished and humbled with observing how nearly man in this condition approaches to the brute creation. But in severer climates, where subsistence cannot be procured with the same ease, where men must unite more closely, and act with greater concert, necessity calls forth their talents and sharpens their invention, so that the intellectual powers are more exercised and improved. The North American tribes, and the natives of Chili, who inhabit the temperate regions in the two great districts of America, are people of cultivated and enlarged understandings, when viewed in comparison with some of those seated in the islands, or on the banks of the Maragnon and Orinoco. Their occupations are more various, their system of policy, as well as of war, more complex, their arts more numerous. But even among them, the intellectual powers are extremely limited in their operations, and, unless when turned directly to those objects which interest a savage, are held in no estimation. Both the North Americans and Chilese, when not engaged in some of the functions belonging to a warrior or hunter, loiter away their time in thoughtless indolence, unacquainted with any other subject worthy of their attention, or capable of occupying their minds.‡ If even among them reason is so much circumscribed in its exertions, and never arrives, in its highest attainments, at the knowledge of those general principles and maxims which serve as the foundation of science, we may conclude that the intellectual powers of man in the savage state are destitute of their proper object, and cannot acquire any considerable degree of vigour and enlargement.

From the same causes, the active efforts of the mind are few, and on most occasions languid. If we examine into the motives which rouse men to activity in civilized life, and prompt them to persevere in fatiguing exertions of their ingenuity or strength, we shall find that they arise chiefly from acquired wants and appetites. These are numerous and importunate; they keep the mind in perpetual agitation, and, in order to gratify them, invention must be always on the stretch, and industry must be incessantly employed. But the desires of simple nature are few, and where a favourable climate yields almost spontaneously what suffices to gratify them, they scarcely stir the soul, or excite any violent emotion. Hence the people of several tribes in America waste their life in a listless indolence. To be free from occupation, seems to be all the enjoyment

* Herrera, dec. 2. lib. II. c. 15.   † Torquem. Mon. Ind. III. 198.   ‡ Lafitau, ii. 2.

towards which they aspire. They will continue whole days stretched out in their hammocks, or seated on the earth in perfect idleness, without changing their posture, or raising their eyes from the ground, or uttering a single word.*

Such is their aversion to labour that neither the hope of future good nor the apprehension of future evil can surmount it. They appear equally indifferent to both, discovering little solicitude, and taking no precautions to avoid the one or to secure the other. The cravings of hunger may rouse them ; but as they devour, with little distinction, whatever will appease its instinctive demands, the exertions which these occasion are of short duration. Destitute of ardour, as well as variety of desire, they feel not the force of those powerful springs which give vigour to the movements of the mind, and urge the patient hand of industry to persevere in its efforts. Man, in some parts of America, appears in a form so rude that we can discover no effects of his activity, and the principle of understanding, which should direct it, seems hardly to be unfolded. Like the other animals, he has no fixed residence ; he has erected no habitation to shelter him from the inclemency of the weather ; he has taken no measures for securing certain subsistence ; he neither sows nor reaps ; but roams about as led in search of the plants and fruits which the earth brings forth in succession ; and in quest of the game which he kills in the forest, or of the fish which he catches in the rivers.

This description, however, applies only to some tribes. Man cannot continue long in this state of feeble and uninformed infancy. He was made for industry and action, and the powers of his nature, as well as the necessity of his condition, urge him to fulfil his destiny. Accordingly, among most of the American nations, especially those seated in rigorous climates, some efforts are employed, and some previous precautions are taken, for securing subsistence. The career of regular industry is begun, and the laborious arm has made the first essays of its power. Still, however, the improvident and slothful genius of the savage state predominates. Even among those more improved tribes, labour is deemed ignominious and degrading. It is only to work of a certain kind that a man will deign to put his hand. The greater part is devolved entirely upon the women. One-half of the community remains inactive, while the other is oppressed with the multitude and variety of its occupations. Thus their industry is partial, and the foresight which regulates it is no less limited. A remarkable instance of this occurs in the chief arrangement with respect to their manner of living. They depend for their subsistence, during one part of the year, on fishing; during another, on hunting; during a third, on the produce of their agriculture. Though experience has taught them to foresee the return of those various seasons, and to make some provision for the respective exigencies of each, they either want sagacity to proportion this provision to their consumption, or are so incapable of any command over their appetites, that, from their inconsiderate waste, they often feel the calamities of famine as severely as the rudest of the savage tribes. What they suffer one year does not augment their industry, or render them more provident to prevent similar distresses.† This inconsiderate thoughtlessness about futurity, the effect of ignorance and the cause of sloth, accompanies and characterizes man in every stage of savage life ;‡ and, by a capricious singularity in his operations, he is then least solicitous about supplying his wants, when the means of satisfying them are most precarious, and procured with the greatest difficulty [52].

III. After viewing the bodily constitution of the Americans, and con-

---

* Bouguer Voy. au Pérou, 102. Borde, 15.   † Charlev. N. Fr. iii. 338. Lettr. Edif. 23. 298. Descript. of N. France, Osborn's Collect. ii. 880. De la Potherie, ii. 63.   ‡ Bancroft's Nat. Hist. of Guiana, 326. XX.

AMERICA.

templating the powers of their minds, we are led, in the natural order of inquiry, to consider them as united together in society. Hitherto our researches have been confined to the operations of understanding respecting themselves as individuals; now they will extend to the degree of their sensibility and affection towards their species.

The domestic state is the first and most simple form of human association. The union of the sexes among different animals is of longer or shorter duration in proportion to the ease or difficulty of rearing their offspring. Among those tribes where the season of infancy is short, and the young soon acquire vigour or agility, no permanent union is formed. Nature commits the care of training up the offspring to the mother alone, and her tenderness, without any other assistance, is equal to the task. But where the state of infancy is long and helpless, and the joint assiduity of both parents is requisite in tending their feeble progeny, there a more intimate connexion takes place, and continues until the purpose of nature be accomplished, and the new race grow up to full maturity. As the infancy of man is more feeble and helpless than that of any other animal, and he is dependent during a much longer period on the care and foresight of his parents, the union between husband and wife came early to be considered not only as a solemn but as a permanent contract. A general state of promiscuous intercourse between the sexes never existed but in the imagination of poets. In the infancy of society, when men, destitute of arts and industry, lead a hard precarious life, the rearing of their progeny demands the attention and efforts of both parents; and if their union had not been formed and continued with this view, the race could not have been preserved. Accordingly in America, even among the rudest tribes, a regular union between husband and wife was universal, and the rights of marriage were understood and recognised. In those districts where subsistence was scanty, and the difficulty of maintaining a family was great, the man confined himself to one wife. In warmer and more fertile provinces, the facility of procuring food concurred with the influence of climate in inducing the inhabitants to increase the number of their wives.*
In some countries the marriage-union subsisted during life; in others, the impatience of the Americans under restraint of any species, together with their natural levity and caprice, prompted them to dissolve it on very slight pretexts, and often without assigning any cause.†

But in whatever light the Americans considered the obligation of this contract, either as perpetual or only as temporary, the condition of women was equally humiliating and miserable. Whether man has been improved by the progress of arts and civilization in society, is a question which, in the wantonness of disputation, has been agitated among philosophers. That women are indebted to the refinements of polished manners, for a happy change in their state, is a point which can admit of no doubt. To despise and to degrade the female sex is a characteristic of the savage state in every part of the globe. Man, proud of excelling in strength and in courage, the chief marks of pre-eminence among rude people, treats woman, as an inferior, with disdain. The Americans, perhaps from that coldness and insensibility which has been considered as peculiar to their constitution, add neglect and harshness to contempt. The most intelligent travellers have been struck with this inattention of the Americans to their women. It is not, as I have already observed, by a studied display of tenderness and attachment that the American endeavours to gain the heart of the woman whom he wishes to marry. Marriage itself, instead of being a union of affection and interests between equals, becomes among them the unnatural conjunction of a master with his slave. It is the observation of

* Lettr. Edif. 23. 318. Lafitau Mœurs, i. 554. Lery ap. de Bry, iii. 234. Journal de Grillet et Bechamel, p. 88. † Lafitau, i. 520. Joutel Journ. Histor. 345. Lozano Desc. del Gran Chaco, 70. Hennepin Mœurs des Sauvages, p. 30. 33.

Vol. I.—20

an author whose opinions are deservedly of great weight, that wherever wives are purchased their condition is extremely depressed.* They become the property and the slaves of those who buy them. In whatever part of the globe this custom prevails, the observation holds. In countries where refinement has made some progress, women when purchased are excluded from society, shut up in sequestered apartments, and kept under the vigilant guard of their masters. In ruder nations they are degraded to the meanest functions. Among many people of America the marriage contract is properly a purchase. The man buys his wife of her parents. Though unacquainted with the use of money, or with such commercial transactions as take place in more improved society, he knows how to give an equivalent for any object which he desires to possess. In some places, the suitor devotes his service for a certain time to the parents of the maid whom he courts; in others he hunts for them occasionally, or assists in cultivating their fields and forming their canoes; in others, he offers presents of such things as are deemed most valuable on account of their usefulness or rarity.† In return for these he receives his wife; and this circumstance, added to the low estimation of women among savages, leads him to consider her as a female servant whom he has purchased, and whom he has a title to treat as an inferior. In all unpolished nations, it is true, the functions in domestic economy which fall naturally to the share of women are so many, that they are subjected to hard labour, and must bear more than their full portion of the common burden. But in America their condition is so peculiarly grievous, and their depression so complete, that servitude is a name too mild to describe their wretched state. A wife among most tribes is no better than a beast of burden, destined to every office of labour and fatigue. While the men loiter out the day in sloth, or spend it in amusement, the women are condemned to incessant toil. Tasks are imposed upon them without pity, and services are received without complacence or gratitude.‡ Every circumstance reminds women of this mortifying inferiority. They must approach their lords with reverence; they must regard them as more exalted beings, and are not permitted to eat in their presence.§ There are districts in America where this dominion is so grievous, and so sensibly felt, that some women, in a wild emotion of maternal tenderness, have destroyed their female children in their infancy, in order to deliver them from that intolerable bondage to which they knew they were doomed.‖ Thus the first institution of social life is perverted. That state of domestic union towards which nature leads the human species, in order to soften the heart to gentleness and humanity, is rendered so unequal as to establish a cruel distinction between the sexes, which forms the one to be harsh and unfeeling, and humbles the other to servility and subjection.

It is owing, perhaps, in some measure, to this state of depression, that women in rude nations are far from being prolific.¶ The vigour of their constitution is exhausted by excessive fatigue, and the wants and distresses of savage life are so numerous as to force them to take various precautions in order to prevent too rapid an increase of their progeny. Among wandering tribes, or such as depend chiefly upon hunting for subsistence, the mother cannot attempt to rear a second child until the first has attained such a degree of vigour as to be in some measure independent of her care From this motive, it is the universal practice of the American women to suckle their children during several years;** and, as they seldom marry early, the period of their fertility is over before they can finish the long

---

* Sketches of Hist. of Man, i. 184.   † Lafitau Mœurs, &c. i. 560, &c.   Charlev. iii. 285, &c. Herrera, dec. 4. lib. iv. c. 7.   Dumont, ii. 156.   ‡ Tertre, ii.. 382.   Borde Relat. des Mœurs des Caraibes, p. 21.   Biet. 357.   Condamine, p. 110.   Fermin. i. 79.   § Gumilla, i. 153.   Barrere, 164.   Labat, Voy. ii. 78.   Chanvalon, 51.   Tertre, ii. 300.   ‖ Gumilla, ii. 233. 238.   Herrera, dec. 7. lib. ix. c. iv.   ¶ Lafitau, i. 590.   Charlevoix, iii. 304.   ** Herrera, dec. 6. lib. i. c. 4

but necessary attendance upon two or three children.* Among some of the least polished tribes, whose industry and foresight do not extend so far as to make any regular provision for their own subsistence, it is a maxim not to burden themselves with rearing more than two children;† and no such numerous families as are frequent in civilized societies are to be found among men in the savage state.‡ When twins are born, one of them commonly is abandoned, because the mother is not equal to the task of rearing both§ [53]. When a mother dies while she is nursing a child, all hope of preserving its life fails, and it is buried together with her in the same grave.‖ As the parents are frequently exposed to want by their own improvident indolence, the difficulty of sustaining their children becomes so great that it is not uncommon to abandon or destroy them.¶ Thus their experience of the difficulty of training up an infant to maturity, amidst the hardships of savage life, often stifles the voice of nature among the Americans, and suppresses the strong emotions of parental tenderness.

But though necessity compels the inhabitants of America thus to set bounds to the increase of their families, they are not deficient in affection and attachment to their offspring. They feel the power of this instinct in its full force, and as long as their progeny continue feeble and helpless, no people exceed them in tenderness and care.** But in rude nations the dependence of children upon their parents is of shorter continuance than in polished societies. When men must be trained to the various functions of civil life by previous discipline and education, when the knowledge of abstruse sciences must be taught, and dexterity in intricate arts must be acquired, before a young man is prepared to begin his career of action, the attentive feelings of a parent are not confined to the years of infancy, but extend to what is more remote, the establishment of his child in the world. Even then his solicitude does not terminate. His protection may still be requisite, and his wisdom and experience still prove useful guides. Thus a permanent connection is formed; parental tenderness is exercised, and filial respect returned, throughout the whole course of life. But in the simplicity of the savage state the affection of parents, like the instinctive fondness of animals, ceases almost entirely as soon as their offspring attain maturity. Little instruction fits them for that mode of life to which they are destined. The parents, as if their duty were accomplished, when they have conducted their children through the helpless years of infancy, leave them afterwards at entire liberty. Even in their tender age, they seldom advise or admonish, they never chide or chastise them. They suffer them to be absolute masters of their own actions.†† In an American hut, a father, a mother, and their posterity, live together like persons assembled by accident, without seeming to feel the obligation of the duties mutually arising from this connection.‡‡ As filial love is not cherished by the continuance of attention or good offices, the recollection of benefits received in early infancy is too faint to excite it. Conscious of their own liberty, and impatient of restraint, the youth of America are accustomed to act as if they were totally independent. Their parents are not objects of greater regard than other persons. They treat them always with neglect, and often with such harshness and insolence as to fill those who have been witnesses of their conduct with horror.§§ Thus the ideas which seem to be natural to man in his savage state, as they result necessarily from his circumstances and condition in that period of his progress,

* Charlev. iii. 303. Dumont, Mém. sur Louisiane, ii. 270. Deny's Hist. Natur. de l'Amérique, &c. ii. 365. Charlev. Hist. de Parag. ii. 422. † Techo's Account of Paraguay, &c. Church. Collect. vi. 108. Lett. Edif. xxxiv. 200. Lozano Descr. 92. ‡ Maccleur's Journal, 63. § Lett. Edif. x. 200. ‖ Charlev. iii. 368. Lett. Ediff. x. 200. P. Melch. Hernandez Memor. de Cheriqul. Colbert. Collect. Orig. Pap. i. ¶ Venega's Hist. of Californ. i. 82. ** Gumilla, i. 211. Biet. 390. †† Charlev. iii. 272. Biet. 390. Gumilla, i. 212. Lafitau, i. 602. Creuxii Hist. Canad. p. 71. Fernandez, Relac. Hist. de los Chequit. 33. ‡‡ Charlev. Hist. N. Fr. iii. 273. §§ Gumilla, i. 212. Tertre, ii. 376. Charlev. Hist. de N. France, iii. 309. Charlev. Hist. de Parag. i. 115. Lozano Descript. del Gran. Chaco, p. 68, 100, 101. Fernand. Relac. Histor. de los Chequit. 496.

affect the two capital relations in domestic life. They render the union between husband and wife unequal. They shorten the duration and weaken the force of the connection between parents and children.

IV. From the domestic state of the Americans, the transition to the consideration of their civil government and political institutions is natural. In every inquiry concerning the operations of men when united together in society, the first object of attention should be their mode of subsistence. Accordingly as that varies, their laws and policy must be different. The institution suited to the ideas and exigencies of tribes which subsist chiefly by fishing or hunting, and which have as yet acquired but an imperfect conception of any species of property, will be much more simple than those which must take place when the earth is cultivated with regular industry; and a right of property, not only in its productions, but in the soil itself, is completely ascertained.

All the people of America, now under review, belong to the former class. But though they may all be comprehended under the general denomination of savage, the advances which they had made in the art of procuring to themselves a certain and plentiful subsistence were very unequal. On the extensive plains of South America man appears in one of the rudest states in which he has been ever observed, or perhaps can exist. Several tribes depend entirely upon the bounty of nature for subsistence. They discover no solicitude, they employ little foresight, they scarcely exert any industry to secure what is necessary for their support. The *Topuyers*, of Brazil, the *Guaxeros*, of Tierra Firme, the *Caiguas*, the *Moxos*, and several other people of Paraguay, are unacquainted with every species of cultivation. They neither sow nor plant. Even the culture of the manioc, of which cassada bread is made, is an art too intricate for their ingenuity, or too fatiguing to their indolence. The roots which the earth produces spontaneously, the fruits, the berries, and the seeds which they gather in the woods; together with lizards and other reptiles, which multiply amazingly with the heat of the climate in a fat soil moistened by frequent rains, supply them with food during some part of the year.* At other times they subsist by fishing; and nature seems to have indulged the laziness of the South American tribes by the liberality with which she ministers in this way to their wants. The vast rivers of that region in America abound with an infinite variety of the most delicate fish. The lakes and marshes formed by the annual overflowing of the waters are filled with all the different species, where they remain shut up, as in natural reservoirs, for the use of the inhabitants. They swarm in such shoals, that in some places they are catched without art or industry [54]. In others, the natives have discovered a method of infecting the water with the juice of certain plants, by which the fish are so intoxicated that they float on the surface and are taken with the hand [55]. Some tribes have ingenuity enough to preserve them without salt, by drying or smoking them upon hurdles over a slow fire.† The prolific quality of the rivers in South America induces many of the natives to resort to their banks, and to depend almost entirely for nourishment on what their waters supply with such profusion.‡ In this part of the globe hunting seems not to have been the first employment of men, or the first effort of their invention and labour to obtain food. They were fishers before they became hunters; and as the occupations of the former do not call for equal exertions of activity or talents with those of the latter, people in that state appear to possess neither the same degree of enterprise nor of ingenuity. The

---

* Nieuhoff. Hist. of Brazil. Church. Coll. ii. 134. Simon Conquista de Tierra Firmé, p. 166. Techo, Account of Paraguay, &c. Church. vi. 78. Lettr. Edif. 23. 384. 10. 190. Lozano, Descrip. del. Gran Chaco, p. 81. Ribas Histor. de los Triumfos, &c. p. 7.   † Condam. 159. Gumilla, ii. 37. Lettr. Edif. 14. 199. 23. 393. Acugna, Relat. de la Riv. des Amas. 138.   ‡ Barrere, Relat. de Fr. Equin. p. 155.

petty nations adjacent to the Maragnon and Orinoco are manifestly the most inactive and least intelligent of all the Americans.

None but tribes contiguous to great rivers can sustain themselves in this manner. The greater part of the American nations, dispersed over the forests with which their country is covered, do not procure subsistence with the same facility. For although these forests, especially in the southern continent of America, are stored plentifully with game,* considerable efforts of activity and ingenuity are requisite in pursuit of it. Necessity incited the natives to the one, and taught them the other. Hunting became their principal occupation; and as it called forth strenuous exertions of courage, of force, and of invention, it was deemed no less honourable than necessary. This occupation was peculiar to the men. They were trained to it from their earliest youth. A bold and dexterous hunter ranked next in fame to the distinguished warrior, and an alliance with the former is often courted in preference to one with the latter.† Hardly any device, which the ingenuity of man has discovered for ensnaring or destroying wild animals, was unknown to the Americans. While engaged in this favourite exercise, they shake off the indolence peculiar to their nature, the latent powers and vigour of their minds are roused, and they become active, persevering, and indefatigable. Their sagacity in finding their prey and their address in killing it are equal. Their reason and their senses being constantly directed towards this one object, the former displays such fertility of invention and the latter acquire such a degree of acuteness as appear almost incredible. They discern the footsteps of a wild beast, which escape every other eye, and can follow them with certainty through the pathless forest. If they attack their game openly, their arrow seldom errs from the mark :‡ if they endeavour to circumvent it by art, it is almost impossible to avoid their toils. Among several tribes, their young men were not permitted to marry until they had given such proofs of their skill in hunting as put it beyond doubt that they were capable of providing for a family. Their ingenuity, always on the stretch, and sharpened by emulation as well as necessity, has struck out many inventions which greatly facilitate success in the chase. The most singular of these is the discovery of a poison, in which they dip the arrows employed in hunting. The slightest wound with those envenomed shafts is mortal. If they only pierce the skin, the blood fixes and congeals in a moment, and the strongest animal falls motionless to the ground. Nor does this poison, notwithstanding its violence and subtlety, infect the flesh of the animal which it kills. That may be eaten with perfect safety, and retain its native relish and qualities. All the nations situated upon the banks of the Maragnon and Orinoco are acquainted with this composition, the chief ingredient in which is the juice extracted from the root of the *curare*, a species of withe.§ In other parts of America they employ the juice of the *manchenille* for the same purpose, and it operates with no less fatal activity. To people possessed of those secrets the bow is a more destructive weapon than the musket, and, in their skilful hands, does great execution among the birds and beasts which abound in the forests of America.

But the life of a hunter gradually leads man to a state more advanced. The chase, even where prey is abundant, and the dexterity of the hunter much improved, affords but an uncertain maintenance, and at some seasons it must be suspended altogether. If a savage trusts to his bow alone for food, he and his family will be often reduced to extreme distress [56]. Hardly any region of the earth furnishes man spontaneously with what his wants require. In the mildest climates, and most fertile soils, his own

---

* P. Martyr, Decad. p. 324. Gumilla, ii. 4, &c. Acugna, i. 156.   † Charlev. Histoire de la N. France, iii. 115.   ‡ Biet. Voy. de France Equin. 357. Davies's Discov. of the River of Amaz. Purchas, iv. p. 1287.   § Gumilla, ii. 1, &c. Condam. 208. Recherch. Philos. ii. 239. Bancroft's Nat. Hist. of Guiana, 281, &c.

industry and foresight must be exerted in some degree to secure a regular supply of food. Their experience of this surmounts the abhorrence of labour natural to savage nations, and compels them to have recourse to culture, as subsidiary to hunting. In particular situations, some small tribes may subsist by fishing, independent of any production of the earth raised by their own industry. But throughout all America, we scarcely meet with any nation of hunters which does not practise some species of cultivation.

The agriculture of the Americans, however, is neither extensive nor laborious. As game and fish are their principal food, all they aim at by cultivation is to supply any occasional defect of these. In the southern continent of America, the natives confined their industry to rearing a few plants, which, in a rich soil and warm climate, were easily trained to maturity. The chief of these is *maize*, well known in Europe by the name of Turkey or Indian wheat, a grain extremely prolific, of simple culture, agreeable to the taste, and affording a strong hearty nourishment. The second is the *manioc*, which grows to the size of a large shrub or small tree, and produces roots somewhat resembling parsnips. After carefully squeezing out the juice, these roots are grated down to a fine powder, and formed into thin cakes called *cassada* bread, which, though insipid to the taste, proves no contemptible food.* As the juice of the manioc is a deadly poison, some authors have celebrated the ingenuity of the Americans in converting a noxious plant into wholesome nourishment. But it should rather be considered as one of the desperate expedients for procuring subsistence, to which necessity reduces rude nations; or, perhaps, men were led to the use of it by a progress in which there is nothing marvellous. One species of manioc is altogether free of any poisonous quality, and may be eaten without any preparation but that of roasting it in the embers. This, it is probable, was first used by the Americans as food; and, necessity having gradually taught them the art of separating its pernicious juice from the other species, they have by experience found it to be more prolific as well as more nourishing† [57]. The third is the *plantain*, which, though it rises to the height of a tree, is of such quick growth, that in less than a year it rewards the industry of the cultivator with its fruit. This, when roasted, supplies the place of bread, and is both palatable and nourishing [58]. The fourth is the *potatoe*, whose culture and qualities are too well known to need any description. The fifth is *pimento*, a small tree yielding a strong aromatic spice. The Americans, who, like other inhabitants of warm climates, delight in whatever is hot and of poignant flavour, deem this seasoning a necessary of life, and mingle it copiously with every kind of food they take.‡

Such are the various productions, which were the chief object of culture among the hunting tribes on the continent of America; and with a moderate exertion of active and provident industry these might have yielded a full supply to the wants of a numerous people. But men, accustomed to the free and vagrant life of hunters, are incapable of regular application to labour, and consider agriculture as a secondary and inferior occupation. Accordingly, the provision for subsistence, arising from cultivation, was so limited and scanty among the Americans, that, upon any accidental failure of their usual success in hunting, they were often reduced to extreme distress.

In the islands, the mode of subsisting was considerably different. None of the large animals which abound on the continent were known there. Only four species of quadrupeds, besides a kind of small dumb dog,

---

* Sloane Hist. of Jam. Introd. p. 18. Labat, i. 394. Acosta, Hist. Ind. Occid. Natur. lib. iv. c. 17. Ulloa, i. 62. Aublet, Mem. sur le Magnioc. Hist. des Plantes, tom. ii. p. 65, &c. † Martyr, Decad. 301. Labet, i. 411. Gumilla, iii. 192. Machuchs Millc. Indiana, 164. ‡ Gumilla, iii. 171. Acosta, lib. iv. c. 20.

existed in the islands, the biggest of which did not exceed the size of a rabbit.* To hunt such a diminutive prey was an occupation which required no effort either of activity or courage. The chief employment of a hunter in the isles was to kill birds, which on the continent are deemed ignoble game, and left chiefly to the pursuit of boys.† This want of animals, as well as their peculiar situation, led the islanders to depend principally upon fishing for their subsistence.‡ Their rivers, and the sea with which they are surrounded, supplied them with this species of food. At some particular seasons, turtle, crabs, and other shellfish abounded in such numbers that the natives could support themselves with a facility in which their indolence delighted.§ At other times, they ate lizards and various reptiles of odious forms.‖ To fishing the inhabitants of the islands added some degree of agriculture. Maize [59], manioc, and other plants were cultivated in the same manner as on the continent. But all the fruits of their industry, together with what their soil and climate produced spontaneously, afforded them but a scanty maintenance. Though their demands for food were very sparing, they hardly raised what was sufficient for their own consumption. If a few Spaniards settled in any district, such a small addition of supernumerary mouths soon exhausted their scanty stores, and brought on a famine.

Two circumstances, common to all the savage nations of America, concurred with those which I have already mentioned, not only in rendering their agriculture imperfect, but in circumscribing their power in all their operations. They had no tame animals; and they were unacquainted with the useful metals.

In other parts of the globe, man, in his rudest state, appears as lord of the creation, giving law to various tribes of animals, which he has tamed and reduced to subjection. The Tartar follows his prey on the horse which he has reared; or tends his numerous herds, which furnish him both with food and clothing: the Arab has rendered the camel docile; and avails himself of its persevering strength: the Laplander has formed the reindeer to be subservient to his will; and even the people of Kamchatka have trained their dogs to labour. This command over the inferior creatures is one of the noblest prerogatives of man, and among the greatest efforts of his wisdom and power. Without this his dominion is incomplete. He is a monarch who has no subjects, a master without servants, and must perform every operation by the strength of his own arm. Such was the condition of all the rude nations in America. Their reason was so little improved, or their union so incomplete, that they seem not to have been conscious of the superiority of their nature, and suffered all the animal creation to retain its liberty, without establishing their own authority over any one species. Most of the animals, indeed, which have been rendered domestic in our continent, do not exist in the New World; but those peculiar to it are neither so fierce nor so formidable as to have exempted them from servitude. There are some animals of the same species on both continents. But the rein-deer, which has been tamed and broken to the yoke in the one hemisphere, runs wild in the other. The *bison* of America is manifestly of the same species with the horned cattle of the other hemisphere.¶ The latter, even among the rudest nations in our continent, have been rendered domestic; and, in consequence of his dominion over them, man can accomplish works of labour with greater facility, and has made a great addition to his means of subsistence. The inhabitants of many regions of the New World, where the bison abounds, might have derived the same advantages from it. It is not of a nature so indocile, but that it might have been trained to be as subservient to man

---

* Oviedo, lib. xii. in proëm. † Ribas Hist. de los Triumph. p. 13. De la Potherie, ii. 33. lii. 20. ‡ Oviedo, lib. xiii. c. 1. Gomara, Hist. Gener. c. 28. § Gomara, Hist. Gener. c 9. Labat, ii. 221, &c. ‖ Oviedo, lib. xiii c 3 ¶ Buffon. artic. *Bison*.

as our cattle.* But a savage, in that uncultivated state wherein the Americans were discovered, is the enemy of the other animals, not their superior. He wastes and destroys, but knows not how to multiply or to govern them.†

This, perhaps, is the most notable distinction between the inhabitants of the Ancient and New Worlds, and a high pre-eminence of civilized men above such as continue rude. The greatest operations of man in changing and improving the face of nature, as well as his most considerable efforts in cultivating the earth, are accomplished by means of the aid which he receives from the animals that he has tamed, and employs in labour. It is by their strength that he subdues the stubborn soil, and converts the desert or marsh into a fruitful field. But man, in his civilized state, is so accustomed to the service of the domestic animals, that he seldom reflects upon the vast benefits which he derives from it. If we were to suppose him, even when most improved, to be deprived of their useful ministry, his empire over nature must in some measure cease, and he would remain a feeble animal, at a loss how to subsist, and incapable of attempting such arduous undertakings as their assistance enables him to execute with ease.

It is a doubtful point, whether the dominion of man over the animal creation, or his acquiring the useful metals, has contributed most to extend his power. The era of this important discovery is unknown, and in our hemisphere very remote. It is only by tradition, or by digging up some rude instruments of our forefathers, that we learn that mankind were originally unacquainted with the use of metals, and endeavoured to supply the want of them by employing flints, shells, bones, and other hard substances, for the same purposes which metals serve among polished nations. Nature completes the formation of some metals. Gold, silver, and copper, are found in their perfect state in the clefts of rocks, in the sides of mountains, or the channels of rivers. These were accordingly the metals first known, and first applied to use. But iron, the most serviceable of all, and to which man is most indebted, is never discovered in its perfect form; its gross and stubborn ore must feel twice the force of fire, and go through two laborious processes, before it becomes fit for use. Man was long acquainted with the other metals before he acquired the art of fabricating iron, or attained such ingenuity as to perfect an invention, to which he is indebted for those instruments wherewith he subdues the earth, and commands all its inhabitants. But in this, as well as in many other respects, the inferiority of the Americans was conspicuous. All the savage tribes, scattered over the continent and islands, were totally unacquainted with the metals which their soil produces in great abundance, if we except some trifling quantity of gold, which they picked up in the torrents that descended from their mountains, and formed into ornaments. Their devices to supply this want of the serviceable metals were extremely rude and awkward. The most simple operation was to them an undertaking of immense difficulty and labour. To fell a tree with no other instruments than hatchets of stone, was employment for a month.‡ To form a canoe into shape, and to hollow it, consumed years; and it frequently began to rot before they were able to finish it.§ Their operations in agriculture were equally slow and defective. In a country covered with woods of the hardest timber, the clearing of a small field destined for culture required the united efforts of a tribe, and was a work of much time and great toil. This was the business of the men, and their indolence was satisfied with performing it in a very slovenly manner. The labour of cultivation was left to the women, who, after digging, or rather stirring the

---

* Nouv. Découverte par Hennepin, p. 192. Kalm, i. 207. † Buffon Hist. Nat. ix. 85. Hist. Philos. et Polit. des Etablissem. des Europ. dans les deux Indes, vi. 364 ‡ Gumilla, iii. 196. § Borde Relat. des Caraibes, p. 22.

field, with wooden mattocks, and stakes hardened in the fire, sowed or planted it; but they were more indebted for the increase to the fertility of the soil than to their own rude industry.*

Agriculture, even when the strength of man is seconded by that of the animals which he has subjected to the yoke, and his power augmented by the use of the various instruments with which the discovery of metals has furnished him, is still a work of great labour; and it is with the sweat of his brow that he renders the earth fertile. It is not wonderful, then, that people destitute of both these advantages should have made so little progress in cultivation, that they must be considered as depending for subsistence on fishing and hunting, rather than on the fruits of their own labour.

From this description of the mode of subsisting among the rude American tribes, the form and genius of their political institutions may be deduced, and we are enabled to trace various circumstances of distinction between them and more civilized nations.

1. They were divided into small independent communities. While hunting is the chief source of subsistence, a vast extent of territory is requisite for supporting a small number of people. In proportion as men multiply and unite, the wild animals on which they depend for food diminish, or fly at a greater distance from the haunts of their enemy. The increase of a society in this state is limited by its own nature, and the members of it must either disperse, like the game which they pursue, or fall upon some better method of procuring food than by hunting. Beasts of prey are by nature solitary and unsocial, they go not forth to the chase in herds, but delight in those recesses of the forest where they can roam and destroy undisturbed. A nation of hunters resembles them both in occupation and in genius. They cannot form into large communities, because it would be impossible to find subsistence; and they must drive to a distance every rival who may encroach on those domains, which they consider as their own. This was the state of all the American tribes; the numbers in each were inconsiderable, though scattered over countries of great extent; they were far removed from one another, and engaged in perpetual hostilities or rivalship.† In America, the word *nation* is not of the same import as in other parts of the globe. It is applied to small societies, not exceeding, perhaps, two or three hundred persons, but occupying provinces, greater than some kingdoms in Europe. The country of Guiana, though of larger extent than the kingdom of France, and divided among a greater number of nations, did not contain above twenty-five thousand inhabitants.‡ In the provinces which border on the Orinoco, one may travel several hundred miles in different directions, without finding a single hut, or observing the footsteps of a human creature.§ In North America, where the climate is more rigorous, and the soil less fertile, the desolation is still greater. There, journeys of some hundred leagues have been made through uninhabited plains and forests‖ [60]. As long as hunting continues to be the chief employment of man, to which he trusts for subsistence, he can hardly be said to have occupied the earth [61].

2. Nations which depend upon hunting are in a great measure strangers to the idea of property. As the animals on which the hunter feeds are not bred under his inspection, nor nourished by his care, he can claim no right to them while they run wild in the forest. Where game is so plentiful that it may be catched with little trouble, men never dream of appropriating what is of small value, or of easy acquisition. Where it is so rare, that the labour or danger of the chase requires the united efforts of a tribe, or village, what is killed is a common stock belonging equally to all, who, by their

* Gumilla, lil. 166, &c. Lettr. Edif. xii. 10. † Lozano Descrip. del Gran Chaco, 59. 62. Fernandez Relac. Hist. de los Chequit. 162. ‡ Voyages de Marchais, iv. 353. § Gumilla, li. 101. ‖ M. Fabry, quoted by Buffon, iii. 448. Lafitau, ii. 179. Bossu, Travels through Louisiana, l. 111.

skill or their courage, have contributed to the success of the excursion. The forest or hunting-grounds are deemed the property of the tribe, from which it has a title to exclude every rival nation. But no individual arrogates a right to any district of these in preference to his fellow-citizens. They belong alike to all; and thither, as to a general and undivided store, all repair in quest of sustenance. The same principles by which they regulate their chief occupation extend to that which is subordinate. Even agriculture has not introduced among them a complete idea of property. As the men hunt, the women labour together, and after they have shared the toils of the seed time, they enjoy the harvest in common.* Among some tribes, the increase of their cultivated lands is deposited in a public granary, and divided among them at stated times, according to their wants† [62]. Among others, though they lay up separate stores, they do not acquire such an exclusive right of property, but that they can enjoy superfluity while those around them suffer want.‡ Thus the distinctions arising from the inequality of possessions are unknown. The terms rich or poor enter not into their language; and being strangers to property, they are unacquainted with what is the great object of laws and policy, as well as the chief motive which induced mankind to establish the various arrangements of regular government.§

3. People in this state retain a high sense of equality and independence. Wherever the idea of property is not established, there can be no distinction among men but what arises from personal qualities. These can be conspicuous only on such occasions as call them forth into exertion. In times of danger, or in affairs of intricacy, the wisdom and experience of age are consulted, and prescribe the measures which ought to be pursued. When a tribe of savages takes the field against the enemies of their country, the warrior of most approved courage leads the youth to the combat.‖ If they go forth in a body to the chase, the most expert and adventurous hunter is foremost, and directs their motions. But during seasons of tranquillity and inaction, when there is no occasion to display those talents, all pre-eminence ceases. Every circumstance indicates that all the members of the community are on a level. They are clothed in the same simple garb. They feed on the same plain fare. Their houses and furniture are exactly similar. No distinction can arise from the inequality of possessions. Whatever forms dependence on one part, or constitutes superiority on the other, is unknown. All are freemen, all feel themselves to be such, and assert with firmness the rights which belong to that condition.¶ This sentiment of independence is imprinted so deeply in their nature that no change of condition can eradicate it, and bend their minds to servitude. Accustomed to be absolute masters of their own conduct, they disdain to execute the orders of another; and having never known control, they will not submit to correction. [68] Many of the Americans, when they found that they were treated as slaves by the Spaniards, died of grief; many destroyed themselves in despair.**

4. Among people in this state, government can assume little authority, and the sense of civil subordination must remain very imperfect. While the idea of property is unknown, or incompletely conceived; while the spontaneous productions of the earth, as well as the fruits of industry, are considered as belonging to the public stock, there can hardly be any such subject of difference or discussion among the members of the same community, as will require the hand of authority to interpose in order to adjust it. Where the right of separate and exclusive possession is not introduced, the

---

* Dr. Furguson's Essay, 125.   † Gumilla, i. 265. Brickell, Hist. of N. Carol. 327.   ‡ Deny's Hist. Natur. ii. 392, 393.   § P. Martyr, Decad. p. 45. Veneg. Hist. of Californ. i. 66. Lery, Navig. in Brazil, c. 17.   ‖ Acosta Hist. lib. vi. c. 10.   Stadius Hist. Brazil, lib. ii. c. 13. De Bry, lii. p. 110. Biet, 361.   ¶ Labat, vi. 124. Brickell, Hist. of Carol. 310.   ** Oviedo, lib. iii. c. 6. p. 97. Vega Conquist. de la Florida, i. 30. ii. 416. Labat, ii. 138. Bonzo. Hist. Nov. Orb. lib. iv. c. 25.

great object of law and jurisdiction does not exist. When the members of a tribe are called into the field, either to invade the territories of their enemies, or to repel their attacks; when they are engaged together in the toil and dangers of the chase, they then perceive that they are part of a political body. They are conscious of their own connexion with the companions in conjunction with whom they act; and they follow and reverence such as excel in conduct and valour. But during the intervals between such common efforts they seem scarcely to feel the ties of political union* [64]. No visible form of government is established. The names of *magistrate* and *subject* are not in use. Every one seems to enjoy his natural independence almost entire. If a scheme of public utility be proposed, the members of the community are left at liberty to choose whether they will or will not assist in carrying it into execution. No statute imposes any service as a duty, no compulsory laws oblige them to perform it. All their resolutions are voluntary, and flow from the impulse of their own minds.† The first step towards establishing a public jurisdiction has not been taken in those rude societies. The right of revenge is left in private hands.‡ If violence is committed, or blood is shed, the community does not assume the power either of inflicting or of moderating the punishment. It belongs to the family and friends of the person injured or slain to avenge the wrong, or to accept of the reparation offered by the aggressor. If the elders interpose, it is to advise, not to decide, and it is seldom their counsels are listened to; for, as it is deemed pusillanimous to suffer an offender to escape with impunity, resentment is implacable and everlasting.§ The object of government among savages is rather foreign than domestic. They do not aim at maintaining interior order and police by public regulations, or the exertions of any permanent authority, but labour to preserve such union among the members of their tribe, that they may watch the motions of their enemies, and act against them with concert and vigour.

Such was the form of political order established among the greater part of the American nations. In this state were almost all the tribes spread over the provinces extending eastward of the Mississippi, from the mouth of the St. Lawrence to the confines of Florida. In a similar condition were the people of Brazil, the inhabitants of Chili, several tribes in Paragua and Guiana, and in the countries which stretch from the mouth of the Orinoco to the peninsula of Yucatan. Among such an infinite number of petty associations, there may be peculiarities which constitute a distinction, and mark the various degrees of their civilization and improvement. But an attempt to trace and enumerate these would be vain, as they have not been observed by persons capable of discerning the minute and delicate circumstances which serve to discriminate nations resembling one another in their general character and features. The description which I have given of the political institutions that took place among those rude tribes in America, concerning which we have received most complete information, will apply, with little variation, to every people, both in its northern and southern division, who have advanced no further in civilization than to add some slender degree of agriculture to fishing and hunting.

Imperfect as those institutions may appear, several tribes were not so far advanced in their political progress. Among all those petty nations which trusted for subsistence entirely to fishing and hunting without any species of cultivation, the union was so incomplete, and their sense of mutual dependence so feeble, that hardly any appearance of government or order can be discerned in their proceedings. Their wants are few, their objects of pursuit simple, they form into separate tribes, and act together, from

---

* Lozano Descr. del Gran. Chaco, 93. Melendez Teforos Verdaderos, ll. 23. † Charlev. Hist. N. France. iii. 266 268. ‡ Herrera, dec. 8. lib. iv. c. 8. § Charlev. Hist. N. France, iii. 271, 272. Lafit. l. 486. Casalni, Hist. de Nuovo Reyno de Granada, 226.

instinct, habit, or conveniency, rather than from any formal concert and association. To this class belong the Californians, several of the small nations in the extensive country of Paragua, some of the people on the banks of the Orinoco, and on the river St. Magdalene, in the new kingdom of Granada.*

But though among these last mentioned tribes there was hardly any shadow of regular government, and even among those which I first described its authority is slender and confined within narrow bounds, there were, however, some places in America where government was carried far beyond the degree of perfection which seems natural to rude nations. In surveying the political operations of man, either in his savage or civilized state, we discover singular and eccentric institutions, which start as it were from their station, and fly off so wide, that we labour in vain to bring them within the general laws of any system, or to account for them by those principles which influence other communities in a similar situation. Some instances of this occur among those people of America whom I have included under the common denomination of savage. These are so curious and important that I shall describe them, and attempt to explain their origin.

In the New World, as well as in other parts of the globe, cold or temperate countries appear to be the favourite seat of freedom and independence. There the mind, like the body, is firm and vigorous. There men, conscious of their own dignity, and capable of the greatest efforts in asserting it, aspire to independence, and their stubborn spirits stoop with reluctance to the yoke of servitude. In warmer climates, by whose influence the whole frame is so much enervated that present pleasure is the supreme felicity, and mere repose is enjoyment, men acquiesce, almost without a struggle, in the dominion of a superior. Accordingly, if we proceed from north to south along the continent of America, we shall find the power of those vested with authority gradually increasing, and the spirit of the people becoming more tame and passive. In Florida, the authority of the sachems, caziques, or chiefs, was not only permanent, but hereditary. They were distinguished by peculiar ornaments, they enjoyed prerogatives of various kinds, and were treated by their subjects with that reverence which people accustomed to subjection pay to a master.†

Among the Natchez, a powerful tribe now extinct, formerly situated on the banks of the Mississippi, a difference of rank took place, with which the northern tribes were altogether unacquainted. Some families were reputed noble, and enjoyed hereditary dignity. The body of the people was considered as vile, and formed only for subjection. This distinction was marked by appellations which intimated the high elevation of the one state, and the ignominious depression of the other. The former were called *Respectable;* the latter, the *Stinkards.* The great Chief, in whom the supreme authority was vested, is reputed to be a being of superior nature, the brother of the sun, the sole object of their worship. They approach this great Chief with religious veneration, and honour him as the representative of their deity. His will is a law, to which all submit with implicit obedience. The lives of his subjects are so absolutely at his disposal, that if any one has incurred his displeasure, the offender comes with profound humility and offers him his head. Nor does the dominion of the Chiefs end with their lives; their principal officers, their favourite wives, together with many domestics of inferior rank, are sacrificed at their tombs, that they may be attended in the next world by the same persons who served them in this; and such is the reverence in which they are held,

* Venegas, i. 68.   Lettr. Edif. ii. 176.   Techo Hist. of Parag. Churchill, vi. 78.   Hist. Gen. des Voyages, xlv. 74.   † Cardenas y Cano Ensayo Chronol. à la Hist. de Florida, p. 46.   Le Moyne de Morgues Icones Floridæ, ap. de Bry, p. 1. 4, &c.   Charlev. Hist. N. France, iii. 467, 468.

that those victims welcome death with exultation, deeming it a recompense of their fidelity and a mark of distinction to be selected to accompany their deceased master.* Thus a perfect despotism, with its full train of superstition, arrogance, and cruelty, is established among the Natchez, and, by a singular fatality, that people has tasted of the worst calamities incident to polished nations, though they themselves are not far advanced beyond the tribes around them in civility and improvement. In Hispaniola, Cuba, and the larger islands, their caziques or chiefs possessed extensive power. The dignity was transmitted by hereditary right from father to son. Its honours and prerogatives were considerable. Their subjects paid great respect to the caziques, and executed their orders without hesitation or reserve.† They were distinguished by peculiar ornaments, and in order to preserve or augment the veneration of the people, they had the address to call in the aid of superstition to uphold their authority. They delivered their mandates as the oracles of heaven, and pretended to possess the power of regulating the seasons, and of dispensing rain or sunshine, according as their subjects stood in need of them.

In some parts of the southern continent, the power of the caziques seems to have been as extensive as in the isles. In Bogota, which is now a province of the new kingdom of Granada, there was settled a nation more considerable in number, and more improved in the various arts of life, than any in America, except the Mexicans and Peruvians. The people of Bogota subsisted chiefly by agriculture. The idea of property was introduced among them, and its rights, secured by laws, handed down by tradition, and observed with great care.‡ They lived in towns which may be termed large when compared with those in other parts of America. They were clothed in a decent manner, and their houses may be termed commodious when compared with those of the small tribes around them. The effects of this uncommon civilization were conspicuous. Government had assumed a regular form. A jurisdiction was established, which took cognizance of different crimes, and punished them with rigour. A distinction of ranks was known; their chief, to whom the Spaniards gave the title of monarch, and who merited that name on account of his splendour as well as power, reigned with absolute authority. He was attended by officers of various conditions ; he never appeared in public without a numerous retinue ; he was carried in a sort of palanquin with much pomp, and harbingers went before him to sweep the road and strew it with flowers. This uncommon pomp was supported by presents or taxes received from his subjects, to whom their prince was such an object of veneration that none of them presumed to look him directly in the face, or ever approached him but with an averted countenance.§ There were other tribes on the same continent, among which, though far less advanced than the people of Bogota in their progress towards refinement, the freedom and inde pendence natural to man in his savage state was much abridged, and their caziques had assumed extensive authority.

It is not easy to point out the circumstances, or to discover the causes which contributed to introduce and establish among each of those people a form of government so different from that of the tribes around them, and so repugnant to the genius of rude nations. If the persons who had an opportunity of observing them in their original state had been more attentive and more discerning, we might have received information from their conquerors sufficient to guide us in this inquiry. If the transactions of people unacquainted with the use of letters were not involved in impenetrable obscurity, we might have derived some information from this

* Dumont Memoir. Hist. sur Louisiane, i, 175. Charlev. Hist. N. France, iii. 419, &c. Lettr. Edif. 20. 106. 111. † Herrera, dec. 1. lib. 1. c. 16. lib. iii. c. 44. p. 88. Life of Columbus, ch. 32. ‡ Piedrahita Hist. de las Conquist. del Reyno de Granada, p. 46. § Herrera, dec. 6. lib. i. c. 2. lib. v. c. 56. Piedrablita, c. 5. p. 25, &c. Gomara, Hist. c. 72.

domestic source. But as nothing satisfactory can be gathered either from the accounts of the Spaniards, or from their own traditions, we must have recourse to conjectures in order to explain the irregular appearances in the political state of the people whom I have mentioned. As all those tribes which had lost their native liberty and independence were seated in the torrid zone, or in countries approaching to it, the climate may be supposed to have had some influence in forming their minds to that servitude which seems to be the destiny of man in those regions of the globe. But though the influence of climate, more powerful than that of any other natural cause, is not to be overlooked, that alone cannot be admitted as a solution of the point in question. The operations of men are so complex that we must not attribute the form which they assume to the force of a single principle or cause. Although despotism be confined in America to the torrid zone, and to the warm regions bordering upon it, I have already observed that these countries contain various tribes, some of which possess a high degree of freedom, and others are altogether unacquainted with the restraints of government. The indolence and timidity peculiar to the inhabitants of the islands, render them so incapable of the sentiments or efforts necessary for maintaining independence, that there is no occasion to search for any other cause of their tame submission to the will of a superior. The subjection of the Natchez, and of the people of Bogota, seems to have been the consequence of a difference in their state from that of the other Americans. They were settled nations, residing constantly in one place. Hunting was not the chief occupation of the former, and the latter seem hardly to have trusted to it for any part of their subsistence. Both had made such progress in agriculture and arts that the idea of property was introduced in some degree in the one community, and fully established in the other. Among people in this state, avarice and ambition have acquired objects, and have begun to exert their power; views of interest allure the selfish; the desire of pre-eminence excites the enterprising; dominion is courted by both; and passions unknown to man in his savage state prompt the interested and ambitious to encroach on the rights of their fellow-citizens. Motives, with which rude nations are equally unacquainted, induce the people to submit tamely to the usurped authority of their superiors. But even among nations in this state, the spirit of subjects could not have been rendered so obsequious, or the power of rulers so unbounded, without the intervention of superstition. By its fatal influence the human mind, in every stage of its progress, is depressed, and its native vigour and independence subdued. Whoever can acquire the direction of this formidable engine, is secure of dominion over his species. Unfortunately for the people whose institutions are the subject of inquiry, this power was in the hands of their chiefs. The caziques of the isles could put what responses they pleased into the mouths of their *Cemis* or gods; and it was by their interposition, and in their name, that they imposed any tribute or burden on their people.* The same power and prerogative was exercised by the great chief of the Natchez, as the principal minister as well as the representative of the Sun, their deity. The respect which the people of Bogota paid to their monarchs was likewise inspired by religion, and the heir apparent of the kingdom was educated in the innermost recess of their principal temple, under such austere discipline, and with such peculiar rites, as tended to fill his subjects with high sentiments concerning the sanctity of his character and the dignity of his station.† Thus superstition, which in the rudest period of society, is either altogether unknown, or wastes its force in childish unmeaning practices, had acquired such an ascendant over those people of America, who had made some little progress towards refinement, that it became the chief instrument of bending

---

* Herrera, dec. 1. lib. iii. c. 3.   † Piedrahita, p. 27

their minds to an untimely servitude, and subjected them, in the beginning of their political career, to a despotism hardly less rigorous than that which awaits nations in the last stage of their corruption and decline.

V. After examining the political institutions of the rude nations in America, the next object of attention is their art of war, or their provision for public security and defence. The small tribes dispersed over America are not only independent and unconnected, but engaged in perpetual hostilities with one another.* Though mostly strangers to the idea of separate property, vested in any individual, the rudest of the American nations are well acquainted with the rights of each community to its own domains. This right they hold to be perfect and exclusive, entitling the possessor to oppose the encroachment of neighbouring tribes. As it is of the utmost consequence to prevent them from destroying or disturbing the game in their hunting grounds, they guard this national property with a jealous attention. But as their territories are extensive, and the boundaries of them not exactly ascertained, innumerable subjects of dispute arise, which seldom terminate without bloodshed. Even in this simple and primitive state of society, interest is a source of discord, and often prompts savage tribes to take arms in order to repel or punish such as encroach on the forests or plains to which they trust for subsistence.

But interest is not either the most frequent or the most powerful motive of the incessant hostilities among rude nations. These must be imputed to the passion of revenge, which rages with such violence in the breast of savages, that eagerness to gratify it may be considered as the distinguishing characteristic of men in their uncivilized state. Circumstances of powerful influence, both in the interior government of rude tribes, and in their external operations against foreign enemies, concur in cherishing and adding strength to a passion fatal to the general tranquillity. When the right of redressing his own wrongs is left in the hands of every individual, injuries are felt with exquisite sensibility, and vengeance exercised with unrelenting rancour. No time can obliterate the memory of an offence, and it is seldom that it can be expiated but by the blood of the offender. In carrying on their public wars, savage nations are influenced by the same ideas, and animated with the same spirit, as in prosecuting private vengeance. In small communities, every man is touched with the injury or affront offered to the body of which he is a member, as if it were a personal attack upon his own honour or safety. The desire of revenge is communicated from breast to breast, and soon kindles into rage. As feeble societies can take the field only in small parties, each warrior is conscious of the importance of his own arm, and feels that to it is committed a considerable portion of the public vengeance. War, which between extensive kingdoms is carried on with little animosity, is prosecuted by small tribes with all the rancour of a private quarrel. The resentment of nations is as implacable as that of individuals. It may be dissembled or suppressed, but is never extinguished; and often, when least expected or dreaded, it bursts out with redoubled fury.† When polished nations have obtained the glory of victory, or have acquired an addition of territory, they may terminate a war with honour. But savages are not satisfied until they extirpate the community which is the object of their hatred. They fight, not to conquer, but to destroy. If they engage in hostilities, it is with a resolution never to see the face of the enemy in peace, but to prosecute the quarrel with immortal enmity.‡ The desire of vengeance is the first and almost the only principle which a savage instils into the minds of his children.§ This grows up

---

* Ribas Hist. de los Triumph. p. 9. † Boucher Hist. Nat. de N. France, p. 93. Charlev. Hist. de N. France, iii. 215. 251. Lery ap. de Bry, iii. 204. Creux. Hist. Canad. p. 72. Lozano Descr. del Gran Chaco, 25. Hennep. Mœurs des Sauv. 40. ‡ Charlev. Hist. N. Fr. iii. 251. Colden. i. 108. ii. 126. Barrere, p. 170. 173. § Charlev. Hist. N. Fr. iii. 326. Lery ap. de Bry, iii. 236. Lozano Hist. de Parag. i. 144.

with him as he advances in life; and as his attention is directed to few objects, it requires a degree of force unknown among men whose passions are dissipated and weakened by the variety of their occupations and pursuits. The desire of vengeance, which takes possession of the heart of savages, resembles the instinctive rage of an animal rather than the passion of a man. It turns, with undiscerning fury, even against inanimate objects. If hurt accidentally by a stone, they often seize it in a transport of anger, and endeavour to wreak their vengeance upon it.* If struck with an arrow in a battle, they will tear it from the wound, break and bite it with their teeth, and dash it on the ground.† With respect to their enemies the rage of vengeance knows no bounds. When under the dominion of this passion, man becomes the most cruel of all animals. He neither pities, nor forgives, nor spares.

The force of this passion is so well understood by the Americans themselves, that they always apply to it in order to excite their people to take arms. If the elders of any tribe attempt to rouse their youth from sloth, if a chief wishes to allure a band of warriors to follow him in invading an enemy's country, the most persuasive topics of their martial eloquence are drawn from revenge. " The bones of our countrymen," say they, " lie uncovered; their bloody bed has not been washed clean. Their spirits cry against us; they must be appeased. Let us go and devour the people by whom they were slain. Sit no longer inactive upon your mats; lift the hatchet, console the spirits of the dead, and tell them that they shall be avenged."‡

Animated with such exhortations, the youth snatch their arms in a transport of fury, raise the song of war, and burn with impatience to imbrue their hands in the blood of their enemies. Private chiefs often assemble small parties and invade a hostile tribe without consulting the rulers of the community. A single warrior, prompted by caprice or revenge, will take the field alone, and march several hundred miles to surprise and cut off a straggling enemy [65]. The exploits of a noted warrior, in such solitary excursions, often form the chief part in the history of an American campaign [66]; and their elders connive at such irregular sallies, as they tend to cherish a martial spirit, and accustom their people to enterprise and danger.§ But when a war is national, and undertaken by public authority, the deliberations are formal and slow. The elders assemble, they deliver their opinions in solemn speeches, they weigh with maturity the nature of the enterprise, and balance its beneficial or disadvantageous consequences with no inconsiderable portion of political discernment or sagacity. Their priests and soothsayers are consulted, and sometimes they ask the advice even of their women.‖ If the determination be for war, they prepare for it with much ceremony. A leader offers to conduct the expedition, and is accepted. But no man is constrained to follow him; the resolution of the community to commence hostilities imposes no obligation upon any member to take part in the war. Each individual is still master of his own conduct, and his engagement in the service is perfectly voluntary.¶

The maxims by which they regulate their military operations, though extremely different from those which take place among more civilized and populous nations, are well suited to their own political state, and the nature of the country in which they act. They never take the field in numerous bodies, as it would require a greater effort of foresight and industry than is usual among savages, to provide for their subsistence during a march of some hundred miles through dreary forests, or during a long voyage upon their lakes and rivers. Their armies are not encumbered with baggage or

* Lery ap. de Bry, iii. 190   † Ibid. iii. 208.   Herrera, dec. 1. lib. vi. c. 8.   ‡ Charlev. Hist. N. Fr. iii. 216, 217. Lery ap. de Bry, iii. 204.   § Bossu, i. 140. Lery ap. de Bry, 215. Hennepin Mœurs des Sauv. 41. Lafitau, ii. 169.   ‖ Charlev. Hist. N. Fr. 215. 268. Blet. 367. 380.   ¶ Charlev. Hist. N. Fr. 217, 218.

military stores. Each warrior, besides his arms, carries a mat and a small bag of pounded maize, and with these is completely equipped for any service. While at a distance from the enemy's frontier, they disperse through the woods, and support themselves with the game which they kill, or the fish which they catch. As they approach nearer to the territories of the nation which they intend to attack, they collect their troops, and advance with greater caution. Even in their hottest and most active wars they proceed wholly by stratagem and ambuscade. They place not their glory in attacking their enemies with open force. To surprise and destroy is the greatest merit of a commander, and the highest pride of his followers. War and hunting are their only occupations, and they conduct both with the same spirit and the same arts. They follow the track of their enemies through the forest. They endeavour to discover their haunts, they lurk in some thicket near to these, and, with the patience of a sportsman lying in wait for game, will continue in their station day after day until they can rush upon their prey when most secure, and least able to resist them. If they meet no straggling party of the enemy, they advance towards their villages, but with such solicitude to conceal their own approach, that they often creep on their hands and feet through the woods, and paint their skins of the same colour with the withered leaves, in order to avoid detection.*
If so fortunate as to remain unobserved, they set on fire the enemies' huts in the dead of night, and massacre the inhabitants as they fly naked and defenceless from the flames. If they hope to effect a retreat without being pursued, they carry off some prisoners, whom they reserve for a more dreadful fate. But if, notwithstanding all their address and precautions, they find that their motions are discovered, that the enemy has taken the alarm, and is prepared to oppose them, they usually deem it most prudent to retire. They regard it as extreme folly to meet an enemy who is on his guard, upon equal terms, or to give battle in an open field. The most distinguished success is a disgrace to a leader if it has been purchased with any considerable loss of his followers [67], and they never boast of a victory if stained with the blood of their own countrymen.† To fall in battle, instead of being reckoned an honourable death, is a misfortune which subjects the memory of a warrior to the imputation of rashness or imprudence‡ [68].

This system of war was universal in America; and the small uncivilized tribes, dispersed through all its different regions and climates, display more craft than boldness in carrying on their hostilities. Struck with this conduct, so opposite to the ideas and maxims of Europeans,* several authors contend that it flows from a feeble and dastardly spirit peculiar to the Americans, which is incapable of any generous or manly exertion.§ But when we reflect that many of these tribes, on occasions which call for extraordinary efforts, not only defend themselves with obstinate resolution, but attack their enemies with the most daring courage, and that they possess fortitude of mind superior to the sense of danger or the fear of death, we must ascribe their habitual caution to some other cause than constitutional timidity.‖ The number of men in each tribe is so small, the difficulty of rearing new members amidst the hardships and dangers of savage life is so great, that the life of a citizen is extremely precious, and the preservation of it becomes a capital object in their policy. Had the point of honour been the same among the feeble American tribes as among the powerful nations of Europe, had they been taught to court fame or victory in contempt of danger and death, they must have been ruined by maxims so ill adapted to their condition. But wherever their com-

* Charlev. Hist. N. Fr. iii. 237, 238. Hennep. Mœurs des Sauv. p. 59 † Charlev. Hist. N. Fr. iii. 238. 307. Biet, 381. Laflau Mœurs des Sauv. ii. 248. ‡ Charlev. iii. 376. § Recherches Philos. sur les Améric. i. 115. Voyage de March. iv, 410. ‖ Laflau Mœurs des Sauv. ii. 248, 249. Charlev, N. Fr. iii. 307.

munities are more populous, so that they can act with considerable force, and can sustain the loss of several of their members without being sensibly weakened, the military operations of the Americans more nearly resemble those of other nations.' The Brazilians, as well as the tribes situated upon the banks of the river De la Plata, often take the field in such numerous bodies as deserve the name of armies.* They defy their enemies to the combat, engage in regular battles, and maintain the conflict with that desperate ferocity which is natural to men who, having no idea of war but that of exterminating their enemies, never give or take quarter [69]. In the powerful empires of Mexico and Peru, great armies were assembled, frequent battles were fought, and the theory as well as practice of war were different from what took place in those petty societies which assume the name of nations.

But though vigilance and attention are the qualities chiefly requisite where the object of war is to deceive and to surprise; and though the Americans, when acting singly, display an amazing degree of address in concealing their own motions, and discovering those of an enemy, yet it is remarkable that, when they take the field in parties, they can seldom be brought to observe the precautions most essential to their own security. Such is the difficulty of accustoming savages to subordination, or to act in concert; such is their impatience under restraint, and such their caprice and presumption, that it is rarely they can be brought to conform themselves to the counsels and directions of their leaders. They never station sentinels around the place where they rest at night, and after marching some hundred miles to surprise an enemy, are often surprised themselves, and cut off, while sunk in as profound sleep as if they were not within reach of danger.†

If, notwithstanding this negligence and security, which often frustrate their most artful schemes, they catch the enemy unprepared, they rush upon them with the utmost ferocity, and tearing off the scalps of all those who fall victims to their rage [70], they carry home those strange trophies in triumph. These they preserve as monuments, not only of their own prowess, but of the vengeance which their arm has inflicted upon the people who were objects of public resentment.‡ They are still more solicitous to seize prisoners. During their retreat, if they hope to effect it unmolested, the prisoners are commonly exempt from any insult, and treated with some degree of humanity, though guarded with the most strict attention.

But after this temporary suspension, the rage of the conquerors rekindles with new fury. As soon as they approach their own frontier, some of their number are despatched to inform their countrymen with respect to the success of the expedition. Then the prisoners begin to feel the wretchedness of their condition. The women of the village, together with the youth who have not attained to the age of bearing arms, assemble, and forming themselves into two lines, through which the prisoners must pass, beat and bruise them with sticks or stones in a cruel manner.§ After this first gratification of their rage against their enemies, follow lamentations for the loss of such of their own countrymen as have fallen in the service, accompanied with words and actions which seem to express the utmost anguish and grief. But in a moment, upon a signal given, their tears cease; they pass, with a sudden and unaccountable transition, from the depths of sorrow to the transports of joy; and begin to celebrate their victory with all the wild exultation of a barbarous triumph.‖ The fate of the prisoners remains still undecided. The old men deliberate concerning it. Some are destined to be tortured to death, in order to satiate

---

* Fabri Veriss. Descrip. Indiæ ap. de Bry, vii. p. 42. † Charlev. N. Fr. iii. 236, 237. Lettr. Edif. xvii. 308. xx. 130. Lafit. Mœurs, 247. Lahontan, ii. 176.   ‡ Lafitau Mœurs, ii. 256.
§ Lahontan, ii. 184.   ‖ Charlev. Hist. N. Fr. iii. 241. Lafitau Mœurs, ii. 264.

the revenge of the conquerors; some to replace the members which the community has lost in that or former wars. They who are reserved for this milder fate, are led to the huts of those whose friends have been killed. The women meet them at the door, and if they receive them, their sufferings are at an end. They are adopted into the family, and, according to their phrase, are seated upon the mat of the deceased. They assume his name, they hold the same rank, and are treated thenceforward with all the tenderness due to a father, a brother, a husband, or a friend. But, if either from caprice or an unrelenting desire of revenge, the women of any family refuse to accept of the prisoner who is offered to them; his doom is fixed. No power can then save him from torture and death.

While their lot is in suspense, the prisoners themselves appear altogether unconcerned about what may befall them. They talk, they eat, they sleep, as if they were perfectly at ease, and no danger impending. When the fatal sentence is intimated to them, they receive it with an unaltered countenance, raise their death song, and prepare to suffer like men. Their conquerors assemble as to a solemn festival, resolved to put the fortitude of the captive to the utmost proof. A scene ensues, the bare description of which is enough to chill the heart with horror, wherever men have been accustomed, by milder institutions, to respect their species, and to melt into tenderness at the sight of human sufferings. The prisoners are tied naked to a stake, but so as to be at liberty to move round it. All who are present, men, women, and children, rush upon them like furies. Every species of torture is applied that the rancour of revenge can invent. Some burn their limbs with redhot irons, some mangle their bodies with knives, others tear their flesh from their bones, pluck out their nails by the roots, and rend and twist their sinews. They vie with one another in refinements of torture. Nothing sets bounds to their rage but the dread of abridging the duration of their vengeance by hastening the death of the sufferers; and such is their cruel ingenuity in tormenting, that, by avoiding industriously to hurt any vital part, they often prolong this scene of anguish for several days. In spite of all that they suffer, the victims continue to chant their death song with a firm voice, they boast of their own exploits, they insult their tormentors for their want of skill in avenging their friends and relations, they warn them of the vengeance which awaits them on account of what they are now doing, and excite their ferocity by the most provoking reproaches and threats. To display undaunted fortitude, in such dreadful situations, is the noblest triumph of a warrior. To avoid the trial by a voluntary death, or to shrink under it, is deemed infamous and cowardly. If any one betray symptoms of timidity, his tormentors often despatch him at once with contempt, as unworthy of being treated like a man.* Animated with those ideas, they endure without a groan what it seems almost impossible that human nature should sustain. They appear to be not only insensible of pain, but to court it. "Forbear," said an aged chief of the Iroquois, when his insults had provoked one of his tormentors to wound him with a knife, "forbear these stabs of your knife, and rather let me die by fire, that those dogs, your allies, from beyond the sea, may learn by my example to suffer like men."† This magnanimity, of which there are frequent instances among the American warriors, instead of exciting admiration, or calling forth sympathy, exasperates the fierce spirits of their torturers to fresh acts of cruelty.‡ Weary, at length of contending with men whose constancy of mind they cannot vanquish, some chief, in a rage, puts a period to their sufferings, by despatching them with his dagger or club.§

* De la Potherie, ii. 237. iii. 43. † Colden, Hist. of Five Nations, i 200. ‡ Voyages de Lahont, i. 236. § Charlev. Hist. N. Fr. iii. 243, &c. 385. Lafitau Mœurs, ii. 265. Creuxij Hist. Canad. p. 73. Hennep. Mœurs des Sauv. p. 64, &c. Lahont, i 233, &c. Tertre, ii. 405. De la Potherie, ii, 22, &c.

This barbarous scene is often succeeded by one no less shocking. As it is impossible to appease the fell spirit of revenge which rages in the heart of a savage, this frequently prompts the Americans to devour those unhappy persons who have been the victims of their cruelty. In the ancient world, tradition has preserved the memory of barbarous nations of cannibals, who fed on human flesh. But in every part of the New World there were people to whom this custom was familiar. It prevailed in the southern continent,* in several of the islands,† and in various districts of North America.‡ Even in those parts where circumstances with which we are unacquainted had in a great measure abolished this practice, it seems formerly to have been so well known that it is incorporated into the idiom of their language. Among the Iroquois, the phrase by which they express their resolution of making war against an enemy is, "Let us go and eat that nation." If they solicit the aid of a neighbouring tribe, they invite it "to eat broth made of the flesh of their enemies"§ [71]. Nor was the practice peculiar to rude unpolished tribes; the principle from which they took rise is so deeply rooted in the minds of the Americans, that it subsisted in Mexico, one of the civilized empires in the New World, and relics of it may be discovered among the more mild inhabitants of Peru. It was not scarcity of food, as some authors imagine, and the importunate cravings of hunger, which forced the Americans to those horrid repasts on their fellow-creatures. Human flesh was never used as common food in any country, and the various relations concerning people who reckoned it among the stated means of subsistence, flow from the credulity and mistakes of travellers. The rancour of revenge first prompted men to this barbarous action.‖ The fiercest tribes devoured none but prisoners taken in war, or such as they regarded as enemies [72]. Women and children who were not the objects of enmity, if not cut off in the fury of their first inroad into a hostile country, seldom suffered by the deliberate effects of their revenge.¶

The people of South America gratify their revenge in a manner somewhat different, but with no less unrelenting rancour. Their prisoners, after meeting at their first entrance with the same rough reception as among the North Americans,** are not only exempt from injury, but treated with the greatest kindness. They are feasted and caressed, and some beautiful young women are appointed to attend and solace them. It is not easy to account for this part of their conduct, unless we impute it to a refinement in cruelty. For, while they seem studious to attach the captives to life, by supplying them with every enjoyment that can render it agreeable, their doom is irrevocably fixed. On a day appointed the victorious tribe assembles, the prisoner is brought forth with great solemnity, he views the preparations for the sacrifice with as much indifference as if he himself were not the victim, and meeting his fate with undaunted firmness, is despatched with a single blow. The moment he falls, the women seize the body and dress it for the feast. They besmear their children with the blood, in order to kindle in their bosoms a hatred of their enemies, which is never extinguished, and all join in feeding upon the flesh with amazing greediness and exultation.†† To devour the body of a slaughtered enemy they deem the most complete and exquisite gratification of revenge. Wherever this practice prevails, captives never escape death, but they are not tortured with the same cruelty as among tribes which are less accustomed to such horrid feasts [73].

* Stadius ap: de Bry, iii. 123. Lery, ibid. 210. Biet, 384. Lettr. Edif. xxiii. 341. Piso, 8. Condam, 84. 97. Ribas, Hist. de los Triumph. 473. † Life of Columb. 529. Mart. Dec. p. 18. Tertre, ii. 405. ‡ Dumont. Mem. l. 254. Charlev. Hist. N. France, i. 259. ii. 14. iii. 21. De la Potherie, ii. 50. § Charlev. Hist. N. Fr. iii. 208, 209. Lettr. Edif. xxiii. p. 277. De la Potherie, ii. 218. ‖ Biet, 383. Bianco, Conversion de Piritu, p. 28. Bancroft, Nat. Hist. of Guiana, p. 259, &c. ¶ Biet, 389. Bandini, Vita di Americo, 84. Tertre, 405. Fermin. Descrip. de Surin. i. 54. ** Stadius ap. de Bry, iii. 40. 123. †† Stadius ap. de Bry, iii. 128, &c. Lery ap. de Bry, iii. 210.

As the constancy of every American warrior may be put to such severe proof, the great object of military education and discipline in the New World is to form the mind to sustain it. When nations carry on war with open force, defy their enemies to the combat, and vanquish them by the superiority of their skill or courage, soldiers are trained to be active, vigorous, and enterprising. But in America, where the genius and maxims of war are extremely different, passive fortitude is the quality in highest estimation. Accordingly, it is early the study of the Americans to acquire sentiments and habits which will enable them to behave like men when their resolution shall be put to the proof. As the youth of other nations exercise themselves in feats of activity and force, those of America vie with one another in exhibitions of their patience under sufferings. They harden their nerves by those voluntary trials, and gradually accustom themselves to endure the sharpest pain without complaining. A boy and girl will bind their naked arms together, and place a burning coal between them, in order to try who first discovers such impatience as to shake it off.* All the trials customary in America, when a youth is admitted into the class of warriors, or when a warrior is promoted to the dignity of captain or chief, are accommodated to this idea of manliness. They are not displays of valour, but of patience ; they are not exhibitions of their ability to offend, but of their capacity to suffer. Among the tribes on the banks of the Orinoco, if a warrior aspires to the rank of captain, his probation begins with a long fast, more rigid than any ever observed by the most abstemious hermit. At the close of this the chiefs assemble, each gives him three lashes with a large whip, applied so vigorously that his body is almost flayed, and if he betrays the least symptoms of impatience or even sensibility, he is disgraced for ever, and rejected as unworthy of the honour to which he aspires. After some interval, the constancy of the candidate is proved by a more excruciating trial. He is laid in a hammoc with his hands bound fast, and an innumerable multitude of venomous ants, whose bite occasions exquisite pain, and produces a violent inflammation, are thrown upon him. The judges of his merit stand around the hammoc, and, while these cruel insects fasten upon the most sensible parts of his body, a sigh, a groan, an involuntary motion, expressive of what he suffers, would exclude him for ever from the rank of captain. Even after this evidence of his fortitude, it is not deemed to be completely ascertained, but must stand another test more dreadful than any he has hitherto undergone. He is again suspended in his hammoc, and covered with leaves of the palmetto. A fire of stinking herbs is kindled underneath, so as he may feel its heat and be involved in its smoke. Though scorched and almost suffocated, he must continue to endure with the same patient insensibility. Many perish in this rude essay of their firmness and courage, but such as go through it with applause, receive the ensigns of their new dignity with much solemnity, and are ever after regarded as leaders of approved resolution, whose behaviour in the most trying situations will do honour to their country.† In North America the previous trial of a warrior is neither so formal nor so severe. Though even there, before a youth is permitted to bear arms, his patience and fortitude are proved by blows, by fire, and by insults more intolerable to a haughty spirit than both.‡

The amazing steadiness with which the Americans endure the most exquisite torments, has induced some authors to suppose that, from the peculiar feebleness of their frame, their sensibility is not so acute as that of other people ; as women, and persons of a relaxed habit, are observed to be less affected with pain than robust men, whose nerves are more firmly braced. But the constitution of the Americans is not so different

---

* Charlev. Hist. N. Fr. iii. 307. † Gumilla, ii. 286, &c. Blet, 376, &c. ‡ Charlev. Hist. N. Fr. iii. 219.

in its texture from that of the rest of the human species, as to account for this diversity in their behaviour. It flows from a principle of honour, instilled early and cultivated with such care, as to inspire man in his rudest state with an heroic magnanimity, to which philosophy hath endeavoured in vain to form him, when more highly improved and polished. This invincible constancy he has been taught to consider as the chief distinction of a man, and the highest attainment of a warrior. The ideas which influence his conduct, and the passions which take possession of his heart, are few. They operate of course with more decisive effect than when the mind is crowded with a multiplicity of objects, or distracted by the variety of its pursuits; and when every motive that acts with any force in forming the sentiments of a savage, prompts him to suffer with dignity, he will bear what might seem to be impossible for human patience to sustain. But wherever the fortitude of the Americans is not roused to exertion by their ideas of honour, their feelings of pain are the same with those of the rest of mankind [74]. Nor is that patience under sufferings for which the Americans have been so justly celebrated, a universal attainment. The constancy of many of the victims is overcome by the agonies of torture. Their weakness and lamentations complete the triumph of their enemies, and reflect disgrace upon their own country.*

The perpetual hostilities carried on among the American tribes are productive of very fatal effects. Even in seasons of public tranquillity, their imperfect industry does not supply them with any superfluous store of provisions; but when the irruption of an enemy desolates their cultivated lands, or disturbs them in their hunting excursions, such a calamity reduces a community, naturally unprovident and destitute of resources, to extreme want. All the people of the district that is invaded are frequently forced to take refuge in woods and mountains, which can afford them little subsistence, and where many of them perish. Notwithstanding their excessive caution in conducting their military operations, and the solicitude of every leader to preserve the lives of his followers, as the rude tribes in America seldom enjoy any interval of peace, the loss of men among them is considerable in proportion to the degree of population. Thus famine and the sword combine in thinning their numbers. All their communities are feeble, and nothing now remains of several nations which were once considerable, but the name.†

Sensible of this continual decay, there are tribes which endeavour to recruit their national force when exhausted, by adopting prisoners taken in war, and by this expedient prevent their total extinction. The practice, however, is not universally received. Resentment operates more powerfully among savages than considerations of policy. Far the greater part of their captives was anciently sacrificed to their vengeance, and it is only since their numbers began to decline fast, that they have generally adopted milder maxims. But such as they do naturalize renounce for ever their native tribe, and assume the manners as well as passions of the people by whom they are adopted‡ so entirely, that they often join them in expeditions against their own countrymen. Such a sudden transition, and so repugnant to one of the most powerful instincts implanted by nature, would be deemed strange among many people; but among the members of small communities, where national enmity is violent and deep rooted, it has the appearance of being still more unaccountable. It seems, however, to result naturally from the principles upon which war is carried on in America. When nations aim at exterminating their enemies, no exchange of prisoners can ever take place. From the moment one is made a prisoner, his country and his friends consider him as dead [75]. He has incurred indelible

---

* Charlev. Hist. N. Fr. iii. 248, 385. De la Potherie, iii. 48. † Charlev. Hist. N. Fr. iii. 202, 203. 429. Gumilla, ii. 227, &c. ‡ Charlev. Hist. N. Fr. iii. 243, &c. Lafit. ii. 308.

disgrace by suffering himself to be surprised or to be taken by an enemy; and were he to return home, after such a stain upon his honour, his nearest relations would not receive or even acknowledge that they knew him.* Some tribes were still more rigid, and if a prisoner returned, the infamy which he had brought on his country was expiated, by putting him instantly to death.† As the unfortunate captive is thus an outcast from his own country, and the ties which bound him to it are irreparably broken, he feels less reluctance in forming a new connexion with people, who, as an evidence of their friendly sentiments, not only deliver him from a cruel death, but offer to admit him to all the rights of a fellow-citizen. The perfect similarity of manners among savage nations facilitates and completes the union, and induces a captive to transfer not only his allegiance, but his affection to the community into the bosom of which he is received.

But though war be the chief occupation of men in their rude state, and to excel in it their highest distinction and pride, their inferiority is always manifest when they engage in competition with polished nations. Destitute of that foresight which discerns and provides for remote events, strangers to the union and mutual confidence requisite in forming any extensive plan of operations, and incapable of the subordination no less requisite in carrying such plans into execution, savage nations may astonish a disciplined enemy by their valour, but seldom prove formidable to him by their conduct; and whenever the contest is of long continuance, must yield to superior art [76]. The empires of Peru and Mexico, though their progress in civilization, when measured by the European or Asiatic standards, was inconsiderable, acquired such an ascendency over the rude tribes around them, that they subjected most of them with great facility to their power. When the people of Europe overran the various provinces of America, this superiority was still more conspicuous. Neither the courage nor number of the natives could repel a handful of invaders. The alienation and enmity, prevalent among barbarians, prevented them from uniting in any common scheme of defence, and while each tribe fought separately, all were subdued.

VI. The arts of rude nations unacquainted with the use of metals, hardly merit any attention on their own account, but are worthy of some notice, as far as they serve to display the genius and manners of man in this stage of his progress. The first distress a savage must feel, will arise from the manner in which his body is affected by the heat, or cold, or moisture of the climate under which he lives; and his first care will be to provide some covering for his own defence. In the warmer, and more mild climates of America, none of the rude tribes were clothed. To most of them nature had not even suggested any idea of impropriety in being altogether uncovered.‡ As under a mild climate there was little need of any defence from the injuries of the air, and their extreme indolence shunned every species of labour to which it was not urged by absolute necessity, all the inhabitants of the isles, and a considerable part of the people on the continent, remained in this state of naked simplicity. Others were satisfied with some slight covering, such as decency required. But though naked, they were not unadorned. They dressed their hair in many different forms. They fastened bits of gold, or shells, or shining stones, in their ears, their noses, and cheeks.§ They stained their skins with a great variety of figures; and they spent much time, and submitted to great pain, in ornamenting their persons in this fantastic manner. Vanity, however, which finds endless occupation for ingenuity and invention in nations where dress has become a complex and intricate art, is circumscribed within so

---

* Lahont, ii. 185, 186. † Herrera, dec. 3. lib. iv. c. 16. p. 173. ‡ Lery Navigat. ap. de Bry, iii. p. 164. Life of Columbus, c. 24. Venegas Hist. of Californ. p. 70. § Lery ap. de Bry, iii. p. 165. Lettr. Edifiantes, xx. p. 221.

narrow bounds, and confined to so few articles among naked savages, that they are not satisfied with those simple decorations, and have a wonderful propensity to alter the natural form of their bodies, in order to render it (as they imagine) more perfect and beautiful. This practice was universal among the rudest of the American tribes. Their operations for that purpose begin as soon as an infant is born. By compressing the bones of the skull, while still soft and flexible, some flatten the crown of their heads; some squeeze them into the shape of a cone; others mould them as much as possible into a square figure;* and they often endanger the lives of their posterity by their violent and absurd efforts to derange the plan of nature, or to improve upon her designs. But in all their attempts either to adorn or to new model their persons, it seems to have been less the object of the Americans to please, or to appear beautiful, than to give an air of dignity and terror to their aspect. Their attention to dress had more reference to war than to gallantry. The difference in rank and estimation between the two sexes was so great, as seems to have extinguished, in some measure, their solicitude to appear mutually amiable. The man deemed it beneath him to adorn his person, for the sake of one on whom he was accustomed to look down as a slave. It was when the warrior had in view to enter the council of his nation, or to take the field against its enemies, that he assumed his choicest ornaments, and decked his person with the nicest care.† The decorations of the women were few and simple; whatever was precious or splendid was reserved for the men. In several tribes the women were obliged to spend a considerable part of their time every day in adorning and painting their husbands, and could bestow little attention upon ornamenting themselves. Among a race of men so haughty as to despise, or so cold as to neglect them, the women naturally became careless and slovenly, and the love of finery and show, which had been deemed their favourite passion, was confined chiefly to the other sex.‡ To deck his person was the distinction of a warrior, as well as one of his most serious occupations [77]. In one part of their dress, which at first sight appears the most singular and capricious, the Americans have discovered considerable sagacity in providing against the chief inconveniences of their climate, which is often sultry and moist to excess. All the different tribes, which remain unclothed, are accustomed to anoint and rub their bodies with the grease of animals, with viscous gums, and with oils of different kinds. By this they check that profuse perspiration, which in the torrid zone wastes the vigour of the frame, and abridges the period of human life. By this, too, they provide a defence against the extreme moisture during the rainy season [78]. They likewise, at certain seasons, temper paint of different colours with those unctuous substances, and bedaub themselves plentifully with that composition. Sheathed with this impenetrable varnish, their skins are not only protected from the penetrating heat of the sun, but as all the innumerable tribes of insects have an antipathy to the smell or taste of that mixture, they are delivered from their teasing persecution, which amidst forests and marshes, especially in the warmer regions, would have been altogether intolerable in a state of perfect nakedness.§

The next object to dress that will engage the attention of a savage, is to prepare some habitation which may afford him shelter by day, and a retreat at night. Whatever is connected with his ideas of personal dignity, whatever bears any reference to his military character, the savage warrior deems an object of importance. Whatever relates only to peaceable and inactive

* Oviedo Hist. lib. III. c. 5. Ulloa, i. 329. Voyage de Labat, ii. 72. Charlevoix, iii. 323. Gumilla, i. 197, &c. . Acugna Relat. de la Riv. des Amaz. ii. 83. Lawson's Voyage to Carolina, p. 33. † Wafer's Voyage, p. 142. Lery ap. de Bry, iii. 167. Charlev. Hist. N. Fran. iii. 316. 322. ‡ Charlev. Hist. de la Nouv. France, iii. 278. 327. Lafitau, ii. 53. Kalm's Voyage, iii. 273. Lery ap. de Bry, iii. 169, 170. Purch. Pilgr. iv. 1287. Ribas Hist. de los Triumph, &c. 479 § Labat, ii. 73. Gumilla, i. 190. 202. Bancroft Nat. Hist. of Guiana, 81. 290.

life, he views with indifference. Hence, though finically attentive to dress, he is little solicitous about the elegance or disposition of his habitation. Savage nations, far from that state of improvement, in which the mode of living is considered as a mark of distinction, and unacquainted with those wants, which require a variety of accommodation, regulate the construction of their houses according to their limited ideas of necessity. Some of the American tribes were so extremely rude, and had advanced so little beyond the primæval simplicity of nature, that they had no houses at all. During the day, they take shelter from the scorching rays of the sun under thick trees; at night they form a shed with their branches and leaves [79]. In the rainy season they retire into coves, formed by the hand of Nature, or hollowed out by their own industry.* Others, who have no fixed abode, and roam through the forest in quest of game, sojourn in temporary huts, which they erect with little labour, and abandon without any concern. The inhabitants of those vast plains, which are deluged by the overflowing of rivers during the heavy rains that fall periodically between the tropics, raise houses upon piles fastened in the ground, or place them among the boughs of trees, and are thus safe amidst that wide extended inundation which surrounds them.† Such were the first essays of the rudest Americans towards providing themselves with habitations. But even among tribes which are more improved, and whose residence is become altogether fixed, the structure of their houses is extremely mean and simple. They are wretched huts, sometimes of an oblong and sometimes of a circular form, intended merely for shelter, with no view to elegance, and little attention to conveniency. The doors are so low that it is necessary to bend or to creep on the hands and feet in order to enter them. They are without windows, and have a large hole in the middle of the roof, to convey out the smoke. To follow travellers in other minute circumstances of their descriptions, is not only beneath the dignity of history, but would be foreign to the object of my researches. One circumstance merits attention, as it is singular, and illustrates the character of the people. Some of their houses are so large as to contain accommodation for fourscore or a hundred persons. These are built for the reception of different families, which dwell together under the same roof [80], and often around a common fire, without separate apartments, or any kind of screen or partition between the spaces which they respectively occupy. As soon as men have acquired distinct ideas of property; or when they are so much attached to their females, as to watch them with care and jealousy; families of course divide and settle in separate houses, where they can secure and guard whatever they wish to preserve. This singular mode of a habitation, among several people of America, may therefore be considered not only as the effect of their imperfect notions concerning property, but as a proof of inattention, and indifference towards their women. If they had not been accustomed to perfect equality, such an arrangement could not have taken place. If their sensibility had been apt to have taken alarm, they would not have trusted the virtue of their women amidst the temptations and opportunities of such a promiscuous intercourse. At the same time, the perpetual concord, which reigns in habitations where so many families are crowded together, is surprising, and affords a striking evidence that they must be people of either a very gentle, or of a very phlegmatic temper, who in such a situation, are unacquainted with animosity, brawling, and discord.‡

After making some provision for his dress and habitation, a savage

* Lettres Edif. v. 273. Venegas Hist. of Califor. i. 76. Lozano, Descrip. del Gran. Chaco, p. 55. Lettres Edif. ii. 176. Gumilla, i. 383. Bancroft, Nat. Hist. of Guiana, 277. † Gumilla, i. 225. Herrera, dec. 1. lib. ix. c. 6. Oviedo Somar. p. 53. C. ‡ Journ. de Grillet et Bechamel dans la Goyane, p. 65. Lafitau Mœurs, ii. 4. Torquem. Monarq. i. 247. Journal Hist. de Jouts, 917. Lery Hist. Brazil, ap. de Bry, iii. 238. Lozano Descr. del Gran. Chaco, 67.

Vol. I.--2ᵃ

will perceive the necessity of preparing proper arms with which to assault or repel an enemy. This, accordingly, has early exercised the ingenuity and invention of all rude nations. The first offensive weapons were doubtless such as chance presented, and the first efforts of art to improve upon these, were extremely awkward and simple. Clubs made of some heavy wood, stakes hardened in the fire, lances whose heads were armed with flint or the bones of some animal, are weapons known to the rudest nations. All these, however, are of use only in close encounter. But men wished to annoy their enemies while at a distance, and the bow and arrow is the most early invention for this purpose. This weapon is in the hands of people whose advances in improvement are extremely inconsiderable, and is familiar to the inhabitants of every quarter of the globe. It is remarkable, however, that some tribes in America were so destitute of art and ingenuity, that they had not attained to the discovery of this simple invention,* and seem to have been unacquainted with the use of any missile weapon. The sling, though in its construction not more complex than the bow, and among many nations of equal antiquity, was little known to the people of North America,† or the islands, but appears to have been used by a few tribes in the southern continent‡ [81]. The people, in some provinces of Chili, and those of Patagonia, towards the southern extremity of America, use a weapon peculiar to themselves. They fasten stones, about the size of a fist, to each end of a leather thong of eight feet in length, and swing these round their heads, throw them with such dexterity, that they seldom miss the object at which they aim.§

Among people who had hardly any occupation but war or hunting, the chief exertions of their invention [82], as well as industry, were naturally directed towards these objects. With respect to every thing else, their wants and desires were so limited, that their invention was not upon the stretch. As their food and habitations are perfectly simple, their domestic utensils are few and rude. Some of the southern tribes had discovered the art of forming vessels of earthen ware, and baking them in the sun, so as they could endure the fire. In North America, they hollowed a piece of hard wood in the form of a kettle, and filling it with water, brought it to boil, by putting red-hot stones into it [83]. These vessels they used in preparing part of their provisions ; and this may be considered as a step towards refinement and luxury ; for men in their rudest state were not acquainted with any method of dressing their victuals but by roasting them on the fire ; and among several tribes in America, this is the only species of cookery yet known.‖ But the masterpiece of art, among the savages of America, is the construction of the canoes. An Esquimaux, shut up in his boat of whalebone, covered with the skins of seals, can brave that stormy ocean on which the barrenness of his country compels him to depend for the chief part of his subsistence.¶ The people of Canada venture upon their rivers and lakes in boats made of the bark of trees, and so light that two men can carry them, wherever shallows or cataracts obstruct the navigation [84]. In these frail vessels they undertake and accomplish long voyages.** The inhabitants of the isles and of the southern continent form their canoes by hollowing the trunk of a large tree, with infinite labour; and though in appearance they are extremely awkward and unwieldy, they paddle and steer them with such dexterity, that Europeans, well acquainted with all the improvements in the science of navigation, have been astonished at the rapidity of their motion, and the quickness of their evolutions. Their *pirogues*, or war boats, are so large as to carry forty or fifty men ; their canoes, employed in fishing and in short voyages are less capa-

* Piedrahita Conq. del Nuevo Reyno, ix. 12.   † Nauf. de Alv. Nun. Cabeca de Vaca, c, x. p. 12.   ‡ Piedrah. p. 16.   § Ovalle's Relation of Chili. Church. Collect. iii. 82. Falkner's Descript. of Patagon. p. 130.   ‖ Charlev. Hist. N. Fr. iii. 332.   ¶ Ellis Voy. 133.   ** Lafitau Mœurs, &c. ii. 213.

cious.* The form as well as materials of all these various kinds of vessels, is well adapted to the service for which they are destined; and the more minutely they are examined, the mechanism of their structure, as well as neatness of their fabric, will appear the more surprising.

But, in every attempt towards industry among the Americans, one striking quality in their character is conspicuous. They apply to work without ardour, carry it on with little activity, and, like children, are easily diverted from it. Even in operations which seem the most interesting, and where the most powerful motives urge them to vigorous exertions, they labour with a languid listlessness. Their work advances under their hand with such slowness, that an eyewitness compares it to the imperceptible progress of vegetation.† They will spend so many years in forming a canoe, that it often begins to rot with age before they finish it. They will suffer one part of a roof to decay and perish, before they complete the other.‡ The slightest manual operation consumes an amazing length of time, and what in polished nations would hardly be an effort of industry, is among savages an arduous undertaking. This slowness of the Americans in executing works of every kind may be imputed to various causes. Among savages, who do not depend for subsistence upon the efforts of regular industry, time is of so little importance that they set no value upon it; and provided they can finish a design, they never regard how long they are employed about it. The tools which they employ are so awkward and defective that every work in which they engage must necessarily be tedious. The hand of the most industrious and skilful artist, were it furnished with no better instrument than a stone hatchet, a shell, or the bone of some animal, would find it difficult to perfect the most simple work. It is by length of labour that he must endeavour to supply his defect of power. But above all, the cold phlegmatic temper peculiar to the Americans, renders their operations languid. It is almost impossible to rouse them from that habitual indolence to which they are sunk; and unless when engaged in war or in hunting, they seem incapable of exerting any vigorous effort. Their ardour of application is not so great as to call forth that inventive spirit which suggests expedients for facilitating and abridging labour. They will return to a task day after day, but all their methods of executing it are tedious and operose [85]. Even since the Europeans have communicated to them the knowledge of their instruments, and taught them to imitate their arts, the peculiar genius of the Americans is conspicuous in every attempt they make. They may be patient and assiduous in labour, they can copy with a servile and minute accuracy, but discover little invention and no talents for despatch. In spite of instruction and example, the spirit of the race predominates; their motions are naturally tardy, and it is in vain to urge them to quicken their pace. Among the Spaniards in America, *the work of an Indian* is a phrase by which they describe any thing, in the execution of which an immense time has been employed and much labour wasted.§

VII. No circumstance respecting rude nations has been the object of greater curiosity than their religious tenets and rites; and none, perhaps, has been so imperfectly understood, or represented with so little fidelity. Priests and missionaries are the persons who have had the best opportunities of carrying on this inquiry among the most uncivilized of the American tribes. Their minds, engrossed by the doctrines of their own religion, and habituated to its institutions, are apt to discover something which resembles those objects of their veneration, in the opinions and rites of every people. Whatever they contemplate they view through one medium, and draw and accommodate it to their own system. They study to reconcile the

* Labat, Voyages, ll. 91, &c. 131.   † Gumilla, ii. 297.   ‡ Borde Relat. des Caraibes, p. 22.   § Voyages de Ulloa, i. 335. Lettr. Edif. &c. xv. 348.

institutions which fall under their observation to their own creed, not to explain them according to the rude notions of the people themselves. They ascribe to them ideas which they are incapable of forming, and suppose them to be acquainted with principles and facts, which it is impossible that they should know. Hence, some missionaries have been induced to believe, that even among the most barbarous nations in America, they had discovered traces, no less distinct than amazing, of their acquaintance with the sublime mysteries and peculiar institutions of Christianity. From their own interpretation of certain expressions and ceremonies, they have concluded that these people had some knowledge of the doctrine of the Trinity, of the incarnation of the Son of God, of his expiatory sacrifice, of the virtue of the cross, and of the efficacy of the sacraments.* In such unintelligent and credulous guides we can place little confidence.

But even when we make our choice of conductors with the greatest care, we must not follow them with implicit faith. An inquiry into the religious notions of rude nations is involved in peculiar intricacies, and we must often pause in order to separate the facts which our informers relate from the reasonings with which they are accompanied, or the theories which they build upon them. Several pious writers, more attentive to the importance of the subject than to the condition of the people whose sentiments they were endeavouring to discover, have bestowed much unprofitable labour in researches of this nature [86].

There are two fundamental doctrines, upon which the whole system of religion, as far as it can be discovered by the light of nature, is established. The one respects the being of a God, the other the immortality of the soul. To discover the ideas of the uncultivated nations under our review, with regard to those important points, is not only an object of curiosity, but may afford instruction. To these two articles I shall confine my researches, leaving subordinate opinions, and the detail of local superstitions, to more minute inquirers. Whoever has had any opportunity of examining into the religious opinions of persons in the inferior ranks of life, even in the most enlightened and civilized nations, will find that their system of belief is derived from instruction, not discovered by inquiry. That numerous part of the human species, whose lot is labour, whose principal and almost sole occupation is to secure subsistence, views the arrangement and operations of nature with little reflection, and has neither leisure nor capacity for entering into that path of refined and intricate speculation which conducts to the knowledge of the principles of natural religion. In the early and most rude periods of savage life, such disquisitions are altogether unknown. When the intellectual powers are just beginning to unfold, and their first feeble exertions are directed towards a few objects of primary necessity and use; when the faculties of the mind are so limited as not to have formed abstract or general ideas; when language is so barren as to be destitute of names to distinguish any thing that is not perceived by some of the senses; it is preposterous to expect that man should be capable of tracing with accuracy the relation between cause and effect; or to suppose that he should rise from the contemplation of the one to the knowledge of the other, and form just conceptions of a Deity, as the Creator and Governor of the universe. The idea of creation is so familiar, wherever the mind is enlarged by science and illuminated with revelation, that we seldom reflect how profound and abstruse this idea is, or consider what progress man must have made in observation and research, before he could arrive at any knowledge of this elementary principle in religion. Accordingly, several tribes have been discovered in America, which have no idea whatever of a Supreme Being, and no rites of religious worship. Inattentive to that

* Venegas, i. 88. 92. Torquemada, ii. 445. Garcia Origen. 122. Herrera, dec. 4. lib. ix. c. 7. dec. 5. lib. iv. c. 7.

magnificent spectacle of beauty and order presented to their view, unaccustomed to reflect either upon what they themselves are, or to inquire who is the author of their existence, men, in their savage state, pass their days like the animals around them, without knowledge or veneration of any superior power. Some rude tribes have not in their language any name for the Deity, nor have the most accurate observers been able to discover any practice or institution which seemed to imply that they recognised his authority, or were solicitous to obtain his favour* [87]. It is however only among men in the most uncultivated state of nature, and while their intellectual faculties are so feeble and limited as hardly to elevate them above the irrational creation, that we discover this total insensibility to the impressions of any invisible power.

But the human mind, formed for religion, soon opens to the reception of ideas, which are destined, when corrected and refined, to be the great source of consolation amidst the calamities of life. Among some of the American tribes, still in the infancy of improvement, we discern apprehensions of some invisible and powerful beings. These apprehensions are originally indistinct and perplexed, and seem to be suggested rather by the dread of impending evils than to flow from gratitude for blessings received. While nature holds on her course with uniform and undisturbed regularity, men enjoy the benefits resulting from it, without inquiring concerning its cause. But every deviation from this regular course rouses and astonishes them. When they behold events to which they are not accustomed, they search for the reasons of them with eager curiosity. Their understanding is unable to penetrate into these; but imagination, a more forward and ardent faculty of the mind, decides without hesitation. It ascribes the extraordinary occurrences in nature to the influence of invisible beings, and supposes that the thunder, the hurricane, and the earthquake are effects of their interposition. Some such confused notion of spiritual or invisible power, superintending over those natural calamities which frequently desolate the earth, and terrify its inhabitants, may be traced among many rude nations [88]. But besides this, the disasters and dangers of savage life are so many, and men often find themselves in situations so formidable, that the mind, sensible of its own weakness, has no resource but in the guidance and protection of wisdom and power superior to what is human. Dejected with calamities which oppress him, and exposed to dangers which he cannot repel, the savage no longer relies upon himself; he feels his own impotence, and sees no prospect of being extricated, but by the interposition of some unseen arm. Hence, in all unenlightened nations, the first rites or practices which bear any resemblance to acts of religion, have it for their object to avert evils which men suffer or dread. The *Manitous* or *Okkis* of the North Americans were amulets or charms, which they imagined to be of such virtue as to preserve the persons who reposed confidence in them from any disastrous event, or they were considered as tutelary spirits, whose aid they might implore in circumstances of distress.† The *Cemis* of the islanders were reputed by them to be the authors of every calamity that afflicts the human race; they were represented under the most frightful forms, and religious homage was paid to them with no other view than to appease these furious deities.‡ Even among those tribes whose religious system was more enlarged, and who had formed some conception of benevolent beings, which delighted in conferring benefits, as well as of malicious powers prone to inflict evil; superstition still appears

* Blet, 539. Lery ap. de Bry, iii. 221. Nieuhoff. Church. Coll. ii. 132. Lettr. Edif. 2. 177. Id. 12, 13. Venegas, i. 87. Lozano Descr. del Gran Chaco, 59. Fernand. Mission. de Chequit. 39. Gumilla, ii. 156. Rochefort Hist. des Antilles, p. 468. Margrave Hist. in Append. de Chilensibus, 286. Ulloa, Notic. Amer. 335, &c. Barrere, 218, 219. Harcourt Voy. to Guiana, Purch. Pilgr. iv. p. 1273. Account of Brazil, by a Portuguese. Ibid. p. 1289. Jones's Journal, p. 50. † Charlev. N. Fr. ill. 343, &c. Creuxii Hist. Canab. p. 82, &c. ‡ Oviedo, lib. iii. c. 1. p. 111. P. Martyr, decad. p. 102, &c.

as the offspring of fear, and all its efforts were employed to avert calamities. They were persuaded that their good deities, prompted by the beneficence of their nature, would bestow every blessing in their power, without solicitation or acknowledgment; and their only anxiety was to soothe and deprecate the wrath of the powers whom they regarded as the enemies of mankind.*

Such were the imperfect conceptions of the greater part of the Americans with respect to the interposition of invisible agents, and such, almost universally, was the mean and illiberal object of their superstitions. Were we to trace back the ideas of other nations to that rude state in which history first presents them to our view, we should discover a surprising resemblance in their tenets and practices; and should be convinced, that in similar circumstances, the faculties of the human mind hold nearly the same course in their progress, and arrive at almost the same conclusions. The impressions of fear are conspicuous in all the systems of superstition formed in this situation. The most exalted notions of men rise no higher than to a perplexed apprehension of certain beings, whose power, though supernatural, is limited as well as partial.

But, among other tribes, which have been longer united, or have made greater progress in improvement, we discern some feeble pointing towards more just and adequate conceptions of the power that presides in nature. They seem to perceive that there must be some universal cause to whom all things are indebted for their being. If we may judge by some of their expressions, they appear to acknowledge a divine power to be the maker of the world, and the disposer of all events. They denominate him the *Great Spirit*.† But these ideas are faint and confused, and when they attempt to explain them, it is manifest that among them the word *spirit* has a meaning very different from that in which we employ it, and that they have no conception of any deity but what is corporeal. They believe their gods to be of the human form, though of a nature more excellent than man, and retail such wild incoherent fables concerning their functions and operations, as are altogether unworthy of a place in history. Even among these tribes, there is no established form of public worship; there are no temples erected in honour of their deities; and no ministers peculiarly consecrated to their service. They have the knowledge, however, of several superstitious ceremonies and practices handed down to them by tradition, and to these they have recourse with a childish credulity, when roused by any emergence from their usual insensibility, and excited to acknowledge the power, and to implore the protection of superior beings.‡

The tribe of the Natchez, and the people of Bogota, had advanced beyond the other uncultivated nations of America in their ideas of religion, as well as in their political institutions; and it is no less difficult to explain the cause of this distinction than of that which we have already considered. The Sun was the chief object of religious worship among the Natchez. In their temples, which were constructed with some magnificence, and decorated with various ornaments, according to their mode of architecture, they preserved a perpetual fire, as the purest emblem of their divinity. Ministers were appointed to watch and feed this sacred flame. The first function of the great chief of the nation, every morning, was an act of obeisance to the Sun; and festivals returned at stated seasons, which were celebrated by the whole community with solemn but unbloody rites.§ This is the most refined species of superstition known in America, and perhaps one of the most natural as well as most seducing. The Sun is the apparent source of the joy, fertility, and life, diffused through nature; and

---

* Tertre, ii. 365. Borde, p. 14. State of Virginia, by a Native, book III. p. 32, 33. Dumont, i. 165. Bancroft Nat. Hist. of Guiana, 309. † Charlev. N. Fr. iii. 343. Sagard, Voy. du Pays des Hurons, 226. ‡ Charlev. N. Fr. iii. 345. Colden, i. 17. § Dumont, i. 158, &c. Charlev N. Fr. iii. 417, &c. 429. Lafitau, i. 167.

while the human mind, in its earlier essays towards inquiry, contemplates and admires his universal and animating energy, its admiration is apt to stop short at what is visible, without reaching to the unseen cause; and pays that adoration to the most glorious and beneficial work of God, which is due only to him who formed it. As fire is the purest and most active of the elements, and in some of its qualities and effects resembles the Sun, it was, not improperly, chosen to be the emblem of his powerful operation. The ancient Persians, a people far superior, in every respect, to that rude tribe whose rites I am describing, founded their religious system on similar principles, and established a form of public worship, less gross and exceptionable than that of any people destitute of guidance from revelation. This surprising coincidence in sentiment between two nations, in such different states of improvement, is one of the many singular and unaccountable circumstances which occur in the history of human affairs.

Among the people of Bogota, the Sun and Moon were, likewise, the chief objects of veneration. Their system of religion was more regular and complete, though less pure, than that of the Natchez. They had temples, altars, priests, sacrifices, and that long train of ceremonies, which superstition introduces wherever she has fully established her dominion over the minds of men. But the rites of their worship were cruel and bloody. They offered human victims to their deities, and many of their practices nearly resembled the barbarous institutions of the Mexicans, the genius of which we shall have an opportunity of considering more attentively in its proper place.*

With respect to the other great doctrine of religion, concerning the immortality of the soul, the sentiments of the Americans were more united: the human mind, even when least improved and invigorated by culture, shrinks from the thoughts of annihilation, and looks forward with hope and expectation to a state of future existence. This sentiment, resulting from a secret consciousness of its own dignity, from an instinctive longing after immortality, is universal, and may be deemed natural. Upon this are founded the most exalted hopes of man in his highest state of improvement; nor has nature withheld from him this soothing consolation, in the most early and rude period of his progress. We can trace this opinion from one extremity of America to the other, in some regions more faint and obscure, in others more perfectly developed, but nowhere unknown. The most uncivilized of its savage tribes do not apprehend death as the extinction of being. All entertain hopes of a future and more happy state, where they shall be for ever exempt from the calamities which imbitter human life in its present condition. This future state they conceive to be a delightful country, blessed with perpetual spring, whose forests abound with game, whose rivers swarm with fish, where famine is never felt, and uninterrupted plenty shall be enjoyed without labour or toil. But as men, in forming their first imperfect ideas concerning the invisible world, suppose that there they shall continue to feel the same desires, and to be engaged in the same occupations, as in the present world; they naturally ascribe eminence and distinction, in that state, to the same qualities and talents which are here the object of their esteem. The Americans, accordingly, allotted the highest place, in their country of spirits, to the skilful hunter, to the adventurous and successful warrior, and to such as had tortured the greatest number of captives, and devoured their flesh.† These notions were so prevalent that they gave rise to a universal custom, which is at once the strongest evidence that the Americans believe in a future state, and the best illustration of what they expect there. As they imagine, that departed spirits begin their career anew in the world whither they are gone, that their friends may not enter upon it defenceless and unprovided,

* Piedrahita, Conq. del N. Reyno, p. 17. Herrera, dec. 6. lib. v. c. 6. † Lery ap. de Bry, III. 223. Charlev. N. Fr. iii. 351, &c. De la Potherie, ii. 45, &c. iii. 5.

they bury together with the bodies of the dead their bow, their arrows, and other weapons used in hunting or war; they deposit in their tombs the skins or stuffs of which they make garments, Indian corn, manioc, venison, domestic utensils, and whatever is reckoned among the necessaries in their simple mode of life.* In some provinces, upon the decease of a cazique or chief, a certain number of his wives, of his favourites, and of his slaves, were put to death, and interred together with him, that he might appear with the same dignity in his future station, and be waited upon by the same attendants.† This persuasion is so deep rooted that many of the deceased person's retainers offer themselves as voluntary victims, and court the privilege of accompanying their departed master, as a high distinction. It has been found difficult, on some occasions, to set bounds to this enthusiasm of affectionate duty, and to reduce the train of a favourite leader to such a number as the tribe could afford to spare [89].

Among the Americans, as well as other uncivilized nations, many of the rites and observances which bear some resemblance to acts of religion, have no connection with devotion, but proceed from a fond desire of prying into futurity. The human mind is most apt to feel and to discover this vain curiosity, when its own powers are most feeble and uninformed. Astonished with occurrences of which it is unable to comprehend the cause, it naturally fancies that there is something mysterious and wonderful in their origin. Alarmed at events of which it cannot discern the issue or the consequences, it has recourse to other means of discovering them than the exercise of its own sagacity. Wherever superstition is so established as to form a regular system, this desire of penetrating into the secrets of futurity is connected with it. Divination becomes a religious act. Priests, as the ministers of heaven, pretend to deliver its oracles to men. They are the only soothsayers, augurs, and magicians, who profess the sacred and important art of disclosing what is hid from other eyes.

But, among rude nations, who pay no veneration to any superintending power, and who have no established rites or ministers of religion, their curiosity, to discover what is future and unknown, is cherished by a different principle, and derives strength from another alliance. As the diseases of men, in the savage state, are (as has been already observed) like those of the animal creation, few, but extremely violent, their impatience under what they suffer, and solicitude for the recovery of health, soon inspired them with extraordinary reverence for such as pretended to understand the nature of their maladies, and to be possessed of knowledge sufficient to preserve or deliver them from their sudden and fatal effects. These ignorant pretenders, however, were such utter strangers to the. structure of the human frame, as to be equally unacquainted with the causes of its disorders, and the manner in which they will terminate. Superstition, mingled frequently with some portion of craft, supplied what they wanted in science. They imputed the origin of diseases to supernatural influence, and prescribed or performed a variety of mysterious rites, which they gave out to be of such efficacy as to remove the most dangerous and inveterate maladies. The credulity and love of the marvellous, natural to uninformed men, favoured the deception, and prepared them to be the dupes of those impostors. Among savages, their first physicians are a kind of conjurers or wizards, who boast that they know what is past, and can foretell what is to come. Incantations, sorcery, and mummeries of diverse kinds, no less strange than frivolous, are the means which they employ to expel the imaginary causes of malignity;‡ and, relying upon

* Chronica de Cieca de Leon, c. 28. Sagard, 233. Creux. Hist. Canad. p. 91. Rochefort. Hist. des Antiles, 568. Biet, 391. De la Potherie, ii. 44. iii. 8. Blanco Convers. de Piritu, p. 35.
† Dumont Louisiane, i. 208, &c. Oviedo, lib. v. c. 3. Gomara Hist. Gen. c. 28. P. Mart. decad. 304. Charlev. N. Fr. iii. 421. Herrera, dec. 1. lib. iii. c. 3. P. Melchior Hernandez Memor. d. Cheriqui. Coll. Orig. Papers, 1. Chron. de Cieca de Leon, c. 33. ‡ P. Melch. Hernandez Memo rial de Cheriqui. Collect. Orig. Pap. 1.

the efficacy of these, they predict with confidence what will be the fate of their deluded patients. Thus superstition, in its earliest form, flowed from the solicitude of man to be delivered from present distress, not from his dread of evils awaiting him in a future life, and was originally ingrafted on medicine, not on religion. One of the first and most intelligent historians of America, was struck with this alliance between the art of divination and that of physic, among the people of Hispaniola.* But this was not peculiar to them. The *Alexis*, the *Piayas*, the *Autmoins*, or whatever was the distinguishing name of their diviners and charmers in other parts of America, were all the physicians of their respective tribes, in the same manner as the *Bubitos* of Hispaniola. As their function led them to apply to the human mind when enfeebled by sickness, and as they found it, in that season of dejection, prone to be alarmed with imaginary fears, or amused with vain hopes, they easily induced it to rely with implicit confidence on the virtue of their spells, and the certainty of their predictions.†
Whenever men acknowledge the reality of supernatural power and discernment in one instance, they have a propensity to admit it in others. The Americans did not long suppose the efficacy of conjuration to be confined to one subject. They had recourse to it in every situation of danger or distress. When the events of war were peculiarly disastrous, when they met with unforeseen disappointment in hunting, when inundations or drought threatened their crops with destruction, they called upon their conjurors to begin their incantations, in order to discover the causes of those calamities, or to foretell what would be their issue.‡ Their confidence in this delusive art gradually increased, and manifested itself in all the occurrences of life. When involved in any difficulty, or about to enter upon any transaction of moment, every individual regularly consulted the sorcerer, and depended upon his instructions to extricate him from the former, as well as to direct his conduct in the latter. Even among the rudest tribes in America, superstition appears in this form, and divination is an art in high esteem. Long before man had acquired such knowledge of a deity as inspires reverence, and leads to adoration, we observe him stretching out a presumptuous hand to draw aside that veil with which Providence kindly conceals its purposes from human knowledge ; and we find him labouring with fruitless anxiety to penetrate into the mysteries of the divine administration. To discern and to worship a superintending power is an evidence of the enlargement and maturity of the human understanding ; a vain desire of prying into futurity is the error of its infancy, and a proof of its weakness.

From this weakness proceeded likewise the faith of the Americans in dreams, their observation of omens, their attention to the chirping of birds, and the cries of animals, all which they suppose to be indications of future events ; and if any one of these prognostics is deemed unfavourable, they instantly abandon the pursuit of those measures on which they are most eagerly bent.§

VIII. But if we would form a complete idea of the uncultivated nations of America, we must not pass unobserved some singular customs, which, though universal and characteristic, could not be reduced, with propriety, to any of the articles into which I have divided my inquiry concerning their manners.

Among savages, in every part of the globe, the love of dancing is a favourite passion. As, during a great part of their time, they languish in

---

* Oviedo, lib. v. c. 1. † Herrera, dec. 1. lib. iii. c. 4. Osborne Coll. ii. 860. Dumont, i. 169, &c. Charlev. N. Fr. lll. 361. 364, &c. Lawson, N. Carol. 214. Ribas, Triumf. p. 17. Biet, 386. De la Potherie, ii. 35, &c. ‡ Charlev. N. Fr. iii. 3. Dumont, i. 173. Fernand. Relac. de los Chequit. p. 40. Lozano, 84. Margrave, 279. § Charlev. N. Fr. iii. 262. 353. Stadius ap de Bry, iii. 120. Creuxj. Hist. Canad. 84. Techo Hist. of Parag. Church. Coll. vi. 37. De la Potherie, iii. 6.

a state of inactivity and indolence, without any occupation to rouse or interest them, they delight universally in a pastime which calls forth the active powers of their nature into exercise. The Spaniards, when they first visited America, were astonished at the fondness of the natives for dancing; and beheld with wonder a people, cold and unanimated in most of their other pursuits, kindle into life, and exert themselves with ardour, as often as this favourite amusement recurred. Among them, indeed, dancing ought not to be denominated an amusement. It is a serious and important occupation which mingles in every occurrence of public or private life. If any intercourse be necessary between two American tribes, the ambassadors of the one approach in a solemn dance, and present the calumet or emblem of peace; the sachems of the other receive it with the same ceremony.* If war is denounced against an enemy, it is by a dance expressive of the resentment which they feel, and of the vengeance which they meditate.† If the wrath of their gods is to be appeased, or their beneficence to be celebrated; if they rejoice at the birth of a child, or mourn the death of a friend,‡ they have dances appropriated to each of these situations, and suited to the different sentiments with which they are then animated. If a person 's indisposed, a dance is prescribed as the most effectual means of restoring him to health; and if he himself cannot endure the fatigue of such an exercise, the physician or conjuror performs it in his name, as if the virtue of his activity could be transferred to his patient.§

All their dances are imitations of some action; and though the music by which they are regulated is extremely simple, and tiresome to the ear by its dull monotony, some of their dances appear wonderfully expressive and animated. The war dance is, perhaps, the most striking. It is the representation of a complete American campaign. The departure of the warriors from their village, their march into the enemy's country, the caution with which they encamp, the address with which they station some of their party in ambush, the manner of surprising the enemy, the noise and ferocity of the combat, the scalping of those who are slain, the seizing of prisoners, the triumphant return of the conquerors, and the torture of the victims, are successively exhibited. The performers enter with such enthusiastic ardour into their several parts; their gestures, their countenance, their voice, are so wild and so well adapted to their various situations, that Europeans can hardly believe it to be a mimic scene, or view it without emotions of fear and horror.‖

But however expressive some of the American dances may be, there is one circumstance in them remarkable, and connected with the character of the race. - The songs, the dances, the amusements of other nations, expressive of the sentiments which animate their hearts, are often adapted to display or excite that sensbility which mutually attaches the sexes. Among some people, such is the ardour of this passion, that love is almost the sole object of festivity and joy; and as rude nations are strangers to delicacy, and unaccustomed to disguise any emotion of their minds, their dances are often extremely wanton and indecent. Such is the *Calenda*, of which the natives of Africa are so passionately fond;¶ and such the feats of the dancing girls which the Asiatics contemplate with so much avidity of desire. But among the Americans, more cold and indifferent to their females, from causes which I have already explained, the passion of love mingles but little with their festivals and pastimes. Their songs and

* De la Potherie Hist. ii. 17, &c: Charlev. N. Fr. iii. 211. 297. La Hontan, i. 100 137. Hennepin Decou. 146, &c. † Charlev. N. Fr. iii. 298. Lafitau, i. 523. ‡ Joutel, 343. Gomara Hist. Gen. c. 196. § Denys Hist. Nat. 189. Brickell, 372. De la Potherie, ii. 36. ‖ De la Potherie, ii. 116. Charlev. N. F. iii. 297. Lafitau, i. 523. ¶ Adamson Voyage to Senegal. iii. 287. Labat, Voyages, iv. 463. Sloane Hist. Nat. of Jam. Introd. p. 48. Formin Descript. de Surin, i. 139.

dances are mostly solemn and martial; they are connected with some of the serious and important affairs of life;* and, having no relation to love or gallantry, are seldom common to the two sexes, but executed by the men and women apart† [90]. If, on some occasions, the women are permitted to join in the festival, the character of the entertainment is still the same, and no movement or gesture is expressive of attachment, or encourages familiarity.‡

An immoderate love of play, especially at games of hazard, which seems to be natural to all people unaccustomed to the occupations of regular industry, is likewise universal among the Americans. The same causes, which so often prompt persons in civilized life, who are at their ease, to have recourse to this pastime, render it the delight of the savage. The former are independent of labour, the latter do not feel the necessity of it; and as both are unemployed, they run with transport to whatever is interesting enough to stir and to agitate their minds. Hence the Americans, who at other times are so indifferent, so phlegmatic, so silent, and animated with so few desires, as soon as they engage in play become rapacious, impatient, noisy, and almost frantic with eagerness. Their furs, their domestic untensils, their clothes, their arms, are staked at the gaming table, and when all is lost, high as their sense of independence is, in a wild emotion of despair or of hope, they will often risk their personal liberty upon a single cast.§ Among several tribes, such gaming parties frequently recur, and become their most acceptable entertainment at every great festival. Superstition, which is apt to take hold of those passions which are most vigorous, frequently lends its aid to confirm and strengthen this favourite inclination. Their conjurors are accustomed to prescribe a solemn match at play as one of the most efficacious methods of appeasing their gods, or of restoring the sick to health.‖

From causes similar to those which render them fond of play, the Americans are extremely addicted to drunkenness. It seems to have been one of the first exertions of human ingenuity to discover some composition of an intoxicating quality; and there is hardly any nation so rude, or so destitute of invention, as not to have succeeded in this fatal research. The most barbarous of the American tribes have been so unfortunate as to attain this art; and even those which are so deficient in knowledge, as to be unacquainted with the method of giving an inebriating strength to liquors by fermentation, can accomplish the same end by other means. The people of the islands of North America, and of California, used, for this purpose, the smoke of tobacco, drawn up with a certain instrument into the nostrils, the fumes of which ascending to the brain, they felt all the transports and phrensy of intoxication¶ [91]. In almost every other part of the New World, the natives possessed the art of extracting an intoxicating liquor from maize or the manioc root, the same substances which they convert into bread. The operation by which they effect this nearly resembles the common one of brewing, but with this difference, that, in place of yeast, they use a nauseous infusion of a certain quantity of maize or manioc chewed by their women. The saliva excites a vigorous fermentation, and in a few days the liquor becomes fit for drinking. It is not disagreeable to the taste, and, when swallowed in large quantities, is of an intoxicating quality.** This is the general beverage of the Americans, which they distinguish by various names, and for which they feel such a violent and insatiable desire as it is not easy either to conceive or

---

* Descript. of N. France. Osborne Coll. ii. 883. Charlev. N. Fr. iii. 84. † Wafer's Account of Isthmus, &c. 169. Lery ap. de Bry, iii. 177. Lozano Hist. de Parag. L 149. Herrera, dec. 2. lib. vii. c. 8. dec. 4. lib. x. c. 4. ‡ Barrere, Fr. Equin. p. 191. § Charlev. N. Fr. iii. 261. 318. Lafitau, ii. 338. &c. Ribas Triumf. 12. Brickell, 335. ‖ Charlev. N. Fr. iii. 362. ¶ Oviedo Hist. ap. Ramus, iii. 113. Venegas, i. 68. Naufrag. de Cabeca de Vaca, cap. 26. ** Stadius ap. de Bry, iii. 111. Lery, ibid. 175.

describe. Among polished nations, where a succession of various functions and amusements keeps the mind in continual occupation, the desire for strong drink is regulated in a great measure by the climate, and increases or diminishes according to the variations of its temperature. In warm regions, the delicate and sensible frame of the inhabitants does not require the stimulation of fermented liquors. In colder countries, the constitution of the natives, more robust and more sluggish, stands in need of generous liquors to quicken and animate it. But among savages, the desire of something that is of power to intoxicate is in every situation the same. All the people of America, if we except some small tribes near the Straits of Magellan, whether natives of the torrid zone, or inhabitants of its more temperate regions, or placed by a harder fate in the severe climates towards its northern or southern extremity, appear to be equally under the dominion of this appetite.* Such a similarity of taste, among people in such different situations, must be ascribed to the influence of some moral cause, and cannot be considered as the effect of any physical or constitutional want. While engaged in war or in the chase, the savage is often in the most interesting situations, and all the powers of his nature are roused to the most vigorous exertions. But those animating scenes are succeeded by long intervals of repose, during which the warrior meets with nothing that he deems of sufficient dignity or importance to merit his attention. He languishes and mopes in this season of indolence. The posture of his body is an emblem of the state of his mind. In one climate, cowering over the fire in his cabin; in another, stretched under the shade of some tree, he dozes away his time in sleep, or in an unthinking joyless inactivity not far removed from it. As strong liquors awake him from this torpid state, give a brisker motion to his spirits, and enliven him more thoroughly than either dancing or gaming, his love of them is excessive. A savage, when not engaged in action, is a pensive melancholy animal; but as soon as he tastes, or has a prospect of tasting, the intoxicating draught, he becomes gay and frolicsome.† Whatever be the occasion or pretexts on which the Americans assemble, the meeting always terminates in a debauch. Many of their festivals have no other object, and they welcome the return of them with transports of joy. As they are not accustomed to restrain any appetite, they set no bounds to this. The riot often continues without intermission several days; and whatever may be the fatal effects of their excess, they never cease from drinking as long as one drop of liquor remains. The persons of greatest eminence, the most distinguished warriors, and the chiefs most renowned for their wisdom, have no greater command of themselves than the most obscure members of the community. Their eagerness for present enjoyment renders them blind to its fatal consequences; and those very men, who in other situations seem to possess a force of mind more than human, are in this instance inferior to children, in foresight as well as consideration, and mere slaves of brutal appetite.‡ When their passions, naturally strong, are heightened and inflamed by drink, they are guilty of the most enormous outrages, and the festivity seldom concludes without deeds of violence or bloodshed.§

But, amidst this wild debauch, there is one circumstance remarkable; the women, in most of the American tribes, are not permitted to partake of it [92]. Their province is to prepare the liquor, to serve it about to the guests, and to take care of their husbands and friends when their reason is overpowered. This exclusion of the women from an enjoyment so highly valued by savages, may be justly considered as a mark of their inferiority, and as an additional evidence of that contempt with which they were

---

* Gumilla, i. 257. Lozano Descrip. del Gran. Chaco, 56. 103. Ribas, 8. Ulloa, i. 249. 337. Marchais, iv. 436. Fernandez Mission. de las Chequit. 35. Barrere, p. 203. Blanco Convers. de Piritu, 31. † Melendez Tesores Verdad. iii. 360. ‡ Ribas, 9. Ulloa, 1 338. § Lettr. Edif. ii. 178. Torquemada Mond. Ind. i. 339.

treated in the New World. The people of North America, when first discovered, were not acquainted with any intoxicating drink; but as the Europeans early found it their interest to supply them with spirituous liquors, drunkenness soon became as universal among them as among their countrymen to the south; and their women, having acquired this new taste, indulge it with as little decency and moderation as the men.*

It were endless to enumerate all the detached customs which have excited the wonder of travellers in America; but I cannot omit one seemingly as singular as any that has been mentioned. When their parents and other relations become old, or labour under any distemper which their slender knowledge of the healing art cannot remove, the Americans cut short their days with a violent hand, in order to be relieved from the burden of supporting and tending them. This practice prevailed among the ruder tribes in every part of the continent, from Hudson's Bay to the river De la Plata; and however shocking it may be to those sentiments of tenderness and attachment, which, in civilized life, we are apt to consider as congenial with our frame, the condition of man in the savage state leads and reconciles him to it. The same hardships and difficulty of procuring subsistence, which deter savages, in some cases, from rearing their children, prompt them to destroy the aged and infirm. The declining state of the one is as helpless as the infancy of the other. The former are no less unable than the latter to perform the functions that belong to a warrior or hunter, or to endure those various distresses in which savages are so often involved by their own want of foresight and industry. Their relations feel this; and, incapable of attending to the wants or weaknesses of others, their impatience under an additional burden prompts them to extinguish that life which they find it difficult to sustain. This is not regarded as a deed of cruelty, but as an act of mercy. An American, broken with years and infirmities, conscious that he can no longer depend on the aid of those around him, places himself contentedly in his grave; and it is by the hands of his children or nearest relations that the thong is pulled, or the blow inflicted, which releases him for ever from the sorrows of life.†

IX. After contemplating the rude American tribes in such various lights; after taking a view of their customs and manners from so many different stations, nothing remains but to form a general estimate of their character compared with that of more polished nations. A human being, as he comes originally from the hand of nature, is every where the same. At his first appearance in the state of infancy, whether it be among the rudest savages or in the most civilized nation, we can discern no quality which marks any distinction or superiority. The capacity of improvement seems to be the same; and the talents he may afterwards acquire, as well as the virtues he may be rendered capable of exercising, depend, in a great measure, upon the state of society in which he is placed. To this state his mind naturally accommodates itself, and from it receives discipline and culture. In proportion to the wants which it accustoms a human being to feel, and the functions in which these engage him, his intellectual powers are called forth. According to the connexions which it establishes between him and the rest of his species, the affections of his heart are exerted. It is only by attending to this great principle that we can discover what is the character of man in every different period of his progress.

If we apply it to savage life, and measure the attainments of the human mind in that state by this standard, we shall find, according to an observation which I have already made, that the intellectual powers of man must be extremely limited in their operations. They are confined

* Hutchinson Hist. of Massachus. 469. Lafitau, ḷḷ. 125. Sagard, 146. † Cassani Histor. de N. Reyno de Gran, p. 300. Piso, p. 6. Ellis Voy. 191. Gumilla, 1. 333.

within the narrow sphere of what he deems necessary for supplying his own wants. Whatever has not some relation to these neither attracts his attention, nor is the object of his inquiries. But however narrow the bounds may be within which the knowledge of a savage is circumscribed, he possesses thoroughly that small portion which he has attained. It was not communicated to him by formal instruction; he does not attend to it as a matter of mere speculation and curiosity; it is the result of his own observation, the fruit of his own experience, and accommodated to his condition and exigencies. While employed in the active occupations of war or of hunting, he often finds himself in difficult and perilous situations, from which the efforts of his own sagacity must extricate him. He is frequently engaged in measures, where every step depends upon his own ability to decide, where he must rely solely upon his own penetration to discern the dangers to which he is exposed, and upon his own wisdom in providing against them. In consequence of this, he feels the knowledge which he possesses, and the efforts which he makes, and either in deliberation or action rests on himself alone.

As the talents of individuals are exercised and improved by such exertions, much political wisdom is said to be displayed in conducting the affairs of their small communities. The council of old men in an American tribe, deliberating upon its interests, and determining with respect to peace or war, has been compared to the senate in more polished republics. The proceedings of the former, we are told, are often no less formal and sagacious than those of the latter. Great political wisdom is exhibited in pondering the various measures proposed, and in balancing their probable advantages against the evils of which they may be productive. Much address and eloquence are employed by the leaders, who aspire at acquiring such confidence with their countrymen as to have an ascendant in those assemblies.* But, among savage tribes, the field for displaying political talents cannot be extensive. Where the idea of private property is incomplete, and no criminal jurisdiction is established, there is hardly any function of internal government to exercise. Where there is no commerce, and scarcely any intercourse among separate tribes; where enmity is implacable, and hostilities are carried on almost without intermission; there will be few points of public concern to adjust with their neighbours; and that department of their affairs which may be denominated foreign, cannot be so intricate as to require much refined policy in conducting it. Where individuals are so thoughtless and improvident as seldom to take effectual precautions for self-preservation, it is vain to expect that public measures and deliberations will be regulated by the contemplation of remote events. It is the genius of savages to act from the impulse of present passion. They have neither foresight nor temper to form complicated arrangements with respect to their future conduct. The consultations of the Americans, indeed, are so frequent, and their negotiations are so many [93], and so long protracted, as to give their proceedings an extraordinary aspect of wisdom. But this is not owing so much to the depth of their schemes, as to the coldness and phlegm of their temper, which render them slow in determining.† If we except the celebrated league, that united the Five Nations in Canada, into a federal republic, which shall be considered in its proper place, we can discern few such traces of political wisdom, among the rude American tribes, as discover any great degree of foresight or extent of intellectual abilities. Even among them, we shall find public measures more frequently directed by the impetuous ferocity of their youth, than regulated by the experience and wisdom of their old men.

As the condition of man in the savage state is unfavourable to the

* Charlev. Hist. N. Fr. iii. 269, &c.   † Ibid. iii. 271.

progress of the understanding, it has a tendency likewise, in some respects, to check the exercise of affection, and to render the heart contracted. The strongest feeling in the mind of a savage is a sense of his own independence. He has sacrificed so small a portion of his natural liberty by becoming a member of society, that he remains, in a great degree, the sole master of his own actions.* He often takes his resolutions alone, without consulting or feeling any connection with the persons around him. In many of his operations he stands as much detached from the rest of his species as if he had formed no union with them. Conscious how little he depends upon other men, he is apt to view them with a careless indifference. Even the force of his mind contributes to increase this unconcern; and as he looks not beyond himself in deliberating with respect to the part which he should act, his solicitude about the consequences of it seldom extends further. He pursues his own career, and indulges his own fancy, without inquiring or regarding whether what he does be agreeable or offensive to others, whether they may derive benefit or receive hurt from it. Hence the ungovernable caprice of savages, their impatience under any species of restraint, their inability to suppress or moderate any inclination, the scorn or neglect with which they receive advice, their high estimation of themselves, and their contempt of other men. Among them, the pride of independence produces almost the same effects with interestedness in a more advanced state of society; it refers every thing to a man himself, it leads him to be indifferent about the manner in which his actions may affect other men, and renders the gratification of his own wishes the measure and end of conduct.

To the same cause may be imputed the hardness of heart and insensibility remarkable in all savage nations. Their minds, roused only by strong emotions, are little susceptible of gentle, delicate, or tender affections.† Their union is so incomplete that each individual acts as if he retained all his natural rights entire and undiminished. If a favour is conferred upon him, or any beneficial service is performed on his account, he receives it with much satisfaction, because it contributes to his enjoyment; but this sentiment extends not beyond himself, it excites no sense of obligation, he neither feels gratitude, nor thinks of making any return‡ [94]. Even among persons the most closely connected, the exchange of those good offices which strengthen attachment, mollify the heart, and sweeten the intercourse of life, is not frequent. The high ideas of independence among the Americans nourish a sullen reserve, which keeps them at a distance from each other. The nearest relations are mutually afraid to make any demand, or to solicit any service,§ lest it should be considered by the other as imposing a burden, or laying a restraint upon his will.

I have already remarked the influence of this hard unfeeling temper upon domestic life, with respect to the connection between husband and wife, as well as that between parents and children. Its effects are no less conspicuous, in the performance of those mutual offices of tenderness which the infirmities of our nature frequently exact. Among some tribes, when any of their number are seized with any violent disease, they are generally abandoned by all around them, who, careless of their recovery, fly in the utmost consternation from the supposed danger of infection.‖ But even where they are not thus deserted, the cold indifference with which they are attended can afford them little consolation. No look of sympathy, no soothing expressions, no officious services, contribute to alleviate the distress of the sufferers, or to make them forget what they endure.¶ Their nearest relations will often refuse to submit to the smallest inconveniency, or to part with the least trifle, however much it may tend

* Fernandez Mission. de los Chequit. 33.   Charlev. Hist. N. Fr. iii. 300.   ‡ Oviedo, Hist.
¶lb. xvi. c. 2.   § De la Potherie, iii. 28.   ‖ Lettre de P. Cataneo ap. Muratori Christian. i.
30.   Tortre, ii, 410.   Lozano, 100.   Herrera, dec. 4. lib. viii. c. 5. dec. 5. lib. iv. c. 2.   Falkner's
Descript. of Patagonia, 98   ¶ Gumilla, i. 329   Lozano, 100.

to their accommodation or relief.* So little is the breast of a savage susceptible of those sentiments which prompt men to that feeling attention which mitigates the calamities of human life, that, in some provinces of America, the Spaniards have found it necessary to enforce the common duties of humanity by positive laws, and to oblige husbands and wives, parents and children, under severe penalties, to take care of each other during their sickness.† The same harshness of temper is still more conspicuous in their treatment of the animal creation. Prior to their intercourse with the people of Europe, the North Americans had some tame dogs, which accompanied them in their hunting excursions, and served them with all the ardour and fidelity peculiar to the species. But, instead of that fond attachment which the hunter naturally feels towards those useful companions of his toils, they requite their services with neglect, seldom feed, and never caress them.‡ In other provinces the Americans have become acquainted with the domestic animals of Europe, and availed themselves of their service; but it is universally observed that they always treat them harshly,§ and never employ any method either for breaking or managing them, but force and cruelty. In every part of the deportment of man in his savage state, whether towards his equals of the human species, or towards the animals below him, we recognise the same character, and trace the operations of a mind intent on its own gratifications, and regulated by its own caprice, with little attention or sensibility to the sentiments and feelings of the beings around him.

After explaining how unfavourable the savage state is to the cultivation of the understanding, and to the improvement of the heart, I should not have thought it necessary to mention what may be deemed its lesser defects, if the character of nations, as well as of individuals, were not often more distinctly marked by circumstances apparently trivial than by those of greater moment. A savage frequently placed in situations of danger and distress, depending on himself alone, and wrapped up in his own thoughts and schemes, is a serious melancholy animal. His attention to others is small. The range of his own ideas is narrow. Hence that taciturnity which is so disgusting to men accustomed to the open intercourse of social conversation. When they are not engaged in action, the Americans often sit whole days in one posture, without opening their lips.|| When they go forth to war, or to the chase, they usually march in a line at some distance from one another, and without exchanging a word. The same profound silence is observed when they row together in a canoe.¶ It is only when they are animated by intoxicating liquors, or roused by the jollity of the festival and dance, that they become gay and conversible.

To the same causes may be imputed the refined cunning with which they form and execute their schemes. Men who are not habituated to a liberal communication of their own sentiments and wishes, are apt to be so distrustful as to place little confidence in others, and to have recourse to an insidious craft in accomplishing their own puposes. In civilized life, those persons who by their situations have but a few objects of pursuit on which their minds incessantly dwell, are most remarkable for low artifice in carrying on their little projects. Among savages, whose views are equally confined, and their attention no less persevering, those circumstances must operate still more powerfully, and gradually accustom them to a disingenuous subtlety in all their transactions. The force of this is increased by habits which they acquire in carrying on the two most interesting operations wherein they are engaged. With them war is a system of craft, in which they trust for success to stratagem more than to open force, and have their

---

* Garcia Origen, &c. 90. Herrera, dec. 4. lib. viii. c. 5. † Cogulludo Hist. de Yucathan, p. 300.
‡ Charlev. N. Fr. iii. 119, 337. § Ulloa Notic. American. 312. || Voyage de Bouguer, 102.
¶ Charlev. iii. 340.

invention continually on the stretch to circumvent and surprise their enemies. As hunters, it is their constant object to ensnare in order that they may destroy. Accordingly, art and cunning have been universally observed as distinguishing characteristics of all savages. The people of the rude tribes of America are remarkable for their artifice and duplicity. Impenetrably secret in forming their measures, they pursue them with a patient undeviating attention, and there is no refinement of dissimulation which they cannot employ, in order to ensure success. The natives of Peru were engaged above thirty years, in concerting the plan of that insurrection which took place under the vice-royalty of the Marquis de Villa Garcia; and though it was communicated to a great number of persons, in all different ranks, no indication of it ever transpired during that long period; no man betrayed his trust, or, by an unguarded look, or rash word, gave rise to any suspicion of what was intended.* The dissimulation and craft of individuals is no less remarkable than that of nations. When set upon deceiving, they wrap themselves up so artificially, that it is impossible to penetrate into their intentions, or to detect their designs.†

But if there be defects or vices peculiar to the savage state, there are likewise virtues which it inspires, and good qualities, to the exercise of which it is friendly. The bonds of society sit so loose upon the members of the more rude American tribes, that they hardly feel any restraint. Hence the spirit of independence, which is the pride of a savage, and which he considers as the unalienable prerogative of man. Incapable of control, and disdaining to acknowledge any superior, his mind, though limited in its powers, and erring in many of its pursuits, acquires such elevation by the consciousness of its own freedom, that he acts on some occasions with astonishing force, and perseverance, and dignity.

As independence nourishes this high spirit among savages, the perpetual wars in which they are engaged call it forth into action. Such long intervals of tranquillity as are frequent in polished societies are unknown in the savage state. Their enmities, as I have observed, are implacable and immortal. The valour of the young men is never allowed to rust in inaction. The hatchet is always in the hand, either for attack or defence. Even in their hunting excursions, they must be on their guard against surprise from the hostile tribes by which they are surrounded. Accustomed to continual alarms, they grow familiar with danger; courage becomes an habitual virtue, resulting naturally from their situation, and strengthened by constant exertions. The mode of displaying fortitude may not be the same in small and rude communities, as in more powerful and civilized states. Their system of war, and standard of valour may be formed upon different principles; but in no situation does the human mind rise more superior to the sense of danger, or the dread of death, than in its most simple and uncultivated state.

Another virtue remarkable among savages, is attachment to the community of which they are members. From the nature of their political union, one might expect this tie to be extremely feeble. But there are circumstances which render the influence, even of their loose mode of association, very powerful. The American tribes are small; combined against their neighbours, in prosecution of ancient enmities, or in avenging recent injuries, their interests and operations are neither numerous nor complex. These are objects which the uncultivated understanding of a savage can comprehend. His heart is capable of forming connections which are so little diffused. He assents with warmth to public measures, dictated by passions similar to those which direct his own conduct. Hence the ardour with which individuals undertake the most perilous service, when the commu-

* Voyage de Ulloa, ii, 309.   † Gumilla, i. 162. Charlev.

www.ingramcontent.com/pod-product-compliance
Lightning Source LLC
Chambersburg PA
CBHW021838230426
43669CB00008B/1011